New Perspectives on

MICROSOFT® WINDOWS® 98

COMPREHENSIVE

JUNE JAMRICH PARSONS

DAN OJA

JOAN CAREY
Carey Associates, Inc.

A Susan Solomon Book

COURSE TECHNOLOGY

ONE MAIN STREET, CAMBRIDGE, MA 02142

an International Thomson Publishing company I(T)P®

Cambridge • Albany • Bonn • Boston • Cincinnati • London • Madrid • Melbourne • Mexico City
New York • Paris • San Francisco • Singapore • Tokyo • Toronto • Washington

New Perspectives on Microsoft Windows 98 — Comprehensive is published by Course Technology.

Associate Publisher	Mac Mendelsohn
Series Consulting Editor	Susan Solomon
Product Manager	Rachel Crapser
Developmental Editor	Rachel Crapser
Production Editor	Catherine G. DiMassa
Text and Cover Designer	Meral Dabcovich

© 1999 by Course Technology ——— I(T)P®

For more information contact:

Course Technology
One Main Street
Cambridge, MA 02142

ITP Europe
Berkshire House 168-173
High Holborn
London WCIV 7AA
England

Nelson ITP, Australia
102 Dodds Street
South Melbourne, 3205
Victoria, Australia

ITP Nelson Canada
1120 Birchmount Road
Scarborough, Ontario
Canada M1K 5G4

International Thomson Editores
Seneca, 53
Colonia Polanco
11560 Mexico D.F. Mexico

ITP GmbH
Konigswinterer Strasse 418
53227 Bonn
Germany

ITP Asia
60 Albert Street, #15-01
Albert Complex
Singapore 189969

ITP Japan
Hirakawacho Kyowa Building, 3F
2-2-1 Hirakawacho
Chiyoda-ku, Tokyo 102
Japan

ISBN 0-7600-5448-7

Printed in the United States of America

1 2 3 4 5 6 7 8 9 10 BM 02 01 00 99 98

PREFACE

The New Perspectives Series

About New Perspectives

Course Technology's **New Perspectives Series** is an integrated system of instruction that combines text and technology products to teach computer concepts, the Internet, and microcomputer applications. Users consistently praise this series for innovative pedagogy, use of interactive technology, creativity, accuracy, and supportive and engaging style.

How is the New Perspectives Series different from other series?

The **New Perspectives Series** distinguishes itself by **innovative technology**, from the renowned Course Labs to the state-of-the-art multimedia that is integrated with our Concepts texts. Other distinguishing features include **sound instructional design**, **proven pedagogy**, and **consistent quality**. Each tutorial has students learn features in the context of solving a realistic case problem rather than simply learning a laundry list of features. With the **New Perspectives Series**, instructors report that students have a complete, integrative learning experience that stays with them. They credit this high retention and competency to the fact that this series incorporates critical thinking and problem-solving with computer skills mastery. In addition, we work hard to ensure accuracy by using a multi-step quality assurance process during all stages of development. Instructors focus on teaching and students spend more time learning.

Choose the coverage that's right for you

New Perspectives applications books are available in the following categories:

Brief
2-4 tutorials

Brief: approximately 150 pages long, two to four "Level I" tutorials, teaches basic application skills.

Introductory
6 or 7 tutorials, or Brief + 2 or 3 more tutorials

Introductory: approximately 300 pages long, four to seven tutorials, goes beyond the basic skills. These books often build out of the Brief book, adding two or three additional "Level II" tutorials.

Comprehensive
Introductory + 4 or 5 more tutorials. Includes Brief Windows tutorials and Additional Cases

Comprehensive: approximately 600 pages long, eight to twelve tutorials, all tutorials included in the Introductory text plus higher-level "Level III" topics. Also includes two Windows tutorials and three or four fully developed Additional Cases. The book you are holding is a Comprehensive book.

Advanced
Quick Review of basics + in-depth, high-level coverage

Advanced: approximately 600 pages long, covers topics similar to those in the Comprehensive books, but offers the highest-level coverage in the series. Advanced books assume students already know the basics, and therefore go into more depth at a more accelerated rate than the Comprehensive titles. Advanced books are ideal for a second, more technical course.

Office

Office suite components
+ integration + Internet

Custom Editions

Choose from any of the
above to build your own
Custom Editions or
CourseKits

Office: approximately 800 pages long, covers all components of the Office suite as well as integrating the individual software packages with one another and the Internet.

Custom Books The New Perspectives Series offers you two ways to customize a New Perspectives text to fit your course exactly: *CourseKits*™ are two or more texts shrinkwrapped together and offer significant price discounts. *Custom Editions*® offer you flexibility in designing your concepts, Internet, and applications courses. You can build your own book by ordering a combination of topics bound together to cover only the subjects you want. There is no minimum order, and books are spiral bound. Contact your Course Technology sales representative for more information.

What course is this book appropriate for?

Microsoft Windows 98 — Comprehensive can be used in any course in which you want students to learn all the most important topics of Windows 98. These topics include basic navigation and file management skills, using Windows Explorer, customizing the Windows 98 working environment, accessing the Web from the desktop, locating information on local disks and on the Web, working with graphics, hardware, and fonts, OLE, networks, and computer maintenance. An appendix on dial-up networking is also included. It is particularly recommended for a full course on Windows 98.

Proven Pedagogy

CASE

Tutorial Case Each tutorial begins with a problem presented in a case that is meaningful to students. The case turns the task of learning how to use an application into a problem-solving process. The problems increase in complexity with each tutorial. These cases touch on issues important to today's business curriculum.

45-minute Sessions We've divided the tutorials into sessions. Each session is designed to be completed in about 45 minutes to an hour (depending upon student needs and the speed of your lab equipment). Sessions allow instructors to more accurately allocate time in their syllabus, and students to better manage their own study time. Each numbered session begins with a "session box," which quickly describes the skills students will learn in the session.

1.

2.

3.

Step-by-Step Methodology We make sure students can differentiate between what they are to do and what they are to read. Through numbered steps – clearly identified by a gray shaded background – students are constantly guided in solving the case problem. In addition, the numerous screen shots with callouts direct students' attention to what they should look at on the screen.

TROUBLE?

TROUBLE? Paragraphs These paragraphs anticipate the mistakes or problems that students may have and help them continue with the tutorial.

"Read This Before You Begin" Page Located opposite the first tutorial's opening page for each level of the text, the Read This Before You Begin Page helps introduce technology into the classroom. Technical considerations and assumptions about software are listed to save time and eliminate unnecessary aggravation. Notes about the Student Disks help instructors and students get the right files in the right places, so students get started on the right foot.

QUICK CHECK

Quick Check Questions Each session concludes with meaningful, conceptual Quick Check questions that test students' understanding of what they learned in the session. Answers to the Quick Check questions are provided at the end of each tutorial.

RW

Reference Windows Reference Windows are succinct summaries of the most important tasks covered in a tutorial and they preview actions students will perform in the steps to follow.

TASK REFERENCE

Task Reference Located as a table at the end of the book, the Task Reference contains a summary of how to perform common tasks using the most efficient method, as well as references to pages where the task is discussed in more detail.

TUTORIAL

PROJECTS

LAB

End-of-Tutorial Tutorial Assignments, Projects, and Lab Assignments Tutorial Assignments provide students with additional hands-on practice of the skills they learned in the tutorial using the same case presented in the tutorial. These Assignments are followed by additional Projects. In addition, some of the Tutorial Assignments or Projects may include Exploration Exercises that challenge students, encourage them to explore the capabilities of the program they are using, and/or further extend their knowledge. Finally, if a Course Lab accompanies a tutorial, Lab Assignments are included after the Projects.

The Instructor's Resource Kit for this title contains:
- Electronic Instructor's Manual in pdf format
- Level I, Level II, and Level III Make Student Disk Programs
- Course Labs
- Course Test Manager Testbank
- Course Test Manager 1.2 Engine
- Figure files

These supplements come on CD-ROM. If you don't have access to a CD-ROM drive, contact your Course Technology customer service representative for more information.

The New Perspectives Supplements Package

Electronic Instructor's Manual Our Instructor's Manuals include tutorial overviews and outlines, technical notes, lecture notes, solutions, and Extra Case Problems. Many instructors use the Extra Case Problems for performance-based exams or extra credit projects. The Instructor's Manual is available as an electronic file, which you can get from the Instructor Resource Kit (IRK) CD-ROM or download it from **www.course.com**.

Student Files Student Files contain all of the data that students will use to complete the tutorials, Tutorial Assignments, and Projects. The Help file on the Instructor's Resource Kit includes instructions for using the files. See the "Read This Before You Begin" pages for more information on Student Files.

Course Labs: Concepts Come to Life These highly interactive computer-based learning activities bring concepts to life with illustrations, animations, digital images, and simulations. The Labs guide students step-by-step, present them with Quick Check questions, let them explore on their own, test their comprehension, and provide printed feedback. Lab icons at the beginning of the tutorial and in the tutorial margins indicate when a topic has a corresponding Lab. Lab Assignments are included at the end of each relevant tutorial. The Labs available with this book and the tutorials in which they appear are:

Using a Mouse	Using a Keyboard	Using Files	The Internet: World Wide Web
Tutorial 1	Tutorial 1	Tutorial 2	Tutorial 5
Web Pages & HTML	Multimedia	Defragmentation and Disk Operations	Data Backup
Tutorial 5	Tutorial 8	Tutorial 11	Tutorial 11

Figure Files Many figures in the text are provided on the IRK CD-ROM to help illustrate key topics or concepts. Instructors can create traditional overhead transparencies by printing the figure files. Or they can create electronic slide shows by using the figures in a presentation program such as PowerPoint.

Course Test Manager: Testing and Practice at the Computer or on Paper Test Manager is cutting-edge, Windows-based testing software that helps instructors design and administer practice tests and actual examinations. Course Test Manager can automatically grade the tests students take at the computer and can generate statistical information on individual as well as group performance.

Online Companions: Dedicated to Keeping You and Your Students Up-To-Date Visit our faculty sites and student sites on the World Wide Web at www.course.com. Here instructors can browse this text's password-protected Faculty Online Companion to obtain an online Instructor's Manual, Student Files, and more. Students can also access this text's Student Online Companion, which contains Student files, the links needed to perform the steps in Tutorial 5, and other useful links.

More innovative technology

Skills Assessment Manager (SAM) This ground-breaking new assessment tool tests students' ability to perform real-world tasks live in the Microsoft Office 97 applications. You can use SAM to test students out of a course, place them into a course, or test ongoing proficiency during a course. Contact your Sales or Customer Service representative about purchasing passwords or licenses for SAM or for more information, visit our Web site at:
www.course.com/products/sam.html

CyberClass CyberClass is a Web-based tool designed for on-campus or distance learning. Use it to enhance how you currently run your class by posting assignments and your course syllabus or holding online office hours. Or, use it for your distance learning course, and offer mini-lectures, conduct online discussion groups, or give your mid-term exam. For more information, visit our Web site at:
www.course.com/products/cyberclass/index.html

Acknowledgments

We want to thank all of the New Perspectives Team members for their support, guidance, and advice. Their insights and team spirit were invaluable. Thanks to our reviewers: Harry Phillips, Santa Rosa Junior College; Emerson R. Bailey, Casper College; Scott Zimmerman, Brigham Young University; Chuck Hommel, University of Puget Sound; and Joe Adamski, Grand Valley State University. We would especially like to give thanks to Judy Adamski, who "went the extra mile" to ensure accuracy, and Greg Bigelow, whose technical knowledge and willingness to provide extra consultation has been a great blessing. Thanks to Sandy Kruse, whose help in drafting the manuscript and working on the supplements has been invaluable. Thanks to Brian McCooey, Manuscript Quality Assurance Leader, and the quality testers: Jon Greacen, John Bosco, and Alex White. Our appreciation goes to Cathie DiMassa, Melissa Panagos, and the staff at GEX for their excellent production work and efforts in implementing the new design. We are grateful to Mac Mendelsohn, Susan Solomon, and Donna Gridley for their editorial support. We want to save the last note of thanks and praise for our editor, Rachel Crapser, whose excellence as an editor is only matched by her excellence as a schedule manager.

June Parsons, Dan Oja, Joan Carey

I would also like to acknowledge and thank my husband Patrick and my five little sons, Stephen, Michael, Peter, Thomas, and John Paul, for their unfailing love, cheer, and faith in me.

Joan Carey

BRIEF CONTENTS

TABLE OF CONTENTS

Tutorial 1   WIN 98 1.3

Exploring the Basics
Investigating the Windows 98 Operating System

Tutorial 2   WIN 98 2.1

Working with Files
Creating, Saving, and Managing Files

Tutorial 6   WIN 98 6.3

Finding Files and Data
Using the Find Feature to Locate Files for a Speechwriter

Tutorial 7   WIN 98 7.1

Working with Graphics
Creating Advertisment Graphics at Kiana Ski Shop

Tutorial 8   WIN 98 8.1

Object Linking and Embedding
Creating a Multimedia Document for the Jugglers Guild

Tutorial 9   WIN 98 9.1

Hardware, Printers, and Fonts
Installing and Troubleshooting a Printer at Chan & Associates

Tutorial 10   WIN 98 10.1

Network Neighborhood
Exploring Network Resources at Millennium Real Estate

Reference Window List

New Perspectives on

MICROSOFT®
WINDOWS® 98

Read This Before You Begin

To the Student

Make Student Disk Program

To complete the Level I tutorials, Tutorial Assignments, and Projects, you need 2 Student Disks. Your instructor will either provide you with Student Disks or ask you to make your own.

If you are making your own Student Disks you will need 2 blank, formatted high-density disks and access to the Make Student Disk program. If you wish to install the Make Student Disk program to your home computer, you can obtain it from your instructor or from the Web. To download the Make Student Disk program from the Web, go to www.course.com, click Data Disks, and follow the instructions on the screen.

To install the Make Student Disk program, select and click the file you just downloaded from www.course.com, 5446-0.exe. Follow the on-screen instructions to complete the installation. If you have any trouble installing or obtaining the Make Student Disk program, ask your instructor or technical support person for assistance.

Once you have obtained and installed the Make Student Disk program, you can use it to create your student disks according to the steps in the tutorials.

Course Labs

The Level I tutorials in this book feature 3 interactive Course Labs to help you understand selected computer concepts. There are Lab Assignments at the end of Tutorials 1 and 2 that relate to these Labs. To start a Lab, click the **Start** button on the Windows 98 Taskbar, point to **Programs**, point to **Course Labs**, point to **New Perspectives Course Labs**, and click the name of the Lab you want to use.

Using Your Own Computer

If you are going to work through this book using your own computer, you need:

Computer System Microsoft Windows 98 must be installed on a local hard drive or on a network drive.

Student Disks You will not be able to complete the tutorials or exercises in this book using your own computer until you have your Student Disks. See "Make Student Disk Program" above for details on obtaining your student disks.

Course Labs See your instructor or technical support person to obtain the Course Lab software for use on your own computer.

Visit Our World Wide Web Site

Additional materials designed especially for you are available on the World Wide Web. Go to http://www.course.com.

To the Instructor

The Make Student Disk Program and Course Labs for this title are available on the Instructor's Resource Kit for this title. Follow the instructions in the Help file on the CD-ROM to install the programs to your network or standalone computer. For information on using the Make Student Disk Program or the Course Labs, see the "To the Student" section above. Students will be switching the default installation settings to Web style in Tutorial 2. You are granted a license to copy the Student Files and Course Labs to any computer or computer network used by students who have purchased this book.

OBJECTIVES

In this tutorial you will:

- Start and shut down Windows 98

- Identify the objects on the Windows 98 desktop

- Practice mouse functions

- Run software programs and switch between them

- Identify and use the controls in a window

- Use Windows 98 controls such as menus, toolbars, list boxes, scroll bars, option buttons, tabs, and check boxes

- Explore the Windows 98 Help system

LABS

Using a Keyboard

Using a Mouse

EXPLORING THE BASICS

Investigating the Windows 98 Operating System

CASE

Your First Day on the Computer

You walk into the computer lab and sit down at a desk. There's a computer in front of you, and you find yourself staring dubiously at the screen. Where to start? As if in answer to your question, your friend Steve Laslow appears.

"You start with the operating system," says Steve. Noticing your puzzled look, Steve explains that the **operating system** is software that helps the computer carry out operating tasks such as displaying information on the computer screen and saving data on your disks. Your computer uses the **Microsoft Windows 98** operating system—Windows 98, for short.

Steve tells you that Windows 98 has a "gooey" or **graphical user interface (GUI)**, which uses pictures of familiar objects, such as file folders and documents, to represent a desktop on your screen. Microsoft Windows 98 gets its name from the rectangular work areas, called "windows," that appear on your screen.

Steve explains that much of the software available for Windows 98 has a standard graphical user interface. This means that once you have learned how to use one Windows software package, such as word-processing software, you are well on your way to understanding how to use other Windows software. Windows 98 lets you use more than one software package at a time, so you can easily switch between your word-processing software and your appointment book software, for example. Finally, Windows 98 makes it very easy to access the **Internet**, the worldwide collection of computers connected to one another to enable communication. All in all, Windows 98 makes your computer an effective and easy-to-use productivity tool.

Steve recommends that you get started right away by using some tutorials that will teach you the skills essential for using Microsoft Windows 98. He hands you a book and assures you that everything on your computer system is set up and ready to go.

SESSION 1.1

In this session, in addition to learning basic Windows terminology, you will learn how to use a pointing device, how to start and stop a program, and how to use more than one program at a time.

Starting Windows 98

Using a Keyboard

Windows 98 automatically starts when you turn on the computer. Depending on the way your computer is set up, you might be asked to enter your username and password.

To start Windows 98:

1. Turn on your computer.

   TROUBLE? If prompted to do so, type your assigned username and press the Tab key. Then type your password and press the Enter key to continue.

   TROUBLE? If this is the first time you have started your computer with Windows 98, messages might appear on your screen informing you that Windows is setting up components of your computer. If the Welcome to Windows 98 box appears, press and hold down the Alt key on your keyboard and then, while you hold down the Alt key, press the F4 key. The box closes.

After a moment, Windows 98 starts.

The Windows 98 Desktop

In Windows terminology, the area displayed on your screen represents a **desktop**—a workspace for projects and the tools needed to manipulate those projects. When you first start a computer, it uses **default** settings, those preset by the operating system. The default desktop, for example, has a plain teal background. However, Microsoft designed Windows 98 so that you can easily change the appearance of the desktop. You can, for example, add color, patterns, images, and text to the desktop background.

Many institutions design customized desktops for their computers. Figure 1-1 shows the default Windows 98 desktop and two other examples of desktops, one designed for a business, North Pole Novelties, and one designed for a school, the University of Colorado. Although your desktop might not look exactly like any of the examples in Figure 1-1, you should be able to locate objects on your screen similar to those in Figure 1-1. Look at your screen display and locate the objects labeled in Figure 1-1. The objects on your screen might appear larger or smaller than those in Figure 1-1, depending on your monitor's settings.

Figure 1-1	THE WINDOWS 98 DESKTOP

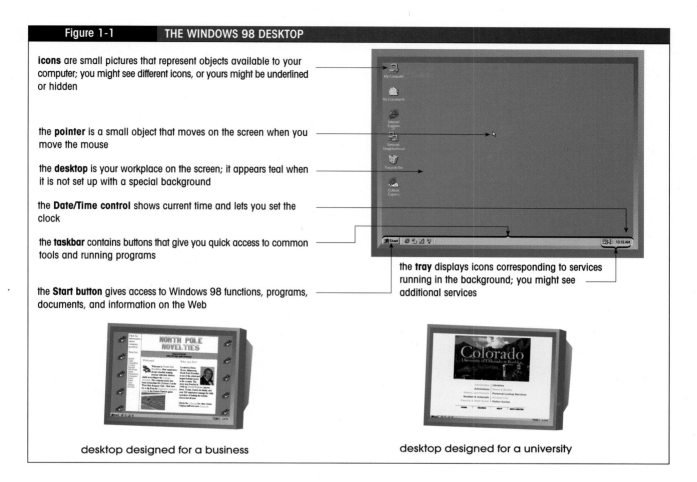

icons are small pictures that represent objects available to your computer; you might see different icons, or yours might be underlined or hidden

the **pointer** is a small object that moves on the screen when you move the mouse

the **desktop** is your workplace on the screen; it appears teal when it is not set up with a special background

the **Date/Time control** shows current time and lets you set the clock

the **taskbar** contains buttons that give you quick access to common tools and running programs

the **Start button** gives access to Windows 98 functions, programs, documents, and information on the Web

the **tray** displays icons corresponding to services running in the background; you might see additional services

desktop designed for a business

desktop designed for a university

If the screen goes blank or starts to display a moving design, press any key to restore the Windows 98 desktop.

Using a Pointing Device

Using a Mouse

A **pointing device** helps you interact with objects on the screen. Pointing devices come in many shapes and sizes; some are designed to ensure that your hand won't suffer fatigue while using them. Some are directly attached to your computer via a cable, whereas others function like a TV remote control and allow you to access your computer without being right next to it. Figure 1-2 shows examples of common pointing devices.

The most common pointing device is called a **mouse**, so this book uses that term. If you are using a different pointing device, such as a trackball, substitute that device whenever you see the term "mouse." In Windows 98 you need to know how to use the mouse to manipulate the objects on the screen. In this session you will learn about pointing and clicking. In Session 1.2 you will learn how to use the mouse to drag objects.

You can also interact with objects by using the keyboard; however, the mouse is more convenient for most tasks, so the tutorials in this book assume you are using one.

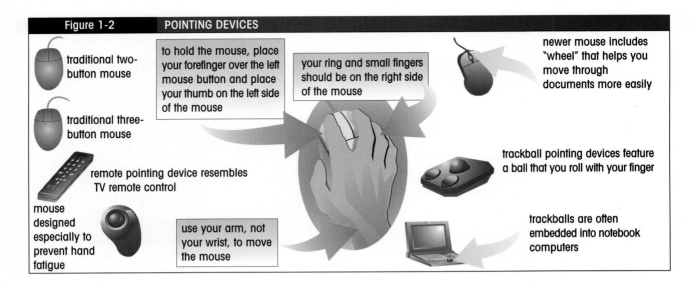

Figure 1-2   POINTING DEVICES

traditional two-button mouse

traditional three-button mouse

remote pointing device resembles TV remote control

mouse designed especially to prevent hand fatigue

to hold the mouse, place your forefinger over the left mouse button and place your thumb on the left side of the mouse

your ring and small fingers should be on the right side of the mouse

use your arm, not your wrist, to move the mouse

newer mouse includes "wheel" that helps you move through documents more easily

trackball pointing devices feature a ball that you roll with your finger

trackballs are often embedded into notebook computers

Pointing

You use a pointing device to move the pointer, in order to manipulate objects on the desktop. The pointer is usually shaped like an arrow ⩩ , although it can change shape depending on where it is on the screen. How skilled you are in using a mouse depends on your ability to position the pointer. Most computer users place the mouse on a **mouse pad**, a flat piece of rubber that helps the mouse move smoothly. As you move the mouse on the mouse pad, the pointer on the screen moves in a corresponding direction.

You begin most Windows operations by positioning the pointer over a specific part of the screen. This is called **pointing**.

To move the pointer:

1. Position your right index finger over the left mouse button, as shown in Figure 1-2. Lightly grasp the sides of the mouse with your thumb and little fingers.

   TROUBLE? If you want to use the mouse with your left hand, ask your instructor or technical support person to help you use the Control Panel to swap the functions of the left and right mouse buttons. Be sure to find out how to change back to the right-handed mouse setting, so that you can reset the mouse each time you are finished in the lab.

2. Place the mouse on the mouse pad and then move the mouse. Watch the movement of the pointer.

   TROUBLE? If you run out of room to move your mouse, lift the mouse and place it in the middle of the mouse pad. Notice that the pointer does not move when the mouse is not in contact with the mouse pad.

When you position the mouse pointer over certain objects, such as the objects on the taskbar, a "tip" appears. These "tips" are called **ToolTips**, and they tell you the purpose or function of an object.

To view ToolTips:

1. Use the mouse to point to the **Start** button . After a few seconds, you see the tip "Click here to begin," as shown in Figure 1-3.

| Figure 1-3 | VIEWING TOOLTIPS |

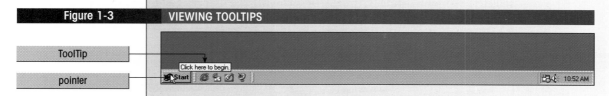

ToolTip

pointer

2. Point to the time on the right end of the taskbar. Notice that today's date (or the date to which your computer's time clock is set) appears.

Clicking

Clicking is when you press a mouse button and immediately release it. Clicking sends a signal to your computer that you want to perform an action on the object you click. In Windows 98 you can click using both the left and right mouse buttons, but most actions are performed using the left mouse button. If you are told to click an object, click it with the left mouse button, unless instructed otherwise.

When you click the Start button, the Start menu appears. A **menu** is a list of options that helps you work with software. The **Start menu** provides you with access to programs, documents, and much more. Try clicking the Start button to open the Start menu.

To open the Start menu:

1. Point to the **Start** button .

2. Click the left mouse button. An arrow ▶ following an option on the Start menu indicates that you can view additional choices by navigating a **submenu**, a menu extending from the main menu. See Figure 1-4.

| Figure 1-4 | START MENU |

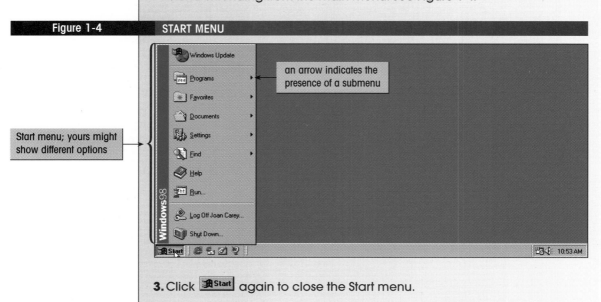

an arrow indicates the presence of a submenu

Start menu; yours might show different options

3. Click  again to close the Start menu.

Next you'll learn how to open a submenu by selecting it.

Selecting

In Windows 98, pointing and clicking are often used to **select** an object, in other words, to choose it as the object you want to work with. Windows 98 shows you which object is selected by highlighting it, usually by changing the object's color, putting a box around it, or making the object appear to be pushed in, as shown in Figure 1-5.

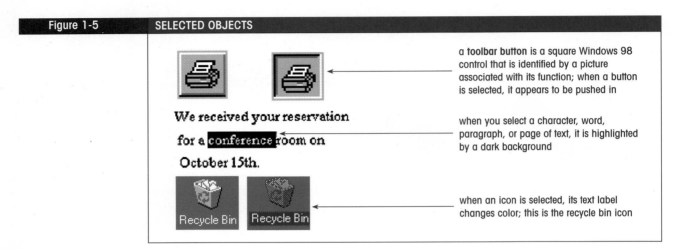

Figure 1-5   SELECTED OBJECTS

a **toolbar button** is a square Windows 98 control that is identified by a picture associated with its function; when a button is selected, it appears to be pushed in

We received your reservation for a conference room on October 15th.

when you select a character, word, paragraph, or page of text, it is highlighted by a dark background

Recycle Bin   Recycle Bin

when an icon is selected, its text label changes color; this is the recycle bin icon

In Windows 98, depending on your computer's settings, some objects are selected when you simply point to them, others when you click them. Practice selecting the Programs option on the Start menu to open the Programs submenu.

To select an option on a menu:

1. Click the **Start** button [Start] and notice how it appears to be pushed in, indicating it is selected.

2. Point to the **Programs** option. After a short pause, the Programs submenu opens, and the Programs option is highlighted to indicate it is selected. See Figure 1-6.

   TROUBLE? If a submenu other than the Programs menu opens, you selected the wrong option. Move the mouse so that the pointer points to Programs.

   TROUBLE? If the Programs option doesn't appear, your Start menu might have too many options to fit on the screen. If that is the case, a small arrow appears at the top or bottom of the Start menu. Click first the top and then the bottom arrow to view additional Start menu options until you locate the Programs menu option, and then point to it.

Figure 1-6	PROGRAMS SUBMENU

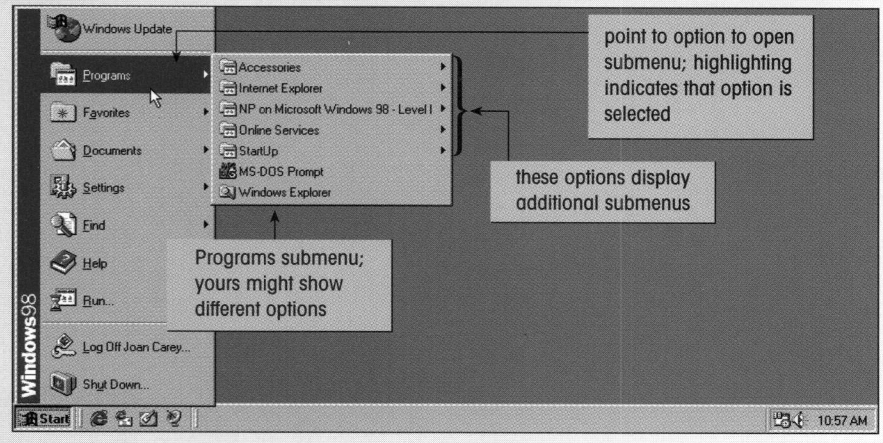

3. Now close the Start menu by clicking [Start] again.

You return to the desktop.

Right-Clicking

Pointing devices were originally designed with a single button, so the term "clicking" had only one meaning: you pressed that button. Innovations in technology, however, led to the addition of a second and even a third button (and more recently, options such as a wheel) that expanded the pointing device's capability. More recent software—especially that designed for Windows 98—takes advantage of additional buttons, especially the right button. However, the term "clicking" continues to refer to the left button; clicking an object with the *right* button is called **right-clicking**.

In Windows 98, right-clicking both selects an object and opens its **shortcut menu**, a list of options directly related to the object you right-clicked. You can right-click practically any object—the Start button, a desktop icon, the taskbar, and even the desktop itself—to view options associated with that object. For example, the first desktop shown in Figure 1-7 illustrates what happens when you click the Start button with the left mouse button to open the Start menu. Clicking the Start button with the right button, however, opens the Start button's shortcut menu, as shown in the second desktop.

| Figure 1-7 | CLICKING WITH THE LEFT AND RIGHT MOUSE BUTTONS |

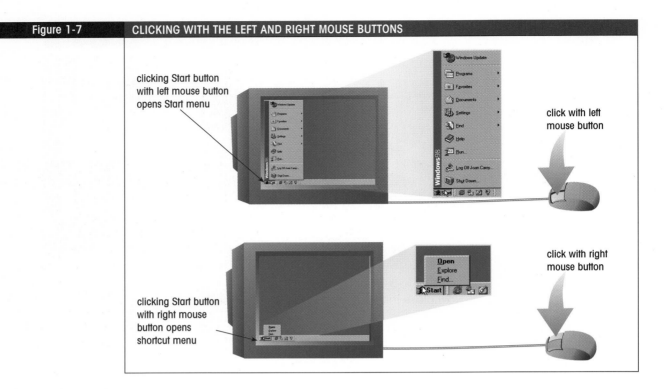

clicking Start button with left mouse button opens Start menu

click with left mouse button

clicking Start button with right mouse button opens shortcut menu

click with right mouse button

Try using right-clicking to open the shortcut menu for the Start button.

To right-click an object:

1. Position the pointer over the Start button.

2. Right-click the **Start** button . The shortcut menu that opens offers a list of options available to the Start button.

TROUBLE? If you are using a trackball or a mouse with three buttons or a wheel, make sure you click the button on the far right, not the one in the middle.

TROUBLE? If your menu looks slightly different from the one in Figure 1-8, don't worry. Computers with different software often have different options.

| Figure 1-8 | START BUTTON SHORTCUT MENU |

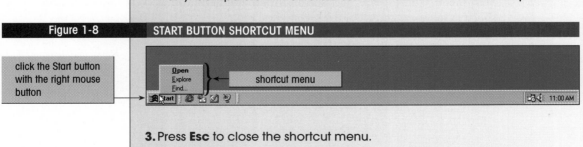

click the Start button with the right mouse button

shortcut menu

3. Press **Esc** to close the shortcut menu.

You again return to the desktop.

Starting **and Closing a Program**

The software you use is sometimes referred to as a **program** or an **application**. To use a program, such as a word-processing program, you must first start it. With Windows 98 you start a program by clicking the Start button.

The Reference Window below explains how to start a program. Don't do the steps in the Reference Window now; they are for your later reference.

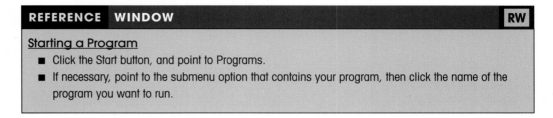

REFERENCE WINDOW **RW**

Starting a Program
- Click the Start button, and point to Programs.
- If necessary, point to the submenu option that contains your program, then click the name of the program you want to run.

Windows 98 includes an easy-to-use word-processing program called WordPad. Suppose you want to start the WordPad program and use it to write a letter or report. You open Windows 98 programs from the Start menu. Programs are usually located on the Programs submenu or on one of its submenus. To start WordPad, for example, you navigate the Programs and Accessories submenus.

To start the WordPad program from the Start menu:

1. Click the **Start** button ![Start] to open the Start menu.

2. Point to **Programs**. The Programs submenu appears.

3. Point to **Accessories**. Another submenu appears. Figure 1-9 shows the open menus.

TROUBLE? If a different menu opens, you might have moved the mouse diagonally so that a different submenu opened. Move the pointer to the right across the Programs option, and then move it up or down to point to Accessories. Once you're more comfortable moving the mouse, you'll find that you can eliminate this problem by moving the mouse quickly.

Figure 1-9	START MENU

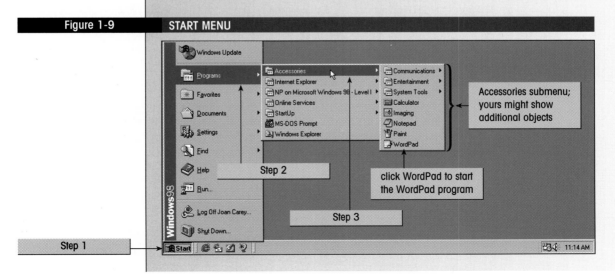

4. Click **WordPad**. The WordPad program opens, as shown in Figure 1-10. If the WordPad window does not fill the entire screen, don't worry. You will learn how to manipulate windows in Session 1.2.

| Figure 1-10 | THE WORDPAD PROGRAM |

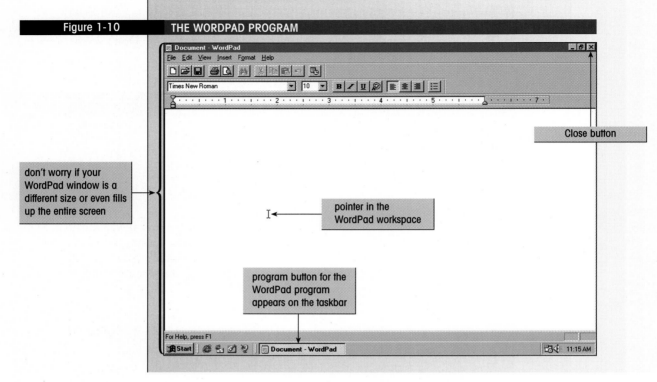

don't worry if your WordPad window is a different size or even fills up the entire screen

Close button

pointer in the WordPad workspace

program button for the WordPad program appears on the taskbar

When a program is started, it is said to be **running**. A program button appears on the taskbar. **Program buttons** give you access to the programs running on the desktop.

When you are finished using a program, the easiest way to close it is to click the Close button ⊠.

To exit the WordPad program:

1. Click the **Close** button ⊠. See Figure 1-10. You return to the Windows 98 desktop.

Running Multiple Programs

One of the most useful features of Windows 98 is its ability to run multiple programs at the same time. This feature, known as **multitasking**, allows you to work on more than one project at a time and to switch quickly between projects. For example, you can start WordPad and leave it running while you then start the Paint program.

To run WordPad and Paint at the same time:

1. Start WordPad, then click the **Start** button Start again.

2. Point to **Programs**, then point to **Accessories**.

3. Click **Paint**. The Paint program appears, as shown in Figure 1-11. Now two programs are running at the same time.

| Figure 1-11 | THE PAINT PROGRAM |

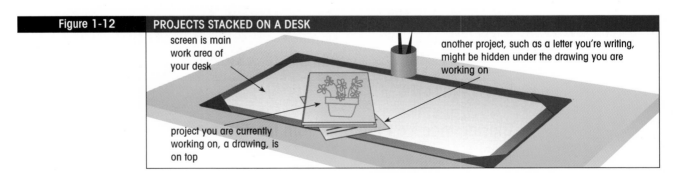

mouse pointer is a pencil when positioned in the drawing area

WordPad program button is not pushed in, indicating that WordPad is running but is not the active program

Paint program button is pushed in, indicating that Paint is the active program

TROUBLE? If the Paint program does not fill the entire screen, don't worry. You will learn how to manipulate windows in Session 1.2.

What happened to WordPad? The WordPad program button is still on the taskbar, so even if you can't see it, WordPad is still running. You can imagine that it is stacked behind the Paint program, as shown in Figure 1-12.

| Figure 1-12 | PROJECTS STACKED ON A DESK |

screen is main work area of your desk

another project, such as a letter you're writing, might be hidden under the drawing you are working on

project you are currently working on, a drawing, is on top

Switching Between Programs

Although Windows 98 allows you to run more than one program, only one program at a time is active. The **active** program is the program with which you are currently working. The easiest way to switch between programs is to use the buttons on the taskbar.

To switch between WordPad and Paint:

1. Click the button labeled **Document - WordPad** on the taskbar. The Document - WordPad button now looks as if it has been pushed in, to indicate that it is the active program, and WordPad moves to the front.

2. Next, click the button labeled **untitled - Paint** on the taskbar to switch to the Paint program.

The Paint program is again the active program.

Accessing the Desktop from the Quick Launch Toolbar

The Windows 98 taskbar, as you've seen, displays buttons for programs currently running. It also can contain **toolbars**, sets of buttons that give single-click access to programs or documents. In its default state, the Windows 98 taskbar displays the **Quick Launch toolbar**, which gives quick access to Web programs and to the desktop. Your taskbar might contain additional toolbars, or none at all.

When you are running more than one program but you want to return to the desktop, perhaps to use one of the desktop icons such as My Computer, you can do so by using one of the Quick Launch toolbar buttons. Clicking the Show Desktop button returns you to the desktop. The open programs are not closed; they are simply inactive.

To return to the desktop:

1. Click the **Show Desktop** button on the Quick Launch toolbar. The desktop appears, and both the Paint and WordPad programs are temporarily inactive. See Figure 1-13.

   TROUBLE? If the Quick Launch toolbar doesn't appear on your taskbar, right-click the taskbar, point to Toolbars, and then click Quick Launch and try Step 1 again.

| Figure 1-13 | ACCESSING THE DESKTOP |

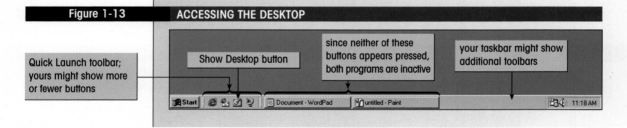

Quick Launch toolbar; yours might show more or fewer buttons

Show Desktop button

since neither of these buttons appears pressed, both programs are inactive

your taskbar might show additional toolbars

Closing Inactive Programs from the Taskbar

It is good practice to close each program when you are finished using it. Each program uses computer resources, such as memory, so Windows 98 works more efficiently when only the programs you need are open. You've already seen how to close an open program using the Close button. You can also close a program, whether active or inactive, by using the shortcut menu associated with the program button on the taskbar.

To close WordPad and Paint using the program button shortcut menus:

1. Right-click the **untitled – Paint** button on the taskbar. To right-click something, remember that you click it with the right mouse button. The shortcut menu for that program button opens. See Figure 1-14.

| Figure 1-14 | PROGRAM BUTTON SHORTCUT MENU |

2. Click **Close**. The button labeled "untitled – Paint" disappears from the taskbar, and the Paint program closes.

3. Right-click the **Document – WordPad** button on the taskbar, and then click **Close**. The WordPad button disappears from the taskbar.

Shutting Down Windows 98

It is very important to shut down Windows 98 before you turn off the computer. If you turn off your computer without correctly shutting down, you might lose data and damage your files.

You should typically use the "Shut down" option when you want to turn off your computer. However, your school might prefer that you select the Log Off option on the Start menu. This option logs you out of Windows 98, leaves the computer turned on, and allows another user to log on without restarting the computer. Check with your instructor or technical support person for the preferred method at your school's computer lab.

To shut down Windows 98:

1. Click the **Start** button [🏁Start] on the taskbar to display the Start menu.

2. Click the **Shut Down** menu option. A box titled "Shut Down Windows" opens.

TROUBLE? If you can't see the Shut Down menu option, your Start menu has more options than your screen can display. A small arrow appears at the bottom of the Start menu. Click this button until the Shut Down menu option appears, and then click Shut Down.

TROUBLE? If you are supposed to log off rather than shut down, click the Log Off option instead and follow your school's logoff procedure.

3. Make sure the **Shut down** option is preceded by a small black bullet. See Figure 1-15.

TROUBLE? If your Shut down option is not preceded by a small black bullet, point to the circle preceding the Shut down option and click it. A small black bullet appears in the circle, indicating that Windows 98 will perform the Shut down option. Your Shut Down Windows dialog box might show additional options, such as Stand by.

| Figure 1-15 | SHUTTING DOWN |

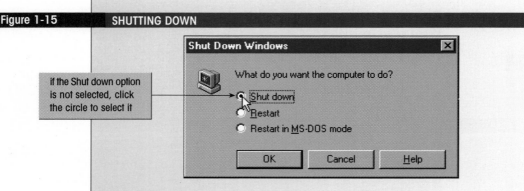

if the Shut down option is not selected, click the circle to select it

4. Click the **OK** button.

5. Click the **Yes** button if you are asked if you are sure you want to shut down.

6. Wait until you see a message indicating it is safe to turn off your computer. If your lab staff has requested you to switch off your computer after shutting down, do so now. Otherwise leave the computer running. Some computers turn themselves off automatically.

QUICK CHECK

1. What is the purpose of the taskbar?

2. The _____ feature of Windows 98 allows you to run more than one program at a time.

3. The _____ is a list of options that provides you with access to programs, documents, submenus, and more.

4. What should you do if you are trying to move the pointer to the left edge of your screen, but your mouse bumps into the keyboard?

5. Even if you can't see an open program on your desktop, the program might be running. How can you tell if a program is running?

6. Why is it good practice to close each program when you are finished using it?

7. Why should you shut down Windows 98 before you turn off your computer?

SESSION 1.2

In this session you will learn how to use many of the Windows 98 controls to manipulate windows and programs. You will also learn how to change the size and shape of a window; how to move a window; and how to use menus, dialog boxes, tabs, buttons, and lists to specify how you want a program to carry out a task.

Anatomy of a Window

When you run a program in Windows 98, it appears in a window. A **window** is a rectangular area of the screen that contains a program or data. Windows, spelled with an uppercase "W," is the name of the Microsoft operating system. The word "window" with a lowercase "w" refers to one of the rectangular areas on the screen. A window also contains controls for manipulating the window and for using the program. Figure 1-16 describes the controls you are likely to see in most windows.

Figure 1-16	WINDOW CONTROLS
CONTROL	**DESCRIPTION**
Menu bar	Contains the titles of menus, such as File, Edit, and Help
Pointer	Lets you manipulate window objects
Program button	Appears on the taskbar to indicate that a program is running on the desktop; appears pressed when program is active and not pressed when program is inactive
Sizing buttons	Let you enlarge, shrink, or close a window
Status bar	Provides you with messages relevant to the task you are performing
Title bar	Contains the window title and basic window control buttons
Toolbar	Contains buttons that provide you with shortcuts to common menu commands
Window title	Identifies the program and document contained in the window
Workspace	Part of the window you use to enter your work—to enter text, draw pictures, set up calculations, and so on

WordPad is a good example of a typical window, so try starting WordPad and identifying these controls in the WordPad window.

To look at window controls:

1. Make sure Windows 98 is running and you are at the Windows 98 desktop.

2. Start WordPad.

   TROUBLE? To start WordPad, click the Start button, point to Programs, point to Accessories, and then click WordPad.

3. On your screen, identify the controls labeled in Figure 1-17. Don't worry if your window fills the entire screen or is a different size. You'll learn to change window size shortly.

Figure 1-17   WORDPAD WINDOW CONTROLS

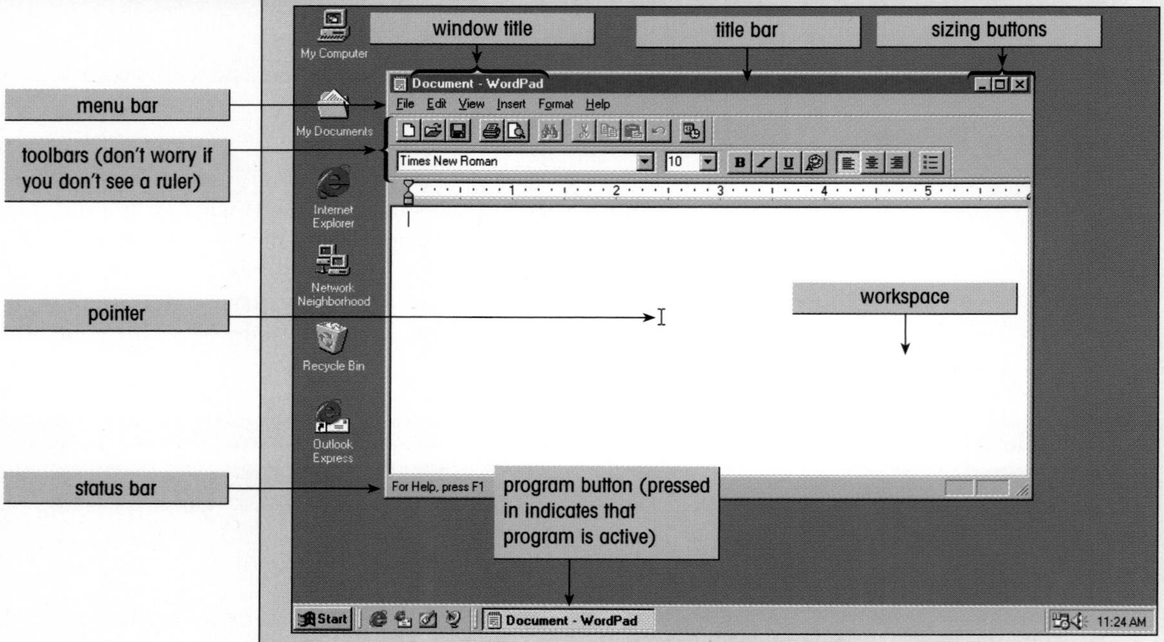

Manipulating a Window

There are three buttons located on the right side of the title bar. You are already familiar with the Close button. The Minimize button hides the window so that only its program button is visible on the taskbar. The other button either maximizes the window or restores it to a predefined size. Figure 1-18 shows how these buttons work.

Minimizing a Window

The Minimize button ▬ hides a window so that only the button on the taskbar remains visible. You can use the Minimize button when you want to temporarily hide a window but keep the program running.

To minimize the WordPad window:

1. Click the **Minimize** button ▬. The WordPad window shrinks so that only the Document - WordPad button on the taskbar is visible.

   TROUBLE? If you accidentally clicked the Close button and closed the window, use the Start button to start WordPad again.

Figure 1-18 WINDOW BUTTONS

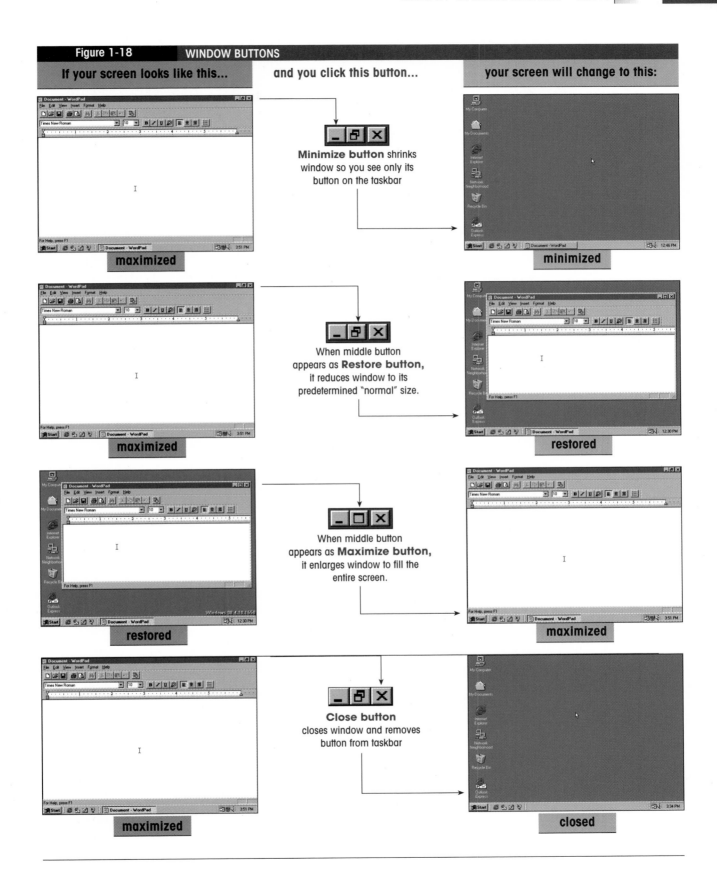

If your screen looks like this...

and you click this button...

your screen will change to this:

maximized

Minimize button shrinks window so you see only its button on the taskbar

minimized

maximized

When middle button appears as **Restore button,** it reduces window to its predetermined "normal" size.

restored

restored

When middle button appears as **Maximize button,** it enlarges window to fill the entire screen.

maximized

maximized

Close button closes window and removes button from taskbar

closed

Redisplaying a Window

You can redisplay a minimized window by clicking the program's button on the taskbar. When you redisplay a window, it becomes the active window.

> ### To redisplay the WordPad window:
>
> **1.** Click the **Document - WordPad** button on the taskbar. The WordPad window is restored to its previous size. The Document - WordPad button looks pushed in as a visual clue that WordPad is now the active window.
>
> **2.** The taskbar button provides another means of switching a window between its minimized and active state: click the **Document - WordPad** button on the taskbar again to minimize the window.
>
> **3.** Click the **Document - WordPad** button once more to redisplay the window.

Maximizing a Window

The Maximize button enlarges a window so that it fills the entire screen. You will probably do most of your work using maximized windows because they allow you to see more of your program and data.

> ### To maximize the WordPad window:
>
> **1.** Click the **Maximize** button 🗖 on the WordPad title bar.
>
> TROUBLE? If the window is already maximized, it will fill the entire screen, and the Maximize button won't appear. Instead, you'll see the Restore button 🗗. Skip Step 1.

Restoring a Window

The Restore button 🗗 reduces the window so it is smaller than the entire screen. This is useful if you want to see more than one window at a time. Also, because of its smaller size, you can drag the window to another location on the screen or change its dimensions.

> ### To restore a window:
>
> **1.** Click the **Restore** button 🗗 on the WordPad title bar. Notice that once a window is restored, 🗗 changes to the Maximize button 🗖.

Moving a Window

You can use the mouse to move a window to a new position on the screen. When you hold down the mouse button while moving the mouse, you are said to be **dragging**. You can move objects on the screen by dragging them to a new location. If you want to move a window, you drag its title bar. You cannot move a maximized window.

To drag the WordPad window to a new location:

1. Position the mouse pointer on the WordPad window title bar.

2. While you hold down the left mouse button, move the mouse to drag the window. A rectangle representing the window moves as you move the mouse.

3. Position the rectangle anywhere on the screen, then release the left mouse button. The WordPad window appears in the new location.

4. Now drag the WordPad window to the upper-left corner of the screen.

Changing the Size of a Window

You can also use the mouse to change the size of a window. Notice the sizing handle [image] at the lower-right corner of the window. The **sizing handle** provides a visible control for changing the size of a window.

To change the size of the WordPad window:

1. Position the pointer over the sizing handle [image]. The pointer changes to a diagonal arrow ↘.

2. While holding down the mouse button, drag the sizing handle down and to the right.

3. Release the mouse button. Now the window is larger.

4. Practice using the sizing handle to make the WordPad window larger or smaller, and then maximize the WordPad window.

You can also drag the window borders left, right, up, or down to change a window's size.

Using Program Menus

Most Windows programs use menus to provide an easy way for you to select program commands. The menu bar is typically located at the top of the program window and shows the titles of menus such as File, Edit, and Help.

Windows menus are relatively standardized—most Windows programs include similar menu options. It's easy to learn new programs, because you can make a pretty good guess about which menu contains the command you want.

Selecting Commands from a Menu

When you click any menu title, choices for that menu appear below the menu bar. These choices are referred to as **menu options** or **commands**. To select a menu option, you click it. For example, the File menu is a standard feature in most Windows programs and contains the options typically related to working with a file: creating, opening, saving, and printing a file or document.

To select the Print Preview menu option from the File menu:

1. Click **File** in the WordPad menu bar to display the File menu. See Figure 1-19.

   TROUBLE? If you open a menu but decide not to select any of the menu options, you can close the menu by clicking its title again.

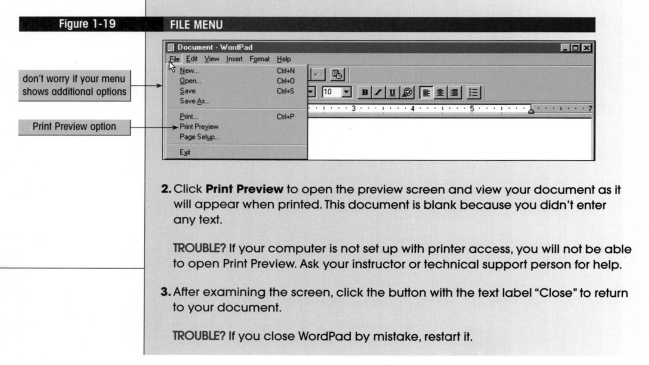

Figure 1-19	FILE MENU

don't worry if your menu shows additional options

Print Preview option

2. Click **Print Preview** to open the preview screen and view your document as it will appear when printed. This document is blank because you didn't enter any text.

   TROUBLE? If your computer is not set up with printer access, you will not be able to open Print Preview. Ask your instructor or technical support person for help.

3. After examining the screen, click the button with the text label "Close" to return to your document.

   TROUBLE? If you close WordPad by mistake, restart it.

Not all menu options immediately carry out an action—some show submenus or ask you for more information about what you want to do. The menu gives you hints about what to expect when you select an option. These hints are sometimes referred to as **menu conventions**. Figure 1-20 describes the Windows 98 menu conventions.

Figure 1-20	MENU CONVENTIONS
CONVENTION	**DESCRIPTION**
Check mark	Indicates a toggle, or "on-off" switch (like a light switch) that is either checked (turned on) or not checked (turned off)
Ellipsis	Three dots that indicate you must make additional selections after you select that option. Options without dots do not require additional choices—they take effect as soon as you click them. If an option is followed by an ellipsis, a dialog box opens that allows you to enter specifications for how you want a task carried out
Triangular arrow	Indicates presence of a submenu. When you point at a menu option that has a triangular arrow, a submenu automatically appears
Grayed-out option	Option that is not available. For example, a graphics program might display the Text Toolbar option in gray if there is no text in the graphic to work with
Keyboard shortcut	A key or combination of keys that you can press to activate the menu option without actually opening the menu

Figure 1-21 shows examples of these menu conventions.

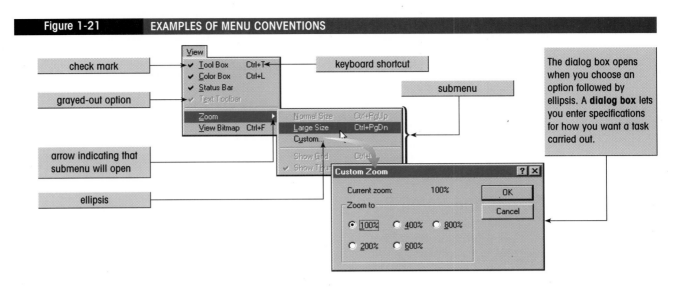

Figure 1-21 — EXAMPLES OF MENU CONVENTIONS

- check mark
- grayed-out option
- arrow indicating that submenu will open
- ellipsis
- keyboard shortcut
- submenu

The dialog box opens when you choose an option followed by ellipsis. A **dialog box** lets you enter specifications for how you want a task carried out.

Using Toolbars

A toolbar, as you've seen, contains buttons that provide quick access to important commands. Although you can usually perform all program commands using menus, the toolbar provides convenient one-click access to frequently used commands. For most Windows 98 functions, there is usually more than one way to accomplish a task. To simplify your introduction to Windows 98 in this tutorial, we will usually show you only one method for performing a task. As you become more accomplished at using Windows 98, you can explore alternate methods.

In Session 1.1 you learned that Windows 98 programs include ToolTips, which indicate the purpose and function of a tool. Now is a good time to explore the WordPad toolbar buttons by looking at their ToolTips.

To find out a toolbar button's function:

1. Position the pointer over any button on the toolbar, such as the Print Preview button. After a short pause, the name of the button appears in a box near the button, and a description of the button appears in the status bar just above the Start button. See Figure 1-22.

Figure 1-22 — TOOLBAR BUTTON AIDS

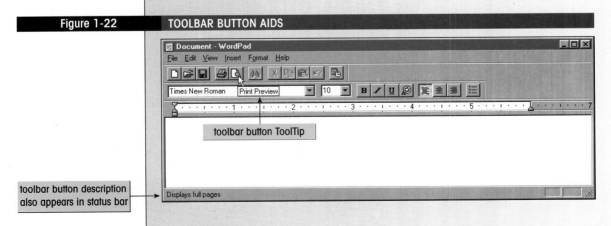

- toolbar button ToolTip
- toolbar button description also appears in status bar

2. Move the pointer to each button on the toolbar to see its name and purpose.

You select a toolbar button by clicking it.

To select the Print Preview toolbar button:

1. Click the **Print Preview** button. The Print Preview screen appears. This is the same screen that appeared when you selected Print Preview from the File menu.

2. After examining the screen, click the button with the text label "Close" to return to your document.

Using List Boxes and Scroll Bars

As you might guess from the name, a **list box** displays a list of choices. In WordPad, date and time formats are shown in the Date/Time list box. List box controls usually include arrow buttons, a scroll bar, and a scroll box, as shown in Figure 1-23.

To use the Date/Time list box:

1. Click the **Date/Time** button to display the Date and Time dialog box. See Figure 1-23.

Figure 1-23	LIST BOX

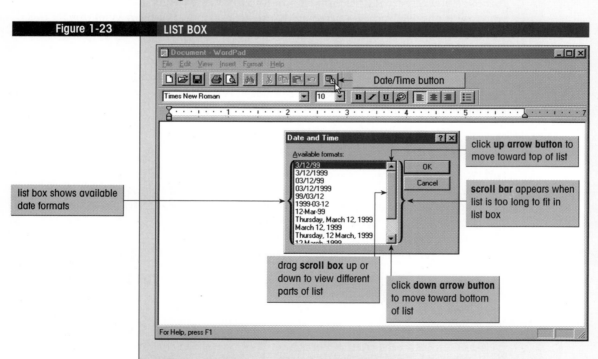

2. To scroll down the list, click the **down arrow** button. See Figure 1-23.

3. Find the scroll box on your screen. See Figure 1-23.

4. Drag the **scroll box** to the top of the scroll bar. Notice how the list scrolls back to the beginning.

> **TROUBLE?** You learned how to drag when you learned to move a window. To drag the scroll box up, point to the scroll box, press and hold down the mouse button, and then move the mouse up.
>
> **5.** Find a date format similar to "March 12, 1999." Click that date format to select it.
>
> **6.** Click the **OK** button to close the Date and Time dialog box. This inserts the current date in your document.

You can access some list boxes directly from the toolbar. When a list box is on the toolbar, only the current option appears in the list box. A **list arrow** appears on the right of the box that you can click to view additional options.

To use the Font Size list box:

1. Click the **list arrow** shown in Figure 1-24.

Figure 1-24	FONT SIZE LIST ARROW

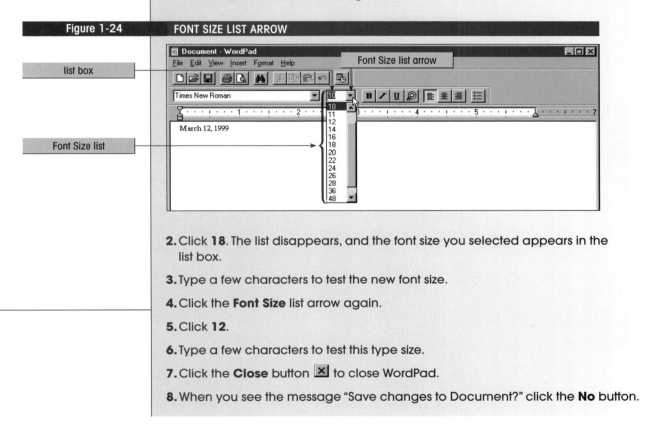

list box

Font Size list arrow

Font Size list

2. Click **18**. The list disappears, and the font size you selected appears in the list box.

3. Type a few characters to test the new font size.

4. Click the **Font Size** list arrow again.

5. Click **12**.

6. Type a few characters to test this type size.

7. Click the **Close** button ⊠ to close WordPad.

8. When you see the message "Save changes to Document?" click the **No** button.

Using Dialog Box Controls

Recall that when you select a menu option or button followed by an ellipsis, a dialog box opens that allows you to provide more information about how a program should carry out a task. Some dialog boxes group different kinds of information into bordered rectangular areas called **panes**. Within these panes, you will usually find tabs, option buttons, check boxes, and other controls that the program uses to collect information about how you want it to perform a task. Figure 1-25 describes common dialog box controls.

Figure 1-25	DIALOG BOX CONTROLS
CONTROL	**DESCRIPTION**
Tabs	Modeled after the tabs on file folders, tab controls are often used as containers for other Windows 98 controls such as list boxes, radio buttons, and check boxes. Click the appropriate tab to view different pages of information or choices.
Option buttons	Also called **radio buttons**, option buttons allow you to select a single option from among one or more options.
Check boxes	Click a check box to select or deselect it; when it is selected, a check mark appears, indicating that the option is turned on; when deselected, the check box is blank and the option is off. When check boxes appear in groups, you can select or deselect as many as you want; they are not mutually exclusive, as option buttons are.
Spin boxes	Allow you to scroll easily through a set of numbers to choose the setting you want
Text boxes	Boxes into which you type additional information

Figure 1-26 displays examples of these controls.

Figure 1-26	EXAMPLES OF DIALOG BOX CONTROLS

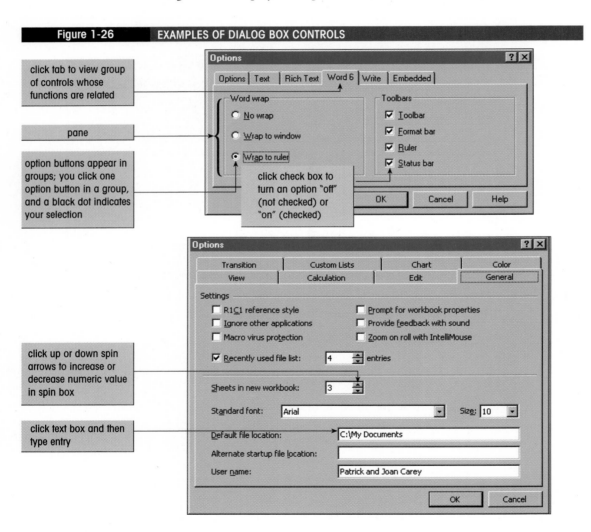

Using **Help**

Windows 98 **Help** provides on-screen information about the program you are using. Help for the Windows 98 operating system is available by clicking the Start button on the taskbar, then selecting Help from the Start menu. If you want Help for a program, such as WordPad, you must first start the program, then click Help on the menu bar.

When you start Help, a Windows Help window opens, which gives you access to help files stored on your computer as well as help information stored on Microsoft's Web site. If you are not connected to the Web, you only have access to the help files stored on your computer.

To start Windows 98 Help:

1. Click the **Start** button.

2. Click **Help**. The Windows Help window opens to the Contents tab. See Figure 1-27.

   TROUBLE? If the Contents tab is not in front, click the Contents tab to view Help contents.

| Figure 1-27 | WINDOWS HELP WINDOW |

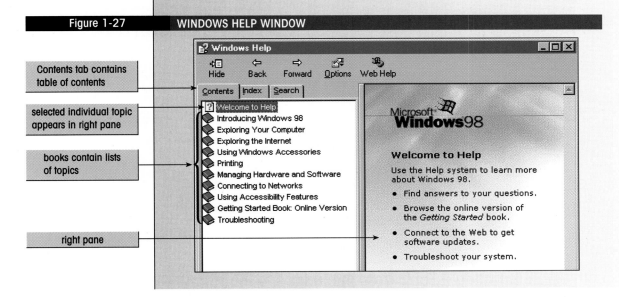

Contents tab contains table of contents

selected individual topic appears in right pane

books contain lists of topics

right pane

Help uses tabs for the three sections of Help: Contents, Index, and Search. The **Contents tab** groups Help topics into a series of books. You select a book 📖 by clicking it. The book opens, and a list of related topics appears from which you can choose. Individual topics are designated with the 🗎 icon.

The **Index tab** displays an alphabetical list of all the Help topics from which you can choose. The **Search tab** allows you to search the entire set of Help topics for all topics that contain a word or words you specify.

Viewing Topics from the Contents Tab

You've already opened two of the Windows accessories, Paint and WordPad. Suppose you're wondering about the other accessory programs. You can use the Contents tab to find more information on a specific topic.

To use the Contents tab:

1. Click the **Using Windows Accessories** book icon 📖. A list of topics and related books appears below the book title. You decide to explore entertainment accessories.

2. Click the **Entertainment** book icon 📖.

3. Click the **CD Player** topic icon 🔖. Information about the CD Player accessory appears in the right pane, explaining how you can use the CD-ROM drive (if you have one) on your computer to play your favorite music CDs. See Figure 1-28.

| Figure 1-28 | LOCATING INFORMATION ABOUT CD PLAYER ACCESSORY |

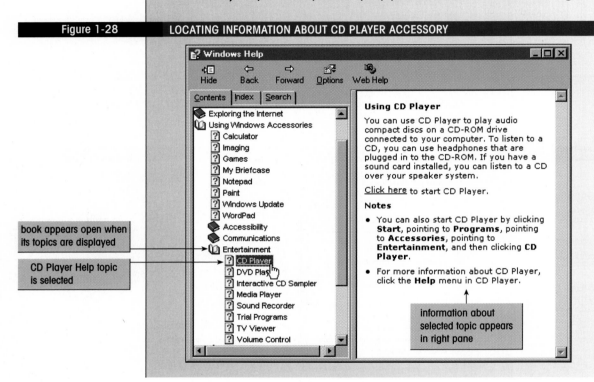

book appears open when its topics are displayed

CD Player Help topic is selected

information about selected topic appears in right pane

Selecting a Topic from the Index

The Index tab allows you to jump to a Help topic by selecting a topic from an indexed list. For example, you can use the Index tab to learn how to arrange the open windows on your desktop.

To find a Help topic using the Index tab:

1. Click the **Index** tab. A long list of indexed Help topics appears.

   TROUBLE? If this is the first time you've used Help on your computer, Windows 98 needs to set up the Index. This takes just a few moments. Wait until you see the list of index entries in the left pane, and then proceed to Step 2.

2. Drag the scroll box down to view additional topics.

3. You can quickly jump to any part of the list by typing the first few characters of a word or phrase in the box above the Index list. Click the box and then type **desktop** to display topics related to the Windows 98 desktop.

4. Click the topic **arranging windows on** and then click the **Display** button. When there is just one topic, it appears immediately in the right pane; otherwise, the Topics Found window opens, listing all topics indexed under the entry you're interested in. In this case, there are two choices.

5. Click **To minimize all open windows**, and then click the **Display** button. The information you requested appears in the right pane. See Figure 1-29. Notice in this topic that there is an underlined word: taskbar. You can click underlined words to view definitions or additional information.

| Figure 1-29 | USING THE INDEX TO LOCATE INFORMATION |

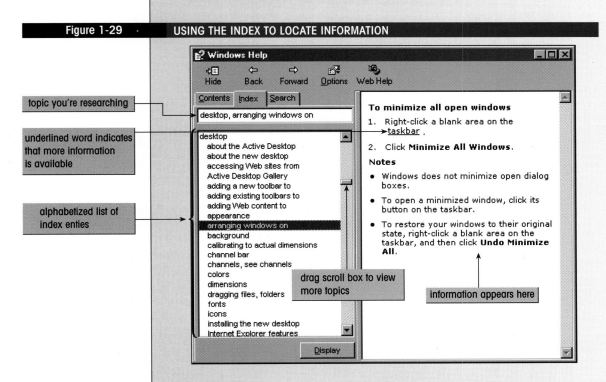

topic you're researching

underlined word indicates that more information is available

alphabetized list of index enties

drag scroll box to view more topics

information appears here

6. Click **taskbar**. A small box appears that defines the term "taskbar." See Figure 1-30.

| Figure 1-30 | VIEWING ADDITIONAL INFORMATION |

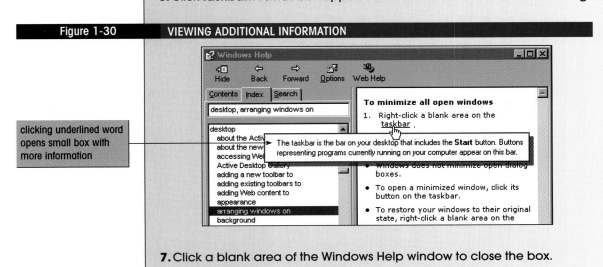

clicking underlined word opens small box with more information

7. Click a blank area of the Windows Help window to close the box.

The third tab, the Search tab, works similarly to the Index tab, except that you type a word, and then the Help system searches for topics containing that word. You'll get a chance to experiment with the Search tab in the Tutorial Assignments.

Returning to a Previous Help Topic

You've looked at a few topics now. Suppose you want to return to the one you just saw. The Help window includes a toolbar of buttons that help you navigate the Help system. One of these buttons is the **Back** button, which returns you to topics you've already viewed. Try returning to the help topic on playing music CDs on your CD-ROM drive.

To return to a help topic:

1. Click the **Back** button. The Using CD Player topic appears.

2. Click the **Close** button ☒ to close the Windows Help window.

3. Log off or shut down Windows 98, depending on your lab's requirements.

Now that you know how Windows 98 Help works, don't forget to use it! Use Help when you need to perform a new task or when you forget how to complete a procedure.

You've finished the tutorial, and as you shut down Windows 98, Steve Laslow returns from class. You take a moment to tell him all you've learned: you know how to start and close programs and how to use multiple programs at the same time. You have learned how to work with windows and the controls they employ. Finally, you've learned how to get help when you need it. Steve congratulates you and comments that you are well on your way to mastering the fundamentals of using the Windows 98 operating system.

QUICK CHECK

1. What is the difference between the title bar and a toolbar?

2. Provide the name and purpose of each button:

   a. ▬   b. ▢   c. ▣   d. ☒

3. Explain each of the following menu conventions:

   a. Ellipsis...   b. Grayed-out   c. ▶   d. ✔

4. A(n) _____ consists of a group of buttons, each of which provides one-click access to important program functions.

5. What is the purpose of the scrollbar?

6. Option buttons allow you to select _____ option(s) at a time.

7. It is a good idea to use _____ when you need to learn how to perform new tasks.

TUTORIAL ASSIGNMENTS

1. **Running Two Programs and Switching Between Them**   In this tutorial you learned how to run more than one program at a time, using WordPad and Paint. You can run other programs at the same time, too. Complete the following steps and write out your answers to questions b through f:

    a. Start the computer. Enter your username and password if prompted to do so.
    b. Click the Start button. How many menu options are on the Start menu?   *13*
    c. Run the Calculator program located on the Accessories menu. How many program buttons are now on the taskbar (don't count toolbar buttons or items in the tray)?   *1*
    d. Run the Paint program and maximize the Paint window. How many programs are running now?   *2*
    e. Switch to Calculator. What are two visual clues that tell you that Calculator is the active program?   *button in blue strip*
    f. Multiply 576 by 1457 using the Calculator accessory. What is the result?   *839232*
    g. Close Calculator, then close Paint.

Explore
2. **WordPad Help**   In Tutorial 1 you learned how to use Windows 98 Help. Just about every Windows 98 program has a help feature. Many computer users can learn to use a program just by using Help. To use Help, you start the program, then click the Help menu at the top of the screen. Try using WordPad Help:

    a. Start WordPad.
    b. Click Help on the WordPad menu bar, and then click Help Topics.
    c. Using WordPad Help, write out your answers to questions 1 through 4.
       1. How do you create a bulleted list?   *1. Click where you want the bulleted list to start*
       2. How do you set the margins in a document?
       3. How do you undo a mistake?
       4. How do you change the font style of a block of text?
    d. Close WordPad.

Explore
3. **The Search Tab**   In addition to the Contents and Index tabs you worked with in this tutorial, Windows 98 Help also includes a Search tab. You may have heard that Windows 98 makes it possible to view television programs on your computer. You could browse through the Contents tab, although you might not know where to look to find information about television. You could also use the Index tab to search through the indexed entry. Or you could use the Search tab to find all Help topics that mention television.

    a. Start Windows 98 Help and use the Index tab to find information about television. How many topics are listed? What is their primary subject matter?
    b. Now use the Search tab to find information about television. Type "television" into the box on the Search tab, and then click the List Topics button.
    c. Write a paragraph comparing the two lists of topics. You don't have to view them all, but in your paragraph, indicate which tab seems to yield more information, and why. Close Help.

4. **Discover Windows 98**   Windows 98 includes an online tour that helps you discover more about your computer and the Windows 98 operating system. You can use this tour to review what you learned in this tutorial and to pick up some new tips for using Windows 98. Complete the following steps and write out your answers to questions d–j.

    a. Click the Start button, point to Programs, point to Accessories, point to System Tools, and then click Welcome to Windows. If an error message appears at any point or if you can't locate this menu option, Welcome to Windows is probably not loaded on your computer. You will not be able to complete this assignment unless you have the Windows 98 CD. Check with your instructor.
    b. Click Discover Windows 98.
    c. Click Computer Essentials and follow the instructions on the screen to step through the tour.
    d. What is the "brain" of your computer, according to the tour information?
    e. What two devices do you use to communicate with your computer?

    f. What is the purpose of the ESC key?

    g. What is double-clicking?

    h. What is the purpose of the top section of the Start menu?

    i. What is another term for "submenu"?

    j. What function key opens the Help feature in most software?

PROJECTS

1. There are many types of pointing devices on the market today. Go to the library and research the types of devices that are available. Consider what devices are appropriate for these situations: desktop or laptop computers, connected or remote devices, and ergonomic or standard designs (look up the word "ergonomic").

   Use up-to-date computer books, trade computer magazines such as *PC Computing* and *PC Magazine*, or the Internet (if you know how) to locate information. Your instructor might suggest specific resources you can use. Write a one-page report describing the types of devices available, the differing needs of users, special features that make pointing devices more useful, price comparisons, and finally, an indication of what you would choose if you needed to buy a pointing device.

2. Using the resources available to you, either through your library or the Internet (if you know how), locate information about the release of Windows 98. Computing trade magazines are an excellent source of information about software. Read several articles about Windows 98 and then write a one-page essay that discusses the features that seem most important to the people who have evaluated the software. If you find reviews of the software, mention the features that reviewers had the strongest reaction to, pro or con.

3. **Upgrading** is the process of placing a more recent version of a product onto your computer. When Windows 98 first came out, people had to decide whether or not they wanted to upgrade their computers to Windows 98. Interview several people you know (at least three) who are well-informed Windows computer users. Ask them whether they are using Windows 98 or an older version of Windows. If they are using an older version, ask why they have chosen not to upgrade. If they are using Windows 98, ask them why they chose to upgrade. Ask such questions as:

   a. What features convinced you to upgrade or made you decide to wait?

   b. What role did the price of the upgrade play?

   c. Would you have had (or did you have) to purchase new hardware to make the upgrade? How did this affect your decision?

   d. If you did upgrade, are you happy with that decision? If you didn't, do you intend to upgrade in the near future? Why, or why not?

   Write a single-page essay summarizing what you learned from these interviews about making the decision to upgrade.

4. Choose a topic you'd like to research using the Windows 98 online Help system. Look for information on your topic using all three tabs: the Contents tab, the Index tab, and the Search tab. Once you've found all the information you can, compare the three methods (Contents, Index, Search) of looking for information. Write a paragraph that discusses which tab proved the most useful. Did you reach the same information topics using all three methods? In a second paragraph, summarize what you learned about your topic. Finally, in a third paragraph, indicate under what circumstances you'd use which tab.

LAB ASSIGNMENTS

Using a Keyboard

Using a Keyboard To become an effective computer user, you must be familiar with your primary input device—the keyboard. See the Read This Before You Begin page for information on installing and starting the lab.

1. The Steps for the Using a Keyboard Lab provide you with a structured introduction to the keyboard layout and the function of special computer keys. Click the Steps button and begin the Steps. As you work through the Steps, answer all of the Quick Check questions that appear. When you complete the Steps, you will see a Summary Report that summarizes your performance on the Quick Checks. Follow the directions on the screen to print the Summary Report.

2. In Explore, start the typing tutor. You can develop your typing skills using the typing tutor in Explore. Take the typing test and print out your results.

3. In Explore, try to improve your typing speed by 10 words per minute. For example, if you currently type 20 words per minute, your goal will be 30 words per minute. Practice each typing lesson until you see a message that indicates that you can proceed to the next lesson. Create a Practice Record, as shown here, to keep track of how much you practice. When you have reached your goal, print out the results of a typing test to verify your results.

Practice Record

Name:

Section:

Start Date:	Start Typing Speed:	wpm
End Date:	End Typing Speed:	wpm
Lesson #:	Date Practiced/Time Practiced	

Using a Mouse

Using a Mouse A mouse is a standard input device on most of today's computers. You need to know how to use a mouse to manipulate graphical user interfaces and to use the rest of the Labs. See the Read This Before You Begin page for information on installing and starting the lab.

1. The Steps for the Using a Mouse Lab show you how to click, double-click, and drag objects using the mouse. Click the Steps button and begin the Steps. As you work through the Steps, answer all of the Quick Check questions that appear. When you complete the Steps, you will see a Summary Report that summarizes your performance on the Quick Checks. Follow the directions on the screen to print the Summary Report.

2. In Explore, create a poster, to demonstrate your ability to use a mouse and to control a Windows program. To create a poster for an upcoming sports event, select a graphic, type the caption for the poster, then select a font, font styles, and a border. Print your completed poster.

QUICK | CHECK ANSWERS

Session 1.1

1. The taskbar contains buttons that give you access to tools and programs.

2. multitasking

3. Start menu

4. Lift the mouse up and move it to the right.

5. Its button appears on the taskbar.

6. To conserve computer resources such as memory.

7. To ensure you don't lose data and damage your files.

Session 1.2

1. The title bar identifies the window and contains window controls; toolbars contain buttons that provide you with shortcuts to common menu commands.

2. a. Minimize button shrinks window so you see button on taskbar

   b. Maximize button enlarges window to fill entire screen

   c. Restore button reduces window to predetermined size

   d. Close button closes window and removes button from taskbar

3. a. ellipsis indicates a dialog box will open

   b. grayed-out indicates option is not currently available

   c. arrow indicates a submenu will open

   d. check mark indicates a toggle option

4. toolbar

5. Scrollbars appear when the contents of a box or window are too long to fit; you drag the scroll box to view different parts of the contents.

6. one

7. online Help

OBJECTIVES

In this tutorial you will:

- Format a disk

- Enter, select, insert, and delete text

- Create and save a file

- Open, edit, and print a file

- Switch to Web style

- Create a Student Disk

- View the list of files on your disk and change view options

- Move, copy, delete, and rename a file

- Navigate Explorer windows

- Make a copy of your Student Disk

LABS

Using Files

WORKING WITH FILES

Creating, Saving, and Managing Files

CASE

Distance Education

You recently purchased a computer in order to gain new skills and stay competitive in the job market. Your friend Shannon suggests that you broaden your horizons by enrolling in a few distance education courses. **Distance education**, Shannon explains, is formalized learning that typically takes place using a computer, replacing normal classroom interaction with modern communications technology. Many distance education courses take advantage of the **Internet**, a vast structure of millions of computers located all over the world that are connected together so that they are able to share information. The **World Wide Web**, usually called the **Web**, is a popular service on the Internet that makes information readily accesssible. Educators can make their course material available on the Web.

Windows 98 makes it possible for your computer to display content in a way that is similar to the way it appears on the Web, and Shannon is eager to show you how. She suggests, however, that first you should get more comfortable with your computer—especially using programs and files. Shannon points out that most of the software installed on your computer was created especially for the Windows 98 operating system. This software is referred to as **Windows 98 applications** or **Windows 98 programs**. You can use software designed for older operating systems, but Windows 98 applications take better advantage of the features of the Windows 98 operating system.

You typically use Windows 98 applications to create files. A **file**, often referred to as a **document**, is a collection of data that has a name and is stored in a computer. Once you create a file, you can open it, edit its contents, print it, and save it again—usually using the same application program you used to create it.

Shannon suggests that you become familiar with how to perform these tasks in Windows 98 applications. Then she'll show you how to set up your computer so it incorporates the look and feel of the Web. Finally, you'll spend time learning how to organize your files.

SESSION 2.1

In Session 2.1 you will learn how to format a disk so it can store files. You will create, save, open, and print a file. You will find out how the insertion point differs from the mouse pointer, and you will learn the basic skills for Windows 98 text entry, such as inserting, deleting, and selecting. *For the steps of this tutorial you will need two blank 3½-inch disks.*

Formatting a Disk

Before you can save files on a disk, the disk must be formatted. When the computer **formats** a disk, the magnetic particles on the disk surface are arranged so data can be stored on the disk. Today, many disks are sold preformatted and can be used right out of the box. However, if you purchase an unformatted disk, or if you have an old disk you want to completely erase and reuse, you can format the disk using the Windows 98 Format command. This command is available through the **My Computer window**, a window that gives you access to the objects on your computer. You open My Computer by using its icon on the desktop. You'll learn more about the My Computer window later in this tutorial.

The following steps tell you how to format a 3½-inch high-density disk using drive A. Your instructor will tell you how to revise the instructions given in these steps if the procedure is different for your lab equipment.

Make sure you are using a blank disk before you perform these steps.

To format a disk:

1. Start Windows 98, if necessary.

2. Write your name on the label of a 3½-inch disk and insert your disk in drive A. See Figure 2-1.

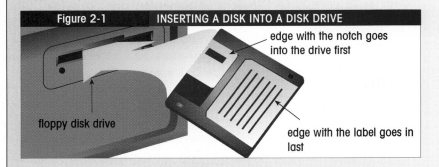

Figure 2-1   INSERTING A DISK INTO A DISK DRIVE

edge with the notch goes into the drive first

floppy disk drive

edge with the label goes in last

TROUBLE? If your disk does not fit in drive A, put it in drive B and substitute drive B for drive A in all of the steps for the rest of the tutorial.

3. Click the **My Computer** icon on the desktop. The icon is selected. Figure 2-2 shows the location of this icon on your desktop.

TROUBLE? If the My Computer window opens, skip Step 4. Your computer is using different settings, which you'll learn to change in Session 2.2.

4. Press **Enter** to open the My Computer window. See Figure 2-2 (don't worry if your window opens maximized).

TROUBLE? If you see a list instead of icons like those in Figure 2-2, click View, then click Large Icons. Don't worry if your toolbars don't exactly match those in Figure 2-2.

TROUBLE? If you see additional information or a graphic image on the left side of the My Computer window, Web view is enabled on your computer. Don't worry. You will learn how to enable and disable Web view in Session 2.2.

Figure 2-2	MY COMPUTER WINDOW

My Computer icon; don't worry if yours appears underlined

3½ Floppy (A:) icon

My Computer window lists icons associated with objects on your computer

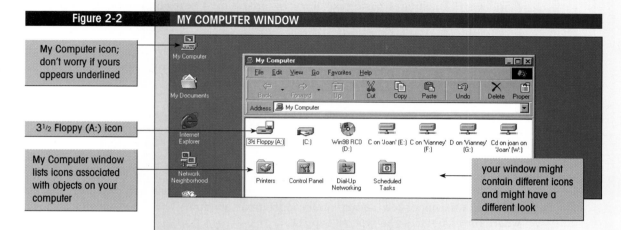

your window might contain different icons and might have a different look

5. Right-click the **3½ Floppy (A:)** icon to open its shortcut menu.

6. Click **Format** on the shortcut menu. The Format dialog box opens.

7. Click the **Full** option button to perform a full format. Make sure the other dialog box settings on your screen match those in Figure 2-3.

Figure 2-3	FORMAT DIALOG BOX

capacity is 1.44 Mb

Format type is Full

only Display box contains check mark

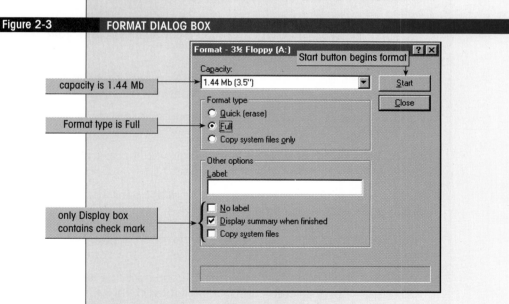

8. On the right side of the dialog box is a Start button. Click this **Start** button to begin formatting the disk. A series of blue boxes at the bottom of the Format window shows you how the format is progressing. When the format is complete, the Format Results dialog box appears.

9. Click the **Close** button, and then close any open windows on the desktop.

TROUBLE? To close the windows, click each Close button ☒.

Working with Text

To accomplish many computing tasks, you need to type text in documents and text boxes. Windows 98 facilitates basic text entry by providing a text-entry area, by showing you where your text will appear on the screen, by helping you move around on the screen, and by providing insert and delete functions.

When you type sentences of text, do not press the Enter key when you reach the right margin of the page. Most software contains a feature called **word wrap**, which automatically continues your text on the next line. Therefore, you should press Enter only when you have completed a paragraph.

If you type the wrong character, press the Backspace key to back up and delete the character. You can also use the Delete key. What's the difference between the Backspace and the Delete keys? The Backspace key deletes the character to the left, while the Delete key deletes the character to the right.

Now you will type some text using WordPad, to practice what you've learned about text entry. When you first start WordPad, notice the flashing vertical bar, called the **insertion point**, in the upper-left corner of the document window. The insertion point indicates where the characters you type will appear.

To type text in WordPad:

1. Start WordPad and locate the insertion point.

   TROUBLE? If the WordPad window does not fill the screen, click the Maximize button 🔲.

   TROUBLE? If you can't find the insertion point, click in the WordPad workspace area.

2. Type your name, using the Shift key to type uppercase letters and using the Spacebar to type spaces, just as on a typewriter.

3. Press the **Enter** key to end the current paragraph and move the insertion point down to the next line.

4. As you type the following sentences, watch what happens when the insertion point reaches the right edge of the page:

   This is a sample typed in WordPad. See what happens when the insertion point reaches the right edge of the page.

   TROUBLE? If you make a mistake, delete the incorrect character(s) by pressing the Backspace key on your keyboard. Then type the correct character(s).

   TROUBLE? If your text doesn't wrap, your screen might be set up to display more information than the screen used for the figures in this tutorial. Type the sentences again until text wraps automatically.

The Insertion Point Versus the Pointer

The insertion point is not the same as the mouse pointer. When the mouse pointer is in the text-entry area, it is called the **I-beam pointer** and looks like I. Figure 2-4 explains the difference between the insertion point and the I-beam pointer.

Figure 2-4 | THE INSERTION POINT VS. THE POINTER

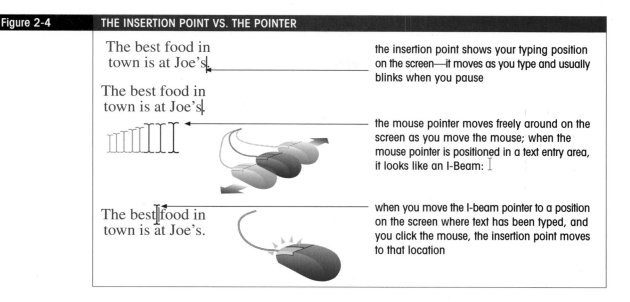

The best food in
town is at Joe's|

the insertion point shows your typing position
on the screen—it moves as you type and usually
blinks when you pause

The best food in
town is at Joe's|

the mouse pointer moves freely around on the
screen as you move the mouse; when the
mouse pointer is positioned in a text entry area,
it looks like an I-Beam: I

The best||food in
town is at Joe's.

when you move the I-beam pointer to a position
on the screen where text has been typed, and
you click the mouse, the insertion point moves
to that location

To enter text, you move the I-beam pointer to the location where you want to type, and then click. The insertion point jumps to the location you clicked and, depending on the program you are using, may blink to indicate the program is ready for you to type. When you enter text, the insertion point moves as you type.

To move the insertion point:

1. Check the locations of the insertion point and the I-beam pointer. The insertion point should be at the end of the sentence you typed in the last set of steps.

   TROUBLE? If you don't see the I-beam pointer, move your mouse until you see it.

2. Use the mouse to move the I-beam pointer to the word "sample," then click the mouse button. The insertion point jumps to the location of the I-beam pointer.

3. Move the I-beam pointer to a blank area near the bottom of the workspace, and click. Notice the insertion point does not jump to the location of the I-beam pointer. Instead the insertion point jumps to the end of the last sentence. The insertion point can move only within existing text. It cannot be moved out of the existing text area.

Selecting Text

Many text operations are performed on a **block** of text, which is one or more consecutive characters, words, sentences, or paragraphs. Once you select a block of text, you can delete it, move it, replace it, underline it, and so on. As you select a block of text, the computer highlights it. If you want to remove the highlighting, just click in the margin of your document.

If you want to delete the phrase "See what happens" in the text you just typed and replace it with the phrase "You can watch word wrap in action," you do not have to delete the first phrase one character at a time. Instead, you can highlight the entire phrase and then type the replacement phrase.

To select and replace a block of text:

1. Move the I-beam pointer just to the left of the word "See."

2. While holding down the mouse button, drag the I-beam pointer over the text to the end of the word "happens." The phrase "See what happens" should now be highlighted. See Figure 2-5.

   TROUBLE? If the space to the right of the word "happens" is also selected, don't worry. Your computer is set up to select spaces in addition to words. After completing Step 4, simply press the Spacebar to type an extra space if required.

Figure 2-5	HIGHLIGHTING TEXT

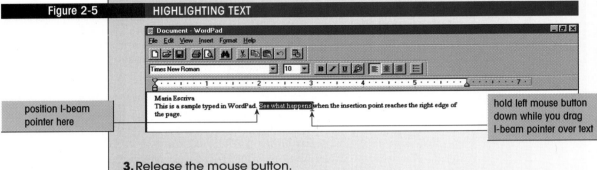

position I-beam pointer here

hold left mouse button down while you drag I-beam pointer over text

3. Release the mouse button.

   TROUBLE? If the phrase is not highlighted correctly, repeat Steps 1 through 3.

4. Type **You can watch word wrap in action**

The text you typed replaces the highlighted text. Notice you did not need to delete the highlighted text before you typed the replacement text.

Inserting a Character

Windows 98 programs usually operate in **insert mode**—when you type a new character, all characters to the right of the insertion point are pushed over to make room.

Suppose you want to insert the word "sentence" before the word "typed" in your practice sentences.

To insert text:

1. Move the I-beam pointer just before the word "typed," then click to position the insertion point.

2. Type **sentence**

3. Press the **Spacebar**.

Notice how the letters in the first line are pushed to the right to make room for the new characters. When a word gets pushed past the right margin, the **word-wrap** feature moves it down to the beginning of the next line.

Saving a File

Using Files

As you type text, it is held temporarily in the computer's memory. For permanent storage, you need to save your work on a disk. In the computer lab, you will probably save your work on a floppy disk in drive A.

When you save a file, you must give it a name. Windows 98 allows you to use up to 255 characters in a filename, although usually the operating system requires some of those characters for designating file location and file type. So, while it is unlikely you would need that many characters, you should be aware that the full 255 characters might not always be available. You may use spaces and certain punctuation symbols in your filenames. You cannot use the symbols \ / ? : * " < > | in a filename, but other symbols such as & ; - and $ are allowed. Furthermore, filenames for files used by older Windows 3.1 or DOS applications (pre-1995 operating systems) must be eight characters or less. Thus when you save a file with a long filename in Windows 98, Windows 98 also creates an eight-character filename that can be used by older applications. The eight-character filename is created from the first six nonspace characters in the long filename, with the addition of a tilde (~) and a number. For example, the filename Car Sales for 1999 would be converted to Carsal~1.

Most filenames have an extension. An **extension** is a suffix, usually of three characters, separated from the filename by a period. In the filename Car Sales for 1999.doc, a period separates the filename from the file extension. The file extension "doc" helps categorize the file by type or by the software that created it. Files created with Microsoft Word software have a .doc extension, such as Resume.doc (pronounced "Resume dot doc"). In general you will not add an extension to your filenames, because the application software automatically does this for you.

Windows 98 keeps track of file extensions, but does not always display them. The steps in these tutorials refer to files using the filename, but not its extension. So if you see the filename Practice Text in the steps, but "Practice Text.doc" on your screen, don't worry—these refer to the same file. Also don't worry if you don't use consistent lowercase and uppercase letters when saving files. Usually the operating system doesn't distinguish between them. Be aware, however, that some programs are "case-sensitive"—they check for case in filenames.

Now you can save the document you typed.

To save a document:

1. Click the **Save** button 🖫 on the toolbar. Figure 2-6 shows the location of this button and the Save As dialog box that appears after you click it.

Figure 2-6	SAVING A FILE

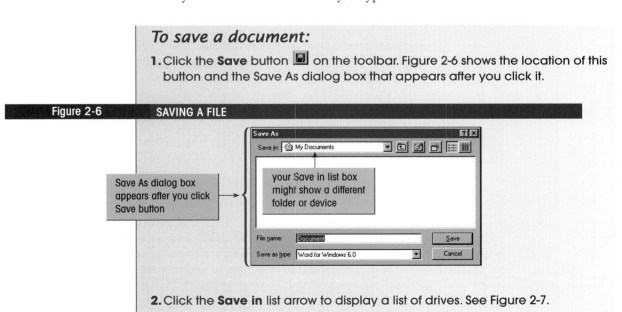

Save As dialog box appears after you click Save button

your Save in list box might show a different folder or device

2. Click the **Save in** list arrow to display a list of drives. See Figure 2-7.

Figure 2-7   SELECTING THE DRIVE

drive containing your
Student Disk

click Save in list arrow
to open list of devices
and folders

Save As

Save in: My Documents

- Desktop
- My Documents
- My Computer
- 3½ Floppy (A:)
- (C:)
  - My Documents
- Audio CD (D:)
- C on 'Joan' (E:)
- C on 'Vianney' (F:)
- D on 'Vianney' (G:)
- Cd on joan on 'Joan' (W:)
- Network Neighborhood

File name

Save as type: Word for Windows 6.0

Save

Cancel

3. Click **3½ Floppy (A:)**, and select the text in the File name box.

   TROUBLE? To select the text, move the I-beam pointer to the beginning of the word "Document." While you hold down the mouse button, drag the I-beam pointer to the end of the word.

4. Type **Practice Text** in the File name box.

5. Click the **Save** button in the lower-right corner of the dialog box. Your file is saved on your Student Disk, and the document title, "Practice Text," appears on the WordPad title bar.

What if you try to close WordPad before you save your file? Windows 98 will display a message—"Save changes to Document?" If you answer "Yes," Windows will display the Save As dialog box so you can give the document a name. If you answer "No," Windows 98 will close WordPad without saving the document. Any changes you made to the document would be lost, so when you are asked if you want to save a file, answer Yes, unless you are absolutely sure you don't need to keep the work you just did.

After you save a file, you can work on another document or close WordPad. Since you have already saved your Practice Text document, you'll continue this tutorial by closing WordPad.

To close WordPad:

1. Click the **Close** button ☒ to close the WordPad window.

Opening a File

Suppose you save and close the Practice Text file, then later you want to revise it. To revise a file you must first open it. When you **open** a file, its contents are copied into the computer's memory. If you revise the file, you need to save the changes before you close the application or work on a different file. If you close a revised file without saving your changes, you will lose them.

Typically, you use one of two methods to open a file. You could select the file from the Documents list or the My Computer window, or you could start an application program and then use the Open button to open the file. Each method has advantages and disadvantages.

The first method for opening the Practice Text file simply requires you to select the file from the Documents list or from the My Computer window. With this method the document, not the application program, is central to the task; hence, this method is sometimes referred to as **document-centric**. You only need to remember the name of your document or file—you do not need to remember which application you used to create the document.

The Documents list contains the names of the last 15 documents used. You access this list from the Start menu. When you have your own computer, the Documents list is very handy. In a computer lab, however, the files other students use quickly replace yours on the list.

If your file is not in the Documents list, you can open the file by selecting it from the My Computer window. Windows 98 starts an application program you can use to revise the file, then automatically opens the file. The advantage of this method is its simplicity. The disadvantage is Windows 98 might not start the application you expect. For example, when you select Practice Text, you might expect Windows 98 to start WordPad because you used WordPad to create it. Depending on the software installed on your computer system, however, Windows 98 might start the Microsoft Word application instead. Usually this is not a problem. Although the application might not be the one you expect, you can still use it to revise your file.

To open the Practice Text file by selecting it from My Computer:

1. From the desktop, open the **My Computer** window.

2. Click the **3½ Floppy (A:)** icon in the My Computer window.

   TROUBLE? If the 3½ Floppy (A:) window opens, skip Step 3.

3. Press **Enter**. The 3½ Floppy (A:) window opens.

4. Click the **Practice Text** file icon.

   TROUBLE? If the Practice Text document appears in a word-processing window, skip Step 5.

5. Press **Enter**. Windows 98 starts an application program, then automatically opens the Practice Text file. You could make revisions to the document at this point, but instead, you'll close all the windows on your desktop so you can try the other method for opening files.

   TROUBLE? If Windows 98 starts Microsoft Word or another word-processing program instead of WordPad, don't worry. You can use Microsoft Word to revise the Practice Text document.

6. Close all open windows on the desktop.

The second method for opening the Practice Text file requires you to open WordPad, then use the Open button to select the Practice Text file. The advantage of this method is you can specify the application program you want to use—WordPad, in this case. This method, however, involves more steps than the method you tried previously.

To start WordPad and open the Practice Text file using the Open button:

1. Start WordPad and maximize the WordPad window.

2. Click the **Open** button 🖼 on the toolbar.

3. Click the **Look in** list arrow to display a list of drives.

4. Click **3½ Floppy (A:)** from the list.

5. Click **Practice Text** to make sure it is highlighted. See Figure 2-8.

Figure 2-8	SELECTING THE FILE

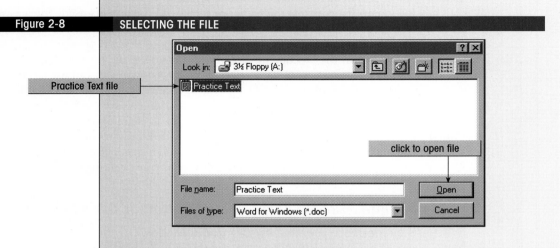

Practice Text file

click to open file

6. Click the **Open** button in the lower-right corner of the dialog box. Your document should appear in the WordPad work area.

Printing a File

Now that the Practice Text file is open, you can print it. It is a good idea to use Print Preview before you send your document to the printer. **Print Preview** shows on the screen exactly how your document will appear on paper. You can check your page layout so you don't waste paper printing a document that is not quite the way you want it. Your instructor might supply you with additional instructions for printing in your school's computer lab.

To preview, then print, the Practice Text file:

1. Click the **Print Preview** button [icon] on the toolbar.

TROUBLE? If an error message appears, printing capabilities might not be set up on your computer. Ask your instructor or lab assistant for help, or skip this set of steps.

2. Look at your print preview. Before you print the document and use paper, you should make sure the font, margins, and other document features look the way you want them to.

TROUBLE? If you can't read the document text on screen, click the Zoom In button.

3. Click the **Print** button. A Print dialog box appears. Study Figure 2-9 to familiarize yourself with the controls in the Print dialog box.

Figure 2-9 PRINTING A FILE

printer name; yours might be different

click to open list of printers available to you; ask your instructor if you need to select a network printer

you can print all or part of a document; to print part, click the Pages option button and then enter the starting and ending pages of the range you want to print

you can print one or more copies, depending on the value in this spin box

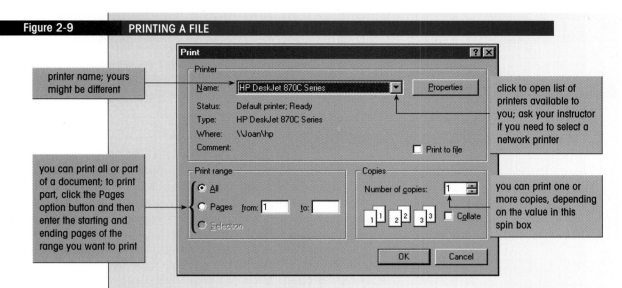

4. Make sure your screen shows the Print range set to "All" and the number of copies set to "1."

5. Click the **OK** button to print your document.

TROUBLE? If your document does not print, make sure the printer has paper and the printer online light is on. If your document still doesn't print, ask your instructor or lab assistant for help.

6. Close WordPad.

TROUBLE? If you see the message "Save changes to Document?" click the No button.

You've now learned how to create, save, open, and print word-processed files—essential skills for students in distance education courses that rely on word-processed reports transmitted across the Internet. Shannon assures you that the techniques you've just learned apply to most Windows 98 programs.

QUICK CHECK

1. A(n) _____ is a collection of data that has a name and is stored on a disk or other storage medium.

2. _____ erases all the data on a disk and arranges the magnetic particles on the disk surface so the disk can store data.

3. True or False: When you move the mouse pointer over a text entry area, the pointer shape changes to an I-bar.

4. What shows you where each character you type will appear?

5. _____ automatically moves text down to the beginning of the next line when you reach the right margin.

6. How do you select a block of text?

7. In the filename New Equipment.doc, doc is a(n) _____.

SESSION 2.2

In this session you will learn how to change settings in the My Computer window to control its appearance and the appearance of desktop objects. You will then learn how to use My Computer to manage the files on your disk; view information about the files on your disk; organize the files into folders; and move, delete, copy, and rename files. *For this session you will use a second blank 3½-inch disk.*

Changing Desktop Style Settings

Shannon tells you that in Windows 98 you work with files by manipulating icons that represent them. These icons appear in many places: the desktop, the My Computer windows, the 3½ Floppy (A:) window, and other similar windows. The techniques you use to manipulate these icons depend on whether your computer is using Classic-style or Web-style settings or a customized hybrid. **Classic style** allows you to use the same techniques in Windows 98 that are used in Windows 95, the previous version of the Windows operating system. **Web style**, on the other hand, allows you to access files on your computer's hard drives just as you access files on the Web. In Classic style, to select an item you click it, and to open an item you click it and then press Enter. In Web style, to select an item you point to it, and to open an item you click it.

Thus, if you wanted to open your Practice Text document from the My Computer window, in Classic style you would click its icon and press Enter, but in Web style you would simply click its icon.

Switching to Web Style

By default, Windows 98 starts using a combination of Classic and Web style settings, but it uses Classic click settings. Your computer might have been set differently. If you have your own computer, you can choose which style you want to use. If you want to minimize the number of mouse actions for a given task, or if you want to explore your computer in the same way you explore the Web, you'll probably want to use Web style. On the other hand, if you are used to Classic style settings, you might want to continue using them. Shannon suggests that you use Web style because you'll be able to use the same techniques on the Web, and you'll be more at ease with your distance learning courses. The next set of steps shows you how to switch to Web style, and the rest of the tutorial assumes that you're using Web-style settings.

To switch styles:

1. Click the **Start** button ⊞Start and then point to **Settings**.

2. Click **Folder Options**. The Folder Options dialog box opens.

   TROUBLE? If you can't open the Folder Options dialog box, or you can't make any changes to it, you probably don't have permission to change these settings. If your computer is set to use Classic style and you can't change this setting, you will notice a few differences in subsequent steps in this tutorial. The TROUBLE? paragraphs will help to ensure that you learn the proper techniques for the settings you are using.

3. On the General tab, click the **Web style** option button. See Figure 2-10.

Figure 2-10   SELECTING WEB STYLE

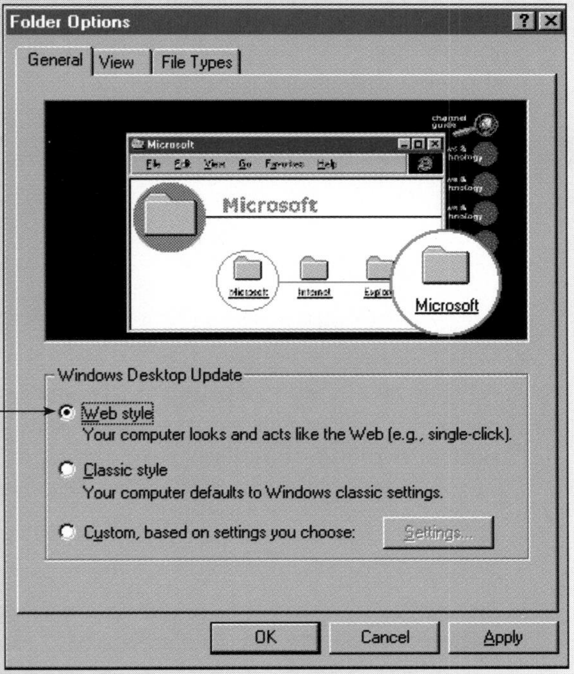

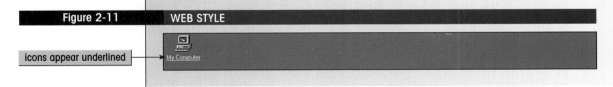

make sure that the Web style option button is selected

TROUBLE? If the Web style option button is already selected, skip Step 3.

4. Click the **OK** button.

5. If the Single-click dialog box appears asking if you are sure you want to use single-click, make sure the **Yes** option button is selected, and then click the **OK** button. You return to the desktop. The icons now appear underlined. See Figure 2-11. It's also possible that a vertical bar called the Channel bar will appear on your desktop. Don't worry; it won't interfere with your work.

Figure 2-11   WEB STYLE

icons appear underlined

You are now using Web-style settings.

Selecting an Icon in Web Style

In Web style, you select an icon representing a device, folder, or file by pointing to the icon long enough for it to become highlighted. This technique is sometimes called **hovering**. The pointer changes from ⬚ to 🖑 when you point to the icon. Try selecting the My Computer icon in Web style.

To select the My Computer icon in Web style:

1. Position the pointer over the My Computer icon on the desktop and notice how the pointer changes from ⌖ to 🖑 and the color of the text label changes to show it is selected. See Figure 2-12.

Figure 2-12 | SELECTING AN ICON IN WEB STYLE

pointer when you point at icon in Web style

TROUBLE? If the My Computer icon is not selected when you point to it, you might not be holding the mouse steadily. You need to steadily "hover" the pointer over the object long enough for the object to become highlighted. Simply passing the mouse over an object will not select it.

TROUBLE? If in Web style you click the My Computer icon instead of simply pointing at it, the My Computer window will open. Close the window and repeat Step 1.

TROUBLE? If you were unable to switch to Web style because you didn't have permission, you'll need to click the My Computer icon to select it.

Note that the Web style selection technique only applies to icons on the desktop and icons in windows such as My Computer.

Opening a File in Web Style

You saw in Session 2.1 that you can open the Practice Text document directly from the 3½ Floppy (A:) window. The steps in Session 2.1 assumed you were using Classic style. Now you'll try opening the Practice Text document using Web style. You open an object by simply clicking it. Try opening your Practice Text file in Web style.

To open the Practice Text file in Web style:

1. Click the **My Computer** icon. The My Computer window opens.

   TROUBLE? If you were unable to switch to Web style, you'll need to press Enter after Steps 1, 2, and 3.

2. Click the **3½ Floppy (A:)** icon. The 3½ Floppy (A:) window opens.

3. Click the **Practice Text** icon. Your word-processing software starts and the Practice Text file opens.

4. Close all open windows.

Now that you've practiced working with icons in Web style, you'll learn other tasks you can perform with these icons to manage your files.

Creating Your Student Disk

For the rest of this session, you must create a Student Disk that contains some practice files. *You can use the disk you formatted in the previous session.*

If you are using your own computer, the NP on Microsoft Windows 98 menu selection will not be available. Before you proceed, you must go to your school's computer lab and find a computer that has the NP on Microsoft Windows 98 program installed. If you cannot get the files from the lab, ask your instructor or lab assistant for help. Once you have made your own Student Disk, you can use it to complete this tutorial on any computer you choose.

To add the practice files to your Student Disk:

1. Write "Disk 1 - Windows 98 Tutorial 2 Student Disk" on the label of your formatted disk (the same disk you used to save your Practice Text file).

2. Place the disk in drive A.

3. Click the **Start** button ![Start] .

4. Point to **Programs**.

5. Point to **NP on Microsoft Windows 98 - Level I**.

   TROUBLE? If NP on Microsoft Windows 98 - Level I is not listed ask your instructor or lab assistant for help.

6. Click **Disk 1 (Tutorial 2)**. A message box opens, asking you to place your disk in drive A.

7. Click the **OK** button. Wait while the program copies the practice files to your formatted disk. When all the files have been copied, the program closes.

Your Student Disk now contains practice files you will use throughout the rest of this tutorial.

My Computer

The My Computer icon, as you have seen, represents your computer, its storage devices, printers, and other objects. The My Computer icon opens into the My Computer window, which contains an icon for each of the storage devices on your computer. On most computer systems, the My Computer window also contains the Control Panel and Printers folders, which help you add printers, control peripheral devices, and customize your Windows 98 work environment. Depending on the services your computer is running, you might see additional folders such as Dial-Up Networking (for some Internet connections) or Scheduled Tasks (for scheduling programs provided with Windows 98) that help you keep your computer running smoothly. Figure 2-13 shows how the My Computer window relates to your computer's hardware.

Figure 2-13   RELATIONSHIP BETWEEN COMPUTER AND MY COMPUTER WINDOW

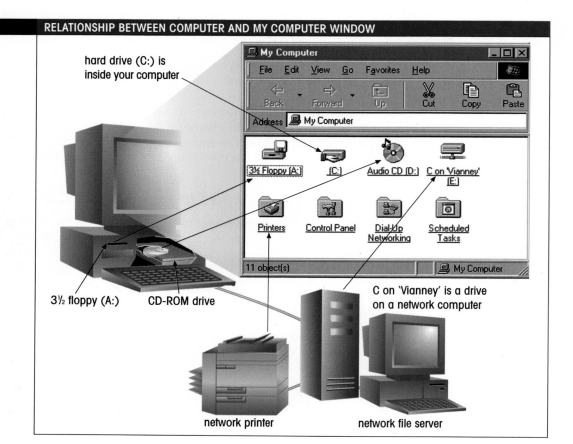

The first floppy drive on a computer is designated as drive A (if you add a second drive it is usually designated as drive B), and the first hard drive is designated drive C (if you add additional hard drives they are usually designated D, E, and so on).

You can use the My Computer window to keep track of where your files are stored and to organize your files. In this section of the tutorial you will move and delete files on your Student Disk in drive A. If you use your own computer at home or work, you will probably store your files on drive C instead of drive A. However, in a school lab environment you usually don't know which computer you will use, so you need to carry your files with you on a floppy disk that you use in drive A. In this session, therefore, you will learn how to work with the files on drive A. Most of what you learn will also work on your home or work computer when you use drive C (or other drives).

Now you'll open the My Computer window.

To open the My Computer window and explore the contents of your Student Disk:

1. Open the My Computer window.

2. Click the **3½ Floppy (A:)** icon. A window appears showing the contents of drive A; maximize this window if necessary. See Figure 2-14.

   TROUBLE? If you are using Classic style, click Settings, click the 3½ Floppy (A:) icon and then press Enter. Your window might look different from Figure 2-14; for example, you might see only files, and not the additional information on the left side of the window.

TROUBLE? If you see a list of filenames instead of icons, click View, then click Large Icons.

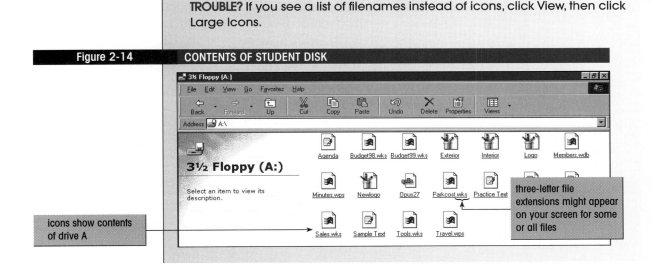

| Figure 2-14 | CONTENTS OF STUDENT DISK |

icons show contents of drive A

three-letter file extensions might appear on your screen for some or all files

Changing My Computer View Options

Windows 98 offers several different options that control how toolbars, icons, and buttons appear in the My Computer window. You can choose to hide or display these options, depending on the task you are performing. To make the My Computer window on your computer look the same as it does in the figures in this book, you need to ensure four things: that only the Address and Standard toolbars are visible and Text Labels is enabled, that Web view is disabled, that Large Icons view is enabled, and that file extensions are hidden.

Controlling the Toolbar Display

The My Computer window, in addition to featuring a Standard toolbar, allows you to display the same toolbars that can appear on the Windows 98 taskbar, such as the Address toolbar or the Links toolbar. These toolbars make it easy to access the Web from the My Computer window. In this tutorial, however, you need to see only the Address and Standard toolbars. You can hide one or all of the My Computer toolbars, and you can determine how they are displayed, with or without text labels. Displaying the toolbars without text labels takes up less room on your screen, but it is not as easy to identify the button's function.

To display only the Address and Standard toolbars and to hide text labels:

1. Click **View**, point to **Toolbars**, and then examine the Toolbars submenu. The Standard Buttons, Address Bar, and Text Labels options should be preceded by a check mark. The Links option should not be checked.

2. If the Standard Buttons option *is not checked*, click it.

3. If necessary, reopen the Toolbars submenu, and then repeat Step 2 with the Address Bar and Text Labels options.

4. Open the Toolbars submenu once again, and if the Links option *is checked*, click it to disable it.

5. Click **View** and then point to **Toolbars** one last time and verify that your Toolbars submenu and the toolbar display look like Figure 2-15.

TROUBLE? If the checkmarks are distributed differently than in Figure 2-15, repeat Steps 1–5 until the correct options are checked.

TROUBLE? If your toolbars are not displayed as shown in Figure 2-15 (for example, both the Standard and Address toolbars might be on the same line, or the Standard toolbar might be above the Address toolbar), you can easily rearrange them. To move a toolbar, drag the vertical bar at the far left of the toolbar. By dragging that vertical bar, you can drag the toolbar left, right, up, or down.

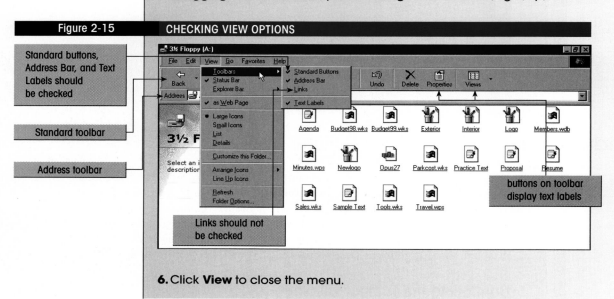

Figure 2-15   CHECKING VIEW OPTIONS

Standard buttons, Address Bar, and Text Labels should be checked

Standard toolbar

Address toolbar

Links should not be checked

buttons on toolbar display text labels

6. Click **View** to close the menu.

Web View

The My Computer window also can be viewed in **Web view**, which allows you to display and customize the My Computer window as a document you would see on the Web. Web view is automatically enabled when you switch to Web style; in its default appearance Web view shows information about the open folder or selected file, along with a decorated background. There are many advantages to Web view, including the ability to place information, graphics, and Web content in a folder window. Shannon says you'll find this feature useful once you've started your distance education courses. For now, however, you don't need to customize Web view, so you'll disable it.

To disable Web view:

1. Click **View**.

2. If the option "as Web Page" is preceded by a check mark, click **as Web Page** to disable Web view.

3. Click **View** again and ensure that as Web Page is not checked.

> **TROUBLE?** If as Web Page is checked, repeat Steps 1 and 2.
>
> **4.** Click **View** again to close the View menu.

Changing the Icon Display

Windows 98 provides four ways to view the contents of a disk—large icons, small icons, list, or details. The default view, Large Icons view, displays a large icon and title for each file. The icon provides a visual cue to the type and contents of the file, as Figure 2-16 illustrates.

Figure 2-16	TYPICAL ICONS AS THEY APPEAR IN MY COMPUTER

FILE AND FOLDER ICONS

	Text documents that you can open using the Notepad accessory are represented by notepad icons.
	Graphic image documents that you can open using the Paint accessory are represented by drawing instruments.
	Word-processed documents that you can open using the WordPad accessory are represented by a formatted notepad icon, unless your computer designates a different word-processing program to open files created with WordPad.
	Word-processed documents that you can open using a program such as Microsoft Word are represented by formatted document icons.
	Files created by programs that Windows does not recognize are represented by the Windows logo.
	A folder icon represents folders.
	Certain folders created by Windows 98 have a special icon design related to the folder's purpose.

PROGRAM ICONS

	Icons for programs usually depict an object related to the function of the program. For example, an icon that looks like a calculator represents the Calculator accessory.
	Non-windows programs are represented by the icon of a blank window.

Large Icons view helps you quickly identify a file and its type, but what if you want more information about a set of files? Details view shows more information than the large icon, small icon, and list views. Details view shows the file icon, the filename, the file size, the application you used to create the file, and the date/time the file was created or last modified.

To view a detailed list of files:

1. Click **View** and then click **Details** to display details for the files on your disk, as shown in Figure 2-17. Your files might be in a different order.

2. Look at the file sizes. Do you see that Exterior and Interior are the largest files?

3. Look at the dates and times the files were modified. Which is the oldest file?

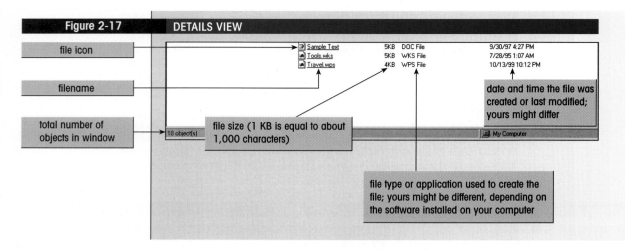

Figure 2-17   DETAILS VIEW

Now that you have looked at the file details, switch back to Large Icon view.

To switch to Large Icon view:

1. Click **View** and then click **Large Icons** to return to the large icon display.

Hiding File Extensions

You have the option to show or hide file extensions for file types that Windows recognizes. Showing them takes up more room but gives more information about the file. In this tutorial, however, you don't need to see file extensions, so you'll hide them. They might already be hidden on your computer.

To hide file extensions:

1. Click **View** and then click **Folder Options**. Note this is the same dialog box you saw when switching to Web style. It is accessible from the Start menu and the My Computer window.

2. Click the **View** tab.

3. Make sure the **Hide file extensions for known file types** check box is checked. If it is not, click it to insert a check mark.

4. Click the **OK** button.

The only file extensions that now appear are those whose file type Windows doesn't recognize.

Folders and Directories

A list of related files located in the same place is referred to as a **directory**. The main directory of a disk is sometimes called the **root directory**, or the **top-level directory**. The root directory is created when you format a disk, and it is designated by a letter—usually A for your floppy disk and C for your hard disk. All of the files on your Student Disk are currently in the root directory of your floppy disk.

If too many files are stored in a directory, the directory list becomes very long and difficult to manage. You can divide a directory into **folders**, into which you group similar files. The directory of files for each folder then becomes much shorter and easier to manage. A folder within a folder is called a **subfolder**. Now, you'll create a folder called Practice to hold your documents.

To create a Practice folder:

1. Click **File**, and then point to **New** to display the submenu.

2. Click **Folder**. A folder icon with the label "New Folder" appears.

3. Type **Practice** as the name of the folder.

   TROUBLE? If nothing happens when you type the folder name, it's possible that the folder name is no longer selected. Right-click the Practice folder, click Rename, and then repeat Step 3.

4. Press the **Enter** key.

When you first create a folder, it doesn't contain any files. In the next set of steps, you will move a file from the root directory to the Practice folder.

Moving and Copying a File

You can move a file from one directory to another, or from one disk to another. When you move a file, it is copied to the new location you specify, and then the version in the old location is erased. The move feature is handy for organizing or reorganizing the files on your disk by moving them into appropriate folders. The easiest way to move a file is to hold down the right mouse button and drag the file from the old location to the new location. A menu appears and you select Move Here.

REFERENCE WINDOW   RW

Moving a File
- Locate the file in the My Compuuter window.
- Hold down the right mouse button while you drag the file icon to its new folder or disk location.
- Click Move Here.

Suppose you want to move the Minutes file from the root directory to the Practice folder. Depending on your computer's settings, this file appears either as Minutes or Minutes.wps. In the following steps, the file is referred to as Minutes.

To move the Minutes file to the Practice folder:

1. Point to the **Minutes** icon.

2. Press and hold the right mouse button while you drag the Minutes icon to the Practice folder. See Figure 2-18.

TROUBLE? If you release the mouse button by mistake before dragging the Minutes icon to the Practice folder, the Minutes shortcut menu opens. Press Esc and then repeat Steps 1 and 2.

| Figure 2-18 | MOVING A FILE |

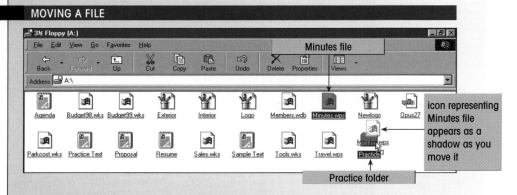

3. Release the right mouse button. A menu appears.

4. Click **Move Here**. The Minutes icon disappears from the window showing the files in the root directory.

Anything you do to an icon in the My Computer window is actually done to the file represented by that icon. If you move an icon, the file is moved; if you delete an icon, the file is deleted.

You can also copy a file from one folder to another, or from one disk to another. When you copy a file, you create an exact duplicate of an existing file in whatever disk or folder you specify. To copy a file from one folder to another on your floppy disk, you use the same procedure as for moving a file, except that you select Copy Here from the menu.

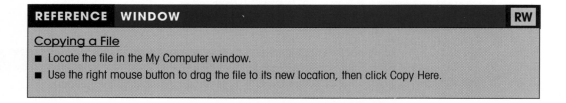

REFERENCE WINDOW   **RW**

Copying a File
■ Locate the file in the My Computer window.
■ Use the right mouse button to drag the file to its new location, then click Copy Here.

Try copying the Resume file into the Practice folder.

To copy the Resume file into the Practice folder:

1. Using the right mouse button, drag the Resume file into the Practice folder.

2. Click **Copy Here**. Notice this time the file icon does not disappear, because you didn't actually move it, you only copied it.

After you move or copy a file, it is a good idea to make sure it was moved to the correct location. You can easily verify that a file is in its new folder by displaying the folder contents.

> *To verify that the Minutes file was moved and the Resume file was copied to the Practice folder:*
>
> 1. Click the **Practice** folder icon. The Practice window appears, and it contains two files—Minutes, which you moved, and Resume, which you copied.
>
> **TROUBLE?** If you are using Classic style, click Settings, click the Practice folder icon and then press Enter to open the Practice window.

Navigating Explorer Windows

The title bar of the open window on your computer, "Practice," identifies the name of the folder you just opened. Before you opened the Practice folder, you were viewing the contents of your floppy disk, so the window's title bar, 3½ Floppy (A:) (or possibly just A:/, depending on how your computer is set up), identified the drive containing your disk, drive A. Before you opened that window you were viewing the My Computer window. Windows that show the objects on your computer are called **Explorer windows** because they allow you to explore the contents of your computer's devices and folders.

You've seen that to navigate through the devices and folders on your computer, you open My Computer and then click the icons representing the objects you want to explore. But what if you want to move back to a previous Explorer window? The Standard toolbar, which stays the same regardless of which Explorer window is open, includes buttons that help you navigate through your Explorer windows. Figure 2-19 summarizes the navigation buttons on the Standard toolbar.

Figure 2-19		NAVIGATIONAL BUTTONS
BUTTON	**ICON**	**DESCRIPTION**
Back	⬅	Returns you to the Explorer window you were most recently viewing. This button is active only when you have viewed more than one Explorer window in the current session.
Forward	➡	Reverses the effect of the Back button.
Up	🔼	Moves you up one level on the hierarchy of your computer's objects; for example, moves you from a folder Explorer window to the drive containing the folder.

Try returning to the 3½ Floppy (A:) window using the Back button.

> *To navigate Explorer windows:*
>
> 1. Click the **Back** button ⬅ to return to the 3½ Floppy (A:) window.
>
> 2. Click the **Forward** button ➡ to reverse the effect of the Back button and return to the Practice window.
>
> 3. Click the **Up** button 🔼 to move up one level. You again return to the 3½ Floppy (A:) window because the Practice folder is contained within the 3½ Floppy (A:) drive.

Deleting a File

You delete a file or folder by deleting its icon. However, be careful when you delete a folder, because you also delete all the files it contains! When you delete a file from a *hard drive* on your computer, the filename is deleted from the directory but the file contents are held in the Recycle Bin. The **Recycle Bin** is an area on your hard drive that holds deleted files until you remove them permanently; an icon on the desktop allows you easy access to the Recycle Bin. If you change your mind and want to retrieve a file deleted from your hard drive, you can recover it by using the Recycle Bin.

When you delete a file from a *floppy disk*, it does not go into the Recycle Bin. Instead, it is deleted as soon as its icon disappears.

Try deleting the file named Agenda from your Student Disk. Because this file is on the floppy disk and not on the hard disk, it will not go into the Recycle Bin, and if you change your mind you won't be able to recover it.

To delete the file Agenda:

1. Right-click the icon for the file Agenda.

2. Click **Delete**.

3. If a message appears asking, "Are you sure you want to delete Agenda?", click **Yes**. The file is deleted and the Agenda icon no longer appears.

Renaming a File

Sometimes you decide to give a file a different name to clarify the file's contents. You can easily rename a file by using the Rename option on the file's shortcut menu or by using the file's label. The same rules apply for renaming a file as applied for naming a file, and you are limited in the number and type of characters you can use.

When you rename a file when file extensions are showing, make sure to include the extension in the new name. If you don't, Windows warns you it might not be able to identify the file type with the new name. Since you set up View options to hide file extensions, this should not be an issue unless you are trying to rename a file whose type Windows doesn't recognize.

Practice using this feature by renaming the Logo file to give it a more descriptive filename.

To rename Logo:

1. Right-click the **Logo** icon.

2. Click **Rename**. After a moment, a box appears around the label.

3. Type **Corporate Logo Draft** as the new filename.

4. Press the **Enter** key. The file now appears with the new name.

5. Click the **Up** button 🖿 to move up one level to the My Computer window.

You can also edit an existing filename when you use the Rename command. Click to place the cursor at the location you want to edit, and then use the text-editing skills you learned with WordPad to edit the filename.

Copying **an Entire Floppy Disk**

You can have trouble accessing the data on your floppy disk if the disk is damaged, is exposed to magnetic fields, or picks up a computer virus. To avoid losing all your data, it is a good idea to make a copy of your floppy disk.

If you wanted to make a copy of an audio cassette, your cassette player would need two cassette drives. You might wonder, therefore, how your computer can make a copy of your disk if you have only one disk drive. Figure 2-20 illustrates how the computer uses only one disk drive to make a copy of a disk.

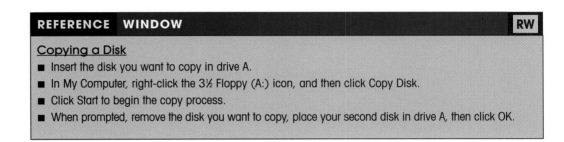

REFERENCE WINDOW   **RW**

Copying a Disk
- Insert the disk you want to copy in drive A.
- In My Computer, right-click the 3½ Floppy (A:) icon, and then click Copy Disk.
- Click Start to begin the copy process.
- When prompted, remove the disk you want to copy, place your second disk in drive A, then click OK.

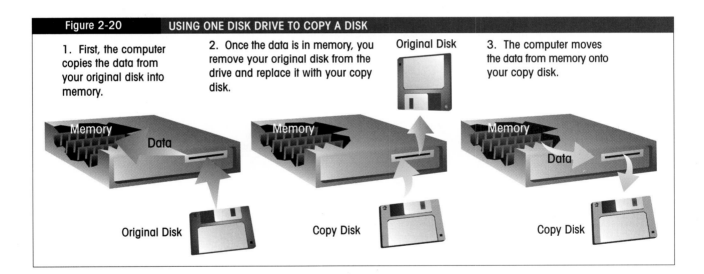

Figure 2-20   **USING ONE DISK DRIVE TO COPY A DISK**

1. First, the computer copies the data from your original disk into memory.

2. Once the data is in memory, you remove your original disk from the drive and replace it with your copy disk.

Original Disk

3. The computer moves the data from memory onto your copy disk.

Memory — Data

Original Disk

Memory

Copy Disk

Memory — Data

Copy Disk

If you have an extra floppy disk, you can make a copy of your Student Disk now. If you change the files on your disk, make sure you copy the disk regularly to keep it updated.

To copy your Student Disk:

1. Write your name and "Windows 98 Disk 1 Student Disk Copy" on the label of your second disk. Make sure the disk is blank and formatted.

   TROUBLE? If you aren't sure the disk is blank, place it in the disk drive and open the 3½ Floppy (A:) window to view its contents. If the disk contains files you need, get a different disk. If it contains files you don't need, you could format the disk now, using the steps you learned at the beginning of this tutorial.

2. Make sure your Student Disk is in drive A and the My Computer window is open.

3. Right-click the **3½ Floppy (A:)** icon, and then click **Copy Disk**. The Copy Disk dialog box opens.

4. Click the **Start** button to begin the copy process.

5. When the message "Insert the disk you want to copy to (destination disk)..." appears, remove your Student Disk and insert your Windows 98 Disk 1 Student Disk Copy in drive A.

6. Click the **OK** button. When the copy is complete, you will see the message "Copy completed successfully." Click the **Close** button.

7. Close the My Computer window.

8. Remove your disk from the drive.

As you finish copying your disk, Shannon emphasizes the importance of making copies of your files frequently, so you won't risk losing important documents for your distance learning course. If your original Student Disk were damaged, you could use the copy you just made to access the files.

Keeping copies of your files is so important that Windows 98 includes with it a program called **Backup** that automates the process of duplicating and storing data. In the Projects at the end of the tutorial you'll have an opportunity to explore the difference between what you just did in copying a disk and the way in which a program such as the Windows 98 Backup program helps you safeguard data.

QUICK CHECK

1. If you want to find out about the storage devices and printers connected to your computer, what window can you open?

2. If you have only one floppy disk drive on your computer, it is usually identified by the letter _____.

3. The letter C is typically used for the _____ drive of a computer.

4. What information does Details view supply about a list of folders and files?

5. The main directory of a disk is referred to as the _____ directory.

6. True or False: You can divide a directory into folders.

7. If you have one floppy disk drive, but you have two disks, can you copy the files on one floppy disk to the other?

TUTORIAL ASSIGNMENTS

1. **Opening, Editing, and Printing a Document**   In this tutorial you learned how to create a document using WordPad. You also learned how to save, open, and print a document. Practice these skills by opening the document called Resume in the Practice folder of your Student Disk. This document is a resume for Jamie Woods. Make the changes shown in Figure 2-21, and then save the document in the Pratice folder with the name "Resume 2" using the Save As command. After you save your revisions, preview and then print the document. Close WordPad.

Figure 2-21

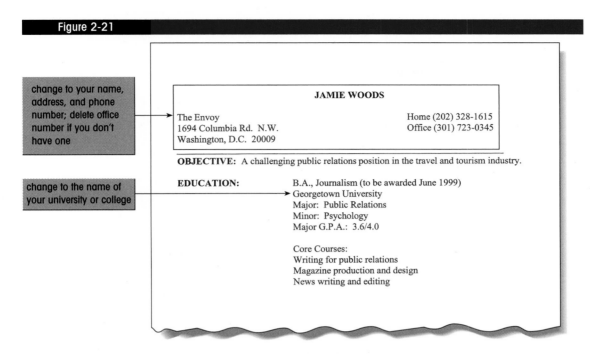

change to your name, address, and phone number; delete office number if you don't have one

change to the name of your university or college

JAMIE WOODS

The Envoy   Home (202) 328-1615
1694 Columbia Rd. N.W.   Office (301) 723-0345
Washington, D.C. 20009

OBJECTIVE: A challenging public relations position in the travel and tourism industry.

EDUCATION: B.A., Journalism (to be awarded June 1999)
                        Georgetown University
                        Major: Public Relations
                        Minor: Psychology
                        Major G.P.A.: 3.6/4.0

                        Core Courses:
                        Writing for public relations
                        Magazine production and design
                        News writing and editing

2. **Creating, Saving, and Printing a Letter**   Use WordPad to write a one-page letter to a relative or a friend. Save the document in the Practice folder on your Student Disk with the name "Letter." Use the Print Preview feature to look at the format of your finished letter, then print it, and be sure to sign it. Close WordPad.

3. **Managing Files and Folders**   Using the copy of the disk you made at the end of the tutorial, complete parts a through f below to practice your file management skills.

   a. Create a folder called Spreadsheets on your Student Disk.
   b. Move the files Parkcost, Budget98, Budget99, and Sales into the Spreadsheets folder.
   c. Create a folder called Park Project.
   d. Move the files Proposal, Members, Tools, Corporate Logo Draft, and Newlogo into the Park Project folder.
   e. Delete the file called Travel.
   f. Switch to the Details view and write out your answers to questions 1 through 5:
      1. What is the largest file or files in the Park Project folder?
      2. What is the newest file or files in the Spreadsheets folder?
      3. How many files (don't include folders) are in the root directory of your Student Disk?
      4. How are the Opus and Exterior icons different? Judging from the appearance of the icons, what would you guess these two files contain?
      5. Which file in the root directory has the most recent date?

4. **More Practice with Files and Folders**   For this assignment, you need a third blank disk. Complete parts a through g below to practice your file management skills.

   a. Write "Windows 98 Tutorial 2 Assignment 4" on the label of the blank disk, and then format the disk if necessary.
   b. Create a new Student Disk, using the Assignment 4 disk. Refer to the section "Creating Your Student Disk" in Session 2.2.
   c. Create three folders on the Assignment 4 Student Disk you just created: Documents, Budgets, and Graphics.
   d. Move the files Interior, Exterior, Logo, and Newlogo to the Graphics folder.
   e. Move the files Travel, Members, and Minutes to the Documents folder.

   f. Move Budget98 and Budget99 to the Budgets folder.

   g. Switch to the Details view and write out your answers to questions 1 through 5:

      1. What is the largest file or files in the Graphics folder?

      2. How many word-processed documents are in the root directory? *Hint*: These documents will appear with the WordPad, Microsoft Word, or some other word-processing icon, depending on what software you have installed.

      3. What is the newest file or files in the root directory (don't include folders)?

      4. How many files in all folders are 5 KB in size?

      5. How many files in the root directory are WKS files? *Hint*: Look in the Type column to identify WKS files.

      6. Do all the files in the Graphics folder have the same icon? What type are they?

5. **Finding a File**   The Help system includes a topic that discusses how to find files on a disk without looking through all the folders. Start Windows Help, then locate this topic, and answer questions a through c:

   a. To display the Find dialog box, you must click the _____ button, then point to _____ from the menu, and finally click _____ from the submenu.

   b. Do you need to type in the entire filename to find the file?

   c. How do you perform a case-sensitive search?

6. **Help with Files and Folders**   In Tutorial 2 you learned how to work with Windows 98 files and folders. What additional information on this topic does Windows 98 Help provide? Use the Start button to access Help. Use the Index tab to locate topics related to files and folders. Find at least two tips or procedures for working with files and folders that were not covered in the tutorial. Write out the tip in your own words and include the title of the Help screen that contains the information.

Explore

7. **Formatting Text**   You can use a word processor such as WordPad to **format** text, that is, to give it a specific look and feel by using bold, italics, and different fonts, and by applying other features. Using WordPad, type the title and words to one of your favorite songs and then save the document on your Student Disk (make sure you use your original Student Disk) with the name Song.

   a. Select the title, and then click the Center 🔲, Bold **B**, and Italic *I* buttons on the toolbar.

   b. Click the Font list arrow and select a different font. Repeat this step several times with different fonts until you locate a font that matches the song.

   c. Experiment with formatting options until you find a look you like for your document. Save and print the final version.

PROJECTS

1. Formatting a floppy disk removes all the data on a disk. Answer the following questions using full sentences:

   a. What other method did you learn in this tutorial to remove data from a disk?

   b. If you wanted to remove all data from a disk, which method would you use? Why?

   c. What method would you use if you wanted to remove only one file? Why?

2. A friend who is new to computers is trying to learn how to enter text into WordPad. She has just finished typing her first paragraph when she notices a mistake in the first sentence. She can't remember how to fix a mistake, so she asks you for help. Write the set of steps she should try.

3. Computer users usually develop habits about how they access their files and programs. Take a minute to practice methods of opening a file, and then evaluate which method you would be likely to use and why.

   a. Using WordPad, create a document containing the words to a favorite poem, and save it on your Student Disk with the name Poem.
   b. Close WordPad and return to the desktop.
   c. Open the document using a *document-centric* approach.
   d. After a successful completion of part c, close the program and reopen the same document using another approach.
   e. Write the steps you used to complete parts c and d of this assignment. Then write a paragraph discussing which approach is most convenient when you are starting from the desktop, and indicate what habits you would develop if you owned your own computer and used it regularly.

Explore

4. The My Computer window gives you access to the objects on your computer. In this tutorial you used My Computer to access your floppy drive so you could view the contents of your Student Disk. The My Computer window gives you access to other objects too. Open My Computer and write a list of the objects you see, including folders. Then click each icon and write a two-sentence description of the contents of each window that opens.

Explore

5. In this tutorial you learned how to copy a disk to protect yourself in the event of data loss. If you had your own computer with an 80 MB hard drive that was being used to capacity, it would take many 1.44 MB floppy disks to copy the contents of the entire hard drive. Is copying a reasonable method to use for protecting the data on your hard disk? Why, or why not?

   a. As mentioned at the end of the tutorial, Windows 98 also includes an accessory called Backup that helps you safeguard your data. Backup doesn't just copy the data—it organizes it so that it takes up much less space than if you simply copied it. This program might not be installed on your computer, but if it is, try starting it (click the Start button, point to Programs, point to Accessories, point to System Tools, and then click Backup) and opening the Help files to learn what you can about how it functions. If it is not installed, skip part a.
   b. Look up the topic of backups in a computer concepts textbook or in computer trade magazines. You could also interview experienced computer owners to find out which method they use to protect their data. When you have finished researching the concept of the backup, write a single-page essay that explains the difference between copying and backing up files, and evaluates which method is preferable for backing up large amounts of data, and why.

LAB ASSIGNMENTS

Using Files   In this Lab you manipulate a simulated computer to view what happens in memory and on disk when you create, save, open, revise, and delete files. Understanding what goes on "inside the box" will help you quickly grasp how to perform basic file operations with most application software. See the Read This Before You Begin page for instructions on starting the Using Files Course Lab.

1. Click the Steps button to learn how to use the simulated computer to view the contents of memory and disk when you perform basic file operations. As you proceed through the Steps, answer all of the Quick Check questions that appear. After you complete the Steps, you will see a Quick Check Summary Report. Follow the instructions on the screen to print this report.

2. Click the Explore button and use the simulated computer to perform the following tasks:

   a. Create a document containing your name and the city in which you were born. Save this document as NAME.
   b. Create another document containing two of your favorite foods. Save this document as FOODS.
   c. Create another file containing your two favorite classes. Call this file CLASSES.
   d. Open the FOOD file and add another one of your favorite foods. Save this file without changing its name.
   e. Open the NAME file. Change this document so it contains your name and the name of your school. Save this as a new document called SCHOOL.
   f. Write down how many files are on the simulated disk and the exact contents of each file.
   g. Delete all the files.

3. In Explore, use the simulated computer to perform the following tasks.

   a. Create a file called MUSIC that contains the name of your favorite CD.
   b. Create another document that contains eight numbers and call this file LOTTERY.
   c. You didn't win the lottery this week. Revise the contents of the LOTTERY file, but save the revision as LOTTERY2.
   d. Revise the MUSIC file so it also contains the name of your favorite musician or composer, and save this file as MUSIC2.
   e. Delete the MUSIC file.
   f. Write down how many files are on the simulated disk and the exact contents of each file.

QUICK | CHECK ANSWERS

Session 2.1

1. file

2. Formatting

3. True

4. insertion point

5. Word wrap

6. Move the I-beam pointer to the left of the first word you want to select, then drag the I-beam pointer over the text to the end of the last word you want to select.

7. file extension

Session 2.2

1. My Computer

2. A

3. hard

4. file name, size, type, and date modified

5. root or top-level

6. True

7. yes

New Perspectives on

MICROSOFT®
WINDOWS® 98

Read This Before You Begin

To the Student

Make Student Disk Program

To complete the Level II tutorials, Tutorial Assignments, and Projects, you need 2 Student Disks. Your instructor will either provide you with Student Disks or ask you to make your own.

If you are making your own Student Disks you will need 2 blank, formatted high-density disks and access to the Make Student Disk program. If you wish to install the Make Student Disk program to your home computer, you can obtain it from your instructor or from the Web. To download the Make Student Disk program from the Web, go to **www.course.com**, click Data Disks, and follow the instructions on the screen.

To install the Make Student Disk program, select and click the file you just downloaded from **www.course.com**, 5447-9.exe. Follow the on-screen instructions to complete the installation. If you have any trouble installing or obtaining the Make Student Disk program, ask your instructor or technical support person for assistance.

Once you have obtained and installed the Make Student Disk program, you can use it to create your student disks according to the steps in the tutorials.

Course Labs

The Level II tutorials in this book feature 2 interactive Course Labs to help you understand selected computer concepts. There are Lab Assignments at the end of Tutorial 5 that relate to these Labs. To start a Lab, click the **Start** button on the Windows 98 Taskbar, point to **Programs**, point to **Course Labs**, point to **New Perspectives Course Labs**, and click the name of the Lab you want to use.

Using Your Own Computer

If you are going to work through this book using your own computer, you need:

Computer System Microsoft Windows 98 must be installed on a local hard drive or on a network drive.

Student Disks You will not be able to complete the tutorials or exercises in this book using your own computer until you have your Student Disks. See "Make Student Disk Program" above for details on obtaining your student disks.

Course Labs See your instructor or technical support person to obtain the Course Lab software for use on your own computer.

To complete the Level II tutorials, you will need to be able to copy files to the hard drive in Tutorial 3, you will need access to Accessibility Options and Accessibility Tools in Tutorial 4, and you will need an Internet connection in Tutorial 5. Tutorial 5 also assumes that Internet Explorer 4 is the default browser.

Visit Our World Wide Web Site

Additional materials designed especially for you are available on the World Wide Web. Go to **http://www.course.com**.

To the Instructor

The Make Student Disk Program and Course Labs for this title are available on the Instructor's Resource Kit for this title. Follow the instructions in the Help file on the CD-ROM to install the programs to your network or standalone computer. For information on using the Make Student Disk Program or the Course Labs, see the "To the Student" section above. In order for students to be able to complete the steps in the Level II tutorials, they will need to be able to copy files to the hard drive in Tutorial 3, have access to Accessibility Options and Accessibility Tools in Tutorial 4, and establish an Internet connection in Tutorial 5. Tutorial 5 also assumes that Internet Explorer 4 is the default browser. You are granted a license to copy the Student Files and Course Labs to any computer or computer network used by students who have purchased this book.

In this tutorial you will:

- "Quick" format a floppy disk

- View the structure of folders and files in Windows Explorer

- Select, create, and rename folders in Windows Explorer

- Navigate through devices and folders using navigation buttons

- Arrange files by name, date modified, size, and type

- Select a single file, group of files, all files, or all files but one

- Create a printout showing the structure of folders and files

- Move and copy one or more files from one folder to another

- Move and copy one or more files from one disk to another

- Delete files and folders

ORGANIZING FILES WITH WINDOWS EXPLORER

Structuring Information on a Disk at Kolbe Climbing School

CASE

Kolbe Climbing School

Bernard Kolbe knew how to climb before he could ride a bike. In college he started what is now one of the most popular guide services in the Front Range, the Kolbe Climbing School, known to locals as "KCS." KCS offers guided climbs in the Front Range area, especially in Rocky Mountain National Park and nearby climbing areas such as Lumpy Ridge. While most clients simply want to learn rock and sport climbing, a few want guides for longer alpine climbs and ice climbing.

Since he started his business, Bernard has handled the paperwork using yellow pads, clipboards, and manila folders. Recent conversations with his insurance agent and accountant, though, convinced him that he needs to keep better records on his employees, clients, and the use and condition of his equipment. The KCS offices adjoin a business services office, so Bernard rented some computer time and began creating the files he needs, storing them on a floppy disk.

Not too long ago, Bernard asked if you could help him out with KCS recordkeeping. You agreed (in exchange for some free climbing lessons) and got to work updating the client files on his floppy disk. When Bernard first gave you the disk he warned you it could use a little organization, so you began by creating a folder structure on the disk.

This morning, you walked into the office to find that Bernard had spent yesterday evening at the rented computer adding new files to his disk. You realize you need to show him the folder structure you created so he can learn to use it. You point out that an important part of computerized recordkeeping is creating and using a system that makes it easy to find important information. Bernard is willing to learn more (it's too cold to climb anyway), so the two of you head over to the business services office to spend some time looking over Bernard's files.

SESSION 3.1

In this session you will learn how Windows Explorer displays the devices and folders your computer can access. Understanding how to manipulate this display is the first step in using Windows Explorer to organize files, which will make you a more productive Windows user. In this tutorial you will work with files and folders on a floppy disk. If you have your own computer or are in a business environment, you will more likely work with files and folders on a hard disk drive. You will discover that file management techniques are the same for floppy disks and hard disks. *For this tutorial you will need two blank 3½-inch disks.*

Creating Your Student Disk with Quick Format

Before you begin, you need to prepare a new Student Disk that contains the sample files you will work with in Tutorials 3 and 4. You can make your Student Disk using the NP on Microsoft Windows 98 menu.

If you are using your own computer, the NP on Microsoft Windows 98 menu will not be available. Before you proceed, bring a blank disk to your school's computer lab and use the NP on Microsoft Windows 98 menu to make your new Student Disk. Once you have made the disk, you can use it to complete this tutorial on any computer that runs Windows 98.

When you want to erase the contents of a floppy disk, you can use the Quick format option rather than the Full format that you use on a new disk. A Quick format takes less time than a Full format because, instead of preparing the entire disk surface, a Quick format erases something called the file allocation table. The **file allocation table** (**FAT**) is a file your operating system uses to track the locations of all the files on the disk. By erasing the FAT, you erase all the information that tells the computer about the files on the disk, and so the disk appears empty to the computer.

To Quick format your Student Disk:

1. Write "Disk 2—Windows 98 Tutorials 3 & 4 Student Disk" on the label of your disk.

2. Place your disk in drive A.

   TROUBLE? If your 3½-inch disk drive is B, place your formatted disk in that drive instead, and for the rest of this tutorial substitute drive B wherever you see drive A.

3. Open the My Computer window.

   TROUBLE? How you open the My Computer window depends on your computer's settings. First try clicking the My Computer icon on the desktop. If you are using Web-style settings, the My Computer window opens. If the window doesn't open, you are using Classic-style settings. Press Enter to open the My Computer window.

4. Right-click the **3½ Floppy (A:)** icon.

5. Click **Format** to display the Format dialog box.

6. Make sure the **Quick (erase)** button and other settings in the dialog box match those shown in Figure 3-1.

Figure 3-1	FORMAT DIALOG BOX

click to Quick format
a disk

```
Format - 3½ Floppy (A:)                           ? X
 Capacity:
 1.44 Mb (3.5")                    ▼        Start
 ┌─ Format type ──────────────┐            Close
 │  ◉ Quick (erase)            │
 │  ○ Full                     │
 │  ○ Copy system files only   │
 └─────────────────────────────┘
 ┌─ Other options ────────────┐
 │  Label:                     │
 │  [                    ]     │
 │                             │
 │  ☐ No label                 │
 │  ☑ Display summary when finished │
 │  ☐ Copy system files        │
 └─────────────────────────────┘
 [                             ]
```

7. Click the **Start** button to begin the Quick format.

   TROUBLE? If an error message appears, it is possible your disk capacity is double-density instead of high-density. Make sure you are using a high-density disk.

8. When the Format Results dialog box appears, click the **Close** button.

9. Click the **Close** button to close the Format dialog box, and then close My Computer.

Now that you have formatted your disk, you can make a Student Disk for Tutorials 3 and 4.

To create your Student Disk:

1. Click the **Start** button [Start], point to **Programs**, point to **NP on Microsoft Windows 98-Level II**, then click **Disk 2 (Tutorials 3 & 4)**.

2. When a message box opens, click the **OK** button. Wait while the program copies the practice files to your formatted disk. When all the files have been copied, the program closes.

Windows Explorer

The root directory of Bernard's disk contains three folders—Clients, Gear, and Guides—plus the files he hasn't yet organized.

The ideal tool for file organization tasks, you tell Bernard, is Windows Explorer. **Windows Explorer** is a program included with Windows 98, designed to simplify file management tasks such as locating, viewing, moving, copying, and deleting files and folders. Using a single window divided into two sections or **panes**, Windows Explorer provides an easy-to-navigate representation of disks, folders, files, Web pages, and other resources available to your computer.

Windows 98 provides more than one way to accomplish most tasks. Although you can use My Computer to look at the contents of a disk, Windows Explorer is a more powerful file management tool. When you're moving just a file or two, My Computer works fine; however, using it to organize many files on several disks often results in a frustrating game of "hide and seek" as you try to navigate through the levels of device and folder windows. For more advanced file management tasks, many people prefer to use Windows Explorer.

Starting Windows Explorer

As with other Windows 98 applications, you start Windows Explorer using the Start menu. It is possible that a Windows Explorer icon is on your desktop, which you can click to start Windows Explorer easily.

To start Windows Explorer:

1. Click the **Start** button [Start], point to **Programs**, then click **Windows Explorer** to open a window titled "Exploring."

2. If the Exploring window is not maximized, click the **Maximize** button ▣.

Changing View Options

Like the My Computer window, the Exploring window can display the Standard, Address, and Links toolbars and a status bar. For this tutorial, you need to make sure you can see the Standard toolbar, the Address bar, and the status bar. You'll also view objects in List view and disable Web view, which you don't need in this tutorial. Finally, you'll display text labels on the Standard toolbar buttons.

To control the toolbar display:

1. Click **View** and then point to **Toolbars**. Make the necessary changes so that the Standard Buttons, Address Bar, and Text Labels options are checked, then remove the checks from the Links options.

2. If necessary, reopen the View menu. Make sure that Status Bar is checked, as Web Page is not checked, and the List option is selected. If Status Bar is not checked, click **Status Bar**.

The Exploring window also allows you to display a variety of Windows 98 Explorer bars. **Explorer bars** help organize information such as your computer's devices, the Web pages you have recently visited, or your favorite files and folders. The **All Folders Explorer bar** appears in the left pane of the Exploring window and displays your computer's devices. To work effectively with folders and files, you need to view the All Folders Explorer bar.

To view the All Folders Explorer bar:

1. Click **View** and then point to **Explorer Bar**.

2. Make sure the All Folders option has a dot next to it. If it does not, click **All Folders**; otherwise click a blank area of the screen to close the View menu. Your Exploring window should now resemble Figure 3-2.

TROUBLE? If your icons aren't underlined, don't worry. The computer shown in the figures is using Web style, so icons appear underlined. If your computer is using Classic style, you might want to switch to Web style to match the steps and figures in this tutorial: click the Start button, point to Settings, click Folder Options, click the Web style option button, and then click the OK button. Click the OK button again if you are asked if you are sure you want to use single-click.

Figure 3-2	WINDOWS EXPLORER OVERVIEW

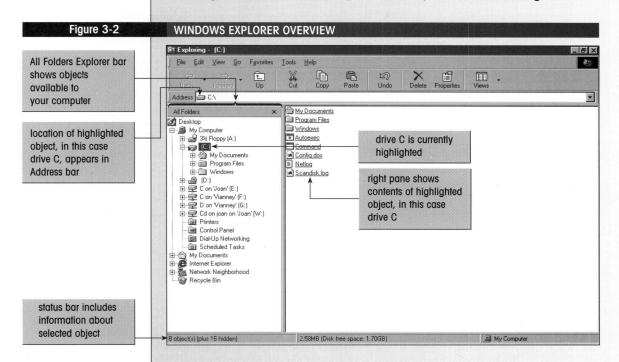

All Folders Explorer bar shows objects available to your computer

location of highlighted object, in this case drive C, appears in Address bar

drive C is currently highlighted

right pane shows contents of highlighted object, in this case drive C

status bar includes information about selected object

TROUBLE? Because your computer system has different files and devices on it than those in the figures, your Exploring window will probably look different. Don't worry.

Study Figure 3-2 and notice how the Exploring window is divided into two sections: the All Folders Explorer bar in the left pane of the window and a list of objects in the right pane. The All Folders Explorer bar contains a list of devices and folders and the other objects available to your computer, including its network and Internet resources. The right pane of the Exploring window displays the contents of the object highlighted in the All Folders Explorer bar (the location of this object is also displayed in the Address bar). If a drive is selected, such as drive C, the folders and files stored on drive C appear, as in Figure 3-2. If a Web page is selected, its contents appear, as you'll see in a later tutorial.

You might have noticed that the left and right panes in Figure 3-2 display the same folders, such as My Documents and Program Files. To some people it is confusing that the same folders are shown in both panes. However, it is important to note that they are not duplicate folders; they are just shown twice. The left pane displays a device's *structure*, that is, its levels of folders and **subfolders** (folders contained in other folders). The right pane, on the other hand, displays the *contents* of a device or folder, including its folders and files.

To see the devices and resources available to your computer, you can scroll through the list of objects on the All Folders Explorer bar in the left pane. Each object in the list has a small icon next to it. In this session you will use the left pane to explore the contents of storage devices on your computer. Explorer uses the icons shown in Figure 3-3 to represent different types of storage devices.

Figure 3-3	STORAGE DEVICE ICONS		
ICON	**REPRESENTS**	**ICON**	**REPRESENTS**
	Floppy disk drive		Network disk drive
	Hard disk drive on your computer		Shared disk drive
	CD-ROM drive		Zip drive

To see a list of storage devices available to your computer:

1. If necessary, use the left pane scroll box to scroll from the bottom to the top of the left pane so you get a look at all the objects on your computer, from the Desktop icon at the top to the Recycle Bin at the bottom.

   TROUBLE? If you don't have a scroll bar, you don't have more than one screen of open devices and files. Skip Step 1.

2. So that you get a better idea of your computer's resources, notice whether your computer has a CD-ROM drive or access to network storage devices.

3. After you look at the list of devices and folders, if necessary, scroll back to the top of the left pane so that you can see at the top of the list.

Viewing the Folders on a Disk Drive

Like a file cabinet, a typical storage device on your computer contains files and folders. These folders can contain additional files and one or more levels of subfolders. If Windows Explorer displayed all your computer's storage devices, folders, and files at once, it could be a very long list. Instead, Windows Explorer allows you to open devices and folders only when you want to see what they contain. Otherwise, you can keep them closed.

As you've seen, the small icon next to each object in the list, called the **device icon** or **folder icon**, represents the device or folder in the All Folders Explorer bar in the left pane. Many of these icons also have a plus box or minus box next to them, which indicates whether the device or folder contains additional folders. Both the device/folder icon and the plus/minus box are controls that you can click to change the display in the Exploring window. You click the plus box to display folders or subfolders, and you click the minus box to hide them. You click the device/folder icon to control the display of object contents in the right pane.

You begin assisting Bernard by showing him how you've structured the folders on drive A. You explain to him how the plus/minus box displays or hides the folders on drive A.

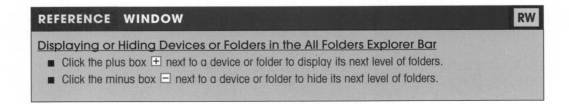

REFERENCE   WINDOW   **RW**

Displaying or Hiding Devices or Folders in the All Folders Explorer Bar
- Click the plus box ⊞ next to a device or folder to display its next level of folders.
- Click the minus box ⊟ next to a device or folder to hide its next level of folders.

To display or hide the levels of folders on drive A:

1. Click ⊞ in front of 3½ Floppy (A:) 💾. The folders in the root directory of drive A appear, and the plus box in front of drive A changes to a minus box ⊟. See Figure 3-4.

   TROUBLE? The 3½ Floppy (A:) device icon 💾 might appear with a different name on your computer. This is the icon representing the device that contains your Student Disk. In the steps in this tutorial, this icon is called simply drive A.

   TROUBLE? If you initially see a minus box in front of the device icon for drive A, your drive A folders are already visible in the left pane. You don't need to click the icon in Step 1.

2. Click ⊟ in front of 3½ Floppy (A:). Now the left pane shows only drive A, without the folders it contains.

3. Click ⊞ in front of 3½ Floppy (A:) one more time.

Figure 3-4	FOLDERS ON DRIVE A

plus/minus box for drive A

plus box indicates that the Clients folder contains subfolders

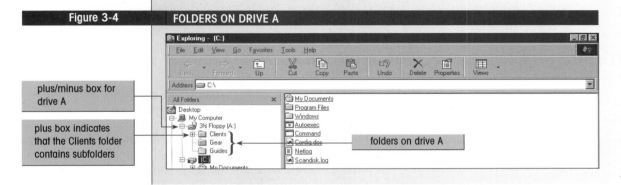

folders on drive A

When you click the plus box ⊞ next to drive A, you do not necessarily see all the folders on the drive. You only see the first level of folders. If one of these folders contains subfolders, a plus box appears next to it. The Clients folder on drive A has a plus box next to it, indicating that it contains subfolders. When you originally created the structure for Bernard's disk, you grouped his clients into Advanced and Basic, and then grouped the Advanced clients by their primary interests—Alpine, Ice, and Sport.

To view the subfolders for Clients:

1. Click ⊞ next to the Clients folder. You see that Clients contains two subfolders: Advanced and Basic.

2. Click ⊞ next to the Advanced folder. Now you see three additional subfolders: Alpine, Ice, and Sport. See Figure 3-5.

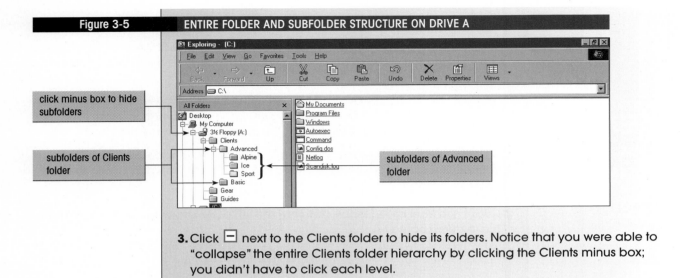

Figure 3-5   ENTIRE FOLDER AND SUBFOLDER STRUCTURE ON DRIVE A

3. Click ⊟ next to the Clients folder to hide its folders. Notice that you were able to "collapse" the entire Clients folder hierarchy by clicking the Clients minus box; you didn't have to click each level.

Selecting a Device or Folder in the All Folders Explorer Bar

To work with a device or folder in the All Folders Explorer bar, you first click it to select it, and Windows highlights it. It is important to understand that using the plus/minus box does not select a device or folder. Notice in Figure 3-5 that drive C is still selected and its contents still appear in the right pane, even though you have been viewing the folder structure of drive A in the left pane.

To select a device or folder, you must click its icon, not its plus/minus box. When you select a device or folder, it becomes active. The **active** device or folder is the one the computer uses when you take an action.

For example, if you want to create a new folder on drive A, you first need to select drive A in the All Folders Explorer bar. It then becomes the active drive. If you don't first activate drive A, the new folder you create will be placed in whatever device or folder is currently active—it could be a folder on the hard drive or network drive. How do you know which device or folder is active? You can know in three ways. First, it is highlighted. Second, its name appears in the Address bar, as shown in Figure 3-6. Finally, its contents appear in the right pane. You'll learn more about the right pane in Session 3.2.

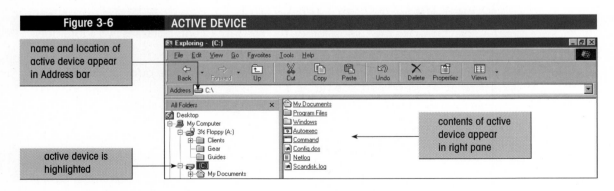

Figure 3-6   ACTIVE DEVICE

You can experiment with changing the active device and folder by selecting drive A and then selecting the Clients folder.

To select devices and folders:

1. Click 🖪 **3½ Floppy (A:)**. To show that drive A is selected, the computer highlights the label and displays it in the Address bar. The right pane shows the contents of drive A. See Figure 3-7.

Figure 3-7	DRIVE A IS THE ACTIVE DEVICE

name of drive A appears in Address bar

click drive A device icon to activate it

contents of drive A appear in right pane

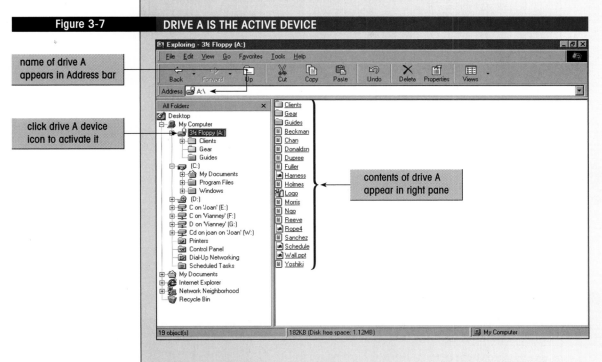

2. Click 📁 **Clients** in the left pane. The computer highlights the label "Clients" and displays it in the Address bar. Its contents appear in the right pane.

Creating New Folders

Bernard tracks gear usage for ropes and other types of equipment such as carabiners, belay plates, and so on. His disk already contains a folder named "Gear" that contains files for each of the KCS ropes. You decide to create two new subfolders within the Gear folder: one for all files having to do with ropes and the other for files having to do with hardware equipment.

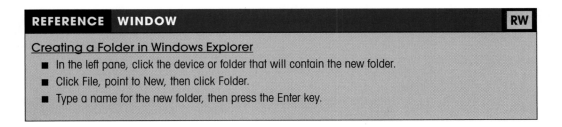

REFERENCE   WINDOW   **RW**

Creating a Folder in Windows Explorer
- In the left pane, click the device or folder that will contain the new folder.
- Click File, point to New, then click Folder.
- Type a name for the new folder, then press the Enter key.

The Clients folder is currently active. If you create a new folder now, it will become a subfolder of Clients. Because you want to create the two subfolders in the Gear folder, you must make the Gear folder active.

To create the new Gear subfolders on Bernard's disk:

1. Click 📁 **Gear** in the left pane to activate the Gear folder.

   TROUBLE? If you clicked ⊞ instead of the folder icon 📁, you did not activate the folder. Be sure you click the folder icon. The Gear folder should appear high-lighted, and the icon should change to 📂 to indicate it is the active folder.

2. Click **File** to open the File menu, point to **New**, and then click **Folder**. A folder icon labeled "New Folder" appears in the right pane.

3. Type **Hardware** as the title of the new folder.

4. Press the **Enter** key. Now create the second subfolder of the Gear folder for all the rope files.

   TROUBLE? If you pressed Enter twice by mistake, Hardware becomes the active folder. Be sure Gear is still the active folder; click the Gear folder icon in the left pane, if necessary.

5. Click **File**, point to **New**, click **Folder**, type **Ropes** as the name of the second folder, and then press the **Enter** key.

6. Click ⊞ next to the Gear folder in the left pane to see the new folders in the left pane. See Figure 3-8.

Figure 3-8	CREATING NEW FOLDERS

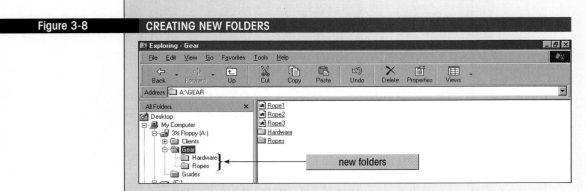

Renaming a Folder

As you and Bernard go over the current folder structure, you realize that a complete inventory of the KCS gear also includes the harnesses climbers wear to attach themselves to the rope for protection in case they fall. Because harnesses aren't considered hardware, you decide that the harness inventory files should go in the same folder with the ropes. Thus, you need to rename the Ropes file "Ropes and Harnesses."

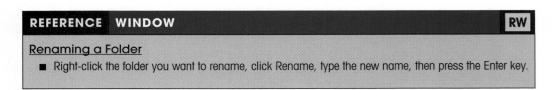

REFERENCE WINDOW   **RW**

Renaming a Folder

■ Right-click the folder you want to rename, click Rename, type the new name, then press the Enter key.

To rename a folder you use the shortcut menu's Rename command, which appears when you click the folder with the right mouse button.

To change the name of the Ropes folder:

1. Right-click **Ropes** in the left pane. (Actually you can right-click Ropes in either the left or right pane; both give you access to the Rename command.)

2. Click **Rename**. The folder name is highlighted, and anything you type will replace the current name.

3. Type **Ropes and Harnesses** as the new folder name.

4. Press the **Enter** key.

The new name now appears in both the left and right panes, though it might be truncated if the panes are too narrow to display it.

Adjusting the Width of the Exploring Window Panes

As you create or view more and more levels of folders, the All Folders Explorer bar might not be wide enough to display all the levels of folders. As a result, you might not be able to see all the device and folder icons. Whether or not this occurs depends on how long your folder names are and how wide the All Folders Explorer bar was in the first place. You can change the width of the Exploring window panes by dragging the dividing bar that separates the two panes.

REFERENCE WINDOW   **RW**

Adjusting the Width of the Exploring Window Panes
- Move the mouse pointer to the dividing bar between the left and right panes.
- When the arrow-shaped pointer ⇖ changes to a double-ended arrow ↔, hold down the left mouse button and drag the dividing line right or left, as necessary.
- When the dividing bar is in the desired position, release the mouse button.

To increase the width of the All Folders Explorer bar:

1. Move the mouse pointer to the dividing bar between the two panes. The pointer changes to a ↔ pointer.

2. Hold down the left mouse button while you drag the dividing bar about one-half inch to the right, as shown in Figure 3-9.

| Figure 3-9 | ADJUSTING THE WIDTH OF THE WINDOWS EXPLORER PANES |

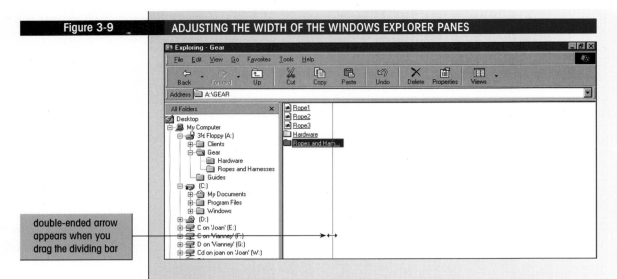

double-ended arrow appears when you drag the dividing bar

3. Release the mouse button. Use this method as necessary when you work with Windows Explorer to adjust the width of the All Folders Explorer bar.

4. Click the **Close** button ☒ to close the Exploring window. You return to the Windows 98 desktop.

QUICK CHECK

1. _____ is an alternative to using *My Computer* for file management tasks.

2. The Exploring window is divided into two panes. Describe each pane, using one sentence for each pane.

3. True or False: If you see folders with the same names in both the right and left panes of the Exploring window, the folders are duplicates and you should erase those in the right pane.

4. True or False: The All Folders Explorer bar displays all the files in a folder.

5. A folder that is contained in another folder is referred to as a(n) _____.

6. You click the _____ to expand the display of folders in the All Folders Explorer bar.

7. If you want to create a new folder on drive A, what should you click in the left pane?

8. True or False: To adjust the width of the All Folders Explorer bar, be sure the mouse pointer looks like ⌐ before you start to drag the dividing bar.

SESSION 3.2

In Session 3.2 you will work with the right pane of the Exploring window, which displays folders and files.

Viewing the Contents of a Device or Folder

As discussed in the previous session, the right pane of the Exploring window shows the contents, both folders and files, of the device or folder that is active in the left pane. Clicking a plus/minus box in the left pane does not affect the right pane. To change the right pane, you must activate a device or folder by clicking its corresponding device or folder icon. Windows Explorer highlights the icon, and the right pane changes to display the contents of the device or folder you clicked. The status bar provides information about the object you selected, including the number of files and folders it contains, the amount of disk space it occupies, and the amount of free disk space.

REFERENCE WINDOW   **RW**

Viewing a List of Files
- Adjust the left pane to display the device or folder whose contents you want to view.
- Click the icon next to the device or folder that contains the files you want to view.

You and Bernard now examine the contents of drive A. You'll need to restart Windows Explorer, and check that your Exploring window settings match those in the following figures.

To view the contents of drive A:

1. Make sure your Student Disk is in drive A, and then start Windows Explorer. Make sure Web view is disabled and the view is List view. Then make sure the Standard toolbar, Address bar, All Folders Explorer bar, and status bar are visible. The Standard toolbar should display text labels.

2. Click 🖳 **3½ Floppy (A:)** in the left pane. See Figure 3-10 if you have trouble locating this icon. The right pane changes to show the contents of drive A, and the status bar displays information about the number and size of objects in drive A. See Figure 3-10.

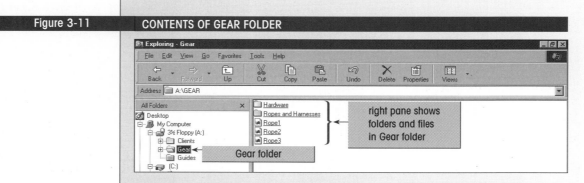

Figure 3-10   CONTENTS OF DRIVE A

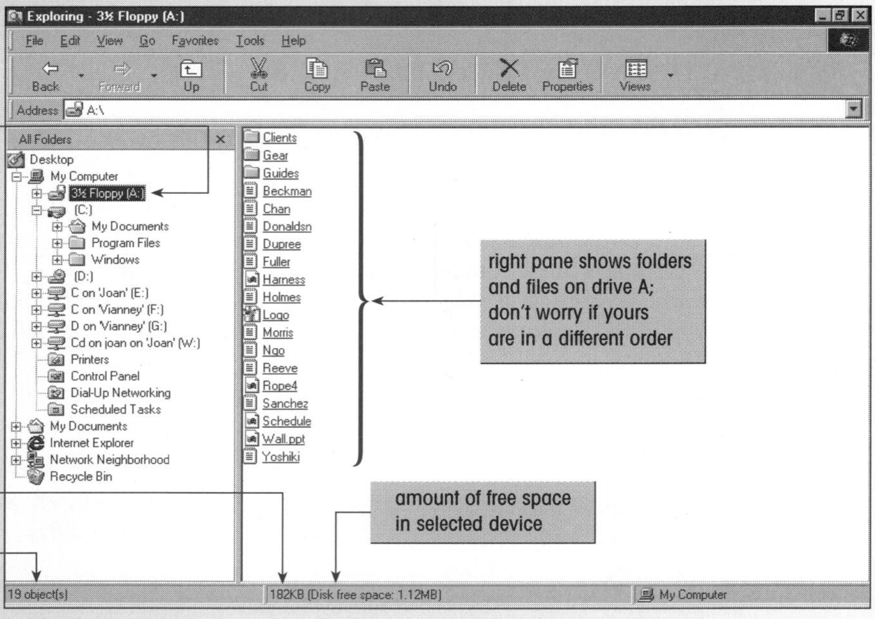

drive A

right pane shows folders and files on drive A; don't worry if yours are in a different order

size of files stored on selected device

amount of free space in selected device

number of objects in the selected drive

You can see that the root directory of drive A contains three folders and several files; however, you cannot see the contents of the folders in this list. To see the contents of a folder, you must select the folder by clicking it in the left pane. Suppose you want to view the contents of the Gear folder.

To view folder contents:

1. Click ⊞ in front of 3½ Floppy (A:) in the left pane to display its folders.

2. Click 📁 **Gear** (not the plus box) in the left pane. The right pane changes to display the files in the Gear folder. In addition to the two subfolders you created earlier, there are three files, one for each type of rope KCS owns. See Figure 3-11.

Figure 3-11   CONTENTS OF GEAR FOLDER

right pane shows folders and files in Gear folder

Gear folder

3. Click 💾 **3½ Floppy (A:)** so that the right pane again displays the contents of the root directory of drive A.

Navigating Through Devices and Folders

So far you've seen how to view a drive or folder's contents by clicking the drive or folder in the left pane. In Windows Explorer, you can also "page" through the devices and folders on your computer, as though they were pages in a magazine. You use the Standard toolbar's navigation buttons to move back or forward through the devices, folders, or files you've visited so far. You can also move up and down through the hierarchy of objects on your computer. See Figure 3-12.

Figure 3-12		STANDARD TOOLBAR NAVIGATION BUTTONS
BUTTON	**ICON**	**DESCRIPTION**
Back	⬅	Returns you to the device, folder, or file you were most recently viewing. If you click it twice, it returns you to the object you were viewing before that, and so on, until you reach the first object you viewed in the current session. This button is active only when you have viewed more than one object in the current session.
Forward	➡	Reverses the effect of the Back button, sending you forward to the object from which you just clicked the Back button. This button is active only when you have used the Back button.
Up	🔼	Moves you up the hierarchy of folders and devices on your computer.

Returning to Previously Viewed Devices and Folders

You are currently viewing the contents of drive A. If you click the Back button once, you will return to the folder you were just viewing—the Gear folder. If you click it more than once, you will return, in reverse chronological order, to previously-viewed folders or devices.

To move back and forward through the devices and folders you've seen so far:

1. Click the **Back** button ⬅. Make sure you click ⬅, and not the arrow to the right of ⬅. You return to the Gear folder. Notice the Forward button is no longer dimmed. You can use it to move forward to where you just were.

   TROUBLE? If you click the list arrow to the right of the Back button by mistake, click it again to close the list and then repeat Step 1.

2. Click ⬅ again. You now return to the device you viewed before viewing the Gear folder: drive A.

3. Click the **Forward** button ➡. The contents of Gear again appear. Click ➡ again and the contents of drive A appear again. The Forward button is now dimmed, indicating you've gone as far forward as you can again.

Windows Explorer remembers where you've been by maintaining a list of the devices and folders you've viewed so far in a session. When you repeatedly click the Back and Forward buttons, you are actually moving through this list. For a more direct route to a previously-viewed device or folder, you can view this list from the File menu or by using the Back and Forward list arrows. The bottom portion of the File menu lists all the devices or folders you've viewed in the current session (up to a number specified by your computer settings), while the Back and Forward lists show, in chronological order, those you've viewed or returned to recently.

To see how these lists help you navigate your computer's devices and folders, try first navigating through the subfolders on your Student Disk. Then try returning to specific devices and folders, using the File menu and Back and Forward lists.

To navigate through the folders on your Student Disk:

1. Click the **Clients** folder in the left pane. The Clients folder opens.

2. Click ⊞ next to Clients in the left pane, and then click the **Advanced** folder in the left pane. Now that you've navigated through several folders, try returning to drive A—this time not using the Back button but instead using the File menu.

3. Click **File** to view the list of the devices and folders you've viewed so far. 3½ Floppy (A:) appears twice in the File menu because you've visited it twice. See Figure 3-13.

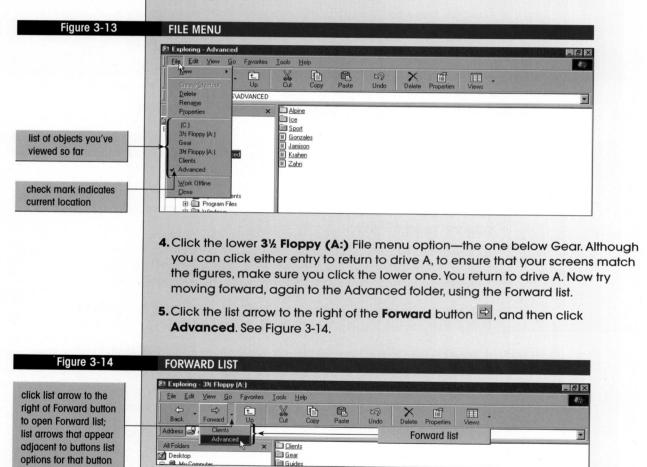

Figure 3-13   FILE MENU

list of objects you've viewed so far

check mark indicates current location

4. Click the lower **3½ Floppy (A:)** File menu option—the one below Gear. Although you can click either entry to return to drive A, to ensure that your screens match the figures, make sure you click the lower one. You return to drive A. Now try moving forward, again to the Advanced folder, using the Forward list.

5. Click the list arrow to the right of the **Forward** button ⇨, and then click **Advanced**. See Figure 3-14.

Figure 3-14   FORWARD LIST

click list arrow to the right of Forward button to open Forward list; list arrows that appear adjacent to buttons list options for that button

Forward list

You have now returned to the Advanced folder. Because you're navigating only a few levels of devices and folders you might not fully appreciate the power of these lists, but if you are exploring multiple folders on multiple local and network drives, you'll find they greatly simplify device and folder navigation.

Navigating Device and Folder Hierarchies

When you use the Back and Forward lists, you are moving in order through objects you've already viewed. You can also move up and down through the hierarchy of devices, folders, and subfolders on your computer. To move down, you click in the left pane, the device, folder, or subfolder you want to view. To move up, you click the Up button 🗁. Unlike the Back button, which moves you to whatever object you were just viewing, the Up button always moves you up in the hierarchy. Thus, if you are viewing a folder on drive A, such as Clients, clicking the Up button always moves you up one level to drive A. Clicking the Up button again moves you up to My Computer. Clicking the Back button, on the other hand, moves you to whatever device or folder you were just viewing. For example, if you are viewing drive A and you then select the Advanced folder, clicking the Up button moves you to Clients, because that is one level above Advanced in the hierarchy. However, clicking the Back button returns you to drive A, because that was the last item you selected.

You are currently viewing the Advanced folder, a subfolder of Clients, which is a folder on drive A. Try moving up the hierarchy from Advanced all the way to the top level, your desktop.

To navigate your computer's hierarchy:

1. Click the **Up** button 🗁. You move up to Clients.

2. Click 🗁 again. You move up to drive A.

3. Click 🗁 again. You move up to My Computer.

4. Click 🗁 one last time. You move up to Desktop. You are now at the top of the hierarchy. The Up button is therefore dimmed.

5. Click the list arrow to the right of the **Back** button ⬅, and then click the top **3½ Floppy (A:)** entry. The contents of drive A reappear.

Arranging Files by File Details

For many file management tasks, you often begin by locating one or more files you want to delete, copy, or move. Explorer helps you locate files by allowing you to arrange files by details such as name, size, date, or type. The arrangement you use will depend on the file management task you are doing.

Before you can arrange files by file details, the right pane must be in Details view. As with My Computer, you can switch views using the View menu or the Standard toolbar Views button 🎬, which, like the Back and Forward buttons, has a list arrow to its right that you can click to select a different view. When you view the files in the right pane in Details view, a button appears at the top of each of the four columns: Name, Size, Type, and Modified. You can click one of these buttons to arrange the files by the corresponding column.

- **Name** button arranges the files by name in ascending order (from A to Z). If you click the Name button a second time, the files appear in descending order (from Z to A).

- **Size** button displays the files in order according to the number of bytes or characters each contains. This is helpful when you need to make more space available on a disk and are trying to decide which files to delete or move to another disk. When the files are arranged in descending order by size, the largest files appear at the top. You might choose to delete those first when you need more disk space.

- **Modified** button displays the files in order by the date and time they were modified. This arrangement is useful, for example, if you are looking for a file you know you created yesterday but whose name you have forgotten.

- **Type** button arranges the files into groups based on which program created the files. Sometimes you want to locate all files of a particular type. For example, you might want to quickly locate all the files created with Microsoft Excel. This sorting arrangement is useful when you know you created a file using a particular application. Explorer identifies the application that created the file in the Type column.

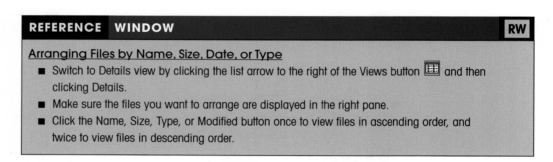

REFERENCE WINDOW   RW

Arranging Files by Name, Size, Date, or Type
- Switch to Details view by clicking the list arrow to the right of the Views button [icon] and then clicking Details.
- Make sure the files you want to arrange are displayed in the right pane.
- Click the Name, Size, Type, or Modified button once to view files in ascending order, and twice to view files in descending order.

Experiment with displaying the files in different orders to see what you can learn about them.

To display the files in a different order:

1. Click the list arrow to the right of the **Views** button [icon], and then click **Details** to view all file details.

2. Click the **Name** button. Notice that folders are alphabetized first, and then files. See Figure 3-15.

   TROUBLE? If you need to change column width to view all the detail information, drag the dividing bars between the Name, Size, Type, and Modified buttons to the left or right.

   TROUBLE? If your files switch to descending order, click the Name button again so they are listed as in Figure 3-15.

Figure 3-15	ARRANGING FILES

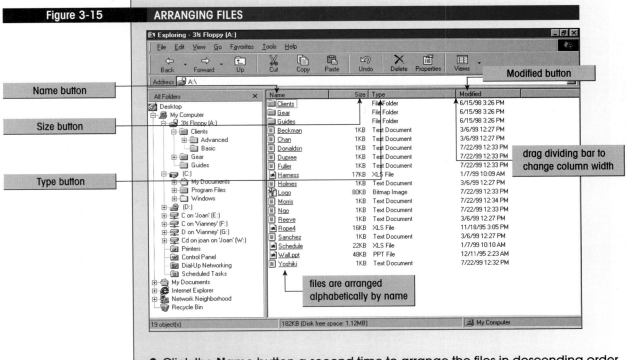

3. Click the **Name** button a second time to arrange the files in descending order by name.

4. Click the **Size** button to arrange the files in ascending order by size. Click the **Size** button a second time to arrange the files in descending order by size. The Logo file is the largest file on the disk.

5. Click the **Type** button. Explorer now groups the files by application type. There is only one bitmap image file.

6. Click the **Modified** button. The files are now listed with the newest or most recently modified file at the top of the list.

TROUBLE? Depending on the width of the columns in the right pane and your computer monitor's settings, you might have to scroll to the right to see the Modified button.

7. Click the **Name** button to restore ascending alphabetical order.

Selecting Files

After you locate the file or files you need for a file management task, you must instruct Explorer which specific file(s) you want to work with. You do this by selecting the file. In Tutorial 2 you learned about the difference between selecting files in Classic style and Web style: When you click a folder or file in the right pane using Classic style, you select it. When you click a folder or file using Web style, however, you open it. This tutorial assumes you are using Web-style settings, but if you are using Classic style, refer to the TROUBLE paragraphs for guidance on how to adjust the steps.

Take a moment to learn some Web-style file selection techniques before working with the files on Bernard's disk. When you select a file in Windows Explorer, information about the file appears in the status bar.

To select one or more files:

1. Point to the **Beckman** file long enough to select it. The file is highlighted to show that it is selected, and information about the file, including its approximate file size, appears in the Status bar.

   TROUBLE? Don't worry if the Beckman file appears as Beckman.txt.

   TROUBLE? If you click the file in Web style instead of simply pointing at it, the Notepad accessory will start and will open the Beckman file. Close Notepad and repeat Step 1.

   TROUBLE? If the Beckman file is not selected when you point to it, you are using Classic style. To select the file, you need to click it.

2. Select the **Morris** file. The Morris file is highlighted to show that it is selected, and Beckman is no longer highlighted.

3. To select all the files and folders on drive A, click **Edit**, then click **Select All**. Explorer highlights the files and folders to show that they are selected.

4. Now deselect the selected files by clicking any blank area in the right pane. The highlighting is removed from all the files to indicate that none is currently selected.

What if you want to work with more than one file, but not with all the files in a folder? For example, suppose Bernard wants to delete three of the files in a folder. In Explorer there are two ways to select a group of files. You can select files listed consecutively using the Shift key, or you can select files scattered throughout the right pane using the Ctrl key. Figure 3-16 shows the two different ways to select a group of files.

Figure 3-16	TWO WAYS TO SELECT A GROUP OF FILES

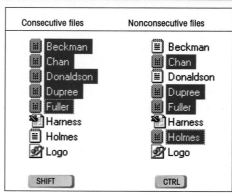

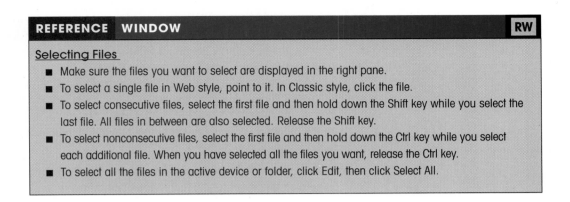

Selecting Files

- Make sure the files you want to select are displayed in the right pane.
- To select a single file in Web style, point to it. In Classic style, click the file.
- To select consecutive files, select the first file and then hold down the Shift key while you select the last file. All files in between are also selected. Release the Shift key.
- To select nonconsecutive files, select the first file and then hold down the Ctrl key while you select each additional file. When you have selected all the files you want, release the Ctrl key.
- To select all the files in the active device or folder, click Edit, then click Select All.

First try selecting a set of consecutive files, and then a set of nonconsecutive files scattered within a folder.

To select groups of files:

1. Select the **Beckman** file.

2. Hold down the **Shift** key while you select the **Fuller** file. Release the **Shift** key. The Beckman and Fuller files and all files in between are highlighted. See Figure 3-17.

Figure 3-17	SELECTING CONSECUTIVE FILES

using the Shift key and the mouse, select these consecutive files

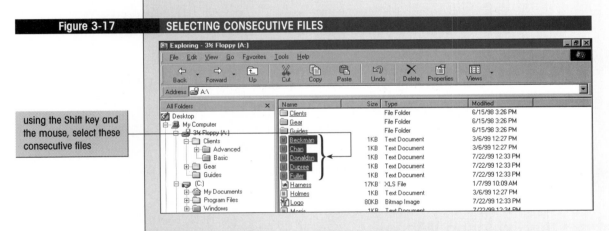

3. Now select a set of nonconsecutive files. First select the **Reeve** file. Notice that selecting this file automatically deselects any selected files.

4. Hold down the **Ctrl** key and select the **Morris** file and then the **Sanchez** file. All three files should be highlighted. Release the **Ctrl** key.

TROUBLE? If you release the Ctrl key by mistake while selecting a set of nonconsecutive files, simply press it again and continue to select the files you want.

TROUBLE? If, in Web style, you pass the pointer too slowly over other files, you might select them too. Try moving the pointer only over a blank area of the screen, or move the mouse quickly over the files you don't want to select. If you do accidentally select a file you don't want to select, point to it again with Ctrl held down, and the file will be deselected. Learning to select nonconsecutive files using Web-style mouse settings can be tricky, so if necessary, practice these steps several times until you feel comfortable.

While selecting multiple files with the Ctrl key, you can deselect any file by pointing to it again while holding down the Ctrl key. You can also select more files by holding down the Ctrl key again, then selecting the additional files. The files do not need to be in consecutive order for you to select them as a group.

To select and deselect additional files:

1. Hold down the **Ctrl** key and point to the **Chan** file to select it. Four files are now selected.

2. Keep holding down the **Ctrl** key and point to the **Sanchez** file to deselect it. Now three files are selected: Chan, Morris, and Reeve.

Suppose you want to select all the files in a folder except one? You can use the Invert Selection menu option to select all the files that are not highlighted.

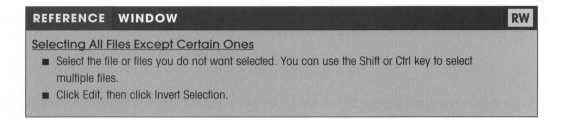

REFERENCE   WINDOW   **RW**

Selecting All Files Except Certain Ones
- Select the file or files you do not want selected. You can use the Shift or Ctrl key to select multiple files.
- Click Edit, then click Invert Selection.

To use Invert Selection to select all files except Dupree:

1. Select the **Dupree** file.

2. Click **Edit**, then click **Invert Selection**. All the folders and files except Dupree are now selected.

3. Click a blank area to remove the highlighting for all the files on drive A.

Printing the Exploring Window

You are almost ready to move the new files Bernard created from the root directory into the appropriate folders. Bernard would like to identify the files that need to be moved. He wonders if there's a quick way to get a hard copy (that is, a paper copy) of the Exploring window so he can write on it. You tell him you can temporarily store an image of your computer screen in memory using the Print Screen key. Then, you can start the WordPad program and paste the image into a blank WordPad document. Finally, you can print the document, which will contain an image of your screen—in this case, the Exploring window. It can be handy to have a printout of the structures of certain important devices for reference, so this is a good procedure to learn.

To print the Exploring window:

1. Make sure the right pane still displays the contents of drive A; if not, click **3½ Floppy (A:)** in the left pane.

2. Click ⊞ next to Clients, Advanced, and Gear as necessary so that all the folders and subfolders on Bernard's disk are visible.

3. Press the **Print Screen** key. Although it seems as if nothing happens, an image of the Exploring window is stored in memory.

   TROUBLE? If you cannot locate the Print Screen key, it might be accessible through another key on your keyboard. Ask your instructor for help.

4. Click the **Start** button ⊞Start, point to **Programs**, point to **Accessories**, and then click **WordPad**. The WordPad window opens.

5. Maximize the WordPad window, type your name and the date at the top of the WordPad window, and then press the **Enter** key twice.

6. Click the **Paste** button 🖺, then scroll to the top of the document (also scroll left, if necessary). The Exploring screen image appears in the WordPad document. See Figure 3-18.

7. Click the **Print** button 🖨. Because the WordPad document contains the graphic image of the Exploring window, it might take longer than usual to print.

8. Close the WordPad window. When you see a message asking if you want to save changes to the document, click the **No** button.

9. Close Windows Explorer.

Figure 3-18	EXPLORING SCREEN IMAGE IN A WORDPAD DOCUMENT

WordPad window

image of Exploring window pasted into WordPad

WordPad scroll bars scroll the image up, down, right, and left

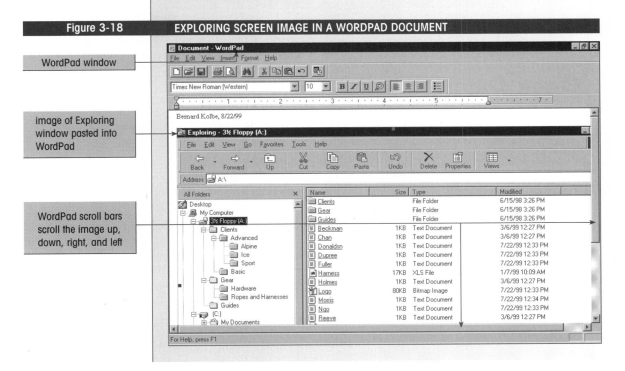

Bernard annotates the printout as shown in Figure 3-19. His notes show you where to move the files in the root directory. You decide to take a break and finish working with Bernard's files tomorrow.

| Figure 3-19 | BERNARD'S PRINTOUT |

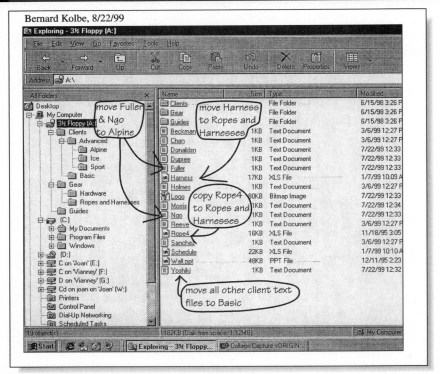

QUICK CHECK

1. True or False: If you click ⊞ next to the Clients folder, Explorer displays a list of files in the Clients folder.

2. What do you click to display a device's or folder's contents in the right pane?

3. True or False: The Explorer toolbar contains buttons you use to select consecutive files in the right pane.

4. _____ view shows the file size and the date when the file was created or last modified.

5. If you hold down the _____ key when you select files, you will select consecutive files, whereas if you hold down the _____ key you will select nonconsecutive files.

6. What view must you be in, and what button do you click, to view files by date?

7. How can you make a printout of your computer screen?

SESSION 3.3

So far in this tutorial, you have learned how to use the All Folders Explorer bar in the left pane to view the structure of folders on a disk and how to view and select files in the right pane of the Exploring window. In Session 3.3 you will put these skills to use in the procedures for copying, moving, and deleting files or folders.

Moving **Files Between Folders**

To organize his disk, Bernard needs to move a number of files to different folders. One procedure for moving a file is to open the folder that contains the file, press and hold down the right mouse button, drag the file to its new location, and then choose the Move Here option from the shortcut menu that opens. You can work with multiple files in the same way you work with single files, if you first select them using the selection techniques you learned in Session 3.2. When you drag, the entire group will be dragged too.

REFERENCE WINDOW   **RW**

Moving One or More Files Between Folders
- Make sure the right pane of the Exploring window shows the files you want to move, and the left pane shows the folders to which you want to move the file(s).
- If you want to move a group of files, first use the Shift or Ctrl keys to select the files to be moved.
- Hold down the right mouse button while you drag the file(s) to the new location.
- Make sure the new location is highlighted before you release the mouse button.
- Click Move Here from the shortcut menu.

Bernard has already marked the printout you created in Session 3.2, to show which files you need to move, shown in Figure 3-19. You begin by moving the Harness file from the root directory to the Equipment folder.

To move the Harness file:

1. Start Windows Explorer and, if necessary, adjust the view settings to match the figures as you did in the previous two sessions.

2. Click 🖫 **3½ Floppy (A:)**, then click ⊞ in front of drive A to display its folders.

3. Click ⊞ next to the Gear folder to display its subfolders.

4. Hold down the right mouse button while you drag **Harness** to the Ropes and Harnesses folder, as shown in Figure 3-20.

Figure 3-20   MOVING A SINGLE FILE

drag Harness so that the Ropes and Harnesses folder is highlighted

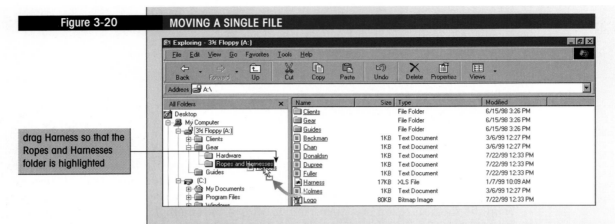

5. Make sure the Ropes and Harnesses folder is highlighted, then release the right mouse button. A shortcut menu appears, as shown in Figure 3-21.

TROUBLE? If you highlighted the wrong folder, click Cancel on the shortcut menu and repeat Steps 4 and 5.

Figure 3-21   SHORTCUT MENU

highlighted Ropes and Harnesses folder

click Move Here

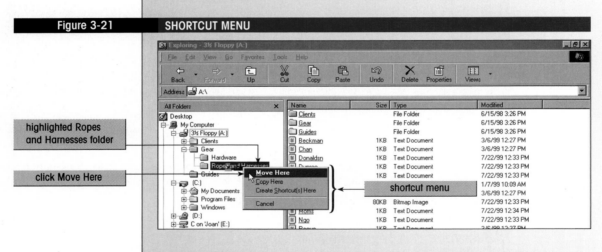

shortcut menu

6. Click **Move Here** to move the Harness file to the Ropes and Harnesses folder. Harness is moved to the new folder, and the Harness file disappears from the right pane.

TROUBLE? If you moved the file to a different folder by mistake, click the Undo 🔄 button on the Explorer toolbar, and then repeat Steps 4 through 6.

7. Click 📁 **Ropes and Harnesses** in the left pane. The Harness file should appear in the right pane.

If you use other Windows applications, you know that in most applications you drag objects with the left mouse button. Although you can drag files in Windows Explorer with the left mouse button, be careful. When you use the left mouse button, Windows Explorer will not open the shortcut menu. Instead, it will simply move or copy the file to the folder you highlight, depending on the circumstances. When you drag a file from one folder to another on the same drive, Explorer moves the file. However, when you drag a file from a folder on one drive to a folder on a different drive, Explorer copies the file; it does not move it. Therefore, to prevent mistakes and lost files, most beginners should use the right mouse button to drag files.

Copying **Files to a Folder**

The procedure for copying a file is similar to the procedure for moving one, except you select Copy Here instead of Move Here from the shortcut menu.

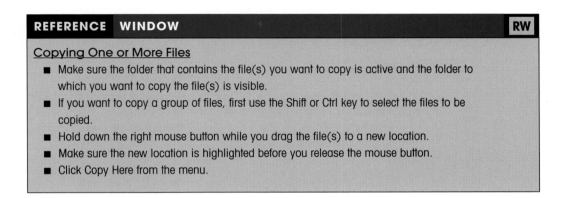

REFERENCE   WINDOW   **RW**

<u>Copying One or More Files</u>
- Make sure the folder that contains the file(s) you want to copy is active and the folder to which you want to copy the file(s) is visible.
- If you want to copy a group of files, first use the Shift or Ctrl key to select the files to be copied.
- Hold down the right mouse button while you drag the file(s) to a new location.
- Make sure the new location is highlighted before you release the mouse button.
- Click Copy Here from the menu.

Bernard recently purchased a fourth rope, and he is tracking its use in the file Rope4. He wants a copy of the Rope4 file in the Ropes folder.

To copy the Rope4 file into the Ropes folder:

1. Click 🖫 **3½ Floppy (A:)** in the left pane to view the files in the root directory once again.

2. Hold down the right mouse button while you drag **Rope4** to the Ropes and Harnesses folder.

3. Make sure the Ropes and Harnesses folder is highlighted, and then release the right mouse button.

4. Click **Copy Here** from the shortcut menu. Rope4 is copied from the root directory to the Ropes and Harnesses folder. Notice that Rope4 is still displayed in the right pane for drive A, because you copied the file rather than moved it.

5. Click 📁 **Ropes and Harnesses** in the left pane and notice that Rope4 now appears in this folder, along with the Harness file.

Moving **Files with Cut and Paste**

Although dragging works well when you can see the file in the right pane and its destination folder in the left pane, this will not always be the case. Instead of dragging, you can use the Cut, Copy, and Paste buttons on the Standard toolbar to move or copy objects. The Cut, Copy, and Paste commands are also available on the selected objects' shortcut menus.

> **REFERENCE WINDOW**   **RW**
>
> <u>Moving or Copying Files with Cut, Copy, and Paste</u>
> - Select the file you want to copy or move. If you want to copy or move a group of files, first use the Shift or Ctrl key to select the files to be moved.
> - Click the Cut button to move the files, or the Copy button to copy them.
> - Select the device or folder into which you want to place the copied or cut files.
> - Click the Paste button.

Bernard wants to move the three rope files from the Gear folder to the Ropes and Harnesses folder. The rope files are listed consecutively, so you should use the Shift key to select these three files before you move them as a group. Then use the Cut and Paste buttons to move the files.

To move the rope files to the Ropes and Harnesses folder:

1. Click 📁 **Gear** to activate the Gear folder and view the other rope files, which also need to be moved into the Ropes and Harnesses folder.

2. Select the three rope files, **Rope1**, **Rope2**, and **Rope3**, using the **Shift** key.

3. Click the **Cut** button ✂️.

4. Click the **Ropes and Harnesses** folder in the left pane.

5. Click the **Paste** button 📋 to move the files to the Ropes and Harnesses folder. The Ropes and Harnesses folder now contains Harness, Rope1, Rope2, Rope3, and Rope4.

If you cut or copy a file or set of files but then neglect to paste them into a destination folder, don't worry. Windows Explorer doesn't actually carry out the cut or copy until you paste. It simply flags the file until it actually performs the action desired. Thus, if you close Windows Explorer without having pasted a file, the file remains in its original position.

You've got Bernard's gear files organized, so now it's time to look at the new client files he added. Mark Fuller and George Ngo are interested exclusively in alpine climbing, so you'll move the Fuller and Ngo client files into the Alpine folder. This time you'll use the shortcut menu to cut and then paste the files; it's quicker.

To move nonconsecutive files from one folder to another:

1. Click 💾 **3½ Floppy (A:)** to display the files it contains in the right pane.

2. Click ➕ in front of Clients and then in front of Advanced.

3. Select the **Fuller** and **Ngo** files.

4. Right-click any one of the selected files and then click **Cut**. See Figure 3-22.

Figure 3-22	CUTTING FILES

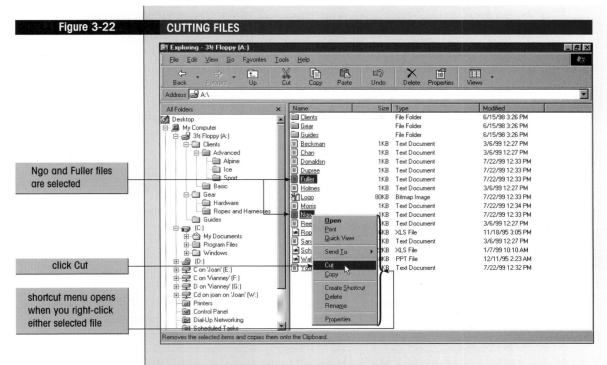

Ngo and Fuller files are selected

click Cut

shortcut menu opens when you right-click either selected file

5. Right-click 📁 **Alpine** and then click **Paste**. The files are moved from the root directory of drive A into the Alpine folder.

You need to move the remaining client files from the root directory into the Basic folder. You can combine some of the methods you have already learned to complete this task most efficiently. If you are in Details view, you'll see that the client files (the ones with people's names) are all text files. If you arrange these files by type, they'll all be next to each other, so you can select them as a group and move them together to the Basic folder.

To move a group of related files to a new folder:

1. Click 💾 **3½ Floppy (A:)** to display the files it contains in the right pane, if necessary.

2. If necessary, click the list arrow to the right of the **Views** button 🔳, and then click **Details**.

3. Click the **Type** button. The client text files are now grouped together.

   TROUBLE? The Type button is at the top of the third column in the right pane.

4. Use the Shift key to select the **Beckman** and **Yoshiki** text files and all the files in between.

5. Right-click the selection, click **Cut**, right-click **Basic**, and then click **Paste**. The files move from the root directory into the Basic folder.

Bernard's disk is now reorganized, with the appropriate files in the gear and client folders.

Moving or Copying Files Between a Floppy Disk and a Hard Disk

In your computer lab you will rarely need to copy a file from your floppy disk to the hard disk of a lab computer. However, if you have a computer at home, you might frequently want to move or copy files from your floppy disk to your hard disk, to take advantage of its speed and large storage capacity.

Moving or copying files from a floppy disk to a hard disk is similar to the procedure for moving or copying files between folders. To practice this task, copy the Excel spreadsheet file named Schedule to the hard disk.

To copy a file from a floppy disk to the hard disk:

1. If necessary, scroll through the left pane so you can see the icon for drive C.

2. Click ▭ **(C:)** in the left pane. Your drive C icon might appear slightly different if it is a network or shared drive.

3. Click **File**, point to **New**, and then click **Folder** to create a new folder on drive C.

   TROUBLE? If a message warns you that you can't create a folder on drive C, you might be on a computer that restricts hard drive access. Ask your instructor or technical support person about other options for working on a hard drive, and read through the rest of this section to learn how you would work on a hard drive if you had the opportunity.

4. Type **Climbing** as the name of the new folder, and then press **Enter** to finalize the name.

   TROUBLE? If there is already a Climbing folder on the hard disk, you must specify a different name. Use the name "Climb" with your initials, such as "ClimbJP." Substitute this folder name for the Climbing folder for the rest of this tutorial.

5. Click ▭ **3½ Floppy (A:)** (you might have to scroll to see it) to display its contents in the right pane.

6. Right-click the **Schedule** file.

7. Click **Copy**. Locate and then right-click the **Climbing** folder on drive C in the left pane (you might have to scroll to see it).

8. Click **Paste**. The original Schedule file remains in the root directory of drive A. A copy of the file now appears in the Climbing folder on drive C.

9. Click ▭ **Climbing** on drive C to ensure that the Schedule file was copied onto the hard drive, then click ▭ **3½ Floppy (A:)** so you can see its contents again.

The Schedule file is now in the Climbing folder on your hard disk.

Copying a File From One Floppy Disk to Another Floppy Disk

You notice that Bernard has a file on his disk called Wall; you ask him about it. He explains that it is a PowerPoint file that contains a slide presentation for the local Parks and Recreation Department, proposing the construction of an indoor climbing wall. You tell Bernard you would love to help him develop the slide show; if he gave you a copy of the file on a new disk, you could work on it on your computer at home. Although you could use the Copy Disk command you used in Tutorial 2 to copy the entire disk, you want only the Wall file on the new disk.

If your computer has only one floppy disk drive, you can't just drag a file from one floppy disk to another, because you can't put both floppy disks in the drive at the same time. So how do you copy the file from one floppy to another? You first copy the file from the first floppy disk—the **source disk**—to a temporary location on the hard drive, then you insert the second floppy disk—the **destination disk**—into drive A; finally, you move the file from the hard disk to the second floppy disk. Figure 3-23 shows this procedure.

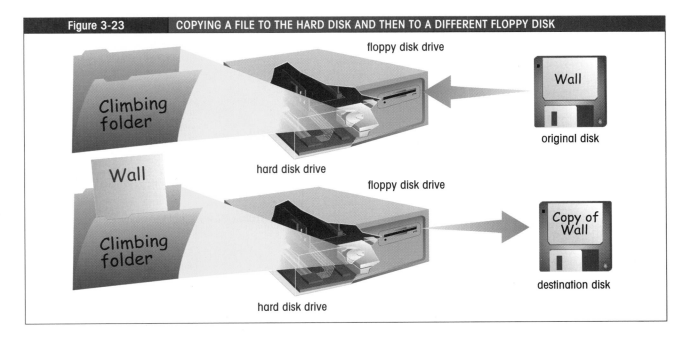

Figure 3-23   COPYING A FILE TO THE HARD DISK AND THEN TO A DIFFERENT FLOPPY DISK

REFERENCE WINDOW   RW

Copying a File from One Floppy Disk to Another
- Make sure you have a folder on the hard drive to which you can copy a file. If necessary, create a new folder on the hard drive.
- Copy the file to the hard drive.
- Take your Student Disk out of the floppy drive and insert the floppy disk to which you want the file copied.
- Click View, and then click Refresh to view the contents of the second disk.
- Move the file from the hard disk to the floppy disk that is now in the floppy disk drive.

To carry out this procedure, you need two disks: your Student Disk and another blank, formatted floppy disk.

To copy one file from your Student Disk, the source disk, to a different floppy disk, the destination disk:

1. Right-click the **Wall** file to select it, and then click **Copy**.

2. Right-click the **Climbing** folder on drive C, and then click **Paste** to copy the file to drive C.

3. After the copy is complete (the drive A light goes out), remove your Student Disk (the source disk).

4. Write "Wall disk" on the label of your second disk, the destination disk. Insert the Wall disk (the destination disk) into drive A.

5. Click **View**, and then click **Refresh** to indicate you have switched disks. The Refresh command examines the contents of the disk again and updates the left and right panes accordingly.

6. Click the **Climbing** folder on drive C.

7. Right-click the **Wall** file and then click **Cut**.

8. Right-click **drive A** and then click **Paste** to move the file to drive A.

9. Click ⊡ **3½ Floppy (A:)** and make sure the Wall file is safely on the disk, then remove the destination disk from drive A.

10. Place your Student Disk back in drive A, click **View**, and then click **Refresh** to view the files on the Student Disk.

Deleting **Files and Folders**

Looking over the contents of the drive A root directory of Bernard's disk, you realize you could delete the Rope4 file, since there's a copy of it in the Ropes and Harnesses folder.

When you delete a file or folder from the hard drive, it goes into the Recycle Bin, so that if you've made a mistake you can always recover the file or folder. Once you delete a file from a floppy disk, however, there is no easy way of recovering it, so use caution before deleting.

REFERENCE   WINDOW   **RW**

Deleting a File or Folder

■ Right-click the file or folder you want to delete. If you are deleting a folder, all the files it contains will be deleted, so make sure you really want to delete the entire folder. To delete multiple files, use the Shift or Ctrl key to select them, and then right-click the selection.

■ Click Delete.

■ Click the Yes button if asked if you are sure.

To delete the Rope4 file:

1. Make sure the right pane displays the files in the drive A root directory.

2. Right-click **Rope4**.

3. Click **Delete** in the shortcut menu.

4. Click the **Yes** button in the Confirm File Delete dialog box.

Two recent ice-climbing accidents have convinced Bernard to stop offering ice climbing, because it's too unpredictable and dangerous. This business decision affects the folder structure on Bernard's disk. You decide to move the client files in the Ice folder into the Advanced folder and then to delete the Ice folder altogether.

To move the files from Ice to Advanced, then delete the Ice folder:

1. Click 📁 **Ice** in the left pane (redisplay the folder hierarchy if necessary).

2. Click **Edit** on the menu bar, and then click **Select All** to select the Kranmer and Wei files.

3. Right-click the selected files, and then click **Cut**.

4. Right-click the **Advanced** folder, and then click **Paste**. Examine the Advanced file contents, and verify that the Kranmer and Wei files have been correctly moved there from the Ice folder.

5. Right-click 📁 **Ice**, and then click **Delete** in the shortcut menu.

6. When you see the message "Are you sure you want to remove the folder 'Ice' and all its contents?" click the **Yes** button.

You've finished organizing Bernard's disk, and as you're getting ready to go, the attendant at the business services center reminds you to be sure to delete any work from the hard drive, so it doesn't get cluttered. You should always "clean up" after a session on a computer that doesn't belong to you. You can do so easily by simply removing the Climbing folder from drive C. If you weren't able to move any files to drive C, you can skip these steps.

To delete the Climbing folder from drive C:

1. Right-click the **Climbing** folder on drive C, scrolling as necessary to locate it in the left pane.

2. Click **Delete** to display the Confirm Folder Delete dialog box. See Figure 3-24.

Figure 3-24	CONFIRM FOLDER DELETE DIALOG BOX

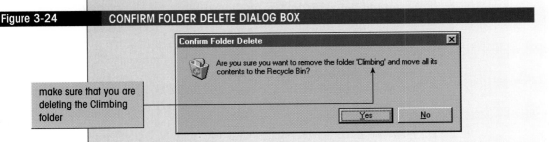

make sure that you are deleting the Climbing folder

TROUBLE? If a message appears telling you that you can't perform this operation, your system administrator might have restricted the deletion privileges from the hard drive. Continue reading the rest of the tutorial.

3. Make sure the Confirm Folder Delete message indicates that the Climbing folder will be moved to the Recycle Bin.

TROUBLE? If a different filename appears in the Confirm Folder Delete dialog box, click the No button and go back to Step 1.

4. Click the **Yes** button to delete the folder from drive C.

5. Close Windows Explorer.

You look over the structure of folders and files on Bernard's disk and realize that, as his business increases, this structure will become increasingly useful. You've used the power of Windows Explorer to simplify tasks such as locating, moving, copying, and deleting files. You can apply these skills to larger file management challenges when you are using a computer of your own and need to organize and work with the files on your hard drive.

QUICK CHECK

1. Why is it a good habit to use the right mouse button, rather than the left, to drag files in Windows Explorer?

2. When you take one floppy disk out of the disk drive and put another disk in, you can use the _____ command to view the files on the new disk.

3. True or False: You can copy a file from one floppy disk to another even if you only have one floppy disk drive in your computer, if you have access to a hard drive.

4. True or False: When you delete a folder, you should first move out any files that you don't want to delete.

5. True or False: When you delete files or folders from the floppy disk, they go into the Recycle Bin.

TUTORIAL ASSIGNMENTS

1. **Copying Files to the Hard Drive** Bernard wants to place his sport-climbing client files (those in the Sport folder) on the hard drive to work with them on an advertisement campaign. The Sport folder is a subfolder of Advanced, which is itself a subfolder of Clients.

a. Using the Wall disk you used in Session 3.3, Quick format the disk, then make a new Student Disk, using the Level II Disk 2 option.

b. Start Windows Explorer, then create a new folder on drive C called "Advertise."

c. Copy the files in the Sport folder on your Student Disk to the Advertise folder on the hard drive.

d. Open the Advertise folder on the hard drive to display the files it contains.

e. Print the Exploring screen, including your name and the date on the printout.

f. Delete the Advertise folder from the hard drive when your printout is complete.

2. **Creating a New Folder and Copying Files**   Bernard now wants a folder that contains all the clients he has, because he'd like to do a general mailing to everyone, advertising an expedition to the Tetons. (*Hint*: The client files are all text files, so consider viewing the files in the root directory by type. Don't forget that there are also client files in the Clients folder and its subfolders.)

   a. Create a folder called "All Clients" on the drive A root directory, and then copy all the text files into the All Clients folder.
   b. Open the Clients folder and all its subfolders one at a time, and copy the text files from those folders into the new All Clients folder.
   c. Print out the Exploring screen showing the All Clients folder arranged by name. Be sure to include your name and the date on your printout.

3. **Copying Between Floppy Disks**   Suppose someone who doesn't know how to use the Windows Explorer (she missed class) wants to copy the Guides folder from her Student Disk to another floppy disk. Try this yourself, and as you go through the procedure, write down each step so that this student will be able to follow the steps and make a copy of Guides without knowing how to use Explorer.

4. **Restructuring a Disk**   Use Quick Format to format the second disk you used in Session 3.3 (the "Wall" disk). Now make a new Student Disk, using the Level I Disk 1 menu option rather than the Level II Disk 2 option. (Disk 1 contains the files you used in Tutorial 2.) Rearrange the files on the disk so they correspond to Figure 3-25. Delete any files or folders not shown in the figure. Print out the Explorer screen that shows your new organization and the files in the Yellowstone Park folder arranged by size.

Figure 3-25

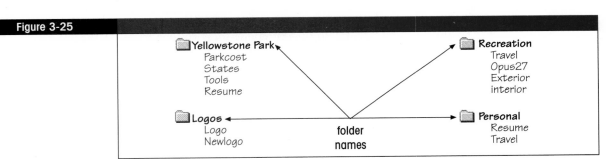

5. **Creating a Folder Structure**   When you complete your computer class, you are likely to use a computer for other courses in your major and for general education requirements such as English and Math. Think about how you would organize the floppy disk that would hold the files for your courses, then prepare a disk to contain your files.

   a. Make a sketch of this organization.
   b. Use Quick Format to erase the contents of the second disk you used in Session 3.3 (the "Wall" disk).
   c. Create the folder structure on your Student Disk (even though you don't have any files to place in the folders right now). Use subfolders to help sort files for class projects (your composition course, for example, might have a midterm and a final paper).
   d. Make sure all folders and subfolders are displayed in the left pane, then place an image of the Exploring screen into WordPad, using the Print Screen key and the methods described in this tutorial. Be sure to include your name and the date on your printout.
   e. Use WordPad to write one or two paragraphs after your name explaining your plan. Your explanation should include information about your major, the courses you plan to take, and how you might use computers in those courses.

6. **Exploring Your Computer's Devices, Folders, and Files**   Answer each of the following questions about the devices, folders, and files on your lab computers. You can find all the answers using the Exploring window.

   a. How many folders (not subfolders) are on drive C?
   b. How many of these folders on drive C have subfolders? What is the easiest way to find the answer to this question?
   c. Do you have a Windows folder on drive C? If so, how many objects does it contain? What is the easiest way to answer this question?
   d. Do you have a folder named My Documents on drive C? If so, what is the size of the largest file in this folder?
   e. Does your computer have a CD-ROM drive? If so, what drive letter is assigned to the CD-ROM drive?
   f. Does your computer have access to a network storage device? If so, indicate the letter(s) of the network storage device(s).
   g. How much space do the files in the root directory of drive C occupy? How much free space is left on drive C?

7. **Separating Program and Data Files**   Hard disk management differs from floppy disk management because a hard disk contains programs and data, whereas a floppy disk (unless it is an installation disk that you got from a software company) generally only contains data files. On a hard disk, a good management practice is to keep programs in folders separate from data files. Keeping this in mind, read the following description, draw a sketch of the folder structure described, then make a sketch of how the current structure could be improved.

   The Marquette Chamber of Commerce uses a computer to maintain its membership list and track dues. It also uses the computer for correspondence. All the programs and data used by the Chamber of Commerce are on drive C. The membership application software is in a folder called Members. The data file for the membership is in a subfolder of Members called Member Data. The accounting program used to track income and expenditures is in a folder called Accounting Programs. The data for the current year is in a folder directly under the drive C icon called Accounting Data 1999. The accounting data from 1997 and 1998 is stored in two subfolders of the folder called Accounting Programs. The word-processing program is in a folder called Word. The documents created with Word are stored in the Member Data folder. Finally, Windows 98 is stored in a folder called Windows, which has ten subfolders.

Explore

8. **Using the Send To Command**   The Send To command provides another way to copy a file to another location. Use the Windows Explorer Help system to learn about the Send To command. Then write the steps you would take to use this command to send a file on your hard drive to a disk in your floppy drive.

PROJECTS

1. Shortly after graduation, you start working for your aunt and uncle, who own a thriving antique store. They hope to store data about their inventory and business on the computer they recently purchased. They have hired you to accomplish this formidable task. Your Aunt Susan asks you to organize her client files and to prepare some financial statements. Your Uncle Gabe wants you to create customized forms for invoicing and inventory. Two part-time employees, Julia and Abigail, have asked you to help develop documents for advertising. You realize that a folder structure would be helpful to keep things straight.

a. Create a folder on your Student Disk named Antiques.

b. Create the following subfolders: Customers, Finances, Invoices, Inventory, and Advertising.

c. Create each of the documents listed below in WordPad and save them to the correct folders on your Student Disk:

Customers subfolder:	Inventory subfolder:
Harrington	Furniture
Searls	Art
Finances subfolder:	Advertising subfolder:
Budget	Anniversary Sale
Profit and Loss	Winter Clearance
Balance Sheet	
Invoices subfolder:	
Sales	
Vendors	

d. In Windows Explorer, display the entire Antiques folder hierarchy in the left pane, and display the contents of the Finances subfolder in the right pane. Press the Print Screen key. Then open a new WordPad document, type your name and the date at the top, and paste an image of the Exploring window into the document. Print the document. Close WordPad, but don't save changes.

2. Uncle Gabe decided to have his financial statements prepared by an accountant, so you need to copy the files in the Finances subfolder onto a different disk that you can give to the accountant. Use the folders and files you created in Project 1. You will need a blank floppy disk and the ability to access your computer's hard drive to complete this project. Uncle Gabe wants to know how to copy files to a new disk, so as you copy the files, write down in detail what you are doing so he can repeat this procedure by following your directions.

a. Create a folder on your hard drive called Accountant.

b. Copy the three files in the Finances folder on your Student Disk to the Accountant folder on your hard disk, using the drag technique.

c. Copy the contents of the Accountant folder to the blank disk, using the cut-and-paste technique.

d. Delete the Accountant folder from your hard disk.

3. You have learned two techniques for moving files between folders: the drag and drop method and the cut-and-paste method. Answer the following questions:

a. Can you think of any situations in which you could not use drag and drop to move a file in Windows Explorer?

b. In such a situation, what should you do instead?

c. Which method do you prefer? Why?

4. You have learned that you can access files from Windows Explorer and My Computer. How do you decide which tool to use for a given situation? Many computer users use the tool that will give them the information they need with the least amount of effort. Others always want to see the most information possible. For each of the following situations, identify which tool you would use, Windows Explorer or My Computer, and why. If you don't think it matters which tool you use, indicate this in your answer.

a. You want to view the files and folders in the root directory of your Student Disk.

b. You want to view all the subfolders on your Student Disk at the same time.

c. You want to copy files from a subfolder on a floppy disk to a folder on a hard disk.

d. You want to view the contents of the Sport folder.

e. You want to open a file without starting the program first.

5. Windows 98 enables users to customize extensively their working environment. For each item, first write the steps you take to make the change, and then comment on the benefits or disadvantages of using the following options in the Exploring window:

   a. Details view or List view

   b. Displaying or hiding the status bar

   c. Displaying or hiding the All Folders Explorer bar

   d. Displaying or hiding the Standard Buttons option (for this option, also address how you accomplish your work without the Standard buttons visible).

QUICK | CHECK ANSWERS

Session 3.1

1. Windows Explorer

2. The left pane, the All Folders Explorer bar, lists the devices and folders and other objects available to your computer; the right pane displays the contents of the object highlighted in the All Folders Explorer bar.

3. False

4. False

5. subfolder

6. plus box

7. the drive A device icon

8. False

Session 3.2

1. False

2. The device or folder icon

3. False

4. Details

5. Shift, Ctrl

6. Details, Modified

7. Press the Print Screen key, paste the image into WordPad, and print the WordPad document.

Session 3.3

1. Using the right mouse button opens a shortcut menu that gives you the choice to move or copy.

2. Refresh

3. True

4. True

5. False

CUSTOMIZING
THE DESKTOP
FOR INCREASED
PRODUCTIVITY

Changing Desktop Settings at Companions, Inc.

CASE

Companions, Inc.

Bow Falls, Arizona, is a popular Sun Belt retirement mecca that is also a college town with several distinguished universities. Beth Yuan, a graduate of Bow Falls University, realized that the unusual mix of the old and young in her town might be perfectly suited to a services business. She formed Companions, Inc. to provide older area residents with trained personal care assistants and help with housecleaning, home maintenance, and running errands. Beth's company now includes employees who work directly with clients and an office staff who help manage the day-to-day tasks of running a business. Many of Beth's employees are students at local colleges who like the flexible hours and enjoy spending time with the elderly residents.

The offices of Companions, Inc. are equipped with computers that are used to maintain client records, schedule employees, manage company finances, develop training materials, and create informational documents about Beth's business. Beth recently upgraded her computers to Windows 98. She has heard that it's easy to change Windows 98 settings to reflect the needs of her office staff. She asks you to find a way to make it easier to access documents and computer resources. She would also like you to give the desktop a corporate look and feel. Finally, she wonders if you can customize Windows 98 to adapt it to users with special needs.

SESSION 4.1

In this session you will learn how to place a Notepad document icon on the desktop and how to stamp the document with the time and date. You will create shortcuts to the objects you use most often, including your computer's floppy disk drive, a document, and a printer. You will learn how to use the icons you create and how to restore your desktop to its original state.

Document-centric **Desktops**

Windows 98 automatically places several icons on your desktop, such as the My Computer and the Recycle Bin icons. You can place additional icons on the desktop that represent objects such as printers, disk drives, programs, and documents. For example, you can create an icon on your desktop that represents your resume. To open this document, you would use its icon. You would no longer have to navigate menus or windows or even locate the program you used to create the document. A desktop that gives this kind of immediate access to documents is called **document-centric**.

Creating a Document Icon on the Desktop

Employees in the Companions, Inc. offices keep a log of their telephone calls, using the Notepad accessory. Notepad, like WordPad, allows you to edit simple text documents, but because it does not include the formatting options provided by WordPad, it is used only for text documents with no formatting. Notepad includes a **time-date stamp** that automatically inserts the time and date whenever you open the document. Figure 4-1 shows you a Notepad document with automatic time-date stamps.

Figure 4-1	NOTEPAD DOCUMENT WITH TIME-DATE STAMP

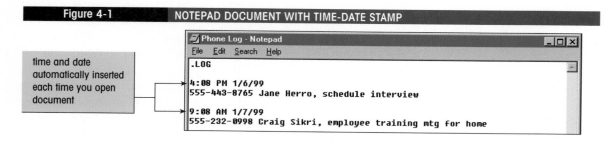

time and date automatically inserted each time you open document

You create a new document on the desktop by right-clicking the desktop and then selecting the type of document you want from a list. An icon, called a **document icon**, appears on the desktop to represent your document. The appearance of the document icon depends on the type of document you create. For example, a Notepad document icon appears as 🗒, whereas a WordPad document icon appears as 🗒. When you open the document represented by the icon, the operating system checks the file's extension to determine which software it should start.

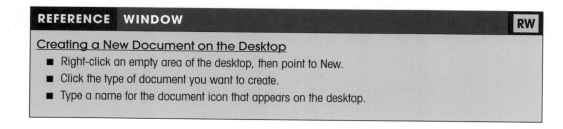

REFERENCE WINDOW   **RW**

Creating a New Document on the Desktop
- Right-click an empty area of the desktop, then point to New.
- Click the type of document you want to create.
- Type a name for the document icon that appears on the desktop.

The phone log is a perfect candidate for a document icon because employees use it so frequently. When you use the document icon to open the document, Windows 98 locates and starts the appropriate software program for you.

To create a Notepad document icon on the desktop:

1. Right-click a blank area of the desktop and point to **New**. The menu shown in Figure 4-2 opens.

> **TROUBLE?** If no menu appears, you might have clicked with the left mouse button instead of the right. Repeat Step 1.

> **TROUBLE?** If your new menu looks different from the one in Figure 4-2, don't worry. The document types that appear on the New menu depend on the software installed on your computer.

> **TROUBLE?** If the objects on your screen take up more or less space than those shown in the figures, don't worry. Your monitor settings are different.

Figure 4-2	CREATING A NEW TEXT DOCUMENT

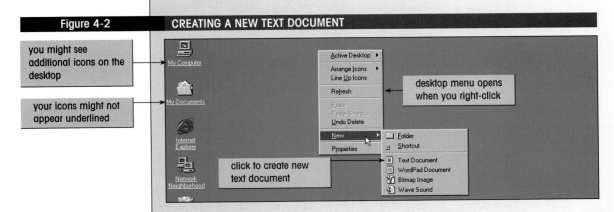

you might see additional icons on the desktop

your icons might not appear underlined

desktop menu opens when you right-click

click to create new text document

2. Click **Text Document**. A document icon for your new text document appears on the desktop. See Figure 4-3.

> **TROUBLE?** If you receive an error message when you try to create a new document on the desktop, your lab might not allow you to make any changes to the desktop. Ask your instructor which sections of this tutorial your lab allows you to complete.

Figure 4-3	DOCUMENT ICON

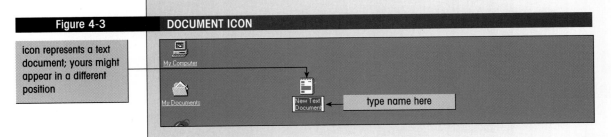

icon represents a text document; yours might appear in a different position

type name here

3. Type **Phone Log** as the name of your document.

> **TROUBLE?** If nothing happens when you type the document name, you might have inadvertently pressed a key or mouse button that deactivated the document icon. Right-click the New Text Document icon, click Rename, and then type Phone Log.

4. Press the **Enter** key. See Figure 4-4.

TROUBLE? If you see a message about changing the filename extension, click No, type Phone Log.txt, and then press Enter. Your computer is set to display file extensions, and because you didn't supply one with the title, the operating system deletes the extension unless you click No and supply a new extension.

Figure 4-4	PHONE LOG DOCUMENT ICON

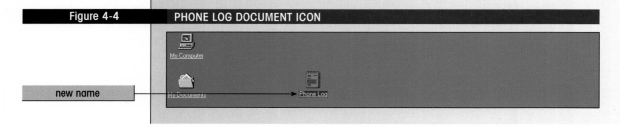

new name

You can often identify an object's type by its icon. The Phone Log document icon 📄 identifies a Notepad text document. Later in this tutorial you'll identify other icons that represent other object types.

Opening a Document on the Desktop

When you use a desktop document icon to open a document, Windows 98 starts the appropriate program, which in this case is Notepad, so you can edit the document.

To open the Phone Log:

1. Click the **Phone Log** icon. Windows 98 starts Notepad. See Figure 4-5.

Figure 4-5	PHONE LOG DOCUMENT OPENS IN NOTEPAD

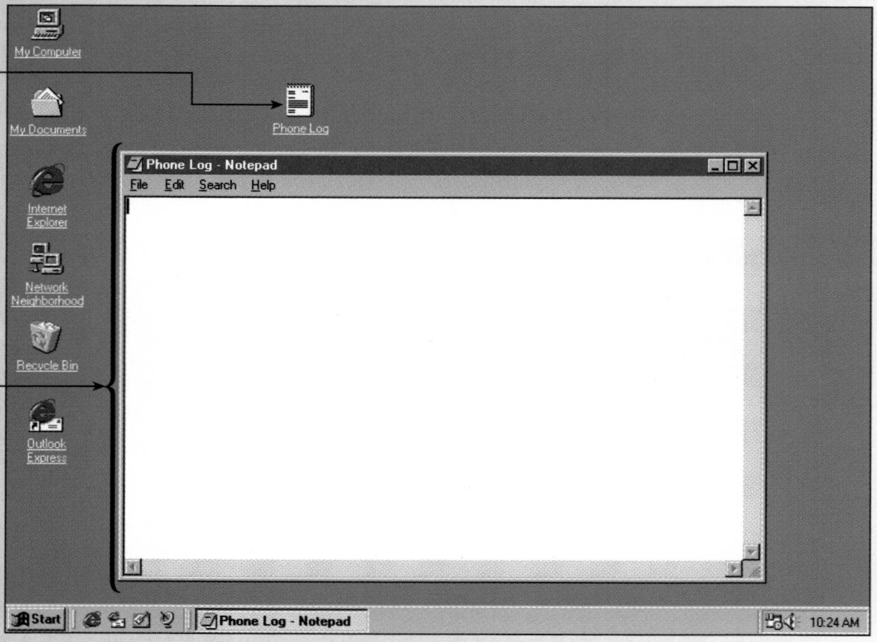

click to open Notepad

Notepad window opens

TROUBLE? If nothing happens when you click the Phone Log icon, your computer may be set to Classic style instead of Web style. This tutorial assumes that your computer is using Web-style settings. To switch to Web style, click the Start button, point to Settings, click Folder Options, click the Web style option button, and then click the OK button. Click the OK button again if you are asked if you are sure you want to use single-click. If you don't have permission to change your computer's settings, press Enter after you click the Phone Log icon. Whenever the steps instruct you to click a desktop icon to open a window, you will also need to press Enter.

TROUBLE? If the Notepad window hides the Phone Log document icon, drag and resize the window as necessary to view both the icon and the window. If the window is maximized, you'll first need to restore it.

Creating a LOG File

Notepad automatically inserts the date when you open a document only if the document begins with .LOG, in uppercase letters. Your next step is to create a document with .LOG at the beginning and to enter some text. Then you will save the document and close it.

To set up the Phone Log document:

1. Type **.LOG**. Be sure to first type the period and to use uppercase letters.

2. Press the **Enter** key to move to the next line.

3. Type **Phone Log for** and then type your name.

4. Press the **Enter** key.

5. Click the **Close** button ☒ to close Notepad.

6. Click **Yes** to save the changes.

Now let's test the Phone Log document to see if an automatic time-date stamp appears when you open it.

To test the .LOG feature:

1. Open the Phone Log document.

   TROUBLE? To open the Phone Log document, click it if you are using Web-style settings; click it and then press Enter if you are using Classic-style settings.

2. Make sure your document contains a time and date stamp. See Figure 4-6.

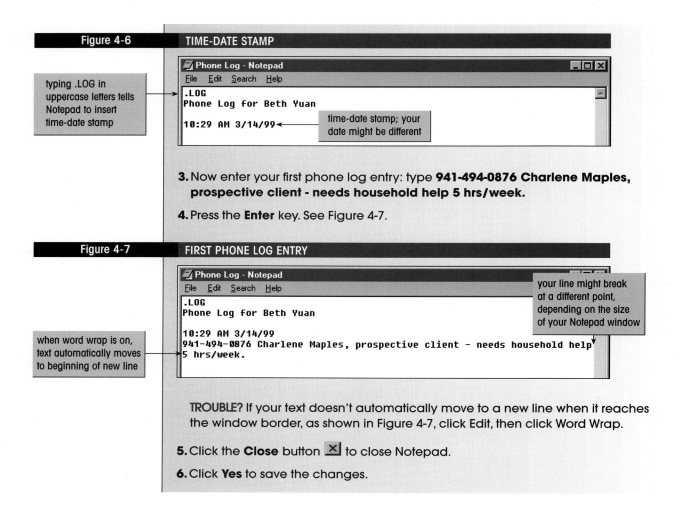

Figure 4-6 TIME-DATE STAMP

typing .LOG in uppercase letters tells Notepad to insert time-date stamp

.LOG
Phone Log for Beth Yuan

10:29 AM 3/14/99 ← time-date stamp; your date might be different

3. Now enter your first phone log entry: type **941-494-0876 Charlene Maples, prospective client - needs household help 5 hrs/week.**

4. Press the **Enter** key. See Figure 4-7.

Figure 4-7 FIRST PHONE LOG ENTRY

your line might break at a different point, depending on the size of your Notepad window

.LOG
Phone Log for Beth Yuan

10:29 AM 3/14/99
941-494-0876 Charlene Maples, prospective client - needs household help
5 hrs/week.

when word wrap is on, text automatically moves to beginning of new line

TROUBLE? If your text doesn't automatically move to a new line when it reaches the window border, as shown in Figure 4-7, click Edit, then click Word Wrap.

5. Click the **Close** button ☒ to close Notepad.

6. Click **Yes** to save the changes.

Creating Shortcuts to Objects

Beth uses her floppy drive regularly and would like an easier way to access it. This is a good reason to create a shortcut icon on the desktop to her floppy drive. A **shortcut icon** provides easy access to the objects on your computer you use most often. You can create shortcut icons for drives, documents, files, Web pages, programs, or other computer resources such as a printer. These "shortcuts" reduce the number of mouse clicks needed to work with files, start programs, and print.

To create a shortcut, you use Windows Explorer or My Computer to find the icon for the document, program, or resource for which you want a shortcut. Then you use the right mouse button to drag the icon onto the desktop.

You might wonder if dragging with the left mouse button creates a shortcut icon in the same way as dragging with the right mouse button. The answer is no. If you drag an icon onto the desktop using the left mouse button, you create a *copy* of the object on the desktop, not a shortcut to the object. This distinction is important to remember so that you don't find yourself working with a copy when you want to be working with the original.

As with other icons on the desktop, to activate a shortcut, you simply click it (and then press Enter if you are using Classic style). The shortcut locates and then opens the document, program, or resource specified by the shortcut icon. Shortcut icons are identified by the arrow in their lower-left corner. Document icons, on the other hand, have no arrow.

REFERENCE   WINDOW   **RW**

Creating a Shortcut

- Use Windows Explorer or My Computer to locate the icon that represents the program, document, or resource for which you want to create a shortcut.
- Make sure you can see the Windows 98 desktop, and that none of the windows are maximized.
- Hold down the right mouse button and drag the icon for the shortcut to the desktop.
- Release the mouse button to display the menu.
- Click Create Shortcut(s) Here.

Creating a Shortcut to a Drive

Now you will create a shortcut to your floppy drive. Once this shortcut is on the desktop, you can open it to view the contents of your Student Disk, or you can move or copy documents to it without having to start Windows Explorer. You'll begin by making a new Student Disk in case the one you used in Tutorial 3 no longer contains the necessary files. You can use your original Student Disk if you don't need it any more, or you can use a new, blank disk.

To make a new Student Disk and then create a shortcut to your floppy drive:

1. Format your disk so that it contains no files.

   TROUBLE? If you don't remember how to format a disk, refer to Tutorial 3.

2. Click the **Start** button 🎛**Start**, point to **Programs**, point to **NP on Microsoft Windows 98-Level II**, and then click **Disk 2 (Tutorials 3 & 4)**.

   TROUBLE? Don't worry if your menu items appear abbreviated.

3. When a message box opens, click the **OK** button. Wait while the program copies the practice files to your formatted disk. When all the files have been copied, the program closes. If necessary, close any open windows.

4. Start the Windows Explorer program.

   TROUBLE? To start Windows Explorer, click the Start button, point to Programs, and then click Windows Explorer.

5. Make sure the Exploring window is open, but not maximized.

   TROUBLE? If the Exploring window is maximized, click 🗗. If necessary, resize the Exploring window so you can see part of the desktop.

6. Locate the device icon 💾 for 3½ Floppy (A:) in the left pane of the Exploring window.

7. Hold down the right mouse button while you drag the device icon 💾 for 3½ Floppy (A:) into an empty area of the desktop. The pointer looks like 💾 3½ Floppy (A:).

8. Release the mouse button. Notice the menu that appears, as shown in Figure 4-8.

Figure 4-8   CREATING A SHORTCUT TO DRIVE A

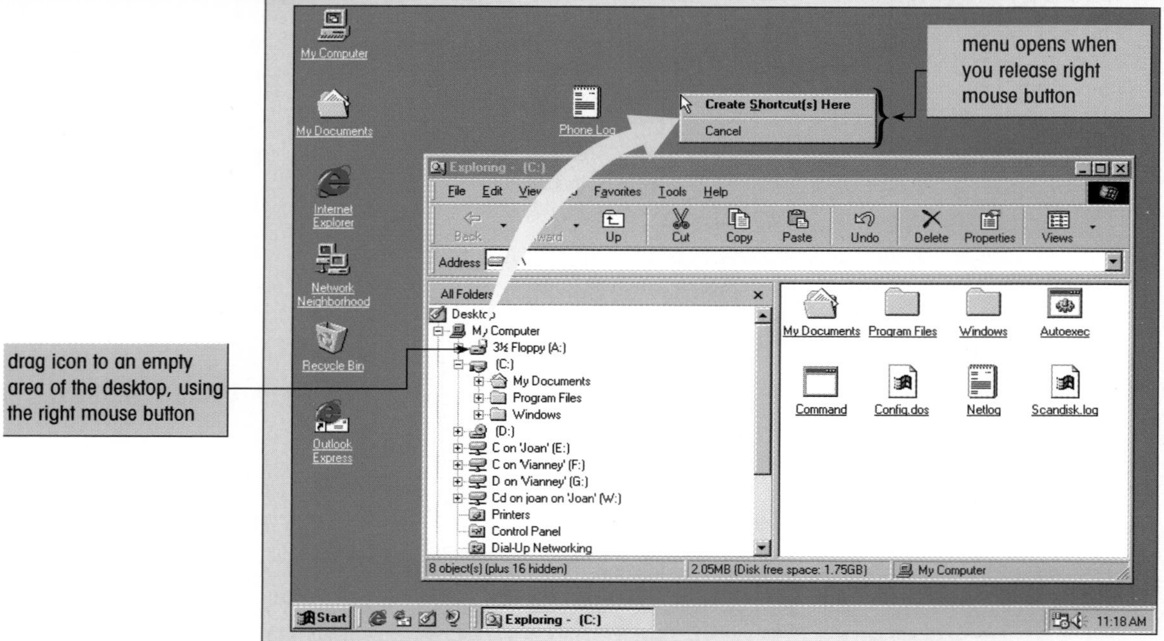

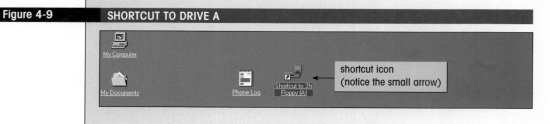

9. Click **Create Shortcut(s) Here**.

10. Click the **Close** button ⊠ to close Windows Explorer. A shortcut labeled "Shortcut to 3½ Floppy (A:)" now appears on the desktop. See Figure 4-9.

Figure 4-9   SHORTCUT TO DRIVE A

Now you can test the shortcut to see if it gives you immediate access to the contents of the disk in drive A.

To test the 3½ Floppy (A:) shortcut:

1. Click the **3½ Floppy (A:)** shortcut icon. A window showing the contents of your 3½ Floppy (A:) drive opens.

2. Click the **Close** button ⊠ to close the 3½ Floppy (A:) window.

Using a Shortcut Icon

Beth often works at her home office and so needs to take the phone log home with her. You tell her that the shortcut makes this easy. All she has to do is move the phone log from the desktop to a floppy disk by dragging the Phone Log icon to the 3½ Floppy (A:) shortcut icon.

To move the document from the desktop to a floppy disk:

1. Hold down the right mouse button and drag the **Phone Log** icon on the desktop to the 3½ Floppy (A:) shortcut you just created. When you release the right mouse button, a menu opens, as shown in Figure 4-10.

TROUBLE? If the Shortcut to 3½ Floppy (A:) icon is not highlighted when you drag the Phone Log icon to it, the Phone Log document will not move to drive A. Repeat Step 1 so that the Shortcut to 3½ Floppy (A:) icon is highlighted, as shown in Figure 4-10, before you proceed to Step 2.

Figure 4-10	MOVING THE PHONE LOG DOCUMENT TO DRIVE A

shortcut icon for drive A is highlighted

click to move Phone Log document from the desktop to drive A

2. Click **Move Here**. The Phone Log icon disappears from the desktop.

When you moved the document icon to the drive A shortcut, the file itself was moved to drive A and off your desktop. You now access the Phone Log by opening drive A. You could open drive A from My Computer or Windows Explorer, but it is handier to use the drive A shortcut. Try using the shortcut method as you add an entry for another phone call.

To open the Phone Log document from the new 3½ Floppy (A:) window and add a new entry:

1. Use the **3-½ Floppy (A:)** shortcut icon to open the drive A window. Scroll through the window if necessary to verify that the Phone Log document is on your Student Disk.

Trouble? If you don't see the Phone Log document on your Student Disk, click the Undo button 🔄 (or click Edit, then click Undo Move if the toolbar isn't displayed), and then repeat the previous set of steps for moving a document to a floppy disk.

2. Open the **Phone Log** document from the 3-½ Floppy (A:) window.

3. If necessary, click the last line of the phone log so you can type a new entry.

4. Type **555-885-0876 Frank Meyers, next week's home care schedule.**

5. Press **Enter**.

6. Click the **Close** button ❌ to close Notepad.

7. Click **Yes** to save the changes.

Creating a Shortcut to a Document

The Phone Log document is now on a floppy disk, as Beth requested; however, it no longer has an icon on the desktop. If you want to access the Phone Log document (now saved on your Student Disk) directly from the desktop, you can create a shortcut that automatically starts Notepad and opens the Phone Log from your Student Disk.

To create a shortcut to the Phone Log document on your Student Disk:

1. Hold down the right mouse button while you drag the Phone Log icon from the 3½ Floppy (A:) window onto the desktop, as shown in Figure 4-11, and then release the mouse button.

| Figure 4-11 | CREATING A SHORTCUT TO THE PHONE LOG DOCUMENT ON DRIVE A |

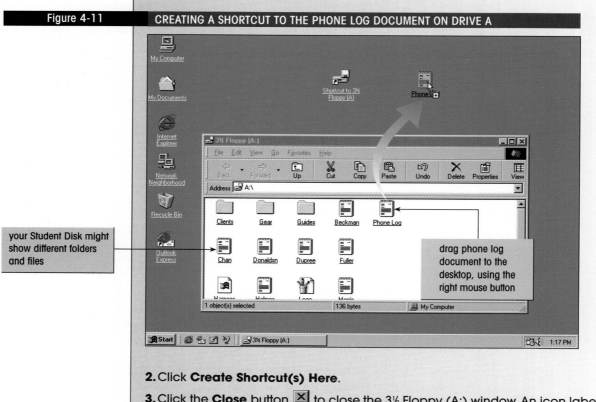

your Student Disk might show different folders and files

drag phone log document to the desktop, using the right mouse button

2. Click **Create Shortcut(s) Here**.

3. Click the **Close** button [X] to close the 3½ Floppy (A:) window. An icon labeled "Shortcut to Phone Log" now appears on the desktop.

Now you can test the shortcut to see if it automatically opens the Phone Log.

To test the Phone Log shortcut:

1. Click the **Shortcut to Phone Log** icon. Windows 98 starts the Notepad program, then opens the Phone Log document.

2. Type: **313-892-7766 Trinity River Accounting** at the end of the list of calls, and then press **Enter**.

3. Click the **Close** button [X] to close Notepad.

4. Click **Yes** to save the changes.

The shortcut icon you just created and tested is different from the Phone Log icon you created at the beginning of this tutorial. That icon was not a shortcut icon. It was a document icon representing a document that was actually located on the desktop. A shortcut icon, on the other hand, can represent a document located anywhere. The shortcut icon currently on your desktop represents a document located on your Student Disk. You can tell the difference between an actual document icon and a shortcut icon by looking for a small arrow in the corner of the icon. If there is no arrow, that icon represents the document.

If you delete a document icon, you also delete the document. If you delete a shortcut icon (with the arrow) you don't delete the document itself, because it is stored elsewhere. You are just deleting the shortcut.

You might notice that some of the icons on your desktop, such as My Computer and the Recycle Bin, don't have arrows and are therefore not shortcut icons. These icons are installed by the operating system and cannot be removed (although they can be hidden).

Creating a Shortcut to a Printer

You now have an efficient way to open the Phone Log and to access your floppy drive. You're sure that Beth will be pleased when you tell her. But first you decide to add a printer shortcut to your growing collection of desktop icons, so that employees can easily print their phone logs and other documents.

You create a printer shortcut in much the same way as you created a shortcut for the floppy drive. First, you locate the printer icon in Windows Explorer. Then you use the right mouse button to drag the icon onto the desktop.

To create a printer shortcut:

1. Start the Windows Explorer program.

2. If the Exploring window is maximized, click the **Restore** button so you can see part of the desktop. Resize and move the window if necessary so you can see the icons you've already created. You might also need to drag the icons you've created to the top of the screen.

3. Locate and then click the **Printers** folder. It is usually located toward the bottom of the left pane of the Exploring window. See Figure 4-12.

Figure 4-12	PRINTERS FOLDER IN WINDOWS EXPLORER

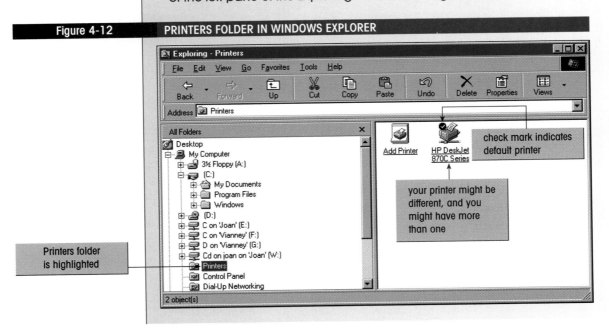

4. Position the pointer over the icon of the printer for which you want to create a shortcut.

   TROUBLE? If you are using a computer that is not connected to a network or printer, read through the following steps for later reference.

   TROUBLE? If more than one printer is listed and you do not know which printer you usually use, use the default printer, identified by the ● icon.

5. Hold down the right mouse button while you drag the printer icon to the desktop.

6. Release the right mouse button to drop the printer icon on the desktop.

7. Click **Create Shortcut(s) Here** on the menu. The printer shortcut appears. See Figure 4-13.

Figure 4-13	CREATING A SHORTCUT TO PRINTER

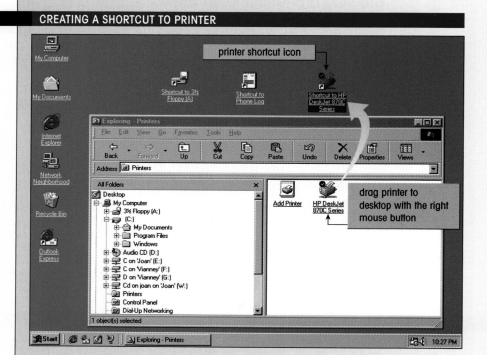

8. Click the **Close** button ☒ to close Windows Explorer.

Once a printer shortcut icon is on the desktop, you can print a document by dragging its icon to the printer shortcut icon. Think of the steps you save by printing this way: you don't have to open any programs or search through menus to locate and open the document or the Print dialog box. You cannot, however, drag shortcuts to documents to the printer shortcut icon—only the documents themselves. Practice printing using the Phone Log document icon on your Student Disk.

To print the Phone Log document using the printer shortcut icon:

1. Open the 3½ Floppy (A:) window, using its shortcut on the desktop.

2. Drag the **Phone Log** document icon, using the left mouse button, to the printer's shortcut icon. See Figure 4-14.

Figure 4-14	PRINTING A DOCUMENT USING SHORTCUTS

3. When you release the mouse button, watch as Windows 98 starts the Notepad program, opens the Phone Log, and then prints the Phone Log. (Normally Windows 98 would simply close the program, but because your document has an automatic time-date stamp, the document is changed every time you open it. Thus, Windows 98 asks if you want to save changes to the document before closing it. You don't need to save it because you don't have any new phone entries to log.)

4. Click **No**. Windows 98 closes Notepad without saving the time-date stamp.

5. Close the 3½ Floppy (A:) window.

Identifying Icons on the Desktop

Your desktop now has three new shortcut icons. Although the names of the shortcut icons help you identify what the shortcuts are for, the icons themselves help you identify the shortcut type. Figure 4-15 shows the types of icons you might see on a desktop and the objects they represent.

Figure 4-15	TYPES OF SHORTCUT ICONS YOU MIGHT SEE ON THE DESKTOP		
ICON	**OBJECT THE ICON REPRESENTS**	**ICON**	**OBJECT THE ICON REPRESENTS**
	Text document		CD-ROM drive
	Floppy drive		Printer
	Hard drive		Folder

When you are opening a document represented by a desktop icon you can usually identify which program Windows 98 will start by looking at the icon representing the document.

Deleting Shortcut Icons

If you are working on your own computer, you can leave the printer and drive icons in place, if you think you'll find them useful. Otherwise, you should delete all the shortcuts you created so that the desktop is restored to its original condition for the next user. You can delete them all at once.

To delete your shortcuts:

1. Point to the printer shortcut icon so that it is highlighted.

   TROUBLE? If pointing does not select the shortcut icon, click a blank area of the desktop and then repeat Step 1.

   TROUBLE? If you are using Classic-style settings, click the printer shortcut icon in Step 1 and the other icons in Step 2.

2. Press and hold down the **Ctrl** key, then point to the floppy drive shortcut icon and the phone log shortcut icon, so that they are also highlighted. Make sure no other icons are highlighted. If they are, deselect them.

3. Press the **Delete** key.

4. Click **Yes** if you are asked if you are sure you want to send these items to the Recycle Bin.

Your desktop is restored to its original appearance.

QUICK CHECK

1. True or False? On a document-centric desktop, the quickest way to open a document is by locating the program that created the document, starting the program, and then using the Open command to locate and open the document.

2. True or False? You can create a document with an automatic time-date stamp in Notepad by typing "log" at the beginning of the document.

3. What happens if you delete a document icon that does not have an arrow on it?

4. What happens if you delete a shortcut icon?

5. What happens if you try to create a shortcut icon by dragging with the left mouse button instead of the right?

SESSION 4.2

In this session you'll change the appearance of your desktop by working with the desktop's property sheets. You'll experiment with your desktop's background and appearance, enable a screen saver, try different colors to see how they look, and modify desktop settings to explore your monitor's capabilities. *As you proceed through this session, check with your instructor or lab manager before you change settings on a school lab computer, and make sure you change them back before you leave.*

Viewing Desktop Properties

In Windows 98, you can think of all the parts of your computer—the operating system, the programs, and the documents—as individual objects. For example, the desktop is an object, the taskbar is an object, a drive is an object, a program is an object, and a document is an object. Each object has **properties**, or characteristics, that you can examine and sometimes change. The desktop itself has many properties, including its color, its size, and the font it uses. Most objects in Windows 98 have property sheets associated with them. A **property sheet** is a dialog box that you open to see or change an object's properties. To open an object's property sheet, you right-click the object and then click Properties on the shortcut menu that appears.

To view desktop properties:

1. Right-click an empty area of the desktop to open the shortcut menu.

2. Click **Properties** to open the Display Properties dialog box. See Figure 4-16.

| Figure 4-16 | DISPLAY PROPERTIES DIALOG BOX |

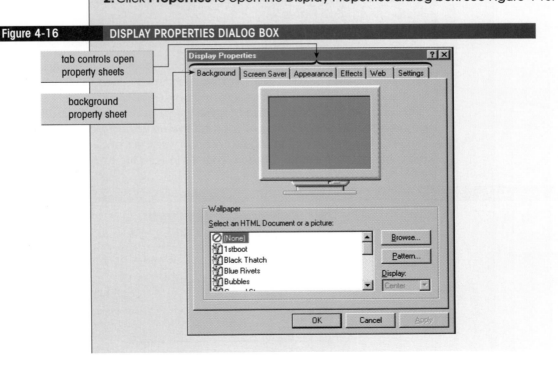

The Display Properties dialog box has several tab controls running along the top of the box. Each tab corresponds to a property sheet. Some objects require only one property sheet, but the desktop has many properties associated with it, so there are more tabs for it. The Background tab appears first, displaying settings for the desktop wallpaper. To view a different property sheet, you click its tab.

Changing Your Desktop's Background

Beth wants the staff computers in the Companions, Inc. offices to have a corporate look. You can change the desktop background color, or you can select a **wallpaper**—a graphic or other type of file that you designate to give your desktop a different appearance—using the Wallpaper list on the Background property sheet. The image of a monitor at the top of the Background property sheet lets you preview the wallpaper. You can also choose a **pattern**, a design or shape that uses the current background color and is repeated over the entire desktop. When you change the background, you are not placing a new object on the desktop, you are simply changing its appearance. If you choose a wallpaper that doesn't occupy the entire background, you can choose a pattern that "fills in" the area around the wallpaper. When a pattern is in effect and you choose a wallpaper that occupies the entire background, the wallpaper covers up the pattern, and not the other way around. You can continue to work with the desktop just as you always did.

You'll first experiment by choosing a pattern, and then by choosing a wallpaper and a graphic.

To select a pattern:

1. Look at the Wallpaper list and notice if a wallpaper is already selected. If one is, write the name down, because you will restore this setting later. Then scroll to the top of the Wallpaper list, click **(None)**, and then click the **Apply** button.

2. Click the **Pattern** button. The Pattern dialog box opens.

3. Click the **Bricks** pattern in the Pattern list. The preview changes to show the Bricks pattern. See Figure 4-17.

   TROUBLE? If the Bricks pattern isn't available, choose a different one.

   TROUBLE? If you have installed desktop themes, a feature that changes the look of your desktop and desktop icons, you need to turn this feature off before you can work with patterns. Click Start, click Settings, and then click Control Panel. Locate and open Desktop Themes, and note the theme your computer is using. To temporarily disable desktop themes, click the Theme list arrow, and then click Windows Default. Click the OK button, close any open windows, and repeat Step 1. When you are finished with this section, restore your themes setting to its original state.

Figure 4-17	SELECTING A PATTERN

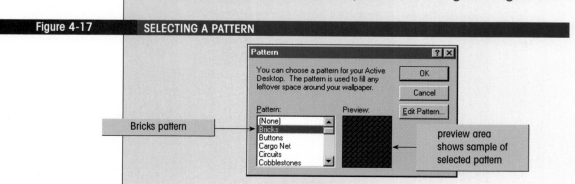

4. Scroll toward the bottom of the **Pattern** list, and then click **Stone**. The preview now shows the Stone pattern.

5. Click the **OK** button and then click the **Apply** button to see how this pattern appears on the entire desktop. See Figure 4-18.

Figure 4-18	STONE PATTERN APPLIED TO DESKTOP

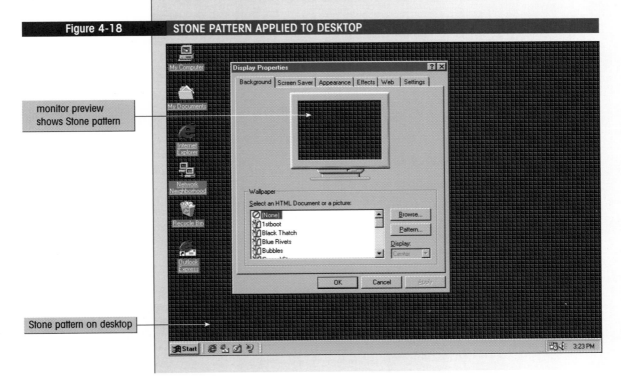

monitor preview shows Stone pattern

Stone pattern on desktop

Beth doesn't think this pattern fits her company very well. You decide to experiment with the Windows 98 wallpapers. Perhaps you can find one that matches the Companions, Inc. corporate look. When you choose a wallpaper, you can either display a single image in the middle of the desktop or you can repeat, or tile, the image across the desktop.

To select a wallpaper:

1. Click **Bubbles** in the Wallpaper list.

   TROUBLE? If the Bubbles wallpaper isn't available, choose a different one.

2. If necessary, click the **Display** list arrow, and then click **Tile** to display multiple copies of the wallpaper image repeated across the entire desktop.

3. Click the **OK** button. The resulting wallpaper is a little overwhelming. You know Beth wouldn't want this look, so you return to the Background property sheet to make a different selection.

4. Right-click an empty area of the desktop, and then click **Properties**.

5. Experiment with the wallpapers available on your computer by clicking them in the Wallpaper list and previewing them.

6. Click **(None)** when you have examined as many as you want.

7. Click the **Pattern** button, scroll to the top of the Pattern list, click **(None)**, click the **OK** button in the Pattern dialog box, and then click the **Apply** button on the background tab. Your desktop is restored to the default position.

None of the wallpapers that come with Windows 98 suit Beth's corporate image, so you ask her if she would like to use the bitmap image of her company logo. She is enthusiastic; it would be great if clients who come to the offices could see the company logo on the office computers.

To use a graphic image as custom wallpaper:

1. If necessary, place your Student Disk in drive A.

2. Click the **Browse** button on the Background property sheet.

3. Click the **Look in** list arrow, and then click **3½ Floppy (A:)**.

4. Click the file **Logo**.

TROUBLE? If Logo appears as Logo.bmp, click Logo.bmp. Your computer is set to display file extensions.

5. Click the **Open** button.

6. Click the **Display** list arrow, and then click **Center** to center the image on the screen.

7. Click the **OK** button to close the Display Properties dialog box. See Figure 4-19. The logo for Companions, Inc. appears in the middle of the desktop.

Figure 4-19   COMPANIONS LOGO APPLIED AS WALLPAPER

Changing Your Desktop's Appearance

Beth looks over your shoulder and comments that the red of the logo doesn't go very well with the teal of the screen background, and she asks if you can try other background colors. The Appearance property sheet gives you control over the color not only of the desktop background but also of all the items on the screen: icons, title bars, borders, menus, scroll bars, and so on.

To view the Appearance property sheet:

1. Right-click an empty area of the desktop, and then click **Properties**.

2. Click the **Appearance** tab. The Appearance property sheet is shown in Figure 4-20.

Figure 4-20	APPEARANCE PROPERTY SHEET

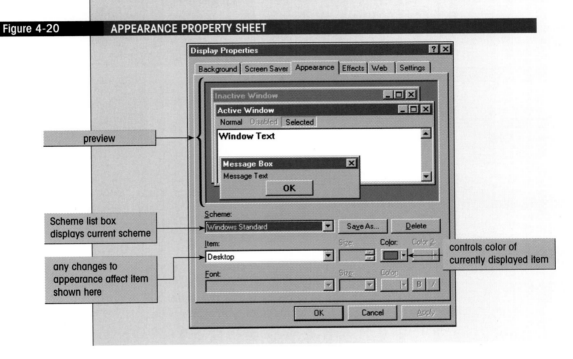

The Appearance property sheet includes several list boxes from which you choose options to change the desktop's appearance. Notice the Scheme list box. A **scheme** is a desktop design. Windows 98 includes a collection of schemes. You can create your own by working with the Appearance property sheet until you arrive at a look you like, and then using the Save As button. The default scheme is Windows Standard. However, if your computer is in a lab, your lab manager might have designed and selected a different scheme. Before you experiment with the appearance of your desktop, you should write down the current scheme so you can restore it later.

The preview in the Appearance property sheet displays many of the elements you are likely to see when working with Windows 98. You can click an item in the preview to change its color, and sometimes its font or size. You want to change the desktop itself to white. The Item list box currently displays "Desktop," so any changes you make in the Color list affect the desktop.

To change the color of your desktop to white:

1. Write down the name of the current scheme, which is displayed in the Scheme list box.

   TROUBLE? If your Scheme list box is empty, your lab manager might have changed scheme settings without saving the scheme. Each time you change an object's color, write down the original color so you can restore that object's color when you are finished.

2. Make sure the Item list box displays "Desktop."

   TROUBLE? If the Item list box does not display "Desktop," click the Item list arrow, scroll until you see "Desktop," and then click Desktop.

3. Click the **Color** list arrow, and then click **white**, the first box in the first row. See Figure 4-21.

| Figure 4-21 | CHANGING THE COLOR OF THE DESKTOP |

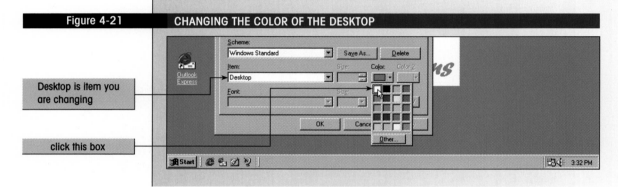

Desktop is item you are changing

click this box

The desktop color in the preview changes to white. Notice that the Scheme list box is now empty because you are no longer using the default scheme. You realize that blue title bars might look strange in contrast to the red and white desktop. You decide to change the title bars to red. To change an element, you either click it in the preview or select it from the Item list.

To change the title bars to red:

1. Click the **Message Box title bar** in the preview. See Figure 4-22 for the location of this title bar. Note that the Item list box now displays "Active Title Bar."

2. Click the **Color** list arrow (next to the Size box), and then click **red**, the first box in the second row. See Figure 4-22.

   TROUBLE? If your Color 2 box displays a color, change it to red too. In Figure 4-22 the Color 2 box is gray because the active title bar uses only one color in the default scheme.

Figure 4-22	CHANGING THE COLOR OF THE TITLE BARS

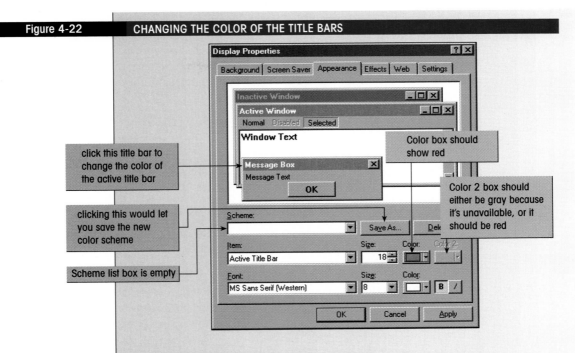

click this title bar to change the color of the active title bar

Color box should show red

clicking this would let you save the new color scheme

Color 2 box should either be gray because it's unavailable, or it should be red

Scheme list box is empty

3. Click the **OK** button to see how the desktop looks. See Figure 4-23.

Figure 4-23	APPEARANCE OF MODIFIED DESKTOP

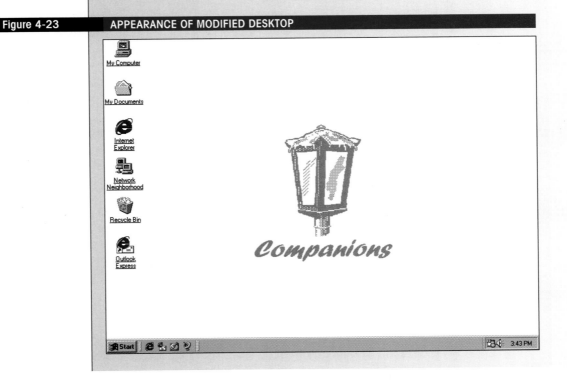

The next time you open a dialog box, you'll see a red title bar. First you'll open My Computer to view the changed title bar, and then you'll restore the desktop to its original settings. You can do this by simply selecting the scheme you wrote down earlier. You could save the colors that match Beth's logo as a scheme if you wanted to. To do this, you would click the Save As button, type a name for your scheme, and then click the OK button.

To restore the desktop colors and wallpaper to their original settings:

1. Open My Computer and observe its red title bar. Then close My Computer.

2. Right-click an empty area of the desktop, and then click **Properties**.

3. Click the **Appearance** tab.

4. Click the **Scheme** list arrow, and then locate and click the scheme you wrote down earlier. Most likely this is Windows Standard, which you will find at the bottom of the list.

   TROUBLE? If your Scheme list box was blank when you began working with the Appearance property sheet, skip Step 3 and instead restore each setting you changed to the original color you wrote down in the beginning of this section. Then proceed to Step 5.

5. Click the **Background** tab to open the Background property sheet.

6. Scroll to the top of the Wallpaper list, then click **(None)**.

7. Click the **Apply** button. The original desktop is restored.

Activating a Screen Saver

A **screen saver** blanks the screen or displays a moving design whenever you haven't worked with the computer for a specified period of time. In older monitors, a screen saver can help prevent "burn-in," or the permanent etching of an image into the screen, which occurs when the same image is displayed for long periods of time. This is not a concern with newer monitors, but if you step away from your computer, the screen saver is handy for hiding your data from the eyes of passers-by. You restore your screen by moving your mouse or pressing a key.

You can select how long you want the computer to sit idle before the screen saver activates. Most users find settings between 3 and 10 minutes to be the most convenient. You can change the setting by clicking the up or down arrow on the Wait box, as you'll see in the next set of steps.

To activate a screen saver:

1. Click the **Screen Saver** tab in the Display Properties dialog box.

2. Click the **Screen Saver** list arrow to display the list of available screen savers. See Figure 4-24.

Figure 4-24	SELECTING A SCREEN SAVER

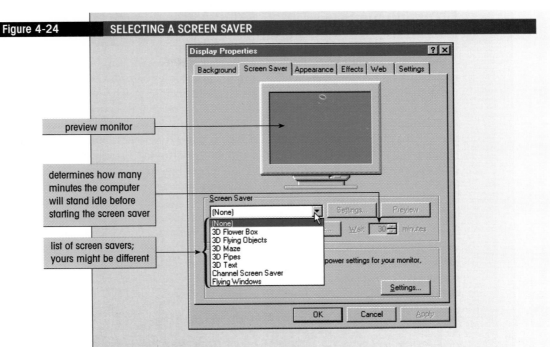

preview monitor

determines how many minutes the computer will stand idle before starting the screen saver

list of screen savers; yours might be different

TROUBLE? If you don't see a list, your computer might not have any screen savers installed, or might have only one.

3. Click any screen saver on the list to select it. Flying Windows is included on the default installation, so click this selection if it is available.

4. Click the **Wait** up or down arrow to change the number in the Wait box to 5. The preview monitor shows how the screen saver will appear.

5. Click the **Preview** button to see the screen saver in motion on the entire screen.

   TROUBLE? If you move the mouse after clicking the Preview button, the screen saver will disappear, sometimes so quickly that you can't even see it. Repeat Step 5, but make sure you don't move the mouse after you click the Preview button.

6. Move the mouse to return to the Display Properties dialog box.

7. Click the **Cancel** button to cancel your screen saver changes. If you were working on your own computer and wanted to save the changes, you would click the Apply button to save the changes or the OK button to save the changes and close the Display Properties dialog box.

Changing **Desktop Settings**

The Settings property sheet allows you to control additional settings that you might never need to consider. But if you want to take full advantage of your monitor type, you should be aware of the options you have on the Settings property sheet. The settings you can change depend on your monitor type and on the **video card** inside your computer that controls visual information you see on the screen. Windows 98 allows you to use more than one monitor, so you might be able to change settings for multiple monitors.

Changing the Size of the Desktop Area

The Screen area slider bar on the Settings property sheet lets you display less or more of the screen on your monitor. If you display less, objects will look bigger, while if you display more, objects will look smaller. You can drag the slider bar between these two extremes. You are actually increasing or decreasing the **resolution**, or sharpness, of the image. Resolution is measured by the number of individual dots, called **pixels**, short for picture elements, that run across and down your monitor. The more pixels, the higher the resolution, the more you see on the screen at one time, and the smaller the objects look.

The 640 × 480 (640 pixels across and 480 pixels down) resolution shows the least information, but uses the largest text and is preferred by most users with 14-inch monitors. The 800 × 600 resolution shows more information but uses smaller text. Many users with 15-inch monitors prefer the 800 × 600 resolution. This is the setting that Beth's computers use. The 1024 × 768 resolution shows the most information, but uses the smallest text. Most users find the 1024 × 768 resolution too small for comfortable use unless they are using a 17-inch or larger monitor. Users with limited vision might prefer the 640 × 480 setting even on larger monitors, because objects and text are bigger and easier to see. You might also want to change your monitor's resolution, depending on what software you are using.

To change the size of the desktop area:

1. Right-click an empty area of the desktop, and then click **Properties**.

2. Click the **Settings** tab to display the Settings properties.

3. Make a note of the original setting in the Screen area, so you can restore it after experimenting with it.

4. To select the 640 × 480 resolution, if it is not already selected, drag the **Screen area** slider to the left. The preview monitor shows the relative size of the 640 × 480 display. See Figure 4-25.

| Figure 4-25 | 640 X 480 RESOLUTION |

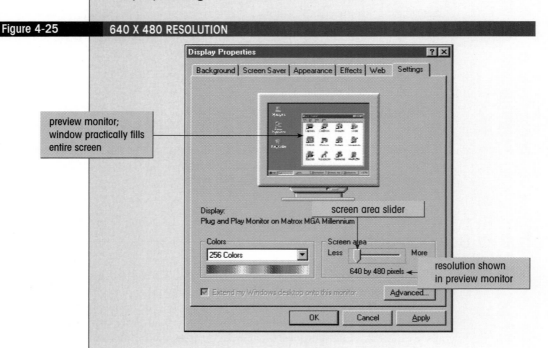

preview monitor; window practically fills entire screen

screen area slider

resolution shown in preview monitor

5. To select the 800 × 600 resolution, drag the **Screen area** slider to the right. The preview monitor shows the relative size of the 800 × 600 display.

6. Return the slider to its original position.

Changing the Color Palette

You can also use the Settings property sheet to change the **color palette**, which specifies the number of colors available to your computer. Beth's computers have a 256-color palette. Figure 4-26 provides additional information on common palettes.

Figure 4-26	COLOR PALETTES
PALETTE	**DESCRIPTION**
16 colors	Very fast, requires the least video memory, sufficient for use with most programs but not adequate for most graphics.
256 colors	Relatively fast, requires a moderate amount of video memory, sufficient for most programs and adequate for the graphics in most games and educational programs. This is a good setting for general use.
High color	Requires higher-quality video card and additional video memory. This setting is useful for sophisticated painting, drawing, and graphics manipulation tasks.
True color	Requires the most video memory and runs most slowly. This setting is useful for professional graphics tasks, but might not be available or might be too slow on some computer systems.

Once you change the color palette, you are prompted to reboot Windows 98. In the next set of steps, you will see how to change the color palette, but to avoid rebooting you won't actually do so.

To view the color palette options:

1. Click the **Colors** list arrow to display the list of color palettes. See Figure 4-27.

Figure 4-27	AVAILABLE COLOR PALETTES

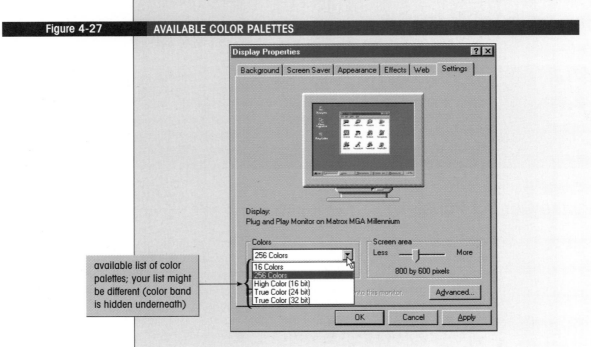

available list of color palettes; your list might be different (color band is hidden underneath)

2. Click **16 Color** and observe that the color band below the Colors list box displays only 16 colors.

   TROUBLE? If 16 Color doesn't appear on your Colors list, skip Step 2.

3. Click the **Colors** list arrow again, and then click **256 Color**. Now the color band displays a greater range of color.

4. Click the **Cancel** button to close the Display Properties dialog box without accepting any changes you might have inadvertently made.

If you are working in a lab, make sure you have changed all settings back to their original state before moving on to Session 4.3.

QUICK CHECK

1. True or False? Although a document is an object, and so is a drive, the desktop is not an object.

2. How do you open an object's property sheet?

3. Name three desktop properties you can change with the desktop property sheets.

4. If you have an older monitor and you want to protect it from harm caused by the same image being displayed for a long time, what can you do?

5. What does it mean to say that a monitor's resolution is 640 × 480?

6. Users with limited vision might want to use which resolution: 640 × 480, 800 × 600, or 1024 × 768? Why?

7. What is the disadvantage of using a color palette with many colors, such as True Color?

SESSION 4.3

In this session you'll learn to control your Windows 98 working environment. You'll learn how to change how your computer uses energy and how the mouse functions. Finally, you'll learn to change to options that make a computer more accessible to users with special needs. *As you proceed through this session, check with your instructor or lab manager before you change any of these settings on a school lab computer, and make sure to change them back before you leave.*

Using the Control Panel

Windows 98 includes a **Control Panel**, available through the Start menu, which centralizes many of your computer's operations and customization features. You'll find the property sheets for many objects, including the desktop, on the Control Panel, as well as other tools that help you control your computer's settings. The Control Panel is so useful that you might want to place a shortcut to it on your desktop.

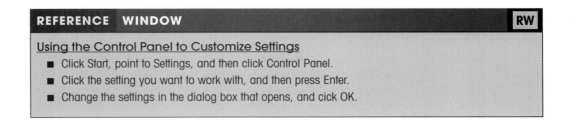

REFERENCE   WINDOW   **RW**

Using the Control Panel to Customize Settings
- Click Start, point to Settings, and then click Control Panel.
- Click the setting you want to work with, and then press Enter.
- Change the settings in the dialog box that opens, and cick OK.

To open the Control Panel:

1. Click the **Start** button [Start], point to **Settings**, and then click **Control Panel**.

   TROUBLE? If a message appears indicating that the Control Panel is not available, you might be in a computer lab with limited customization access. Ask your instructor or technical resource person for options.

2. Click **View** on the menu bar, and make sure **as Web Page** is not selected. If it is, click **as Web Page**. You don't need to view the Control Panel as a Web page to get the information needed for this tutorial.

3. Click **View**, and then click **List** to display the icons, as in Figure 4-28.

   TROUBLE? Because some tools are optional, your Control Panel might display different tools than the ones shown in Figure 4-28.

| Figure 4-28 | CONTROL PANEL |

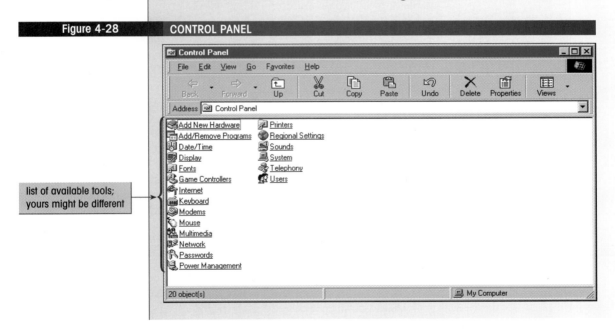

list of available tools;
yours might be different

Using Power Management Features

The Windows 98 **power management** features allow you to control the amount of power your computer and its devices require when you don't need them to be running at full capacity. For example, if you're taking a short break, you might not want to turn your system off completely, because shutting down and then restarting the computer is time-consuming. Instead, you can place the computer on **standby**, which reduces the amount of power consumed by your drives and monitor, but still allows you to return to work quickly because the computer is not actually turned off. Standby is also useful for users who leave their computers on 24 hours a day, because they schedule their computers to perform resource-intensive tasks in the middle of the night, or because they use their computers to receive faxes or download files when they are not actually sitting at their computer. Standby is also useful for conserving battery power in portable computers. **Portable computers**, also called laptops or notebooks, are small and light and can be transported much more easily than a standard desktop computer. You can specify one standby setting for battery power and a different setting for AC power.

You can also put your computer in **hibernation**, which turns off your monitor and hard disk, but unlike standby, also saves your work and turns off your computer. When you restart your computer, it appears just as you left it, reopening any programs or documents you left open. It takes longer to bring your computer out of hibernation than out of standby.

When you tell Beth about these features, she is eager to explore them further, because they conserve both energy and money. You warn her, however, that her computer will be able to use power management features only if its hardware is designed for that purpose.

You change power management settings by working with **power schemes**, or preset power management options. A power scheme controls, for example, the amount of time you want to elapse before the system turns off the monitor. Windows 98 comes with three default power schemes, although you can create and save new ones:

- Portable/Laptop for portable computers
- Home/Office Desk for a computer that has periods of disuse
- Always On for a computer that functions 24 hours a day (this option isn't available on notebook computers)

Your list might show additional schemes.

To view your computer's power management settings:

1. In the Control Panel, click **Power Management**.

2. On the Power Schemes tab, click the **Power schemes** list arrow. Note the schemes available to your computer. The Settings pane below the Power schemes list box shows the options for the currently selected scheme. The number of options you see depends on your computer's hardware. You might have check boxes for standby, hard disks, and monitor, or you might have only one or two of these options. The monitor and hard disks on the computer in Figure 4-29 can both be turned off after a specified amount of idle time.

TROUBLE? If you don't see the Power Schemes tab or the Power schemes list arrow, click the Cancel button and read these steps without performing them.

TROUBLE? Don't worry if your property sheet shows additional tabs, such as a Hibernation tab, or additional or fewer settings. Power management settings appear only when your hardware supports them.

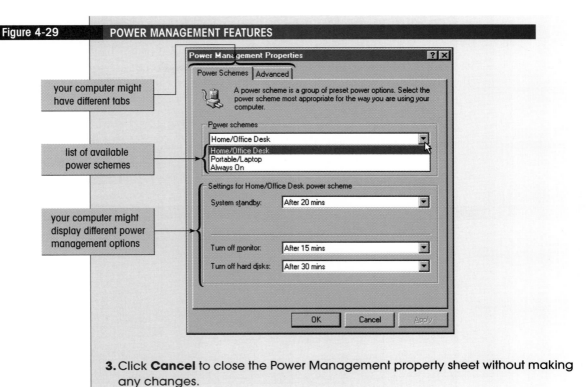

Figure 4-29 | POWER MANAGEMENT FEATURES

your computer might have different tabs

list of available power schemes

your computer might display different power management options

3. Click **Cancel** to close the Power Management property sheet without making any changes.

Because many computer users rely on voice mail and fax management software to receive voice mail messages and faxes, they need the computer to come out of standby when the modem line receives a phone call. In a lab you won't use this feature, but if you have your own computer, you can enable this feature using the Advanced tab on the Power Management Properties dialog box. Then, before the computer goes into standby, make sure the appropriate modem software is running and the modem is turned on (if it is an external modem, attached to the outside of your computer).

Customizing the Mouse

The Mouse Properties dialog box, available through the Control Panel, lets you customize the mouse settings. Using this dialog box you can configure the mouse for the right or left hand, adjust the double-click speed, choose different pointer shapes, turn on pointer trails to make it easier to locate the pointer, and adjust the pointer speed.

If you have a Microsoft IntelliPoint device or some other pointing device, you might see additional features in the Mouse Properties dialog box. For example, the SnapTo, Focus, Sonar, Vanish, PointerWrap, and Odometer options all come with the IntelliPoint device, and settings for these options are usually found with the other mouse settings.

Beth, and two of her employees, are left-handed, so one of the first things you want to do is experiment with the left-handed mouse settings.

Configuring the Mouse for the Right or Left Hand

You can configure the mouse for either right-handed or left-handed users. If you select the left-handed setting, the operations of the left and right mouse buttons are reversed. If you are instructed to click the right mouse button, you must click the *left* mouse button, and vice versa.

To configure the mouse for right-handed or left-handed users:

1. Click the **Mouse** icon in the Control Panel to display the Mouse Properties dialog box. You can set the mouse for right-handed users or left-handed users by clicking the appropriate option button. See Figure 4-30.

| Figure 4-30 | BUTTONS PROPERTY SHEET |

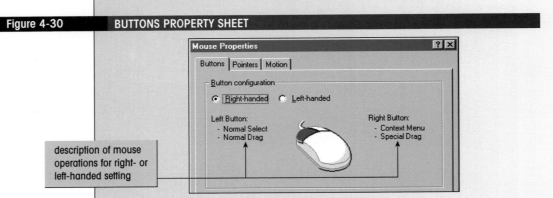

description of mouse operations for right- or left-handed setting

2. Click the **Right-handed** option button if you are right-handed; click the **Left-handed** option button if you are left-handed. Notice that as you change this setting the descriptions of mouse operations change.

3. If you are working on your own computer, click the **Apply** button to apply your changes, then test the new mouse setting by dragging the Mouse Properties dialog box with the appropriate mouse button.

4. Return this setting to its original state, and then click the **Apply** button.

   TROUBLE? If clicking Apply doesn't seem to work, try using the other mouse button!

Adjusting Double-Click Speed

Many Windows programs use **double-clicking**, or clicking the mouse twice in rapid succession, to select or open objects. Some new users have difficulty double-clicking, which is why Microsoft designed Windows 98 to work without double-clicking. However, other users find double-clicking the quickest way to work, especially when their Folder Options desktop settings are set to Classic style. Beth wants you to experiment with slowing down the double-click speed to allow for more time between the two clicks.

To test the current double-click speed:

1. Position the pointer over the purple box in the Test area of the Mouse Properties dialog box, as shown in Figure 4-31.

Figure 4-31	TESTING DOUBLE-CLICK SPEED

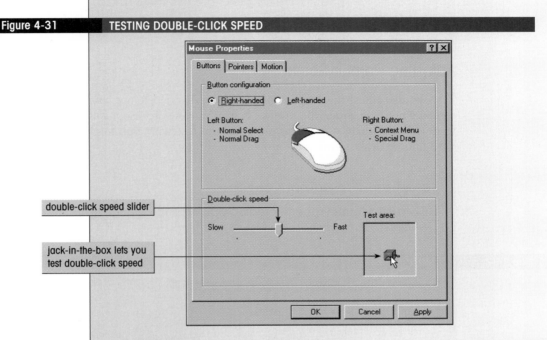

double-click speed slider

jack-in-the-box lets you test double-click speed

2. Place your hand on the mouse and quickly press and release the left mouse button twice.

TROUBLE? If you changed the mouse to left-handed operation, you will need to double-click by quickly pressing and releasing the right mouse button twice.

3. If you double-click successfully, the jack-in-the-box pops out of the box.

4. Double-click the **purple box** again to close it.

TROUBLE? Don't worry if you can't open the jack-in-the-box. In the next series of steps you'll learn how to adjust the double-click speed for your convenience.

If you have trouble double-clicking, you can slow down the double-click speed by using the Double-click speed slider bar.

To slow down the double-click speed:

1. Drag the **Double-click speed** slider toward Slow.

2. Double-click the **jack-in-the-box** to see if you can make it pop up.

3. If you still cannot successfully double-click, drag the **Double-click speed** slider even farther toward Slow, and then repeat Step 2.

4. Once you can successfully double-click, try increasing or decreasing the double-click speed to find the most comfortable speed for you.

5. If you are using your own computer, click the **Apply** button to change the double-click speed to the new setting. If you are in a lab, make sure to restore this setting to its original status.

Adjusting Pointer Speed

You can also adjust the pointer speed or the relative distance that the pointer moves on the screen when you move the mouse. It can be easier to use a slower speed when you need more control, such as in a drawing program. Likewise, you might need faster speed if you have limited desktop space for moving the mouse.

To adjust the pointer speed:

1. From the Mouse Properties dialog box, click the **Motion** tab to display the Motion property sheet. See Figure 4-32.

Figure 4-32	MOTION PROPERTY SHEET

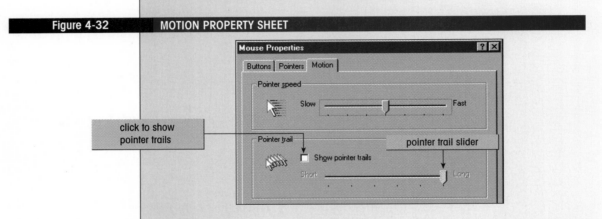

click to show pointer trails

pointer trail slider

2. To decrease the pointer speed, drag the **Pointer speed** slider toward Slow.

3. To increase the pointer speed, drag the **Pointer speed** slider toward Fast.

4. If you are using your own computer, adjust the pointer speed to the setting that is most comfortable for you, then click the **Apply** button. If you are using a lab computer, return this setting to its original position.

Using Pointer Trails

A **pointer trail** is a trail of pointers that appears on the screen in the wake of the pointer as you move it, like the wake of a boat. Locating the pointer is sometimes difficult, especially on some notebook computer displays. You might find the pointer trail helpful if you occasionally have trouble locating the pointer on your screen. For example, if Beth is on a business trip, she might enable the pointer trail while she uses her notebook computer in a dimly lit hotel room. Users with vision problems might also find this feature helpful.

To turn on the pointer trail:

1. Make sure the Motion tab of the Mouse Properties dialog box is displayed.

2. Click the **Show pointer trails** check box to select this option.

3. Move the mouse. A trail of pointers follows the pointer when you move it.

4. To increase the length of the trail, drag the **Pointer trail** slider toward Long.

5. To decrease the length of the trail, drag the **Pointer trail** slider toward Short.

6. Click the **Apply** button if you want to leave pointer trails on, and you are using your own computer. If you are in a lab, make sure to restore this setting to its original status.

7. Make sure all Mouse Properties settings are in their original position, and then click the **OK** button to close the Mouse Properties dialog box.

You can adjust additional mouse settings using the Accessibility Options feature, as you'll see in the next section.

Activating Accessibility Options

Accessibility options are Windows 98 settings that you can change to make it easier to interact with your computer. Although designed primarily for users with vision, hearing, and mobility needs, users without special needs also find it helpful to adjust accessibility settings under certain circumstances, such as when they are working with drawing software and need more control over mouse and keyboard settings, using a portable computer with a small screen, or working in a poorly lit room.

There are two ways to change accessibility settings. You can open the Accessibility Properties dialog box from the Control Panel to access individual accessibility settings, or you can use the Accessibility Settings Wizard's series of questions to determine what settings you should change to work most effectively. Let's first examine some of the individual accessibility settings, and then you'll walk through part of the Accessibility Settings Wizard.

To open the Accessibility Properties dialog box:

1. Make sure that the Control Panel is open.

   TROUBLE? If the Control Panel is not open, click the Start button, click Settings, and then click Control Panel.

2. Click the **Accessibility Options** icon in the Control Panel. The Accessibility Options dialog box opens. See Figure 4-33.

   TROUBLE? If the Accessibility Options icon does not appear in the Control Panel, you might need to ask your lab manager to install Accessibility Options. If you are working on your own computer, you can install it yourself. Make sure you have your Windows 98 Setup disk in the appropriate drive. Click the Add/Remove Programs icon in the Control Panel, click the Windows Setup tab, click the Accessibility check box, click the OK button, and then follow the instructions on the screen to install the Accessibility Options and the Accessibility Tools features.

Figure 4-33   ACCESSIBILITY PROPERTIES DIALOG BOX

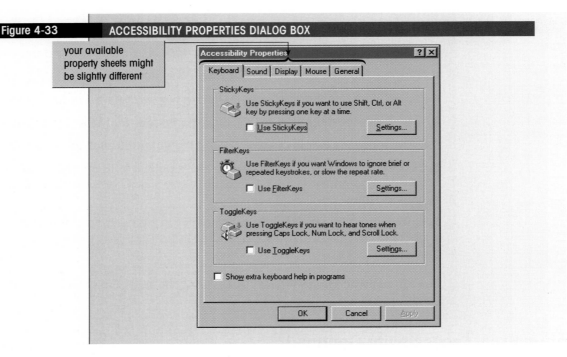

your available
property sheets might
be slightly different

The Accessibility Properties dialog box has five property tabs: Keyboard, Sound, Display, Mouse, and General. Don't worry if you don't have all these tabs. First you'll explore some of the most helpful accessibility options. For example, if you have restricted movement, you can use the keyboard instead of the mouse and can simplify some key press sequences. If you have limited vision, you can select high-contrast mode to make it easier to see the objects and text on the screen.

Using MouseKeys to Control the Pointer

All users occasionally have trouble using the mouse to precisely control the pointer when using programs such as Paint or other drawing or graphics programs. You can turn on MouseKeys to control the pointer with the numeric keypad as well as with the mouse. This is also a useful feature if you have a temporary or permanent hand injury.

To turn on MouseKeys:

1. Click the **Mouse** tab in the Accessibility Properties dialog box.

2. Click the **Use MouseKeys** check box to place a check mark in it.

3. Click the **Apply** button to activate MouseKeys. After a short time, the MouseKeys icon appears in the taskbar tray. See Figure 4-34.

Figure 4-34	TURNING ON MOUSEKEYS

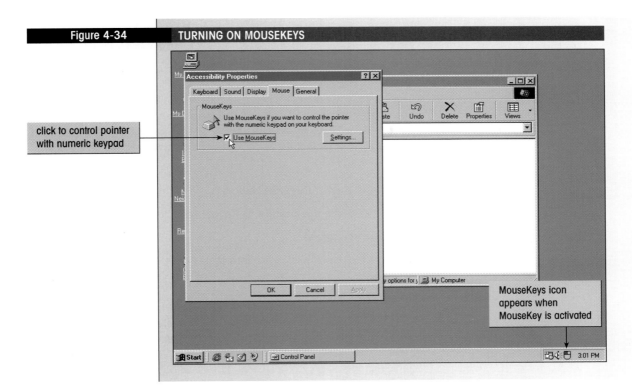

click to control pointer
with numeric keypad

MouseKeys icon
appears when
MouseKey is activated

When the MouseKeys feature is active, you can control the pointer using either the mouse or the keys on the numeric keypad. Before you try working with MouseKeys, study Figure 4-35, which describes some of the mouse actions you can duplicate using keys on the numeric keypad.

Figure 4-35	MOUSEKEYS ACTIONS AND CORRESPONDING KEYS

MOUSE ACTION	CORRESPONDING NUMERIC KEYPAD KEY
Move pointer horizontally	Press 4 to move left, 6 to move right
Move pointer vertically	Press 8 to move up, 2 to move down
Move pointer diagonally	Press 7, 1, 9, and 3
Click	Press 5
Double-click	Press + (plus)
Right-click	Press – (minus), then press 5 (pressing – assigns the right-click function to 5; when you are done right-clicking, press / to restore 5 to clicking)
Begin dragging after pointing to object	Press Insert and then press arrow keys
End dragging	Press Delete to release mouse button
Move a single pixel at a time	Press and hold Shift, then use directional keys

To practice using MouseKeys:

1. Use the numeric keypad to move the pointer over the **Start** button. The End key moves you to the lower left.

TROUBLE? Most keyboards have two keypads: one with only arrows and one with numbers and arrows. Make sure you are using the keypad with numbers. If the pointer doesn't move when you press the number keys, press the NumLock key on the keyboard.

TROUBLE? If MouseKeys isn't working, it's possible that Windows 98 is set to reset accessibility options after a specified amount of time. Return to the Mouse property sheet, and then reset MouseKeys by clicking Apply. Then click the General tab, and check if Automatic reset is enabled. If it is, click the check box to turn it off for now, and then click Apply.

2. Press **5** once the pointer is over the Start button.

3. Hold down the **8** key to move the pointer to **Programs**.

4. Move the pointer to **Accessories**.

5. Move the pointer to **Paint**, and then press **5** to start the Paint program.

6. Practice moving the pointer by pressing the **7 8 9**, **4 6**, and **1 2 3** number keys on the numeric keypad.

7. Press the **Insert** key on the numeric keypad to start drawing. Press the number keys to move the pointer and draw precise vertical, horizontal, and diagonal lines.

8. Press the **Delete** key on the numeric keypad to stop drawing.

MouseKeys is especially useful for drawing precise diagonal lines in a graphics package such as Paint, although you might notice, if you've used Paint before, that it is slower. Now close Paint and deactivate MouseKeys.

To use MouseKeys to close the Paint window:

1. Use the keys on the numeric keypad to move the pointer over the **Close** button ⊠ on the Paint window.

2. Press the **5** key to click ⊠.

3. Use the keys on the numeric keypad to move the pointer over the **No** button on the Paint dialog box, and then press the **5** key to close Paint.

4. Click the **Use MouseKeys** check box to turn this feature off, and then click **Apply**.

Simplifying Key Operation with StickyKeys

StickyKeys is a feature that makes Windows 98 easier for users who have trouble holding down one key while pressing another key. Three keys typically used in conjunction with other keys are the Shift key, the Ctrl key, and the Alt key. These keys are also known as **modifier keys**— you hold them down while pressing another key, to modify the action of the second key. Many actions that you perform with the mouse can also be performed with modifier keys. For example, instead of clicking the Start button to open the Start menu, you can use Ctrl+Esc. Key combinations such as these are often called **keyboard shortcuts**. To more clearly show the effect of StickyKeys, you'll start by using a keyboard shortcut without StickyKeys enabled.

To test the normal behavior of a modifier key:

1. Click the **Control Panel** button on the taskbar to bring the Control Panel window to the foreground, if it is hidden by the Accessibility Properties dialog box.

   TROUBLE? If the Control Panel window minimizes instead of coming to the foreground, click the Control Panel button a second time.

2. Notice the underlined character in each word on the menu bar. For example, notice the underlined F in File and the underlined V in View. You can use the underlined character with a modifier key to open the menu in a single step.

3. Press and hold the **Alt** key, and then press **F** to display the File menu.

4. Press **Esc** to close the File menu.

5. Click the **Minimize** button ▬ to minimize the Control Panel window.

Now try enabling StickyKeys to see how it affects the way you use key combinations such as Alt+F.

To turn on StickyKeys:

1. Click the **Keyboard** tab in the Accessibility Properties dialog box to display the keyboard properties.

2. Click the **Use StickyKeys** check box to place a check mark in it.

3. Click the **Apply** button to activate StickyKeys. After a few moments the StickyKeys icon 🔲 appears in the bottom-right corner of the taskbar.

Once StickyKeys is enabled, you can press and release the modifier key and then press the action key, to take the place of the keyboard shortcut. When you press the modifier key, the lower-right key in the StickyKeys icon is shaded.

To test the effect of StickyKeys:

1. Click the **Control Panel** button on the taskbar to bring the Control Panel window to the foreground.

2. Press and release the **Alt** key. A sound indicates that a StickyKey has been pressed, and the bottom-right box in the StickyKeys icon 🔲 is filled in. The sound and the icon indicate that the next key you press will be combined with the Alt StickyKey.

   TROUBLE? If you didn't hear a sound, sounds might not be enabled on your StickyKeys settings or on your computer. You can enable sounds by clicking the Settings button in the Keyboard property sheet and selecting the sound settings you want.

3. Press the **F** key. Because StickyKeys was activated, you did not have to hold down the Alt key while you pressed the F.

4. Press **Esc** to close the File menu.

5. Click the **Minimize** button ▬ to minimize the Control Panel window.

6. In the Accessibility Properties dialog box, click the **Use StickyKeys** check box to remove the check mark, and then click the **Apply** button to deactivate StickyKeys. The StickyKeys icon disappears from the right end of the task bar.

Enabling High Contrast

The Display property sheet lets you set the screen display to high contrast. **High contrast** uses large white letters on a black background and greatly increases the size of the title bar and window control buttons. In high-contrast mode, objects and text stand out more visibly. If you have limited vision, if you're in a dark office, or if you are without your glasses, high-contrast mode can make it much easier to see what's on your screen.

To turn on high contrast:

1. Click the **Display** tab to see the display properties.

2. Click the **Use High Contrast** check box to place a check mark in it.

3. Click the **Apply** button to activate the high-contrast settings. After a short time, the screen changes to the high-contrast display. See Figure 4-36. On screens set to a lower resolution, high contrast can make the desktop appear crowded.

Figure 4-36	APPLYING HIGH CONTRAST

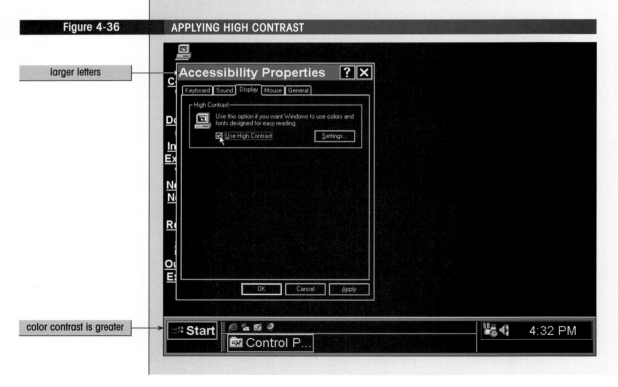

larger letters

color contrast is greater

The high-contrast setting affects all programs, but it does not affect the contents of the document window in a program. Try opening WordPad to see how high contrast works in a program.

To run WordPad with high contrast active:

1. Click the **Start** button 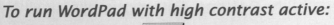, point to **Programs**, and then point to **Accessories**.

2. Click **WordPad** to start the WordPad program.

3. Type your name, and notice that the default font in WordPad itself does not change when high contrast is active, as shown in Figure 4-37.

Figure 4-37 | **OPENING A PROGRAM IN HIGH CONTRAST**

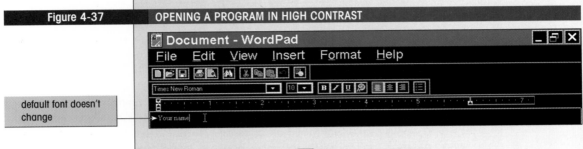

default font doesn't change

4. Click the **Close** button ☒ to close WordPad.

5. Click the **No** button when you are asked if you want to save the document.

You shouldn't leave the desktop display in high-contrast mode if you are in a computer lab at your school. Restore the desktop to its original appearance. When you turn off high contrast, you'll find that the taskbar is larger than it should be. You can easily restore it to its normal size by dragging its top border down.

To turn off the high-contrast setting:

1. Click the **Use High Contrast** check box to remove the check mark.

2. Click the **Apply** button to apply the new setting. After a short time the screen returns to the normal display.

   TROUBLE? If the Apply button is hidden behind the taskbar, drag the title bar of the Accessibility window up until you can see the Apply button.

   TROUBLE? If clicking Apply does not return the screen to its normal display, right-click a blank area of the screen, click Properties, click the Appearance tab, click the Scheme list arrow, and then click Windows Standard.

3. To return the taskbar to its normal height, position the pointer over the top edge of the taskbar, as shown in Figure 4-38, then drag the top edge of the taskbar down to the normal height and release the mouse button.

Figure 4-38 | **RESIZING THE TASKBAR**

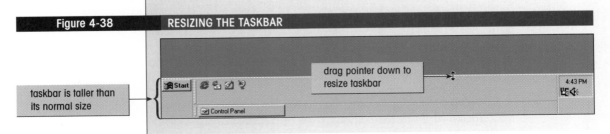

taskbar is taller than its normal size

drag pointer down to resize taskbar

Turning off Accessibility Options Automatically

You can set Accessibility Options to turn off automatically after the computer sits idle for a specified period of time. This is ideal for situations such as computer labs, where you want to use accessibility options but other users don't. You can activate an accessibility option, and when you're done, Windows 98 automatically turns it off if the computer sits idle for a period of time.

To make sure that Accessibility Options turns off after a specified period of time:

1. Click the **General** tab in the Accessibility Properties dialog box.

2. If the **Turn off accessibility features after idle for:** check box is not checked, click it to activate this feature.

3. You can click the **minutes** list arrow to select a period of time from 5 to 30 minutes, after which the accessibility features automatically turn off. Study Figure 4-39 to see how you would make sure that the accessibility features turn off after a specified period of time. Don't make this change, however, if you are using a lab computer.

Figure 4-39	IDLING ACCESSIBILITY OPTIONS

turns Accessibility Options off when selected

select number of minutes of idle time before Accessibility Options disengages

4. Click the **OK** button to close the Accessibility Properties dialog box.

5. Close the Control Panel window by right-clicking its button on the taskbar and then clicking Close.

Starting the Accessibility Wizard

You've now seen how to access one accessibility setting at a time, but you can streamline setting Accessibility Options using the Accessibility Wizard, available on the Accessories menu. You decide to show Beth just the first few steps of this Wizard. You won't actually make any changes as you proceed through the Wizard, and you will cancel the procedure shortly after starting it, to ensure that you leave the desktop unchanged for the next user.

To use the Accessibility Wizard:

1. Click the **Start** button [Start], point to **Programs**, point to **Accessories**, point to **Accessibility**, and then click **Accessibility Wizard**. You are first given the opportunity to select a larger font size. See Figure 4-40.

TROUBLE? If your Accessories menu doesn't have an Accessibility submenu, make sure Accessibility Options and Accessibility Tools are both installed on your computer.

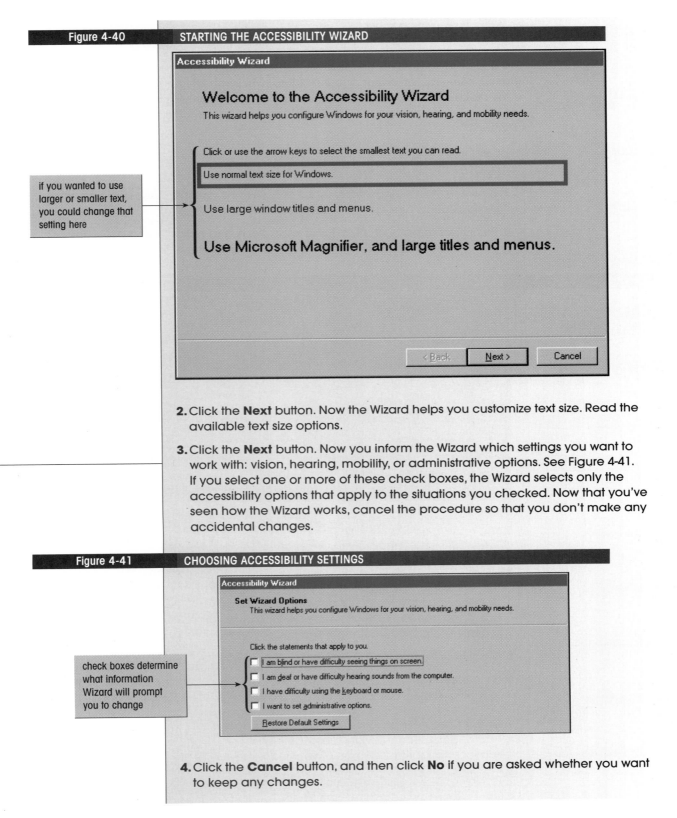

Figure 4-40   STARTING THE ACCESSIBILITY WIZARD

if you wanted to use larger or smaller text, you could change that setting here

2. Click the **Next** button. Now the Wizard helps you customize text size. Read the available text size options.

3. Click the **Next** button. Now you inform the Wizard which settings you want to work with: vision, hearing, mobility, or administrative options. See Figure 4-41. If you select one or more of these check boxes, the Wizard selects only the accessibility options that apply to the situations you checked. Now that you've seen how the Wizard works, cancel the procedure so that you don't make any accidental changes.

Figure 4-41   CHOOSING ACCESSIBILITY SETTINGS

check boxes determine what information Wizard will prompt you to change

4. Click the **Cancel** button, and then click **No** if you are asked whether you want to keep any changes.

You can see how much easier it would be to use the Wizard than to select the options individually from the Control Panel.

Enlarging a Portion of the Screen with Magnifier

You decide to show Beth one final tool that she might find useful when working with a portable computer or giving demonstrations. Microsoft Magnifier enlarges only a portion of the desktop: the area that you are actively using. If you are pointing to a portion of the screen, that portion appears magnified. If you are typing in an area, that portion appears magnified.

> ### To enlarge a portion of the screen:
>
> 1. Click the **Start** button [Start], point to **Programs**, point to **Accessories**, point to **Accessibility**, and then click **Magnifier**.
>
> 2. Point to an area on the Magnifier dialog box and notice how the top part of your screen magnifies just that portion of your screen. See Figure 4-42.

| Figure 4-42 | USING MAGNIFIER |

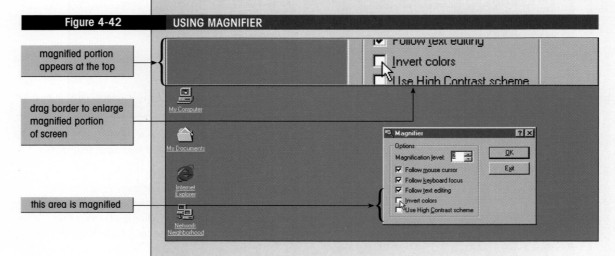

magnified portion appears at the top

drag border to enlarge magnified portion of screen

this area is magnified

> 3. You can adjust the height of the magnified screen: drag the Magnifier border down an inch to enlarge the magnified area.
>
> 4. Click the **OK** button. Move the mouse around and notice how the magnification area follows the mouse. If you are typing, Magnifier follows the insertion point as you type. Verify this by starting WordPad and then typing a sentence or two. If you needed to work on a presentation on a portable computer while on a dimly lit airplane, you might find this option very helpful.
>
> 5. Close WordPad and click **No** if asked if you want to save changes.
>
> 6. Click the **Magnifier** button in the taskbar, and then click the **Exit** button. The Magnifier dialog box closes, and your desktop is returned to normal.
>
> **TROUBLE?** You might notice that some of the icons on your desktop are rearranged. Because Magnifier requires the upper third of the screen for magnification, it might move some of your icons around. To restore them, simply drag them into the proper position.

Beth is impressed with the degree of customization possible with Windows 98. After working with the document-centric desktop she created for herself, she realizes that, trivial as they may seem, the icons on the desktop increase productivity enormously. She's also confident that she could customize one of the Companions, Inc. computers for any of her employees with special needs.

One of the most exciting features of Windows 98 is the way it lends itself to the needs of its users. Your ability to customize Windows 98 in a lab setting is limited and the settings are likely to be changed by the next user. But if you are running Windows 98 on your own computer, you will find that designing a desktop that reflects your needs is time well spent. In creating a document-centric desktop you should keep one thing in mind: having too many icons on the desktop defeats the purpose of giving quick access to your documents. If you have icons crowded all over the desktop, it is difficult to locate quickly the one you want.

If you are working in a lab setting, make sure you return all settings to their original state before leaving the lab.

QUICK CHECK

1. You change most mouse settings using the Control Panel mouse icon. Which mouse setting can you change using the Mouse property sheet in the Accessibility Options dialog box?

2. If you set the mouse for left-handed use, what happens when you click an icon with the left mouse button?

3. Name two settings you can change to make it easier to use Windows 98 if you have limited vision.

4. If you are using MouseKeys, what number on the numeric keypad should you press when you want to select an object?

5. Which keyboard shortcut opens the Start menu?

6. Which modifier key do you use to open a menu?

7. When Magnifier is running, what happens as you type text?

8. What is the difference between standby and hibernation?

TUTORIAL ASSIGNMENTS

1. **Creating Shortcuts**   Practice placing a document on the desktop and printing it, using a printer shortcut icon.

   a. Start Windows Explorer. Create a shortcut to the printer you use regularly.
   b. Create a new text document on your Student Disk, typing your name and the list of classes you are taking in the document. Name this document "Classes."
   c. Drag the Classes document icon to the printer shortcut. Your document prints.
   d. Now use the techniques you learned in the previous tutorial to print an image of your desktop. (Use the Print Screen key to save an image of the desktop, open WordPad, type your name and the date at the top of the document, paste the image into WordPad, and then print the image from WordPad and hand it in to your instructor.)
   e. When you are finished, delete both icons from your desktop.

Explore ▶ 2. **Create a Shortcut to a Folder**   Beth recently assigned Sally Hanson, an undergraduate at one of the local colleges, to provide housekeeping for three clients. Sally plans to be out of the area over spring break, so Beth needs to write a memo to each client asking if they need replacement help. Beth would like to be able to get at the correspondence for Sally Hanson more easily.

   a. Start Windows Explorer, and then create a new folder called "Sally" on your Student Disk.

   b. Start Notepad, and then compose the three memos, typing in your own text. Save the memos to the Sally folder on your Student Disk with the names "Smith," "Arruga," and "Kosta" (the names of the three clients). Close Notepad when you are finished.

   c. Drag the Sally folder from Windows Explorer to the desktop, using the right mouse button, and then click Create Shortcut(s) Here.

   d. Name the shortcut icon "Sally."

   e. Test the shortcut icon by opening the Sally folder, and then open one of the memos. Use two different methods to open these two objects, and write down which methods you used.

   f. Arrange your desktop so you can see the open memo in Notepad, the open folder window, and the shortcut icon. You might need to resize the windows to make them smaller. Then print an image of the desktop, using the techniques you learned in the previous tutorial.

   g. Remove the desktop shortcut to the folder when you are done.

3. **Customizing the Mouse**   One of Beth's older clients, Antonio Castagna, would like part-time work at the offices of Companions, Inc. helping to prepare client schedules. Beth wants to make the mouse easier for him to use. She asks you to adjust the double-click speed and pointer speed to their lowest settings.

   a. Print images of the two property sheets you use to do this, using the techniques you learned in Tutorial 3. On the printouts, draw arrows pointing to the settings you changed.

   b. Restore the settings to their original speed when you are finished.

Explore ▶ 4. **Exploring Accessibility Options**   This tutorial didn't use the FilterKeys and ToggleKeys options on the Keyboard property sheet in the Accessibility Properties dialog box. Explore these options.

   a. Click the Help button (the question mark ❓ in the upper-right corner of the Accessibility Properties dialog box) and then click these two items on the property sheet to discover what they do.

   b. Write a paragraph describing the circumstances under which you'd use these settings.

5. **Create a New Bitmap on the Desktop**   In this tutorial you created a new text document directly on the desktop. In this tutorial assignment, you'll create a new bitmap image document on your Student Disk. You'll use the mouse to write your signature. Then you'll use this bitmap image as the wallpaper on your desktop.

   a. Use My Computer to open drive A and display the contents of your Student Disk.

   b. Right-click an empty area of the drive A window, point to New, and then click Bitmap Image.

   c. Name the new icon "My Signature."

   d. Open My Signature. What program does Windows 98 use to open this file?

Explore ▶   e. Drag the mouse over the empty canvas to write your signature.

   f. Exit the program, and save your changes. Close the drive A window.

   g. Right-click an empty area of the desktop, click Properties, and then make sure the Background property sheet is visible.

   h. Click the Browse button and select the My Signature bitmap image from your Student Disk. Click the Open button. Your signature appears as the wallpaper. Print an image of the screen, using the techniques you learned in Tutorial 3.

   i. Restore the desktop to its original appearance.

Explore

6. **Explore Your Computer's Desktop Properties**   Answer each of the following questions about the desktop properties on your lab computers.

    a. Open the Power Management Properties dialog box. What power scheme is your computer using, if any? What settings are in effect for that power scheme?

    b. In the Power Management Properties dialog box, click the Advanced tab. Turn on the option to show the power meter on the taskbar. A power icon, like a plug, appears in the tray. Point at the power icon. What message appears? Turn this option off and close the Power Management Properties dialog box.

    c. Open the Display Properties dialog box. What resolution is your monitor using? What other resolution settings are available for your monitor? Drag the slider to find out. If it's an older monitor, it might not have higher resolutions available.

    d. What color palette are you using?

    e. Is Windows 98 using a screen saver on your machine? Which one? After how many minutes of idle time does it engage?

    f. What is your desktop's default color scheme?

    g. Does your desktop display a pattern or wallpaper? Which one?

7. **Customizing Your Desktop**   The ability to place icons directly on the desktop gives you the opportunity to create a truly document-centric desktop. Figure 4-43 shows Beth's desktop after she's had a chance to create all the shortcuts you recommended and to add additional shortcuts for programs, folders, files, and other resources she uses regularly.

Figure 4-43

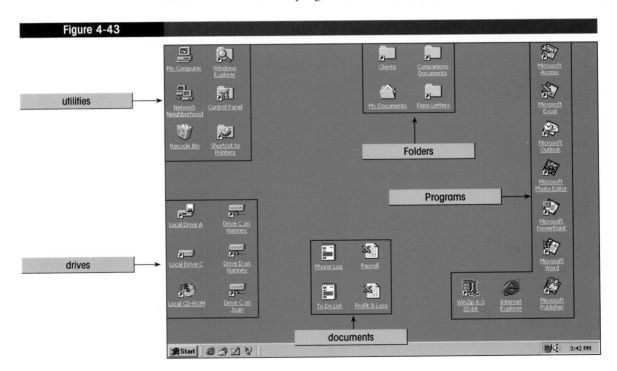

Notice that this desktop has shortcuts not just for drives and documents, but also for programs, utilities, and other Windows 98 objects. The amount of time you save by arranging your desktop in this manner cannot be overestimated, if you spend a lot of time at the computer. If you have your own computer, create a desktop that meets your needs.

Use the following strategy:

    a. Use Windows Explorer to locate the drives on your computer, and then create a shortcut to the local or network drives you use.

b. If you haven't done so already, use Windows Explorer to create folders for the work you usually do on your computer. You might want a folder for each class you're taking, letters you write, projects, or hobbies. Then create a shortcut to each folder you use regularly.

c. Create shortcuts for each document you use repeatedly. Remember not to overcrowd your desktop.

d. If you know how to locate program and utility files, create shortcuts to the programs and utilities you use most often.

e. Group the icons on your desktop so that similar objects are in the same location.

f. Print a copy of your desktop in its final form.

PROJECTS

1. Knowing that you have two years left in your college degree program, your parents decide to splurge and give you a computer, complete with Windows 98, for your birthday. Your parents spent hours getting everything loaded and configured for you, so when you pick it up this weekend you can get right to work on that major project due on Monday. You have about half an hour before your roommate returns with your car, so take out an 8½ by 11 piece of paper, and draw the desktop that will give you the quickest access to all documents, devices, and/or programs needed to carry out the tasks listed below. Indicate shortcut icons with an arrow. Also draw a window showing your floppy disk contents, using the information provided in the "To Do List."

   To Do List

   a. Finish typing paper for American History project, using WordPad.
      —currently saved on floppy
      —will need to print
   b. Finish lab report for Organic Chemistry, using WordPad.
      —currently saved on floppy
      —will need to print
   c. Insert bitmap image saved on floppy into Organic Chemistry lab report.
   d. Review outline for Office Procedures class test, created in WordPad.
      —currently saved on a floppy
      —will need to print

2. You provide computer support at Highland Yearbooks, a company that publishes high school and college yearbooks. Highland has just upgraded to Windows 98, and you'd like to get right to work customizing the desktops of Highland employees for optimal performance. You start with the computer belonging to John McPhee, one of the sales representatives. Create a desktop for John that takes the following circumstances into account. When you are done, print an image of the desktop, using the techniques you learned in the previous tutorial. Then make sure you remove any shortcuts you created and restore the desktop to its original settings. On the back of your printout, write down which options you changed to meet John's needs.

   a. John keeps a Notepad file with a time-date stamp of long-distance phone calls stored on the desktop.
   b. John wants to be able to print the phone log file quickly, without having to open it first.
   c. The company colors at Highland Yearbooks are blue and gold. John would like a blue desktop with gold title bars.
   d. John recently slammed the car door on his fingers and would like to avoid using the mouse until the bruises have healed.

3. In this tutorial you learned ways to work more efficiently. The shortcut menu is another Windows feature that helps you work efficiently. You've learned that a shortcut menu appears when you right-click an object. The operating system, however, changes the shortcut menu depending on the object you right-click and what you are doing with that object. Using WordPad, create a chart that summarizes the features available when you right-click:

    a. an object on the desktop
    b. the taskbar
    c. selected text in a WordPad document
    d. nonselected text in a WordPad document

    Write a paragraph that explains why these shortcut menus are all different from one another.

4. You recently took a part-time job at the local high school, assisting the computer lab manager. After your first day on the job you notice how often the lab manager uses property sheets. You decide to spend the evening exploring property sheets so you can be more useful on the job. For future reference, make a chart in WordPad that describes the information you can glean when you look at the property sheets for:

    a. programs
    b. devices
    c. drives
    d. documents (create your own document on the desktop, if there is none available)

    After your chart, write which tools you used to locate the property sheets for each of these objects.

5. Your cousin, Joey, has Windows 98 on his new computer, but has not taken much time to learn about all of the customizable and time-saving features it offers him. In WordPad, type a letter to Joey, explaining three main features covered in this tutorial. Because you know that he is more likely to try to use these features if he has directions in front of him, include basic instructions on how to access them.

6. You just printed your letter to Joey in Project 5, and then remembered the concept of *document-centric* desktops you learned in this tutorial. You think that if Joey can conceptualize this, it will really expand his Windows 98 horizons. You decide to add a note explaining the difference between the document- and program-centric desktop. Write a paragraph about this difference.

7. You have been asked to give a presentation at a *Computer Users with Special Needs* seminar on campus. You have a half hour to present participants with information on Windows 98 Accessibility Options. In WordPad, prepare a two-page handout for the group that summarizes all the information you want to present, in a clear, concise manner. Use online Help for information about some of the accessibility features not covered in this tutorial. Make sure to include instructions on how Windows 98 users access these options.

8. You are trying to save money on your electric bill and are wondering if you can take advantage of the Windows 98 power management features. Open the Power Management Properties dialog box on your computer (or the one you are using in the lab) and print the screen you see using the techniques you learned earlier in this book. On the printout, write a paragraph describing the power management features available specifically to your computer and how they can help save money.

Explore 9. You would like to learn how to create your own pattern to use as a desktop background.

    a. Open the Pattern dialog box, click any pattern, and then click the Edit Pattern dialog box. The Pattern Editor dialog box opens.

b. Type your name in the Name box and then click anywhere in the Pattern box and observe what happens.

c. Continue to click until you have the design you want, and then print the screen that shows the pattern you designed. Click the Close button to close the Pattern Editor dialog box, and click No so your changes aren't saved.

d. Use online Help to learn how you would save your pattern, apply it, and then remove it from the Pattern list.

QUICK | CHECK ANSWERS

Session 4.1

1. False

2. False

3. You delete not only the icon but also the document.

4. You delete only the icon but not the document.

5. You place a copy of the document on the desktop rather than placing a shortcut to the original document.

Session 4.2

1. False

2. Right-click the object and then click Properties.

3. Here are four: Background, Screen Saver, Appearance, Settings. You could also mention the properties on each of these sheets, such as color palette, resolution, and so on.

4. Activate a screen saver

5. There are 640 pixels across and 480 down.

6. 640 × 480, because it displays the largest objects.

7. It requires extra video memory and runs more slowly.

Session 4.3

1. MouseKeys, which lets you use the number keys on the keypad to take over the function of the mouse

2. You open the shortcut menu.

3. Pointer speed, pointer trails, high contrast, Magnifier

4. 5

5. Ctrl+Esc

6. Alt

7. Magnifier follows the insertion point as you type.

8. Standby reduces the power consumed by your drives and monitor but doesn't turn the computer off. Hibernation turns off your monitor and hard disk and also saves your work and turns off your computer.

B R I N G I N G
THE WORLD WIDE
WEB TO THE DESKTOP

Creating an Active Desktop
at Highland Travel

CASE

Highland Travel

Highland Travel, a touring company that offers guided tour packages to Scotland, recently hired you as an advertising manager. You meet with the company's technical support person, Scott Campbell. After describing the training you'll receive, Scott explains that Highland Travel uses the Internet and the World Wide Web to promote the company, to provide services to clients, and to improve communication among employees. The company recently upgraded its computers to Windows 98, and management wants all employees to be able to use its features to the fullest. When Scott shows you your cubicle at Highland Travel, you are pleased to see that you've been assigned your own Windows 98 computer.

You tell Scott you've heard that one popular feature of Windows 98 is its integration of the operating system with the Web. Scott nods, and tells you that during your first week on the job, you'll go through a training program to familiarize yourself with Windows 98, and particularly with its Web features. He explains that Windows 98 brings the richness of the Web to your desktop with Active Desktop. **Active Desktop** is a technology that transforms the desktop into your own personal "communications central"—not only for launching programs and accessing files, but also for obtaining and displaying any type of Web-based information. The Windows 98 desktop is called "active" because, unlike previous versions of the Windows operating system, the Windows 98 desktop allows you to access the Internet.

Active Desktop manifests itself in several ways on your computer. You can place updatable Web content, such as weather maps, sports news, and stock tickers, on your desktop so it functions as a personalized newspaper. With Active Desktop technology, you learn one method and use one tool—Explorer—to access information anywhere, regardless of location or format. Active Desktop also allows you to view and navigate local files and folders just as you would information on the Web. Scott assures you that the training program will familiarize you with these and more features—and will introduce you to Highland Travel's Web site.

SESSION 5.1

In this session, you will learn how Windows 98 brings the Internet and the World Wide Web to your desktop. You will learn to use the Exploring window to view Web sites. You will activate a link, navigate a Web page with frames, print a Web page, and download a file. *For this tutorial you will need a blank 3½-inch disk.*

The Internet

Microsoft designed Windows 98 so that it integrates use of the Internet with its other functions. For example, in Windows 98 you can choose to extend the way you click on the Internet (single-clicking) to the rest of your computer work. In your training program, you'll discover additional ways that Microsoft has brought the Internet to its Windows 98 operating system.

Scott begins your training by explaining the basic concepts that make the Internet possible. When two or more computers are connected together so that they can exchange information and resources, they create a structure known as a **network**. Networks facilitate the sharing of data and resources among multiple users. Networks can also be connected to each other to share information between computers on different networks; when two or more networks are connected, they create an **internetwork**, or **internet**. "The Internet" (capital "I") has come to refer to the "network of networks" that is made up of millions of computers linked to networks all over the world. Computers and networks on the Internet are connected by fiber-optic cables, satellites, phone lines, and other communication systems, as shown in Figure 5-1. Data travels across these communication systems using whatever route is most efficient.

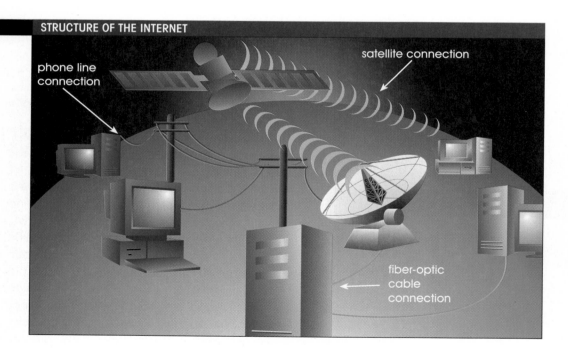

Figure 5-1   STRUCTURE OF THE INTERNET

phone line connection

satellite connection

fiber-optic cable connection

The Internet, by design, is a decentralized structure. There is no Internet "company." Instead, the Internet is a collection of different organizations, such as universities and businesses, that each organize their own information. There are no rules about where information is stored, and no one regulates the quality of information available on the Internet.

Even though the lack of central control can make it hard for beginners to find their way through the resources on the Internet, decentralization has some advantages. The Internet is open to innovation and rapid growth, as different organizations and individuals have the freedom to test new products and services and make them quickly available to a global audience. One such service developed in recent years is the World Wide Web.

The World Wide Web

The World Wide Web makes it easy to share and access data stored on computers around the world with minimal training and support, and for this reason, Microsoft designed Windows 98 to offer easy Web access. The Web is a system of **hypertext documents**—electronic files that contain elements known as **links** that target other parts of a document or other documents altogether. A link can be a word or phrase or a graphic image. Figure 5-2 shows a Colorado touring company hypertext document with several links. Each link targets a separate document that offers more information about the company.

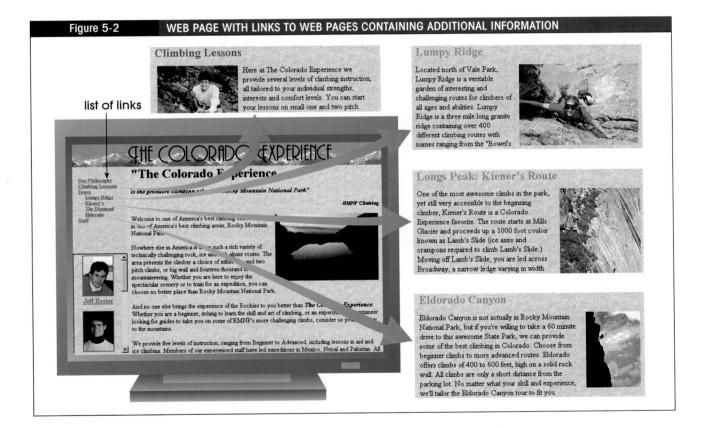

Figure 5-2   **WEB PAGE WITH LINKS TO WEB PAGES CONTAINING ADDITIONAL INFORMATION**

Each hypertext document on the Web is called a **Web page** and is stored on a computer on the Internet called a **Web server**. A Web page can contain links to other Web pages located anywhere on the Internet—on the same computer as the original Web page or on an entirely different computer halfway across the world. The ability to cross-reference other Web pages with links is one of the most important features of the Web.

In using the Windows 98 desktop, you've already seen how the icons on your desktop can look like links, accessible with a single click. When you click a link on a Web page, you can also connect to other file types, including scanned photographs, graphic images, film clips, sounds, online discussion groups, and computer programs.

Navigating Web pages using hypertext is an efficient way to access information. When you read a book you follow a linear progression, reading one page after another. With hypertext, you progress through the pages in whatever order you want. Hypertext allows you to skip from one topic to another, following the information path that interests you, as shown in Figure 5-3.

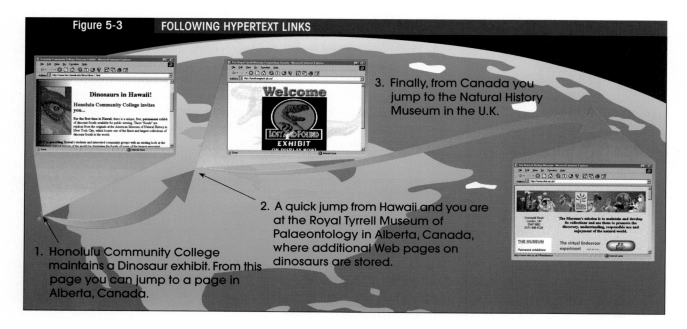

Figure 5-3   FOLLOWING HYPERTEXT LINKS

Dinosaurs in Hawaii!
Honolulu Community College invites you...

3. Finally, from Canada you jump to the Natural History Museum in the U.K.

2. A quick jump from Hawaii and you are at the Royal Tyrrell Museum of Palaeontology in Alberta, Canada, where additional Web pages on dinosaurs are stored.

1. Honolulu Community College maintains a Dinosaur exhibit. From this page you can jump to a page in Alberta, Canada.

Microsoft has taken advantage of this fact by designing its Windows 98 operating system to mimic your experience on the Web. The techniques you'll learn in this tutorial to navigate Web pages are identical to those you learned in previous tutorials to navigate the objects on your computer. Microsoft's goal with Windows 98 is to make the user's experience with local files, network files, and files on computers around the world as uniform as possible.

Browsers

To access documents on the Web, you need a **browser**—software that locates, retrieves, displays, and organizes documents stored on Web servers. Your browser allows you to visit Web sites around the world; view multimedia documents; transfer files, images, and sounds to your computer; conduct searches for specific topics; and run software on other computers. In Figure 5-3, the dinosaur Web documents that you see appear in a browser window. Windows 98 includes a set of communications software called **Internet Explorer** that includes the Internet Explorer browser, as well as tools for other Internet functions such as electronic mail, or **email**, electronic messages sent between users over the Internet. Another popular communications software package is **Netscape Communicator**, which includes the Netscape Navigator browser.

Microsoft has integrated the Internet Explorer browser into the Windows 98 operating system so that its functions are available to many Windows 98 components. For example, the Windows Explorer utility that you used in Tutorial 3 to navigate files on your Student Disk uses Internet Explorer features so that it can function as a browser. The My Computer window works similarly.

There are many advantages to using the same tools to access information regardless of its location. Computer users in the past had to use one tool to access local files, another to access network files, and many additional products to access information on the Internet, such as email, files, and other computers. The Windows 98 operating system allows you to view information anywhere with a single set of techniques.

When you try to view a Web page, your browser locates and retrieves the document from the Web server and displays its contents on your computer. As shown in Figure 5-4, the server stores the Web page in one location, and browsers anywhere in the world can view it.

| Figure 5-4 | USING A BROWSER TO VIEW A WEB DOCUMENT ON A SERVER |

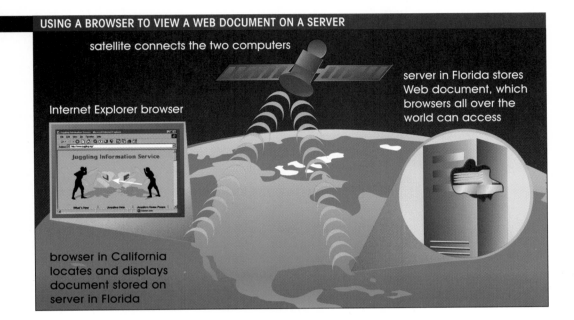

For your browser to connect to the World Wide Web, you must have an Internet connection. In a university setting your connection might come from the campus network on which you have an account. If you are working on a home computer and gaining Internet access from your modem over a phone line, your connection is called a **dial-up connection** and is maintained via an account with an **Internet service provider** (**ISP**), a company that sells Internet access. With a dial-up connection, you are connected to the Internet only as long as your modem "stays on the line," whereas on most institutional networks, you are always connected to the Internet because the network is actually a part of the Internet. If you are using a dial-up connection to connect to your institution's network, you have probably received instructions that help you establish this connection.

Viewing Web Pages

You've already used Windows Explorer to view the files and folders on your disks, and now Scott wants to show you that you can also use it to browse sites on the Web. Scott suggests you start exploring the Web by connecting to the Highland Travel page. When you connect to the Internet without specifying a particular Web page, Windows 98 automatically loads your **home page**—the Web page designated by the operating system as your starting point (you can specify a different home page if you want). Windows 98 designates Microsoft

Corporation's company page as the home page, but you can easily designate a different home page. If you are at an institution such as a university, a home page has probably already been designated for you. A home page can also refer to the Web page that a person, organization, or business has created to give information about itself. Since you are already familiar with Windows Explorer, Scott suggests that you use this tool to view a Web page.

REFERENCE WINDOW   **RW**

Viewing a Web Page with Windows Explorer
- Click the Start button, point to Programs, and then click Windows Explorer.
- Scroll down the All Folders Explorer bar to locate the Internet Explorer icon.
- Click the Internet Explorer icon.

To view your home page in Windows Explorer:

1. Click the **Start** button 🔲Start, point to **Programs**, and then click **Windows Explorer**.

2. If necessary, click the **Maximize** button 🔲 to maximize the Windows Explorer window.

3. If necessary, scroll down the All Folders Explorer bar on the left pane until you locate an entry for Internet Explorer.

   TROUBLE? If the All Folders Explorer bar is not visible, click View, point to Explorer Bar, and then click All Folders.

4. Click the **Internet Explorer** icon 🔲. Wait for a moment as your home page loads and appears in the right pane.

   TROUBLE? If the Internet Explorer icon doesn't appear on the All Folders Explorer bar, Internet service is not set up on your computer. If you are using a lab computer, ask your technical support person for assistance. If you are using your own computer, click the Start button, point to Programs, point to Internet Explorer, click Connection Wizard, read the Welcome dialog box, and proceed through the Wizard by selecting the options that fit your circumstances. If you are not sure which options to choose, check your ISP documentation.

   TROUBLE? If you are in a university setting, you are probably already connected to the Internet, and your home page will appear immediately. If you are working from a computer with a dial-up connection and are not already connected to the Internet, Windows 98 will attempt to connect you. Wait and follow the prompts that appear. If you can't establish a connection, check with your technical support person in the lab, or if you are using your own computer, use Dial-Up Networking as instructed by your ISP, or call your ISP's technical support line for assistance. If an error message appears, it's possible that the server on which your home page is stored is temporarily busy or unavailable.

5. Take a moment to make sure your Exploring window matches the one shown in the figures. Click **View**, point to **Toolbars**, and then make sure the Standard Buttons, Address Bar, and Text Labels options are checked. The Links option should not be checked.

6. If necessary, open the View menu again. Make sure **Status Bar** is checked.

7. So that you can view Web pages in the full Exploring window, hide the All Folders Explorer Bar. Open the View menu again, point to **Explorer Bar**, and then click **None**. Your Exploring window should look like Figure 5-5.

TROUBLE? If your Exploring window shows a different Web page and the Address bar shows a different address, don't worry. Your home page is just different.

Figure 5-5	HOME PAGE DISPLAYED IN EXPLORING WINDOW

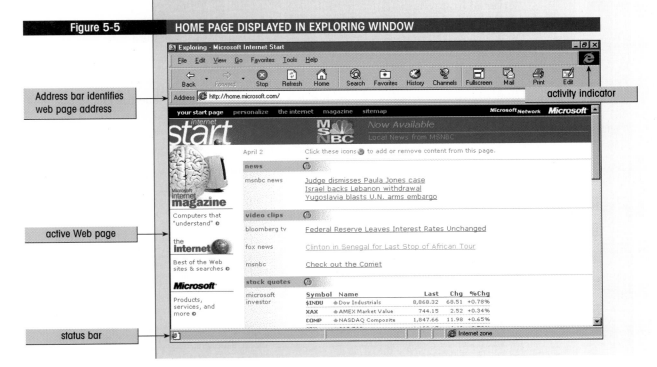

Address bar identifies web page address

activity indicator

active Web page

status bar

Windows Explorer is now functioning as a browser. How does the Exploring window change when you work with Web documents as compared to the local or network documents stored on your Student Disk or hard drives?

■ When you work with local and network drives and folders in the Exploring window, you see in the right pane a list of the files or subfolders those drives and folders contain. To view the contents of a file, you need to click the file icon to start a software application capable of displaying the file contents. But with Windows Explorer you can display Web pages without external software, so when you use it as a browser, you see the actual Web page in the right pane—not just a file icon for that page. If you hide the All Folders Explorer bar, as you just did in the previous set of steps, the Web page fills the entire Exploring window.

■ The Address bar, shown in Figure 5-5, identifies not the local or network drive and folder but the address of the Web page you are viewing.

■ The Back and Forward buttons move you through Web pages you've viewed, instead of through the drives and folders you've viewed.

■ The **activity indicator**, an animation that moves when a Web page is loading, activates so you can see when Windows Explorer is retrieving a page.

■ The status bar shows information about the active Web page rather than about a drive, folder, or file.

Opening a Page on the Web with a URL

When you want to visit a particular site, you need to know its URL. A **URL**, or **uniform resource locator**, is a Web page's address and consists of a protocol identifier, a server address, and a file pathname. Computers use standardized procedures, called **protocols**, to transmit files. Web documents travel between sites using **HyperText Transfer Protocol**, or **HTTP**, so Web page URLs begin with "http://" to identify the protocol they use. The server address tells the exact location of the Internet server and the type of organization that owns and operates it. For example, in the server address "www.northern.edu" the "www" indicates that the server is on the World Wide Web, "northern" indicates the name of the organization that owns the server (Northern University), and "edu" indicates that it's an educational site. Other common site types include "com" for commercial sites, "gov" for government agencies, and "org" for nonprofit organizations. Each file stored on a network server must have a unique pathname, just as files on a disk do. The pathname includes the folder or folders the file is stored in, plus the filename and its extension. The filename extension for Web pages is usually html or just htm. Try deciphering the following URL:

http://www.northern.edu/education/programs.html

The protocol is http, the server address is www.northern.edu, the pathname is education/programs.html, and programs.html is the filename.

Scott tells you that the URL for the Highland Travel page is:

http://www.course.com/NewPerspectives/Win98/Highland

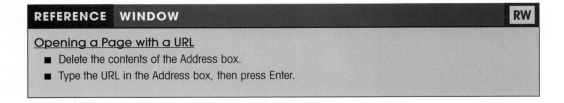

REFERENCE	WINDOW	RW

Opening a Page with a URL
- Delete the contents of the Address box.
- Type the URL in the Address box, then press Enter.

To open a page on the Web with a URL:

1. Click the **Address** box on the Address bar. The contents of the Address box, which should be the URL for your home page, are highlighted. Anything you type will replace the highlighted URL.

   TROUBLE? If the contents of the Address box are not highlighted, highlight the address manually by dragging the mouse from the far left to the far right of the URL. Be sure to highlight the entire URL.

2. Type **http://www.course.com/NewPerspectives/Win98/Highland** in the Address box. Make sure you type the URL exactly as shown.

3. Press **Enter**. Highland Travel's Welcome page opens in the Exploring window. See Figure 5-6.

TROUBLE? If you receive a Not Found error message, the URL might not be typed correctly. Repeat Steps 1 through 3, making sure that the URL in the Address box matches the URL in Step 2. You can correct a minor error by double-clicking in the Address box, using the arrow keys to move to the error, and then making the correction and pressing Enter. If the URL you typed does match the URL in Step 2, and you still receive an error message, it's possible that there is a problem with your Internet connection or with the Web server that stores the Highland Travel page. See the Read This Before You Begin page prior to Tutorial 3, or ask your instructor or technical support person for help.

Figure 5-6	CONNECTING TO THE HIGHLAND TRAVEL SITE

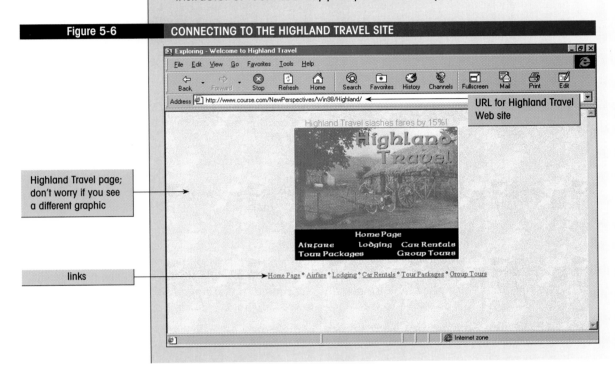

You can access information about the Highland Travel company by navigating through its Web pages. Spend some time doing that now.

Navigating the Web

Once you are connected to the Internet and your browser window is open, you can connect to Web pages by entering a URL in the Address box or by clicking a link. The Highland Travel Web page contains links, so you decide to learn more about the company by activating one of the links on the Welcome page.

Activating a Link

A hypertext link on the Web, like a link in a chain, is a connector between two points. Links can appear in two ways: as text that you click or as a graphic that you click. A **text link** is a word or phrase that is usually underlined and often boldfaced or colored differently. A

graphic link is a graphic image that you click to jump to another location. When you aren't sure whether a graphic image is a link, point to it with the mouse pointer. When you move the mouse pointer over a link—text or graphic—the pointer changes shape from ⬉ to ☝. The ☝ pointer indicates that when you click, you will activate that link and jump to the new location. The destination of the link appears in the status bar, and, for some graphic links, a small identification box appears next to your pointer.

The Highland Travel page contains both text and graphic links. The text links are at the bottom of the page, underlined, and in color. The graphic links are the words in a fancy font at the bottom of the Highland Travel photo, although graphic links are often images or photos. The links give your browser the information it needs to locate the page. When you activate a link, you jump to a new location, the target of the link, which can be another location on the active Web page (for example, often the bottom of a Web page contains a link that jumps you up to the top), a different document or file, or a Web page stored on a remote Web server anywhere in the world. When you activate a link, there are three possible outcomes:

1. You successfully reach the target of the link. The browser contacts the site you want, connects to the site, transfers the data from the site to your computer, and displays the data on your screen.

2. The link's target is busy, perhaps because the server storing the link's target is overwhelmed with too many requests. You can click the Stop button ⊗ to prevent your browser from further attempting to make the connection. You'll have to try a different link, or try this link later.

3. The link points to a target that doesn't exist. Documents are often removed from Web servers as they become obsolete, or they are moved to new locations, and links that point to those documents are not always updated. If you click an obsolete link, a message box appears. If an error message box appears, click the OK button and try a different link. Otherwise click the Back button ⇐ to return to the page you were previously viewing.

The amount of time it takes to complete a link, called the **response time**, can vary, depending upon the number of people trying to connect to the same site, the number of people on the Internet at that time, the site design, and the speed of your Internet connection. In fact, one of the differences you might notice between clicking links on your desktop that target local objects, such as My Computer or a desktop document, and those that target Web pages on the Internet, is the difference in response time. Linking to local objects is usually instantaneous, whereas linking to pages on the Web can take many seconds, because of the time required for the data to be transferred over your Internet connection.

As you can see in Figure 5-7, activating a link starts a multistep process. When you point to a link, the status bar displays a message that it is connecting to the address of the link's target, its URL. When you click the link, the activity indicator animates. The status bar displays a series of messages indicating that your browser is connecting to the site, is waiting for a reply, is transferring data, and finally, is done.

Figure 5-7	ACTIVATING A LINK

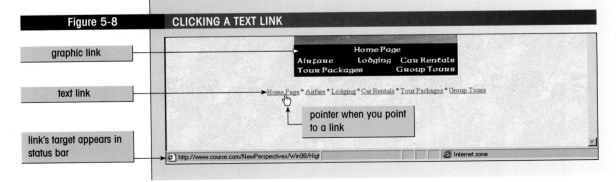

You can see the Web page build as your browser transfers information to the screen in multiple passes. The first wave brings a few pieces to the page, and with each subsequent pass, the browser fills in more detail, until the material is complete. Try activating one of the Highland Travel links to access the company's home page.

To activate a link:

1. Point to the text link **Home Page**—the one at the bottom of the page. (You could also point to the graphic link, the one with the fancy font; both links target the same page). Notice that the pointer changes shape from ⇖ to 🖑, indicating that you are pointing to a hypertext link. The status bar shows the URL for that link. See Figure 5-8.

Figure 5-8	CLICKING A TEXT LINK

graphic link

Home Page
Airfare   Lodging   Car Rentals
Tour Packages   Group Tours

text link

Home Page ° Airfare ° Lodging ° Car Rentals ° Tour Packages ° Group Tours

pointer when you point to a link

link's target appears in status bar

http://www.course.com/NewPerspectives/Win98/High   Internet zone

2. Click the **Home Page** text link to activate the link. The status bar notes the progress of the link. When the status bar displays "Done," the link is complete, and the Web page that is the target of the link appears. See Figure 5-9.

Figure 5-9   COMPLETED LINK

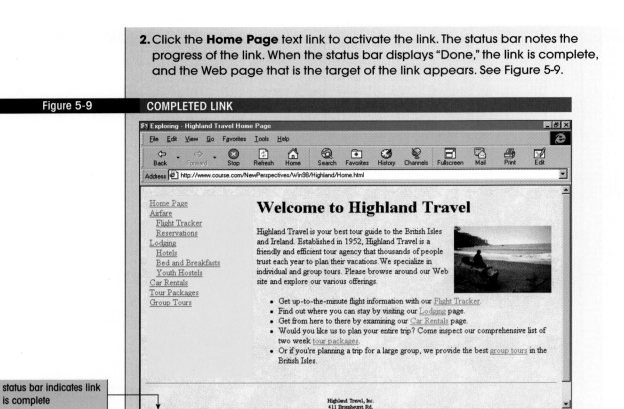

status bar indicates link is complete

Viewing Web Pages with Frames

Scott mentions that if you spend much time using Windows 98 to explore the Web, you'll probably encounter Web pages with frames. A **frame** is a section of the document window that allows Web page designers to organize information more effectively. Each frame can have its own set of scroll bars and can display the contents of a different Web page, as shown in Figure 5-10. The NEC Products page is made up of two pages: the one on the left lists graphic links to other pages, and the one on the right displays the list of product categories.

Figure 5-10	WEB PAGE MADE UP OF FRAMES

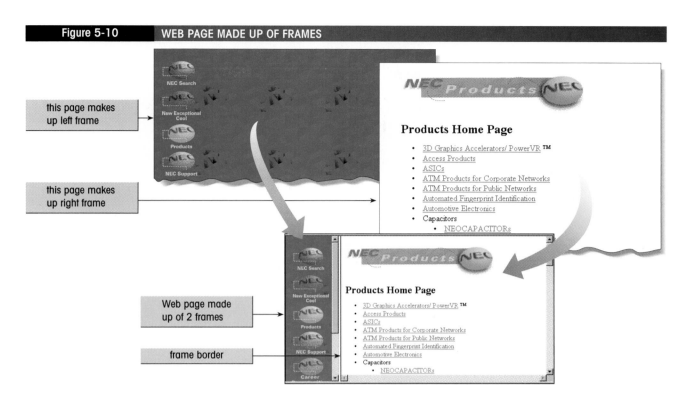

Many Web sites today use frames because they allow the user to see different areas of information simultaneously. When you scroll through the contents of one frame, you do not affect the other frame or frames. Scott suggests you view the Tour Packages page, which employs frames, to learn about this season's Highland Travel tours.

To view a page with frames:

1. Click the **Tour Packages** text link, located in the yellow box on the left of the home page. The Tour Packages page opens. This page consists of four frames that contain the Tour Packages heading at the top, information on the left about the specified tour, a scroll box listing the tour itinerary for each tour on the right, and graphic links to four different tours on the bottom. See Figure 5-11.

   TROUBLE? If no scroll bars appear in the right frame, your screen resolution is so high that it is capable of displaying the entire itinerary. Skip Step 2, and note that in the rest of the Steps you might not find it necessary to scroll.

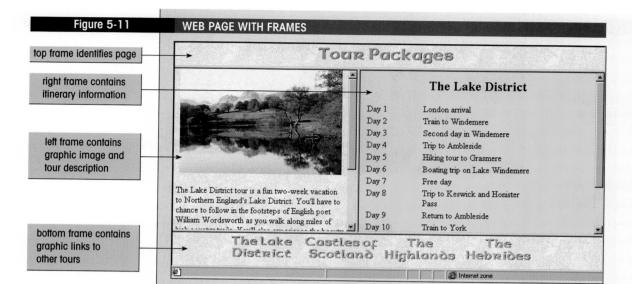

Figure 5-11 **WEB PAGE WITH FRAMES**

top frame identifies page

right frame contains itinerary information

left frame contains graphic image and tour description

bottom frame contains graphic links to other tours

2. Scroll through the information in the right frame. The other three frames remain static while the right frame changes.

3. To change the display, click the **Castles of Scotland** graphic link in the bottom frame. The information in the left frame changes, and the itinerary in the right frame changes. Scroll through the information in the right frame and again notice that the other frames are static.

4. Click **The Highlands** graphic link to view its itinerary, and then click **The Hebrides** graphic link. You have now viewed information on all four tours.

By using frames, the designer of this Web page made it possible for you to view only the information you choose to view.

Returning to a Previously-Viewed Page

In Tutorial 3 you saw that the Exploring window allowed you to navigate the devices and folders on your local and network drives, using the Back and Forward buttons. These buttons are also found in most browsers. The Back button returns you to the Web page you were most recently viewing, and the Forward button reverses the effect of the Back button. Both the Back and Forward buttons contain lists of visited sites; you can return to those sites by clicking the list arrow to the right of either button and clicking the site.

To return to a previously-viewed Web page:

1. Click the **Back** button ⬅ repeatedly, to navigate back through the tour itineraries you viewed. You return to the Highland Travel page, the page you were visiting before you viewed the Tours framed page.

TROUBLE? If you click the small arrow to the right of the Back button, a list opens. Click the arrow again to close the list, and repeat Step 1. This time make sure you click ⬅.

2. Click ⬅ until the Back button dims, indicating that you have reached your starting point, probably your hard drive (usually the first location to open when you start Windows Explorer). Now try moving forward again to return to the Tours page.

3. Click the **Forward** button ➡ repeatedly until the Forward button dims, indicating that you are looking at the last page you visited.

4. Click the **Home** button 🏠 to return to your home page.

5. Now, you'll use the Back list to see how you can return to a page you've visited without having to navigate through all the pages you've seen in a given session. Click the small arrow to the right of the Back button. The Back list opens. See Figure 5-12.

| Figure 5-12 | ACCESSING A PAGE VIA THE BACK LIST |

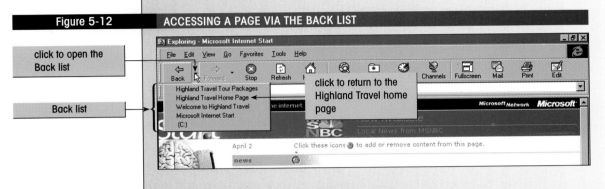

click to open the Back list

Back list

6. Click **Highland Travel Home Page** to return to the Highland Travel home page.

Scott mentions that for information on other methods of navigating Web pages, you can search the Help files for the Search, History, and Favorites features. He does not have time to show you all of these features, but you'll have the chance to work with the Favorites feature in Session 5.2.

Printing a Web Page

Although reducing paper consumption is an advantage of browsing information online, sometimes you'll find it useful to print a Web page. For example, you might want to refer to the information later when you don't have computer access. Although Web pages can be any size, printers tend to use 8½ × 11-inch sheets of paper. When you print, your browser automatically reformats the text of the Web page to fit the paper dimensions. Because lines might break at different places or text size might be altered, the printed Web page might be longer than you expect. You can specify the number of pages you want to print in the Print dialog box. You decide to print the first page of the Highland Travel Web page.

To print a Web page:

1. Click **File** and then click **Print**.

2. If necessary, click the **Pages** option button, type **1** in the from box, press the **Tab** key to move to the to box, and then type **1**. This indicates that you want to print only the page range 1 to 1 of the document, or just the first page of the document.

3. Click the **OK** button to print the first page of the Web page.

Some printers are set up to print headers and footers in addition to the Web page itself, so when you retrieve the page from your printer, you might find the page's title, its URL, the date, and other similar information at the top and bottom of the page.

Downloading a File

Scott explains that Windows 98 also makes it easy to transfer files stored on the Internet to your computer. **Downloading** is the process of saving a file located on a **remote computer** (a computer located elsewhere on the Internet) to your own computer. The method you use to download information you find on the Web depends on how the file appears on the Web page. If you want to save the Web page itself, you use the Save As command on the File menu. If you want to save a graphic image located directly on the Web page, you save it by right-clicking the object you want and then using the Save Picture As command that appears in the shortcut menu.

You liked the Lake District graphic on the Tours page, so you decide to download it so you can use it as a background image on your desktop.

To download a file:

1. Write "Disk 3—Windows 98 Tutorial 5 Student Disk" on the label of a blank, formatted floppy disk. Insert your Student Disk into drive A.

2. Return to the Tour Packages page and make sure The Lake District itinerary is visible.

3. Right-click the Lake District graphic to open its shortcut menu. See Figure 5-13.

Figure 5-13	DOWNLOADING A GRAPHIC IMAGE

click to open Save dialog box

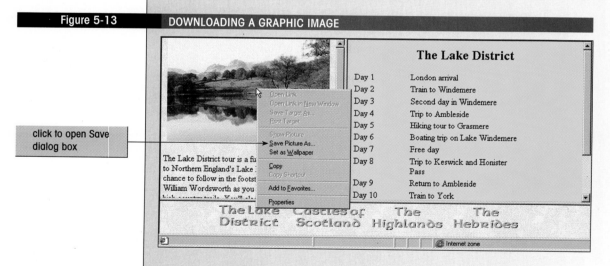

4. Click **Save Picture As**.

5. Click the **Save in** list arrow, and click **3½ Floppy (A:)**. The name "lake" should appear in the File name box, and the type should be JPEG, a common graphic image type on the Web.

TROUBLE? If a name other than "lake" appears in the File name box, replace it with the name "lake".

6. Click the **Save** button. Windows 98 transfers the file over the Internet from the Tour Packages Web page to your Student Disk.

7. Close the Exploring window.

The file is now on your Student Disk, and you could open it in a graphics software program such as Paint and work with it there. Note that content appearing on Web pages is often copyrighted, and you should always make sure you have permission to use it before doing so. Since this graphic is owned by Highland Travel, Scott tells you that you can use it.

QUICK CHECK

1. What is a home page?

2. The address of a Web page is called a(n) _____.

3. Someone has given you the URL of an interesting Web page. How can you view that Web page?

4. When you see a URL with "edu" in it, what can you assume about that site's Web server?

5. You can easily flip through Web pages using the _____ and _____ buttons.

6. How can you download a graphic image that you find on the Web?

SESSION 5.2

In this session you will learn how to set up your computer so that it delivers Web page content to your desktop without your having to go look for it. You will subscribe to a Web site and a channel, add updatable Active Desktop items to your desktop, and learn how to schedule updates.

Subscribing to a Web Site with Internet Explorer

Scott now wants to show you how you can receive content from the Web without having to go look for it. When you connected to the Highland Travel Web page in Session 5.1, you had to go looking for it. You were told where to find the information (that is, you were given a URL), and then you went to that location and "pulled" information from the Web server onto your own computer.

Newer technology, however, makes it possible for you to subscribe to information sites, just as you would to a magazine or newspaper, so that information is delivered to your doorstep—your computer—on a schedule, without your having to seek it. When you **subscribe** to a Web site, you set up your computer so that it checks the site at specific times to see if it has changed. If the site has changed, Explorer can notify you or can download the changed page so you can view it later without having to actually visit the site or be connected to the Internet—this is called **offline viewing**.

To subscribe to a site, you add it to your **Favorites folder**, a folder that contains a list of your favorite places to visit, including Web pages or local documents. When you add a Web page or any file to your Favorites folder, you can access it from the Favorites list, available through all browser windows and from the Start menu.

When you add a page to the Favorites folder, you have three choices:

■ Add the page to your list of favorites without subscribing to it. You then can return to the page without having to type its URL in—you simply select the page from the Favorites list. Windows 98 does not, however, check for updated content.

■ Subscribe to the page and be notified when the page is updated. When Windows 98 discovers that the page has changed, it adds a red gleam ✳ to the page icon. You can also customize your subscription so that you're notified by e-mail when the page has changed; the e-mail message will contain a link to the page so you can view it immediately.

■ Subscribe to the page, be notified when the page is updated, and download the page for offline viewing.

Why is subscribing useful? Suppose you habitually visit 5 or 10 favorite Web sites every day—perhaps a news service such as CNN, the National Geographic site, a recipe site that offers new recipes every day, a page that reports ski conditions for your area's cross-country ski trails, and so on. You could go through the steps of connecting to all those sites every day, one at a time, and perusing their contents—or you could subscribe to each site and schedule them all to update first thing in the morning while you get ready for work. Windows 98 will connect automatically to sites you subscribed to on the schedule you specified and will download the Web pages of any sites that have changed. You can view the downloaded pages later, without having to be connected to the Internet. If you own a portable computer, instead of grabbing a newspaper to read for the daily train commute to work, you could browse through your Web subscriptions instead.

Scott suggests that you subscribe to the Highland Travel page, this time using Internet Explorer rather than Windows Explorer. You'll find that Internet Explorer looks just like the Exploring window you worked with in Session 5.1.

To subscribe to a site:

1. Click the **Start** button 🅁Start, point to **Programs**, point to **Internet Explorer**, and then click **Internet Explorer**.

2. Click the **Address** box to select its contents, and then type **http://www.course.com/NewPerspectives/Win98/Highland** in the Address box. Press **Enter**. The Highland Travel page loads.

   TROUBLE? If the page looks different than it did before, don't worry. It was designed to be updatable.

3. To add the page to your Favorites folder, click **Favorites** on the Internet Explorer menu bar, and then click **Add to Favorites**. The Add Favorite dialog box opens, giving you the opportunity to decide whether you want to just add the page to your Favorites list or to subscribe to the current page. See Figure 5-14.

Figure 5-14	SUBSCRIBING TO A WEB PAGE

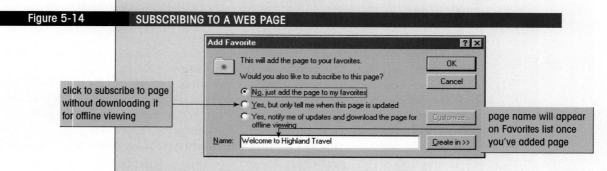

click to subscribe to page without downloading it for offline viewing

page name will appear on Favorites list once you've added page

4. Since you want to subscribe to the page, click the **Yes, but only tell me when this page is updated** option button.

5. Click the **OK** button. Now you'll test the entry you just made to see how easily you can return to a page in the Favorites folder.

6. Click the **Home** button 🏠 to return to your home page.

7. Click **Favorites** on the menu bar. The Welcome to Highland Travel page appears in the Favorites list. See Figure 5-15.

Figure 5-15	FAVORITES LIST

page you just added to Favorites list

Favorites list; yours might look different

8. Click **Welcome to Highland Travel**. You return to the Highland Travel page. Unlike pages that appear in the Back and Forward lists, which are only available until you close Explorer, this page will stay on your Favorites list until you remove it.

9. Close the Internet Explorer browser.

You are now subscribed to the Welcome to Highland Travel page, and Windows 98 will notify you if the page has changed, by placing the red gleam icon ✳ next to the page icon. You can subscribe to any Web site, although some sites might prevent you from doing so, because they might not be set up to handle a large number of automated visits.

Bringing Live Content to the Desktop with Active Desktop Items

Subscribing is the most basic level of a technology called Webcasting. With **Webcasting**, information arrives at your computer without your having to go get it. Basic subscribing, however, is not without problems—for one thing, with basic subscribing you have no control over what kind of content you will receive from the site you've subscribed to; Windows 98 simply downloads it all. Thus many Web site authors are developing their sites to provide more advanced Webcasting technology, called **push technology**, which allows both authors and subscribers to gain more control over content delivery and schedule. Subscribing on its own is not true "push technology."

True push technology occurs when the author of a Web site modifies the site so that it sends information to subscribers on its own, without requiring a subscriber's computer to do the searching.

Scott explains that you're going to begin your exploration of push technology by adding live content to the desktop—Active Desktop items. An **Active Desktop item** is an object that you place on your desktop that receives updates from content providers who push the updates to subscribers on a schedule. For example, you could place a selection of Active Desktop items on your desktop, as in Figure 5-16.

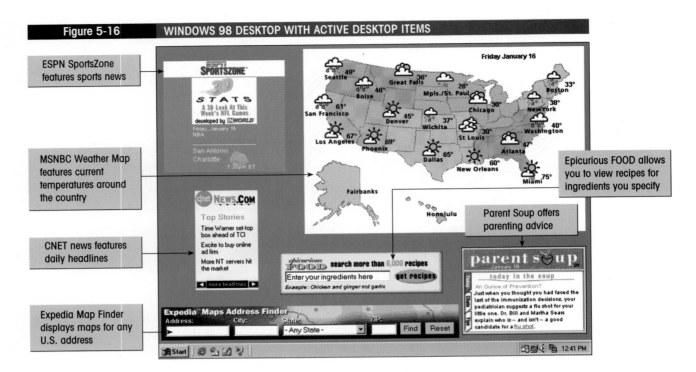

| Figure 5-16 | WINDOWS 98 DESKTOP WITH ACTIVE DESKTOP ITEMS |

ESPN SportsZone features sports news

MSNBC Weather Map features current temperatures around the country

CNET news features daily headlines

Expedia Map Finder displays maps for any U.S. address

Epicurious FOOD allows you to view recipes for ingredients you specify

Parent Soup offers parenting advice

Every morning when this user checks her desktop, each component will have been automatically updated (if, that is, she has set the update schedules that way). The weather map will show the morning's weather instead of weather from the night before, the news service will display the most recent news, and other Active Desktop items will update in a similar fashion. This user has created her own "mini-newspaper," made up of only the information she's interested in.

Some Active Desktop items are interactive, allowing you to enter information and receive a response. The Epicurious FOOD Active Desktop item, for example, allows you to enter ingredients, such as beans and rice, and when you click the Get Recipes button, Internet Explorer starts and displays recipes from the Epicurious site containing those ingredients. Likewise, if you enter a location in the Expedia Maps Address Finder Active Desktop item and then click the Find button, a map will appear showing the location you specified. Microsoft maintains a collection of Active Desktop items at its Active Desktop Gallery Web site.

Enabling Active Desktop

To add Active Desktop items to your desktop, you must first enable the Active Desktop feature, which allows the desktop to receive pushed information.

To enable Active Desktop:

1. Right-click a blank area of the desktop, then point to **Active Desktop**.

2. Make sure the **View As Web Page** option is checked.

It might seem that nothing has changed, but your desktop is now poised to receive whatever information you request, on your schedule.

Adding an Active Desktop Gallery Item to the Desktop

You add an item from the Active Desktop Gallery to your desktop using the Web tab of the Display Properties dialog box. Windows 98 automatically locates and displays the Microsoft Active Desktop Gallery site in your browser. Scott suggests you add a weather map to your desktop.

To add a weather map from the Active Desktop Gallery to your desktop:

1. Right-click a blank area of the desktop.

2. Point to **Active Desktop** and then click **Customize my Desktop**. The Display Properties dialog box opens, displaying the Web tab.

3. Click the **New** button. When you are prompted to open the Active Desktop Gallery, click the **Yes** button. If you are not connected to the Web, Windows 98 connects you. Internet Explorer opens and loads Microsoft's Active Desktop Gallery page. Maximize the Internet Explorer window, if necessary.

   TROUBLE? If Windows 98 has difficulty connecting you, follow the prompts or acknowledge the messages on the screen. If the connection fails, try again later. The Microsoft server might be busy.

4. Scroll down the icon list if necessary, and then click the **Weather** icon, shown in Figure 5-17.

5. Click **MSNBC Weather Map**. After a moment, the weather map appears, along with a button entitled "Add to Active Desktop." See Figure 5-17.

   TROUBLE? If the MSNBC Weather Map doesn't appear, choose a different Active Desktop item.

Figure 5-17	ADDING AN ACTIVE DESKTOP ITEM

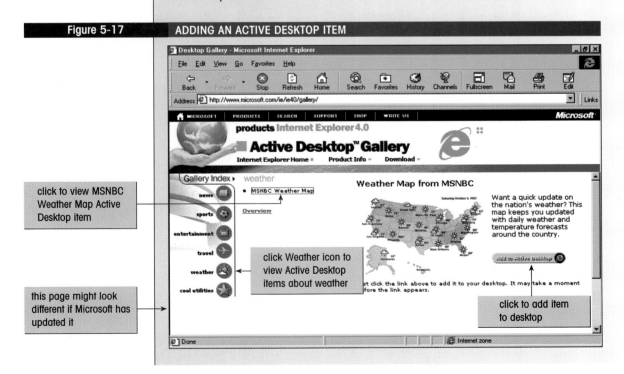

click to view MSNBC Weather Map Active Desktop item

click Weather icon to view Active Desktop items about weather

this page might look different if Microsoft has updated it

click to add item to desktop

6. Click the **Add to Active Desktop** button. Then click the **Yes** button if a Security Alert dialog box asks if you want to add this item to your active desktop. A dialog box appears that asks you to confirm the procedure and gives you the opportunity to change the default schedule.

7. Click the **OK** button to confirm the procedure and accept the default schedule. The Downloading Subscriptions dialog box appears, informing you of the download progress. The download process might take one or several minutes, depending on the speed of your Internet connection.

8. Once the download is complete, close your browser. The item you added appears on your desktop. See Figure 5-18.

TROUBLE? If the Active Desktop item appears but doesn't look like a weather map, the MSNBC site might be busy. A desktop item will still appear, but it won't include the map. Continue with the steps, using the Active Desktop item.

TROUBLE? If scroll bars appear around your Active Desktop item, don't worry. You'll learn momentarily how to resize it.

| Figure 5-18 | WEATHER MAP ACTIVE DESKTOP ITEM |

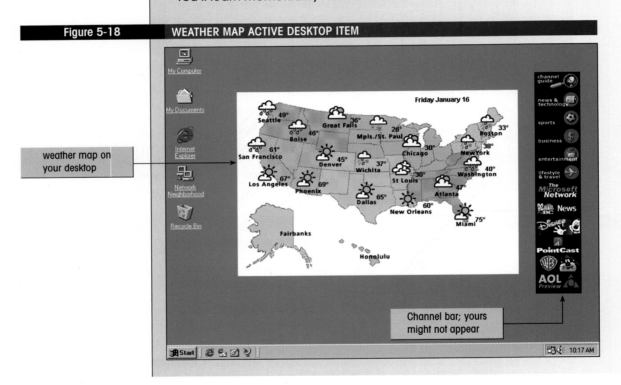

The weather map shows the temperature for sites around the country. This item has been assigned a daily update schedule of 12:00 a.m. (You'll learn how to check the update schedule shortly.) So if you check the weather map every day after 12:00 a.m., you'll find it has been automatically updated (if you are connected to the Internet).

Moving Active Desktop Items

When an Active Desktop item is on your desktop, it occupies a rectangular block that seems to be a part of the background. To move or resize an Active Desktop item, you must first point to it to select it. When an Active Desktop item is selected, a title bar and border appear, which you can manipulate to move and resize the item as you would any other Windows 98 window (such as the My Computer window). Practice moving Active Desktop items by moving the weather map.

To move the weather map:

1. Point to the top of the weather map. A gray border appears around the entire Active Desktop item, and a bar, similar to a window's title bar, appears at the top. This bar includes a Close button ☒ and a list arrow on the left that opens a menu for that item. See Figure 5-19.

   TROUBLE? If the title bar doesn't appear, move the pointer closer to the top of the Active Desktop item. The title bar should appear just before the pointer reaches the top of the item.

| Figure 5-19 | ACTIVATING AN ACTIVE DESKTOP ITEM |

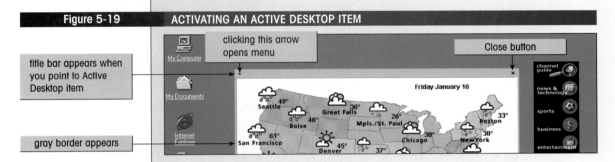

2. Drag the title bar to the left. The entire weather map moves.

Resizing Active Desktop Items

When you activate an Active Desktop item, a border also appears. You use the border to resize the item. For example, you drag the left border to the left to widen the item, you drag the top border up to lengthen the item, or you drag any corner out to enlarge both dimensions simultaneously.

To resize the weather map:

1. Point to the lower-right corner of the weather map. The gray border appears, and the mouse pointer changes from ↖ to ↘.

2. Drag the corner border to the lower right. The Active Desktop item expands in size.

You can also shrink Active Desktop items by dragging borders in instead of out. When you shrink an item so that it can no longer display all the relevant information, scroll bars appear that let you scroll through the information when the item is active. Try shrinking the weather map and then using its scroll bar.

To shrink the weather map:

1. Point to the bottom border of the weather map. The pointer changes from ⇖ to ↕.

2. Drag the bottom border up until some of the map is hidden. A scroll bar appears.

3. Point to the bottom scroll arrow and hold down the mouse button. The weather map scrolls down so you can see the hidden portion.

4. Resize the weather map so that the scroll bar disappears.

Although you can shrink Active Desktop items to make more room on the desktop, keep in mind that Active Desktop items usually display in a default size that displays the right amount of information. If your monitor is set to a resolution of 640 × 480, you might find that when you resize the items so they fit, you can't see enough of each item for it to be meaningful. Adding more than two or three Active Desktop items is impractical unless you have a large monitor at a high resolution.

Closing and Removing Active Desktop Items

When you close an Active Desktop item, you aren't removing it from your system—just from your desktop. To remove an Active Desktop item from your system, you need to open the Display Properties dialog box. Now that you've experimented a little with Active Desktop items, you decide to first close the weather map and then remove it entirely from your desktop.

To close the weather map Active Desktop item:

1. Point to the top of the weather map so that it is activated and the title bar appears.

2. Click the **Close** button ☒. The weather map disappears from the desktop.

Although it is not displayed on your desktop, the weather map Active Desktop item is still on your hard drive and available to you from the Web tab on the Display Properties dialog box. The Web tab lists your current Active Desktop items. If an item's check box is selected, it appears on the desktop and is updated according to the update schedule. If the check box is not selected, the item will not appear on your desktop. If you want to remove an Active Desktop item from your computer, you delete it from your Active Desktop item list on the Web tab.

Now that you know how to use Active Desktop items, Scott suggests you remove the weather map from your computer.

To remove the weather map from your computer:

1. Right-click a blank area of the desktop, point to **Active Desktop**, and then click **Customize my Desktop**.

2. Click the **MSNBC Weather** item—not the check box. The MSNBC Weather item should appear highlighted.

3. Click the **Delete** button. Click **Yes** if asked if you are sure.

4. Click the **OK** button to close the Display Properties dialog box.

The desktop is now restored to its original state.

Subscribing to a Channel

The Active Desktop items you just worked with originate from Web sites called channels. A **channel** is a Web site that broadcasts its content to subscribers. When you subscribed to an Active Desktop item, you were accessing only a tiny part of a channel. When you subscribe to a channel, however, you gain access to an entire Web site that contains content that you can view according to your preferences. In developing Windows 98, Microsoft worked with many leading content providers to develop a collection of channels. This collection is available through the **Channel bar**, an organized list of channels and channel categories. You view channels not on the desktop but in the browser, and, as with any subscription, channel content can be downloaded to your computer for offline viewing.

To use the Channel bar, you must first make sure it is visible on your screen.

To view the Channel bar:

1. Right-click a blank area of the desktop, point to **Active Desktop**, then click **Customize my Desktop**.

2. On the Web tab, click the **Internet Explorer Channel Bar** check box if it is not already selected.

3. Click the **OK** button. The Channel bar appears. See Figure 5-20.

   TROUBLE? If your Channel bar contains different objects, don't worry. Your Channel bar might have been modified.

| Figure 5-20 | CHANNEL BAR |

opens Microsoft's Active Channel Guide

categories of channels

individual channels

The Channel bar contains channels available from the Microsoft Web Active Channel Guide site and individual channels that you can add and delete. To view a channel, you click its button in the Channel bar, and Internet Explorer opens to display the channel content. To receive updated content from the channel, you need to subscribe to it.

Scott suggests you explore the Lifestyle & Travel channels and subscribe to one that might help you with your work at Highland Travel. When you choose a category, the Microsoft Active Channel Guide opens, which helps you select and subscribe to the channels you want. Once you select a channel, a button labeled Add Active Channel appears, which you click to initiate the channel subscription procedure. You then have three choices, similar to the choices you have when you subscribe to a nonchannel Web site, as you did earlier in this session:

■ Add the channel to the Channel bar without subscribing to it.

■ Subscribe to the channel and be notified when updates occur, via the red gleam icon *.

■ Subscribe to the channel, be notified of updates via *, and download the channel for offline viewing.

Some channels offer Active Desktop items; they include an Add to Active Desktop button, which you can click to subscribe just to the Active Desktop item and not to the entire channel.

When you connect to the Active Channel Guide, it appears in the Internet Explorer browser in **Fullscreen mode**, which allows the browser to occupy the entire screen. You can click the Fullscreen button to switch to and from Fullscreen mode.

To subscribe to a Channel bar channel:

1. Click the **Lifestyle & Travel** button on the Channel bar. The Active Channel Guide opens to the Lifestyle & Travel page, which displays icons for channels you can add. See Figure 5-21.

   TROUBLE? If a Welcome to Active Channels message box appears, asking if you want a quick overview, click the No button. The Lifestyle & Travel button should then open.

Figure 5-21	ACTIVE CHANNEL GUIDE

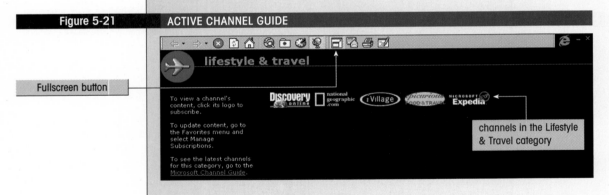

2. Click the **Discovery Online** icon to access the Discovery Online channel.

   TROUBLE? If you receive an error message, click the appropriate button to acknowledge the message. Try continuing with the steps. If you can't, the Discovery Online channel might be busy. Try again later, or try a different channel.

   TROUBLE? If a dialog box appears, asking you to insert the CD-ROM, click the Connect button and do not insert the CD-ROM.

   TROUBLE? The Channels Explorer bar moves into view whenever you point to the left side of the screen. If it obscures your view, click its Close button ⊠ to close it.

3. Click the **Add Active Channel** button. The Modify Channel Usage dialog box opens. See Figure 5-22.

TROUBLE? If the Add Active Channel button doesn't appear, search the entire page; it might appear as a link. Otherwise, click the Back button ⇐ and choose a different channel. Substitute that channel for the Discovery Online channel throughout this tutorial.

Figure 5-22	SUBSCRIBING TO A CHANNEL

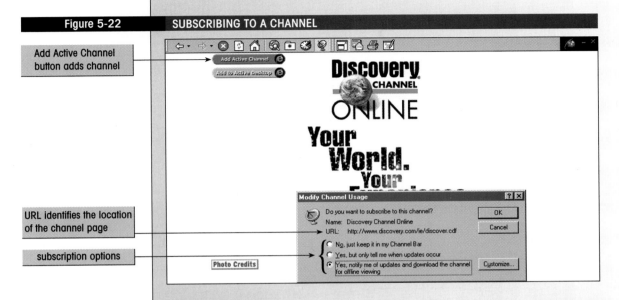

Add Active Channel button adds channel

URL identifies the location of the channel page

subscription options

4. Click the **Yes, but only tell me when updates occur** option button, and then click the **OK** button. The browser opens and displays the channel contents.

TROUBLE? If you are asked if you want to replace your current screen saver with the Channel Screen Saver, click the No button.

Scheduling Updates

Channel designers assign a default update schedule, perhaps daily or hourly, to the channels they maintain. You can accept the default schedule, or you can customize the update to retrieve information more or less frequently, so the content is updated at a time most convenient to you. Windows 98 manages the list of sites to which you've subscribed from the Subscriptions folder, available from any browser window. You can manage updates from there.

Viewing Update Schedules

Most of the time you'll probably just want to accept the publisher's update schedule, but there are situations in which you might want your subscriptions to update at a specific time. For example, if you want to read all your updates over your lunch hour, you might schedule each update for 11:30 a.m., download the updates for offline viewing, and read the updates during lunch.

To view a subscribed object's update schedule:

1. In the browser window, click the **Fullscreen** button to view the entire window.

2. Click **Favorites** on the menu bar, and then click **Manage Subscriptions**. The Subscriptions folder opens, listing the pages, channels, or Active Desktop items to which you are subscribed. There should be at least two items in your Subscriptions folder: the Welcome to Highland Travel page you subscribed to earlier, and the Discovery Channel Online channel.

   TROUBLE? If your view does not show subscription details, click View and then click Details.

3. Right-click the **Welcome to Highland Travel** subscription, and then click **Properties**. The object's Properties dialog box opens, identifying the URL of the channel and the status of the current scheduling and update settings. See Figure 5-23.

Figure 5-23	VIEWING SUBSCRIPTION STATUS

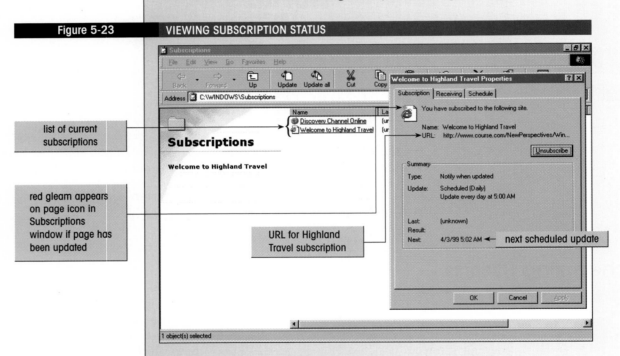

list of current subscriptions

red gleam appears on page icon in Subscriptions window if page has been updated

URL for Highland Travel subscription

next scheduled update

4. Click the **Receiving** tab. On this tab, you can change receiving settings, such as notification options and password settings, if applicable.

5. Click the **Schedule** tab. On this tab, you can time updates differently from the publisher's timing.

6. Click the **Cancel** button so you don't make any inadvertent changes.

Updating a Channel Manually

You can also update your scheduled objects manually—one at a time, or all at once.

To update objects manually:

1. Right-click **Welcome to Highland Travel**, and then click **Update Now**. The Downloading Subscriptions dialog box opens, and Internet Explorer begins downloading any updated information. When the download is complete, the Downloading Subscriptions dialog box closes automatically. Once you've downloaded an update, you can click the object's icon to open and view it. If the subscription has updated content, a red gleam icon ✳ appears. See Figure 5-24.

| Figure 5-24 | UPDATING A SUBSCRIPTION |

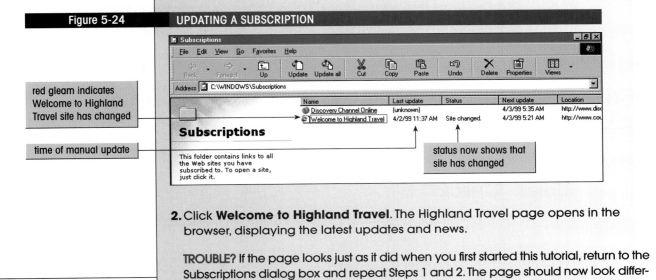

red gleam indicates Welcome to Highland Travel site has changed

time of manual update

status now shows that site has changed

2. Click **Welcome to Highland Travel**. The Highland Travel page opens in the browser, displaying the latest updates and news.

   TROUBLE? If the page looks just as it did when you first started this tutorial, return to the Subscriptions dialog box and repeat Steps 1 and 2. The page should now look different. You can repeat Steps 1 and 2 once again, to see yet a third version of this page. Normally you don't have to update a subscription more than once, but this Web page was designed to illustrate the concept of updating. Because it is a simulation, you might need to update more than once, depending on the circumstances.

You can also update all your subscriptions at once by clicking the Update all button 🔄 on the Subscriptions folder toolbar. Depending on the number of your subscriptions, this can be time-consuming.

Unsubscribing

Before you proceed, you should remove Highland Travel from your Favorites folder, so that you leave the folder in the same state you found it, and you should unsubscribe from the sites you subscribed to.

To restore your Favorites folder and Subscriptions folder to their original state:

1. Click **Favorites** on the browser menu bar.

2. Click **Organize Favorites**. The Organize Favorites dialog box opens.

3. Right-click **Welcome to Highland Travel** in the Favorites list, and then click **Delete**. You have now deleted it from the Favorites list. You still need to delete it from the Subscriptions dialog box.

TROUBLE? If you are asked if you are sure, click the Yes button.

TROUBLE? If you don't see Welcome to Highland Travel in the Favorites list, scroll to the bottom of the list.

4. Click the **Close** button and then close the browser.

5. In the Subscriptions folder, right-click **Welcome to Highland Travel** and then click **Delete**. Click the **Yes** button to confirm the deletion. Now you have deleted your subscription.

6. Delete the Discovery Channel Online channel subscription in the same way.

7. Close the Subscriptions window.

8. Now remove the Channel bar from your desktop, if it wasn't there when you started this session. Right-click the desktop, point to **Active Desktop**, click **Customize my Desktop**, click the **Internet Explorer Channel Bar** check box to remove the check mark, and then click the **OK** button. Your desktop is restored to its original state.

QUICK CHECK

1. Can you subscribe to a Web site that is not a channel? Explain your answer.

2. What is offline viewing?

3. What is push technology?

4. An object on the desktop that receives pushed content from a channel is called a(n) _____.

5. What is the difference between an Active Desktop item and a channel?

6. How do you know if a page or channel you've subscribed to has updated content?

SESSION 5.3

In this session, you will learn to place a Web page on your desktop background and work with the features it contains. Then you'll learn to control folder options and to customize your folders with background images and Web content. Finally, you'll modify the taskbar by adding and removing toolbars and toolbar buttons.

Choosing an HTML File as a Background

Web Pages & HTML

In Tutorial 4 you worked with the Desktop Properties dialog box to change your desktop's color and pattern, and then to display a graphic image file on your desktop. Active Desktop technology extends your control over your desktop's background by allowing you to use Web pages as wallpaper. To create Web pages, you use a language called **HTML**, which stands for Hypertext Markup Language. HTML uses special codes to describe how the page should appear on the screen. Figure 5-25 shows a Web page as it appears on your computer screen, and behind it, the underlying HTML code. It is this code that the browser interprets when a Web page is viewed.

Figure 5-25	WEB PAGE AND THE HTML CODE IT EMPLOYS

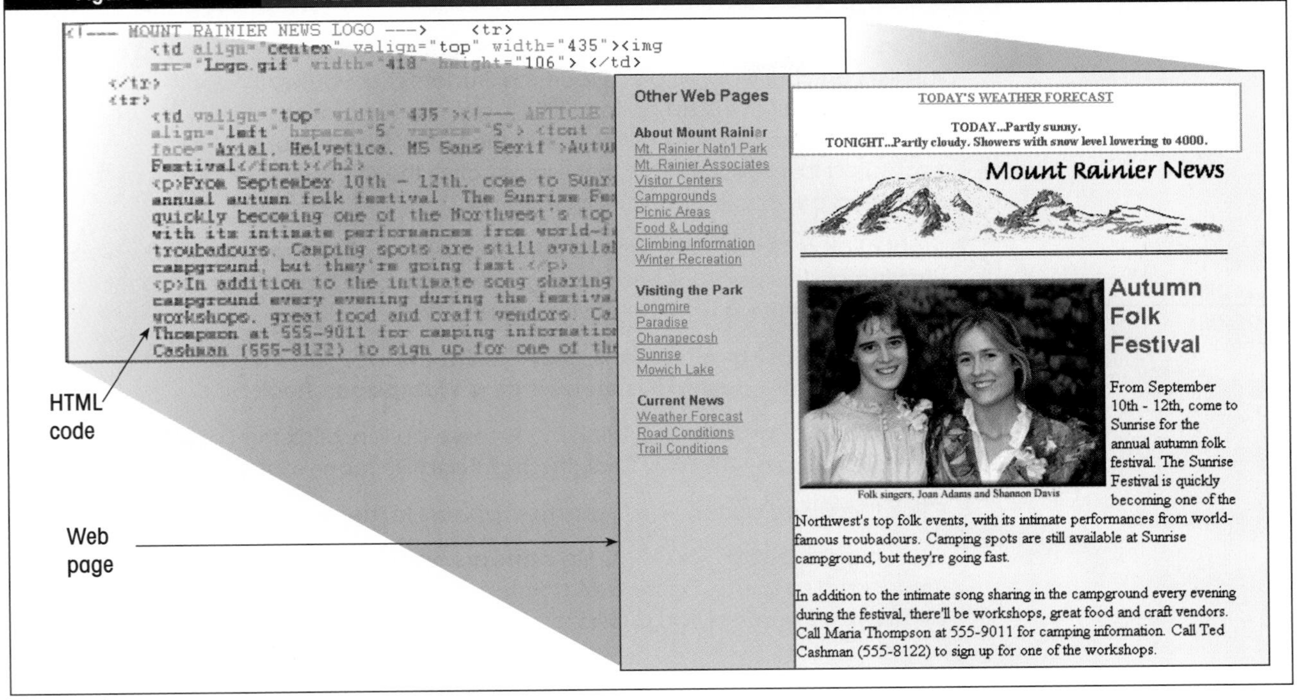

HTML code

Web page

A document created using the HTML language is called an **HTML file** and is saved with the htm or html extension. Most Web pages are HTML files.

Because Windows 98 enables you to use an HTML file as your background wallpaper, your Windows 98 desktop background can feature text, clip art, photos, animated graphics, links, and multimedia objects such as sound and video. Your desktop can also include **applets**, programs attached to the Web page that extend its capabilities. Some applets add movement and interesting visual effects to your page, whereas others are capable of asking you questions, responding to your questions, checking your computer settings, and calculating data. There are even applets that allow you to play interactive games against the computer or against another person logged on to the Web.

You can use a word-processing program such as Microsoft Word to save a document as an HTML file, or you can create a new one using the Web page editor included with Windows 98, FrontPage Express. If you learn the HTML language, you can use a simple text editor (such as Notepad) to create a more complex and sophisticated HTML file. Alternately, you can use the Internet Explorer browser to save an existing Web page as an HTML file that you can then use as your wallpaper.

The added control Windows 98 gives you over background wallpaper makes it possible to make the desktop a launch pad for your most important projects. A corporation, for example, might create an HTML file that contains important company information, an updatable company calendar, links to company documents, a company directory, and so on. Scott wants to show you a Web page he's designing to be used as a background for all Highland Travel computers. He has created an HTML file in his Web page editor and has placed it on a disk for you to examine.

To use a Web page as a background:

1. To view the Highland Travel desktop background Web page, you need to place the files on your Student Disk. Place the Student Disk you worked with in Session 5.1 in drive A. Click the **Start** button ▉Start, point to **Programs**, point to **NP on Microsoft Windows 98 – Level II**, and then click **Disk 3 (Tutorial 5)**. When you are prompted to insert your disk in the drive, click the **OK** button, and wait as the files you need are copied to your Student Disk.

2. Right-click a blank area of the desktop and then click **Properties**. When you are viewing a Web page as your background, you can hide the desktop icons so they don't interfere with the HTML content.

3. To hide the background icons, click the **Effects** tab, and then select the **Hide icons when the desktop is viewed as a Web page** check box.

4. Click the **Background** tab, click the **Browse** button, click the **Look in** list arrow, then click **Floppy 3½ (A:)**. Click the **highland** file icon—not the folder icon.

5. Click the **Open** button. The filename appears in the Wallpaper list.

6. Click the **OK** button. The HTML file appears on your desktop background, and the icons disappear. Figure 5-26 points out some of the features an HTML file allows you to employ on a desktop background.

| Figure 5-26 | PLACING AN HTML FILE ON THE DESKTOP |

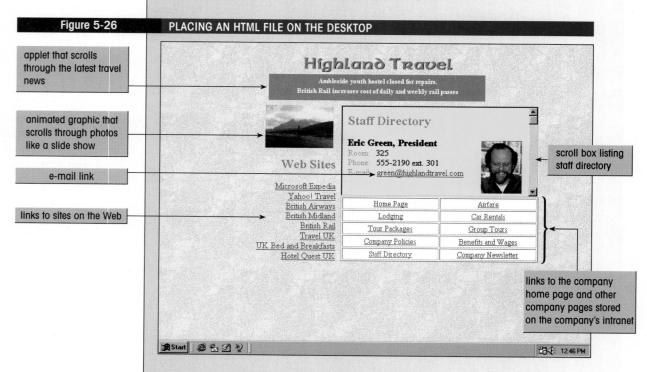

7. Scroll through the Staff Directory to see how you can interact with objects on an HTML background. Notice your experience with these objects is just the same as it would be if you were working with this page in the browser window.

The difference between using an HTML file as your wallpaper and using a graphic file, as you did in Tutorial 4, is that a graphic is simply a picture that adds interest to your desktop background, whereas an HTML file allows you to interact with the information on your background. If the HTML file contains links, you can click those links to connect to the sites they target. Try clicking one of the links on the page.

To activate a desktop link:

1. Click the **Home Page** link. Your browser starts, and after a moment the link's target appears in the browser window—the familiar Highland Travel page.

2. Close your browser. You return to the desktop.

Scott explains that once he finishes developing his page, the company will place it on all company desktops, so all employees have access to the information it contains. Since it isn't finished, he recommends you remove it from your desktop.

To restore the desktop to its original appearance:

1. Right-click a blank area of the desktop and then click **Properties**.

   TROUBLE? If you right-click an area of the Web page that has Web content, properties for that object appear, instead of desktop properties. Make sure the dialog box that opens is the Display Properties dialog box. If it isn't, try right-clicking a different area, and make sure it is blank.

2. Click the **Effects** tab and then click the **Hide icons when the desktop is viewed as a Web page** check box, to remove the check.

3. Click the **Background** tab.

4. Scroll up the Wallpaper list and then click **(None)**.

5. Click the **OK** button.

Changing Folder Settings

Scott explains that in addition to customizing your desktop background with Web content, you can also customize the way your computer's folders function. In Tutorial 2 you learned that the Folder Options dialog box controls the degree to which your operating system mimics the Web environment. Scott wants you to view the customization possibilities you have in this dialog box, so you can choose the settings you're most comfortable with. The Custom setting allows you to enable or disable Active Desktop, choose to have all folders open in the same window or open in different windows, view folders as if they were Web pages (you'll learn more about this later), and control whether the mouse and the icons it selects should function as they do in a browser or as they used to function with Windows 95.

You'll examine the Custom options to see how you can change your settings, but then you'll choose Web style so your screen matches the figures.

To view folder settings:

1. Click the **Start** button [Start], point to **Settings**, and then click **Folder Options**.

2. Click the **Custom** option button, and then click the **Settings** button to examine the available options. See Figure 5-27.

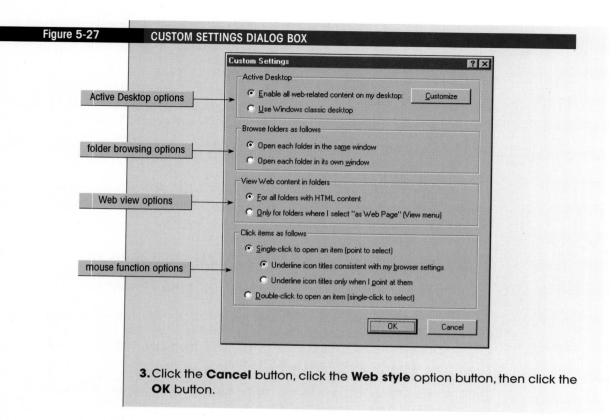

Figure 5-27   CUSTOM SETTINGS DIALOG BOX

Active Desktop options →

folder browsing options →

Web view options →

mouse function options →

3. Click the **Cancel** button, click the **Web style** option button, then click the **OK** button.

Adding Web Content to Folders

Folder windows in Windows 98 can appear with Web content in them. Just as you placed an HTML file on your desktop background, so can you create an HTML file for a given folder that makes Web content available. For example, suppose you are working on the tour package itineraries offered by Highland Travel. As you develop them, you might want to make them available to all the tour agents in the company. You can do this by saving the itineraries as Web pages, placing them in a folder, and then making the folder available to the company's **intranet**, or the internal company network. You could then customize the folder window so that it displayed information about the folder and its contents, links to Web pages that you are using as information sources, and so on.

In order to set a folder up in this way, you need to know how to use the HTML language. Scott doesn't expect you to know HTML, but he does want you to see how folders set up with HTML files can be used.

Choosing a Background Image for a Folder

Microsoft has designed a cloudlike graphic image for folders, which includes a formatted folder label and a preview utility that allows you to point to a file and see a "thumbnail image" of its contents. Before you apply your own background image to the Student Disk folder, take a moment to examine the difference between non-Web view and Web view folder settings.

To examine how Web view changes a folder's appearance:

1. Make sure your Student Disk is in drive A.

2. Open the My Computer window and then click the **3½ Floppy (A:)** icon. The contents of your Student Disk appear. First, view the folder with Web view disabled, so you can see the difference.

3. Click **View** and then, if necessary, click **as Web Page** to remove the check mark. Your Student Disk folder should appear with no HTML information; only the folder and file icons appear.

4. Now enable Web view by clicking **View** and then clicking **as Web Page**. The cloud graphic appears, as well as a folder label.

5. Now try the preview feature. Maximize the window, point to the **brockton** graphic file, and notice that information about that file and a small "thumbnail" of the image appear in the left side of the window. If necessary, scroll down the left side of the window to see an image preview. See Figure 5-28. The preview feature is extremely handy when you are trying to locate a particular file quickly.

| Figure 5-28 | **ENABLING WEB VIEW** |

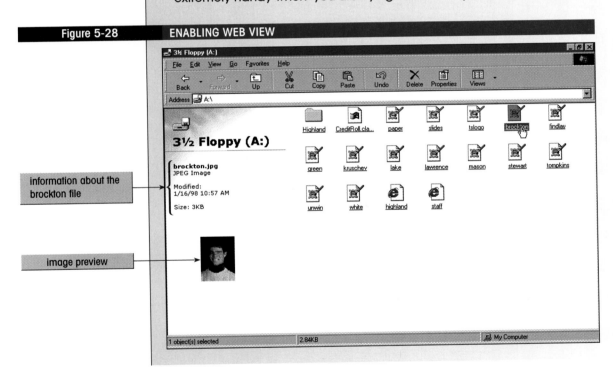

The most basic way to customize a folder is to display it with a background image. Because the purpose of the folder window is to display folder contents, you don't want to create a distracting background, so choose your graphic carefully. Scott suggests you apply the graphic that is used on the Highland Travel Web page background—a tan parchment graphic named "paper." Windows 98 repeatedly inserts the image into the folder's background, in a process called **tiling**, until the entire window is filled up, as shown in Figure 5-29. The graphic image in this figure is Bricks.gif.

Figure 5-29   FILLING A FOLDER BACKGROUND WITH A GRAPHIC IMAGE

the Bricks image is inserted
over and over again
into the Web page until
it fills up the background

Your Sample Web Page

Bricks.gif graphic file

To choose the paper image for your Student Disk:

1. Now you're ready to add a background image to this folder, as Scott suggested. Click **View** and then click **Customize this Folder**.

2. Click the **Choose a background picture** option button, and then click the **Next** button.

3. Click the **Browse** button, click the **Look in** list arrow, click **3½ Floppy (A:)**, click the **Files of type** list arrow, and then click **GIFs**.

4. Click **paper** and then click the **Open** button.

5. Click the **Next** button and then click the **Finish** button. The 3½ Floppy (A:) window now shows the graphic image you selected in the background. See Figure 5-30.

Figure 5-30   ADDING A BACKGROUND IMAGE TO A FOLDER

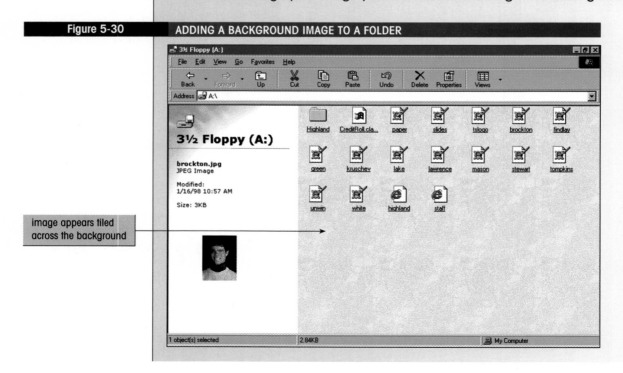

image appears tiled
across the background

6. Now you should remove customization to restore the window to its original settings: in the 3½ Floppy (A:) window, click **View**, click **Customize this Folder**, click
the **Remove customization** option button, click the **Next** button twice, and then
click the **Finish** button. Your Student Disk folder should now appear with the
default Web view settings.

Viewing a Folder Customized with Web Content

In addition to applying a background image to a folder, you can also change the default Web
view settings—if you have experience with the HTML language. Scott has HTML experience, and has customized the Highland folder, which contains the tour itineraries for
upcoming tours. He plans on making this folder available to the company network, and so
wants it to have the company logo and a link to the company Web page. You ask if you can
take a look at it.

To view a Web-content-rich folder and the HTML codes it employs:

1. Click the **Highland** folder icon and notice how Scott has customized this folder.
Point to the **castles** Web page to view the preview. See Figure 5-31.

Figure 5-31	VIEWING A CUSTOMIZED WEB VIEW FOLDER

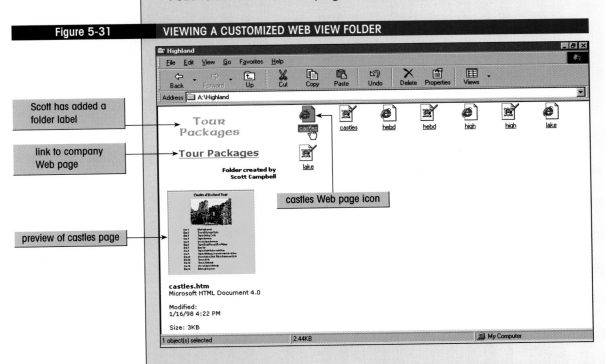

2. Now experiment a little with the Web content in the Highland folder. Click the
Tour Packages link. Your browser starts and displays the link's target, the Tour
Packages page.

3. Close your browser. You return to the desktop.

Scott says that he hopes the company will find these folder customizations useful. You point out that they do give easy access to important Highland Travel documents.

Modifying Taskbar Toolbars to Access the Web

As you've seen in this tutorial, Windows 98 allows you to access the Web from many locations. You can also customize your taskbar to improve your access to the Web and to your favorite files. In its default settings, the Windows 98 taskbar displays only the Start button, the Quick Launch toolbar, and the tray, which contains the time and icons that give you quick access to important utilities. You can, however, add toolbars to the taskbar that give you access to the Web and to programs and documents. You can also create your own toolbars.

Adding Toolbars to the Taskbar

Windows 98 makes four default toolbars available to the taskbar. See Figure 5-32.

Figure 5-32	TOOLBARS AVAILABLE TO THE TASKBAR
TOOLBAR	**DESCRIPTION**
Address	As in a browser, allows you to select or enter an address, such as a URL, to open the browser to that location.
Links	As in a browser, displays buttons for popular Web pages, such as the Microsoft home page. When you click a button on the Links toolbar, your browser opens and displays the location you clicked.
Desktop	Displays buttons that correspond to each desktop icon on the taskbar. This is a useful way to get access to your desktop icons even when application windows fill the desktop.
Quick Launch	Displays buttons for Internet services and for a direct route to the desktop.

First you'll experiment with adding the Address toolbar to the taskbar, and then you'll see how easily you can reach a Web page directly from the taskbar.

To add toolbars to the taskbar:

1. Right-click a blank area of the taskbar.

2. Point to **Toolbars**. The list of available toolbars appears. See Figure 5-33.

Figure 5-33	ENABLING A TOOLBAR

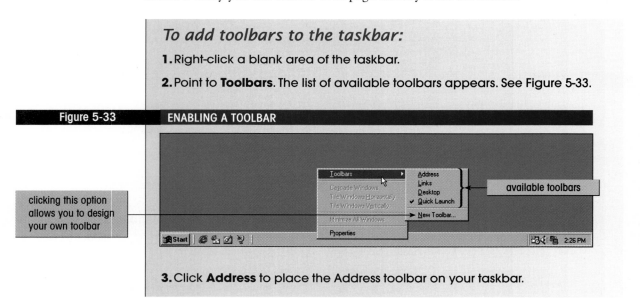

clicking this option allows you to design your own toolbar

available toolbars

3. Click **Address** to place the Address toolbar on your taskbar.

4. Now experiment with the Address toolbar by clicking the Address box. Type **http://www.course.com/NewPerspectives/Win98/Highland** and press **Enter**. Your browser starts and the Highland Travel page appears.

5. Close your browser.

6. Right-click a blank area of the taskbar, point to **Toolbars**, and click **Address** to remove the Address toolbar. Now right-click the taskbar again, point to **Toolbars**, and then click **Links** to display the Links toolbar.

7. Click the **Best of the Web** button. Your browser opens to Microsoft's Best of the Web site. See Figure 5-34.

   TROUBLE? If the Best of the Web button doesn't appear, click a different button on the Links toolbar. Your screen will look different from Figure 5-34.

Figure 5-34	LINKS TOOLBAR

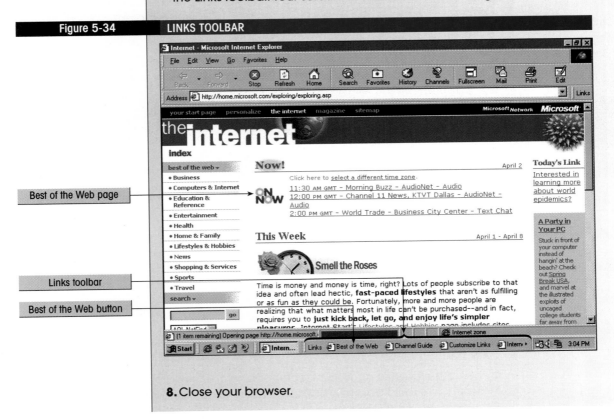

8. Close your browser.

Rearranging Taskbar Toolbars

When you have more than one toolbar displayed on the taskbar, you might need to move the toolbars around to have access to the tools you need. Each toolbar is preceded by a dividing bar, located immediately to the left of the toolbar. You can drag this bar to move toolbars around or to resize a toolbar. Try moving the Links toolbar to the left of the Quick Launch toolbar and then resizing the Quick Launch toolbar.

To rearrange taskbar toolbars:

1. Point to the dividing bar to the left of the Links toolbar. The pointer changes to ↔.

2. Drag the Links toolbar to the left of the Quick Launch toolbar. You can move any toolbar in this way. When a toolbar has more buttons than the taskbar can display, a small arrow appears that you can click to display more buttons. See Figure 5-35.

| Figure 5-35 | MOVING THE LINKS TOOLBAR |

click arrow to view additional toolbar buttons

Links toolbar is now to left

3. Try resizing the Quick Launch toolbar. Drag its dividing bar to the left to enlarge it. As you enlarge it, some of the Links toolbar buttons are hidden, and there is extra space on the Quick Launch toolbar.

4. Remove the Links toolbar.

Adding Buttons to the Quick Launch Toolbar

In Tutorial 4 you saw how to add shortcut icons to the desktop to help you access the documents you use most frequently. You can also add buttons to the taskbar that perform a similar function. Suppose you were helping develop the itinerary for the Castles tour at Highland Travel. You might want easy access to the Web page that contains the itinerary. Try adding a button to the Quick Launch toolbar that targets the Castles Web page, located in the Highland folder on your Student Disk.

To add a button to the Quick Launch toolbar:

1. Open the My Computer window, click the **3½ Floppy (A:)** icon, and then click the **Highland** folder.

2. Point to the **castles** document icon—not the castles graphic icon. The document icon should appear with the Internet Explorer logo 🅔. Drag this icon to the far right of the Quick Launch toolbar. When a vertical black line appears, as in Figure 5-36, release the mouse button. A new button appears on the Quick Launch toolbar.

Figure 5-36   **ADDING A BUTTON TO THE QUICK LAUNCH TOOLBAR**

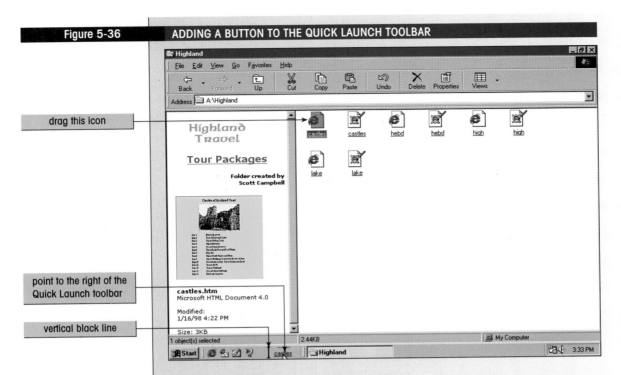

drag this icon

point to the right of the
Quick Launch toolbar

vertical black line

3. Click the button you just added. Because it represents an HTML document, your browser starts and opens the document. See Figure 5-37.

Figure 5-37   **ACTIVATING A DOCUMENT BUTTON ON THE QUICK LAUNCH TOOLBAR**

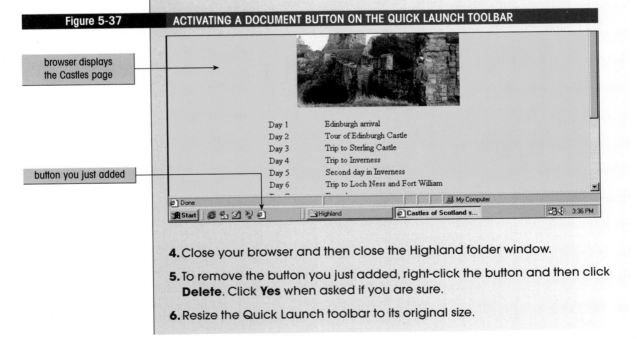

browser displays
the Castles page

button you just added

4. Close your browser and then close the Highland folder window.

5. To remove the button you just added, right-click the button and then click **Delete**. Click **Yes** when asked if you are sure.

6. Resize the Quick Launch toolbar to its original size.

Your desktop is now restored to its original state. Scott and you agree that Windows 98 revolutionizes a computer user's experience with the Web. Windows 98 Web features make information on computers in Toledo, Cairo, Kuala Lumpur, Calcutta, Moscow, or Calgary just as accessible to you as the files on your local hard drive.

QUICK CHECK

1. What language do you use to write Web pages?

2. What is an applet? Give an example.

3. True or False: You can use Microsoft Word to create a desktop background document.

4. What is the difference between using a graphic image as a background and using a Web page as a background?

5. If you want your desktop icons to behave like links, which folder options style should you use?

6. What is the advantage of using Web view?

7. How do you add a document button to the Quick Launch toolbar?

TUTORIAL ASSIGNMENTS

1. **History of the Internet and the World Wide Web**   Computers have been around for several decades now, but how did the Internet and the World Wide Web get started? Microsoft considered the Internet an important enough development to incorporate many of its features into the Windows 98 operating system. Go to the library and locate books or articles on the Internet, and write a single-page essay on the history of the Internet. Answer questions such as:
   a. What role did the ARPANET play in the development of the Internet?
   b. What role did CERN play in the development of the World Wide Web?
   c. Over what period of time did the Internet grow? What about the World Wide Web?
   d. When did browsers first become available?

2. **Connecting to the Internet over a Modem**   This tutorial mentioned that home computer users can connect to the Internet using a dial-up connection via an account with an ISP. Say you had your own computer, and you wanted to connect to the Internet from home. Research ISPs in your area, including their rates and services, and then write a single-page essay describing your findings. Which ISP would you choose, and why?

3. **Exploring Your Home Page**   In this tutorial the figures showed Microsoft Corporation's home page as the home page. Your home page might be different—take some time to explore.
   a. Start the Internet Explorer browser and print your home page.
   b. Follow one of the links on your home page, and continue to click any interesting links that you encounter. Clicking whatever links interest you is often called "surfing." On your print-out, circle the link you followed. Write in the margin where it took you.
   c. Use the Home button to return to your home page, and then follow another link and go where it leads you. Again, circle the link on your printout and indicate where you ended up and what you saw along the way.

4. **Connecting to Specific Web Sites**   You learned in this tutorial that you can enter a URL into the Address box of your browser to connect to a specific Web site. Using the Internet Explorer browser, enter the following URLs, and print the first page of each URL.

   a. http://www.usps.gov
   b. http://www.nps.gov
   c. http://www.cnn.com
   d. Using any one of these pages as a starting point, follow links until you locate a page with frames. Record the URL of the page you found.

Explore

5. **Active Desktop Gallery**   Figure 5-16 showed a desktop with a number of Active Desktop items. One of them was the Expedia Maps Address Finder. Try adding this item to your desktop and then using it to print a map of your hometown neighborhood.

   a. Connect to the Active Desktop Gallery site.
   b. Click the Travel button and then click the Expedia Maps item.
   c. Add this item to your Active Desktop.
   d. Once the item appears on your desktop, enter your address, city, state, and zip code into the appropriate boxes. Click the Find button.
   e. Once the map appears, print it. If Expedia can't locate your neighborhood, enter a different address, such as your school's address, and click the Find button again.
   f. Remove the Active Desktop item from your desktop.

6. **Exploring Active Channels**   At Highland Travel you explored the Lifestyle & Travel group of channels. The Channel bar lists not only groups of channels but also individual channels, such as The Microsoft Network, MSNBC News, Disney, and Warner Brothers. Scott points out that you can explore one of these channels directly by selecting it from the Channel bar.

   a. Make sure the Channel bar is visible on the desktop and then click one of the channels listed on the Channel bar.
   b. Click the Add Active Channel button, and then follow the prompts to reach the site you chose. If asked if you want to subscribe, click No.
   c. Once the channel opens, click links that interest you. Write a paragraph describing what you learned from the channel you connected to.
   d. Close your browser.

7. **Web Page Desktop Backgrounds**   Scott wants you to fully appreciate the benefits of using a Web page as a desktop background.

   a. Apply the Highland Web page (not the folder), located in the root directory of your Student Disk, as your desktop background.
   b. Observe the background carefully and work with the objects that are incorporated into this Web page.
   c. Connect to the Active Desktop Gallery and add a desktop item that would add to the usefulness of this desktop.
   d. Using the Highland desktop you just created as an example, write two paragraphs describing what a Web page background offers that a graphic image file, such as you used in Tutorial 4, does not. Give detailed information about the purpose of each element on the desktop.
   e. Restore your computer's background to its original state.

8. **Modifying a Folder**   You've been at Highland Travel for a week now, and you decide to create and decorate a folder that will contain some of your advertising documents.

   a. Open My Computer and then open the 3½ Floppy (A:) window.
   b. Create a new folder on your Student Disk named "Advertising."
   c. Open the Advertising folder.
   d. Open the Internet Explorer browser and connect to the Highland Web page located at: http://www.course.com/NewPerspectives/Win98/Highland

    e. Locate and download to the Advertising folder on your Student Disk one of the graphic images on the Highland Web page that you think might make a nice background for your folder.

    f. Apply the graphic image as the Advertising folder background.

    g. Use the techniques you learned earlier in this book to print an image of the Advertising folder. Make sure that you type your name into the WordPad document before you print.

9. **Customizing the Taskbar**   In this tutorial you added a Web page icon to the Quick Launch toolbar. Scott points out that you can get instant access to your Advertising folder if you add its folder icon to the Quick Launch toolbar.

    a. Make some extra space on the Quick Launch toolbar.

    b. If necessary, open the Advertising folder you created in the previous tutorial assignment.

    c. Click the Up button to move one level up.

    d. Drag the Advertising folder icon to the Quick Launch toolbar.

    e. Use the techniques you learned earlier in this book to print an image of the screen. Make sure that you type your name into the WordPad document before you print.

PROJECTS

1. You have worked with both Windows Explorer and Internet Explorer over the course of this tutorial. Compare the functions of these two Windows 98 features.

    a. Start Windows Explorer and observe the window carefully.

    b. Now start Internet Explorer and observe the window carefully. Write a paragraph describing how the two windows differ.

    c. Return to Windows Explorer and click the Microsoft icon on the cloud graphic in the upper-right corner of the Windows Explorer window. What happens?

    d. Compare the two windows and write a second paragraph describing how they differ when Windows Explorer is used as a browser.

    e. Microsoft's goal with Windows 98 was to create a "single Explorer." Why do you think Microsoft set this goal? What advantages or disadvantages does the single Explorer have?

2. You have a friend who has used Windows Explorer extensively for managing his own files and folders, and you mention to him that he can also use Windows Explorer as a browser. Write him a note, which you'll e-mail to him, that describes how this is possible. Make sure you describe what happens to elements such as the left and right panes, the Address bar, the activity indicator, and the status bar.

Explore

3. In this tutorial you learned how to access information on the Web when you either knew the URL or you used a guide such as the Channel Guide. Internet Explorer also includes a search tool, accessible via the Search button 🔍, that helps you find the Web pages you need. Use Internet Explorer's online Help to learn about the Search button (look for "Search button" on the Index tab) and about the general topic of searching the Web.

    a. How would you search for information on a given topic?

    b. Once the Search feature displays a list of search results, what should you do to display the Web page containing the information?

    c. Follow the directions you studied in the Help file to search for information on one of your hobbies, such as snowboarding. While you are using the Search Explorer bar, write down the exact steps you take. Was your search successful? Write down the URL of the page you connected to.

Explore

4. You just went to California for a three-week vacation with some friends. On returning, you decide to "capture the moment" by downloading a graphic image that will remind you of your vacation activities.

   a. Use what you learned in Project 3 to locate a graphic image on surfing, rock climbing, wine tasting, or some other vacation activity, and download it to your Student Disk. (If you skipped Project 3, connect to the Highland site or your home page and download a graphic from there.)
   b. Apply the image you located as a desktop background. Then apply it as a background image to the 3½ Floppy (A:) folder.
   c. With the 3½ Floppy (A:) window open, print your screen, using the techniques you learned earlier in this book. Make sure you include your name on the printout.

5. Because most labs can't accommodate subscriptions, you probably will need your own computer to complete this project. Your dream is to plan your investments so you can retire by age 55. To keep yourself posted on the stock market:

   a. Subscribe to a Web site on the stock market. You could try http://www.nasdaq.com or http://www.djia.com.
   b. Create a log in Notepad (perhaps using the LOG feature you learned about in Tutorial 4) to record information such as the closing value of an index such as Nasdaq or the Dow on a given day.
   c. Check your Subscriptions folder two more times during the week, and connect to the site you subscribed to, when it has changed. How did you know it changed?
   d. Record any newly posted, pertinent information in the log.
   e. When you have recorded three entries in the log, open the log window and your Subscriptions folder, and print your screen so your instructor can see which Web page you subscribed to and what information you gained. Make sure you unsubscribe from the Web page once the week is over.

The Internet:
World Wide
Web

LAB ASSIGNMENTS

The Internet: World Wide Web One of the most popular services on the Internet is the World Wide Web. This Lab is a Web simulator that teaches you how to use Web browser software to find information. You can use this Lab whether or not your school provides you with Internet access. See the Read This Before You Begin page for information on starting the lab.

1. Click the Steps button to learn how to use Web browser software. As you proceed through the Steps, answer all of the Quick Check questions that appear. After you complete the Steps, you will see a Quick Check Summary Report. Follow the instructions on the screen to print this report.

2. Click the Explore button on the Welcome screen. Use the Web browser to locate a weather map of the Caribbean Virgin Islands. What is its URL?

3. A SCUBA diver named Wadson Lachouffe has been searching for the fabled treasure of Greybeard the pirate. A link from the Adventure Travel Web site www.atour.com leads to Wadson's Web page called "Hidden Treasure." In Explore, locate the Hidden Treasure page and answer the following questions:

   a. What was the name of Greybeard's ship?
   b. What was Greybeard's favorite food?
   c. What does Wadson think happened to Greybeard's ship?

4. In the Steps, you found a graphic of Jupiter from the photo archives of the Jet Propulsion Laboratory. In the Explore section of the Lab, you can also find a graphic of Saturn. Suppose one of your friends wanted a picture of Saturn for an astronomy report. Make a list of the blue, underlined links your friend must click, in the correct order, to find the Saturn graphic. Assume that your friend will begin at the Web Trainer home page.

5. Enter the URL http://www.atour.com to jump to the Adventure Travel Web site. Write a one-page description of this site. In your paper include a description of the information at the site, the number of pages the site contains, and a diagram of the links it contains.

6. Chris Thomson is a student at UVI and has his own Web pages. In Explore, look at the information Chris has included on his pages. Suppose you could create your own Web page. What would you include? Use word-processing software to design your own Web page. Make sure you indicate the graphics and links you would use.

Web Pages & HTML It's easy to create your own Web pages. There are many software tools to help you become a Web author. In this Lab you'll experiment with a Web-authoring wizard that automates the process of creating a Web page. You'll also try your hand at working directly with HTML code. See the Read This Before You Begin page for information on starting the lab.

1. Click the Steps button to activate the Web-authoring wizard and learn how to create a basic Web page. As you proceed through the Steps, answer all of the Quick Check questions. After you complete the Steps, you will see a Quick Check Summary Report. Follow the instructions on the screen to print this report.

2. In Explore, click the File menu, then click New to start working on a new Web page. Use the wizard to create a home page for a veterinarian who offers dog day-care and boarding services. After you create the page, save it on drive A or C, and print the HTML code. Your site must have the following characteristics:
   a. Title: Dr. Dave's Dog Domain
   b. Background color: Gold
   c. Graphic: Dog.jpg
   d. Body text: Your dog will have the best care day and night at Dr. Dave's Dog Domain. Fine accommodations, good food, playtime, and snacks are all provided. You can board your pet by the day or week. Grooming services also available.
   e. Text link: "Reasonable rates" links to www.cciw.com/np3/rates.htm
   f. E-mail link: "For more information: " links to daveassist@drdave.com

3. In Explore, use the File menu to open the HTML document called Politics.htm. After you use the HTML window (not the wizard) to make the following changes, save the revised page on Drive A or C, and print the HTML code. Refer to the following table for a list of HTML tags you can use:

HTML TAGS	MEANING AND LOCATION
<HTML></HTML>	States that the file is an HTML document. Opening tag begins the page; closing tag ends the page (required).
<HEAD></HEAD>	States that the enclosed text is the header of the page. Appears immediately after the opening HTML tag (required).
<TITLE></TITLE>	States that the enclosed text is the title of the page. Must appear within the opening and closing HEAD tags (required).
<BODY></BODY>	States that the enclosed material (all the text, images, and tags in the rest of the document) is the body of the document (required).
<H1></H1>	States that the enclosed text is a heading.
 	Inserts a line break. Can be used to control line spacing and breaks in lines.
<UL></UL> <OL></OL>	Indicates an unordered list (list items are preceded by bullets) or an ordered list (list items are preceded by numbers or letters).
<LI>	Indicates a list item. Precedes all items in unordered or ordered lists.
<CENTER></CENTER>	Indicates that the enclosed text should be centered on the width of the page.
<B></B>	Indicates that the enclosed text should appear in boldface.
<I></I>	Indicates that the enclosed text should appear in italics.
<A HREF="*URL*"></A>	Indicates that the enclosed text is a hypertext link. The URL of the linked material must appear within the quotation marks after the equal sign.
<IMG SRC="*filename*">	Inserts an inline image into the document where *filename* is the name of the image.
<HR>	Inserts a horizontal rule.

    a. Change the title to Politics 2000.
    b. Center the page heading.
    c. Change the background color to FFE7C6 and the text color to 000000.
    d. Add a line break before the sentence "What's next?"
    e. Add a bold tag to "Additional links on this topic:"
    f. Add one more link to the "Additional links" list. The link should go to the site http://www.elections.ca, and the clickable link should read "Elections Canada".
    g. Change the last graphic to display the image "next.gif".

4. In Explore, use the Web-authoring wizard and the HTML window to create a home page about yourself. You should include at least a screenful of text, a graphic, an external link, and an e-mail link. Save the page on drive A, then print the HTML code. Turn in your disk and printout.

QUICK CHECK ANSWERS

Session 5.1

1. A home page is the Web page designated by the operating system as your starting point, or the Web page that a person, organization, or business has created to give information about itself.

2. URL

3. Type the URL in the Address box, then press Enter.

4. It is an educational site.

5. Back and Forward

6. Right-click the image, click Save Picture As, enter a file name and destination folder, then click Save.

Session 5.2

1. Yes. When you subscribe to a non-channel Web site, you set up your computer so that it checks the site at specific times to see if the site has changed and then downloads the changes. When you subscribe to a channel, you automatically receive content from Web sites that broadcast their content to subscribers.

2. With offline viewing, your computer downloads a page so that you can view it later without being connected to the Internet.

3. Push technology allows both Web site authors and subscribers to gain more control over content delivery and schedule.

4. Active Desktop item

5. An Active Desktop item is part of a channel; a channel is an entire Web site that contains content that you can view according to your preferences.

6. A red gleam icon appears.

Session 5.3

1. HTML

2. An applet is a program attached to a Web page that extends the capabilities of the Web page. An example is a program that allows you to play a game on a Web page.

3. True

4. A graphic only provides visual information; a Web page background can feature text, clip art, photos, animated graphics, links, multimedia objects such as sound and video, and applets.

5. Web style

6. Web view allows you to access Web features in folder windows.

7. Display the document icon in an Explorer window, and then drag the icon to the Quick Launch toolbar.

New Perspectives on

MICROSOFT®
WINDOWS® 98

To the Student

Make Student Disk Program

To complete the Level III tutorials, you will need 4 Student Disks. To complete all Tutorial Assignments and Projects, you will need an additional 3 disks. Your instructor will either provide you with Student Disks or ask you to make your own.

If you are making your own Student Disks you will need 3 blank, formatted high-density disks and access to the Make Student Disk program. If you wish to install the Make Student Disk program to your home computer, you can obtain it from your instructor or from the Web. To download the Make Student Disk program from the Web, go to **www.course.com**, click Data Disks, and follow the instructions on the screen.

To install the Make Student Disk program, select and click the file you just downloaded from **www.course.com**, 5448-7.exe. Follow the on-screen instructions to complete the installation. If you have any trouble installing or obtaining the Make Student Disk program, ask your instructor or technical support person for assistance.

Once you have obtained and installed the Make Student Disk program, you can use it to create your Student Disks according to the steps in the tutorials.

Course Labs

The Level III tutorials in this book feature 3 interactive Course Labs to help you understand Multimedia, Defragmentation and Disk Operations, and Data Backup. There are Lab Assignments at the end of Tutorials 8 and 11 that relate to these Labs.

To start a Lab, click the **Start** button on the Windows 98 Taskbar, point to **Programs**, point to **Course Labs**, point to **New Perspectives Course Labs**, and click the name of the Lab you want to use.

Using Your Own Computer

If you are going to work through this book using your own computer, you need:

Computer System Microsoft Windows 98 must be installed on a local hard drive or on a network drive. You will need access to a network to complete Tutorial 10. To complete the steps of the Dial-Up Networking Appendix, you will need a computer with a modem and access to a phone line and ISP. You may wish to have your Microsoft Windows 98 CD readily available.

Student Disks You will not be able to complete the tutorials or exercises in this book using your own computer until you have your Student Disks. See "Make Student Disk Program" above for details on obtaining your Student Disks.

Course Labs See your instructor or technical support person to obtain the Course Lab software for use on your own computer.

Visit Our World Wide Web Site

Additional materials designed especially for you are available on the World Wide Web. Go to **http://www.course.com**.

To the Instructor

The Make Student Disk Program and Course Labs for this title are available on the Instructor's Resource Kit for this title. Follow the instructions in the Help file on the CD-ROM to install the programs to your network or standalone computer. For information on using the Make Student Disk Program or the Course Labs, see the "To the Student" section above. In order for students to be able to complete the steps in the Level III tutorials, they will need access to Quick View in Tutorial 6, the Clipboard Viewer in Tutorial 8, and a network in Tutorial 10. They will need to be able to place files on the hard drive in Tutorial 11. If your students need to learn how to set up dial-up networking connections, they can complete the Appendix, but they will need a computer with a modem and access to a phone line and ISP. You are granted a license to copy the Student Files and Course Labs to any computer or computer network used by students who have purchased this book.

OBJECTIVES

In this tutorial you will:

- Find specific files by name, contents, and location using several methods, including wildcards

- Open and delete files from the Find window

- Limit a search to a specific folder

- Locate files by date, type, and size

- Open documents with the Documents menu

- View file contents using Quick View

- Search for information on the Internet using query and subject searches

- Search with the Search Explorer bar

- Search for people on the Internet

FINDING FILES AND DATA

Using the Find Feature to Locate Files for a Speechwriter

CASE

Speechwriter's Aide

Like thousands of other college students who are graduating soon, you've been dropping in at the campus job center regularly. Today, you notice that Senator Susannah Bernstein's speechwriter has posted an advertisement for an aide. When you call to inquire, Carolyn King, the senator's speechwriter, asks you to come by the next morning. Your interview goes very well. You learn that the job would primarily entail locating information that Carolyn could use in writing the Senator's speeches. Carolyn explains that her previous aide collected and organized information in a filing cabinet. In addition to the paper archive, the previous aide started an electronic quotations archive that includes over a hundred files on a 3½-inch disk. These files contain anecdotes, jokes, and commentary on a variety of subjects.

You explain to Carolyn that you could maximize the efficiency of the information retrieval process if you had a computer running Windows 98 with an Internet connection. Carolyn doesn't think that should be a problem, but she hasn't used Windows 98 before and asks you to update her on the features that make information retrieval easier.

You explain that Windows 98 includes a powerful search tool called **Find** that helps you find files on the local or network drives to which you have access. When your local or network drives don't yield the information you need, you can expand your search by hunting for information on the Internet. The Internet contains a vast number of computers and networks that store information, much of which can be accessed and retrieved using the search tools that Windows 98 makes available. With Windows 98 and an Internet connection, information from around the world is accessible from your office computer. Carolyn is intrigued, and by the end of the interview she offers you the job.

After a week of training and orientation, Carolyn assigns you office space that includes a computer running Windows 98 and an Internet connection. She promises that your first assignment will come soon, and in the meantime asks that you familiarize yourself with the information available locally.

SESSION 6.1

In this session, you will learn how to start the Windows 98 Find feature and perform simple searches for files by their filenames. You will experiment with different search words and techniques, including wildcards. You will also work with the Results list in order to display the files in the most convenient format. For this tutorial you will need a blank 3½-inch disk.

Preparing Your Student Disk

Before you can begin working, you need to bring a blank 3½-inch disk to the computer lab to create a Student Disk containing the sample files you will work with in this tutorial. In the computer lab, you will make your Student Disk, using the NP on Microsoft Windows 98 menu. If you are using your own computer, however, the NP on Microsoft Windows 98 menu may not be available. Before you proceed, refer to the Read This Before You Begin page for instructions on obtaining the files necessary for your Student Disk.

To make your Student Disk:

1. Write "Disk 4—Windows 98 Tutorial 6 Student Disk" on the label of a blank, formatted 3½-inch disk. Insert your Student Disk into drive A.

   TROUBLE? If your 3½-inch disk drive is B, place your formatted disk in that drive instead, and for the rest of this tutorial substitute drive B wherever you see drive A.

2. Point to the **Start** button [🄰Start], point to **Programs**, point to **NP on Microsoft Windows 98-Level III**, and then click **Disk 4 (Tutorial 6)**. When you are prompted to insert your disk in the drive, click the **OK** button, and wait as the files you need are copied to your Student Disk.

3. Close all the open windows on your screen.

Search Strategies

Windows 98 offers a useful set of search tools, all available on the Find submenu of the Start menu, which help you find several types of information. See Figure 6-1.

On your own computer, the best way to make sure you can find your files quickly and easily is to start with a well-organized folder structure. But even on your own computer, you might forget the names or locations of certain files. One of the options on the Find menu—Files or Folders—opens the Find window, which helps you locate files and folders on the devices available to your computer. Find can help you avoid searching manually through the hundreds of files your hard disk contains. It is also useful when you are working on someone else's computer, a network computer, a computer with multiple users who share documents, or when you have a disk with someone else's data, as is the case with the quotations archive disk.

Figure 6-1	SEARCH TOOLS
FIND OPTION	**DESCRIPTION**
Files or Folders	Locates files or folders on local or network drives
Computer	Locates shared computers or folders on a network (this option appears only if your computer has network capabilities)
Using Microsoft Outlook	Locates Microsoft Outlook items, such as tasks, appointments, and messages (this option appears only if Microsoft Outlook is installed on your computer)
On the Microsoft Network	Locates information on Microsoft's Internet service Web site (this option appears only if your computer uses the Microsoft Network online service)
On the Internet	Locates information on the Internet
People	Locates people, using directory services available on your computer and on the Internet

To search for a file, you provide Find with **search criteria**, one or more conditions you want Find to meet as it searches. For example, you could provide search criteria specifying all or part of a filename and the drive you think the file might be on. Find then locates and displays every file that matches those criteria. Find groups search criteria into three categories—Name & Location, Date, and Advanced—as shown in Figure 6-2.

Figure 6-2	SEARCH CRITERIA AVAILABLE IN THE FIND: ALL FILES DIALOG BOX
TAB	**SEARCH CRITERIA**
Name & Location	All or part of a filename Any words or phrases contained within the text of the file (not the filename) The location (computer, drive, or folder) in which you want Windows 98 to search
Date	The date on which, or range of dates within which the file was created, last modified, or last accessed
Advanced	File type File size

You start browsing through the quotations archive disk. You discover that the disk is organized into several folders. You open a few files and find quotes from a wide variety of people—historical figures such as Eleanor Roosevelt and Gandhi, as well as more modern personalities such as Jay Leno and Alice Walker. As you are reading through one of the files, Carolyn stops by and asks if you could look for appropriate material for a speech the Senator will deliver next week at Stanton College on successful leadership. You see there are so many files on the disk that opening and reading through every one of them would be time-consuming, so you decide to use the Find utility to locate information on the topic of leadership.

Starting Find

You didn't create the quotations files, and you know very little about them, so Find is just the tool to help you locate quotations for Senator Bernstein's speech. You can start Find from the Start menu, or from within Windows Explorer. When you use Windows Explorer, you can choose Find from the Tools menu, or you can right-click the folder or device you want to search, and then click Find. You'll use the Start menu method.

To start Find and specify that you want to search for files or folders:

1. Click the **Start** button ![Start], and then point to **Find**. The Find menu opens. Your Find menu might show different menu options than those shown in Figure 6-3 (it might not show Computer, and it might show Using Microsoft Outlook or On the Microsoft Network). Because you are looking for files, you'll choose the first option, Files or Folders.

Figure 6-3	FIND MENU

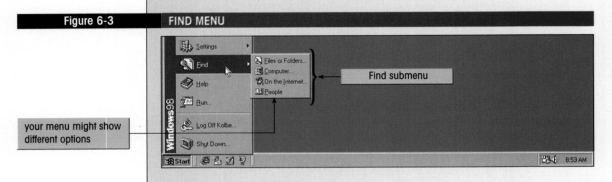

your menu might show different options

Find submenu

2. Click **Files or Folders** on the Find menu. A window opens that lets you specify criteria for the file you are looking for. See Figure 6-4.

Figure 6-4	FIND WINDOW

Find window's title bar changes depending on your search criteria

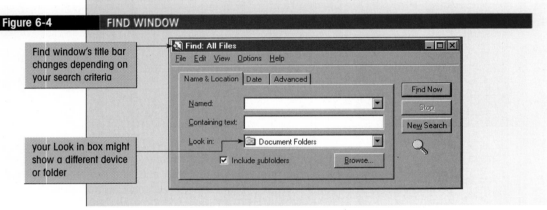

your Look in box might show a different device or folder

The title of the window that opens when you first start Find is Find: All Files. As you will see as you go through this session, when you specify search criteria, the title changes to describe the kind of search you are performing.

The Find window helps you locate a file by entering search criteria. The three tabs at the top of the Find window correspond to the three search criteria categories shown in Figure 6-2. The active tab, Name & Location, lets you specify all or part of a filename and a location in which Find should search.

REFERENCE WINDOW   RW

Specifying Search Criteria

A   B   C   D   E

```
Find: All Files                           _ □ ×
File  Edit  View  Options  Help

  Name & Location │ Date │ Advanced │          Find Now    H

F    Named:              [        ▼]          Stop

     Containing text: [              ]        New Search  I

     Look in:   [□ C:  ◄        ▼]            🔍

G →  ☑ Include subfolders      Browse...
```

A Search by name, location, or contents.
B Search by date modified, created, or last accessed.
C Search by file type or size.
D Search one or all drives on your computer.
E Search a folder on your computer or search the drives on a network computer.
F Search by part or all of a filename.
G Search the subfolders of the location specified in the Look in list box.
H Find all files matching specified search criteria.
I Clear search criteria and reset to default values.

Searching by Name and Location

To find a specific file, you type as much of the filename as you know in the Named box. The letters you type are called a **search string**. Because Find is not case-sensitive when searching for filenames, you can type the search string in either uppercase or lowercase letters. Find lists any files or folders whose names contain the search string.

REFERENCE WINDOW   RW

Searching for a File by Name

■ Click the Start button, point to Find, and then click Files or Folders.
■ Type a search string in the Named box.
■ Click the Look in list arrow, and then click the drive you want to search or click My Computer to select all the drives on your computer.
■ Use the Include subfolders check box to indicate whether you want to search subfolders of the drive or folder in the Look in box.
■ Click the Find Now button.

What search string should you enter when you don't know the filename? You can guess, based on the file contents. Because you are looking for quotes that could be useful in a speech to college students on leadership, you decide to start by looking for files named "leadership." Later you can try other search strings.

To search for files containing "leadership" in the filename:

1. Click the **Named** box, and then type **leadership**.

You've entered a criterion for the filename, and now you need to specify a file location. When you first start Find, a folder or drive name, such as Document Folders, appears in the Look in box, which specifies where Find will search. If your computer has multiple drives and you aren't sure which drive contains the file you're looking for, you can search your entire computer by clicking My Computer on the Look in list. However, if you know which drive contains the file, you can speed up your search by limiting the search to that drive.

All the files you are looking for are located on your Student Disk so you specify your floppy drive as your search location.

To specify drive A as the file location:

1. Click the **Look in** list arrow, and then click **3½ Floppy (A:)** so that Windows 98 searches only the files on your Student Disk.

2. Make sure the **Include subfolders** check box is selected so that Find searches all folders on the Student Disk, not just the files contained in the root directory.

3. Click the **Find Now** button. Find searches for all files on drive A whose names contain the search string you entered. Then it appends a box that shows the search results. The title of the Find window changes to Find: Files named leadership.

4. Click **View** and then click **Details** to ensure that you are viewing file details. See Figure 6-5.

   TROUBLE? If your results show "txt" extensions after the filenames, your computer is set to show file extensions. To hide file extensions, click the Start button, point to Settings, click Folder Options, click the View tab, click the Hide file extensions for known file types check box, and then click the OK button.

Figure 6-5	RESULTS LIST

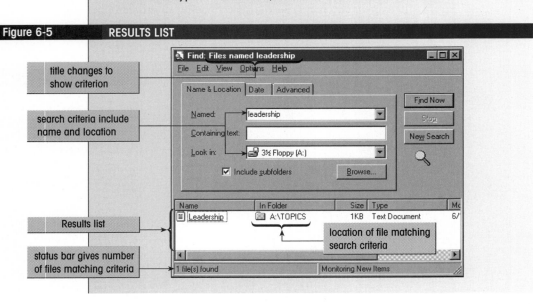

- title changes to show criterion
- search criteria include name and location
- Results list
- status bar gives number of files matching criteria
- location of file matching search criteria

The **Results list**—the box that Find appends that shows search results—shows one file, Leadership. The In Folder column provides the file locations, A:\Topics. The location begins with the drive, in this case, A. If the file is in a folder, a backslash (\) separates the drive from the folder name. Therefore, files in A:\Topics are in the Topics folder on drive A. If there are subfolders, additional backslashes separate the folders from one another. Figure 6-6 shows how this notation works on a drive A that contains two folders, Politics and Speeches, both of which have subfolders.

Figure 6-6	FILE LOCATIONS

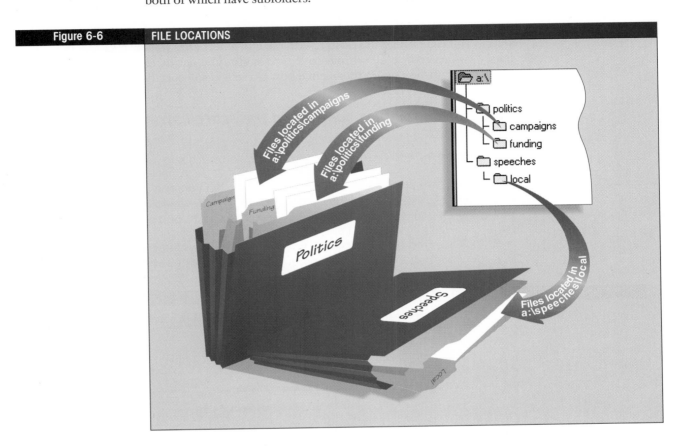

Experimenting **with Search Strings**

You wonder if you would find more files using a different search string. One rule of thumb is to use the root of your search word as your criterion. For example, if you decide to search for files on political topics for Senator Bernstein's speech, should you enter "politics" as your search string? Probably not, because a file named Politician (for example) will not appear in the Results list. However, the root "politic," without the added "s," would yield files named Politician, Political Quotations, or Politics. Figure 6-7 shows several examples of search strings that use the root of a word (you don't need to try any of these now).

Figure 6-7	CHOOSING EFFECTIVE SEARCH STRINGS	
TOPIC	**USE THIS SEARCH STRING:**	**FINDS THESE FILENAMES:**
politics	politic	Politics, Politicians, Political Quotations
education	educ	Education, Educative Issues, Educators
computers	comput	Computers, Computing, Computerization

Of course, the root of the word, if it is very general, might also let in unwanted files. Searching for "lead" instead of "leader," for example, would display a file such as "Lead Corrosion." Fortunately, with Find it's easy to adjust your search string until you find only those files you want.

Now that you know there is a file containing quotations specifically about leadership, you decide to look for files on leaders, using "leader" as your search string. To perform a new search, you can change the existing criteria, add a new criterion, or click the **New Search** button, which returns all settings to their defaults. You decide to change the search string "leadership" to "leader" in the Named box. Drive A is still specified in the Look in box.

To search for files containing the search string "leader" on drive A:

1. Change the entry in the Named box from leadership to leader.

   TROUBLE? To change an entry in a text box, often you can simply click the text box to highlight the contents, and whatever you type replaces the existing entry. Or you can click twice and then edit the text box contents.

2. Click the **Find Now** button. The Results list now shows three files that might contain information on leadership. Scroll to see them if necessary. See Figure 6-8.

Figure 6-8	EXPANDING A SEARCH

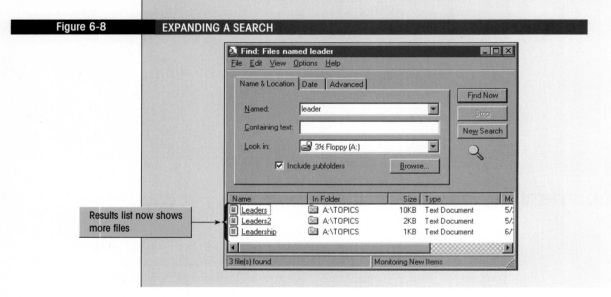

Results list now shows more files

Opening a File from Find

Once you locate a file using the Find utility, you can open it directly from Find. In the document-centric environment of Windows 98, you don't have to start a program before you can open a file. You can simply right-click it in the Results list, and then click Open (or, in Web style, you can click the file; in Classic style, you can click it and then press Enter, or double-click it). Windows 98 locates and starts the program for you. If Windows 98 cannot open your file, it is possible that you don't have the necessary program for that file type installed on your computer. If this is the case, the Open With dialog box opens and gives you the opportunity to specify the program you want Windows 98 to open for that file.

You decide to open the Leadership file to see if it contains any quotes the senator might find useful.

To open a file from the Results list:

1. Right-click the **Leadership** file in the Results list, and then click **Open**. The file opens in Notepad.

   TROUBLE? If the text of the quotations extends beyond the right border of the Notepad window, click Edit then click Word Wrap.

2. Browse through the contents of the file and note that it contains several quotations on leadership. When you are finished, click the Notepad **Close** button ⊠ to close Notepad. Click **No** if you are prompted to save your changes.

You show Carolyn the files you found for the speech at Stanton College.

Using Wildcards

Carolyn is pleased that you found helpful material for her so quickly. She mentions that Senator Bernstein will also be participating in the Atomic Energy symposium next month, so anything you can find on that topic would be useful. You decide to check if there are any files on Albert Einstein, but you can't remember how to spell his name. If you make a spelling error, Find won't locate the files you want. You can, however, use wildcards to approximate a filename. **Wildcards** are characters that you can substitute for all or part of a filename in a search string. Find recognizes two wildcards: the asterisk and the question mark. When you want to locate a group of files whose names follow certain specific patterns, such as all files that begin and end with certain characters, or all files with a specified string in a specified location, you can use wildcards.

The * (asterisk) wildcard stands in place of any number of consecutive characters in a filename. With the search string "m*n" Find could locate files with names such as Men, Magician, or Modern, but not Male or Women. Here, the files that Find locates have a common characteristic: they all begin with "m" and end with "n."

When Find encounters the asterisk wildcard in a search string, it allows additional characters only in those places indicated by the wildcard. Find does not include filenames with characters before the "m" or after the "n." If this is not what you had in mind, you can use additional wildcards. If you specify the search string "*m*n*" then Find includes Men, Magician, Modern, Women, and Mention, but not Male. These files have the letter "m" in common, which appears somewhere in the name, followed at a later point by the letter "n."

You can also control the Results list with the ? (question mark) wildcard, which lets you select files when one character in the filename varies. For example, the search string "m?n" locates Men or Man but not Mistaken or Moon.

Files that match the "m?n" criteria must have the letters "m" and "n" in their filenames, separated by a single character. Unlike the asterisk wildcard, however, the question mark wildcard does not cause Find to exclude files with characters before or after the "m" or "n." So although "m*n" excludes Women and Mental, "m?n" does not, because both of these files contain "m" and "n" separated by a single character.

The question mark wildcard is often used to locate files whose names include version numbers or dates, such as Sales1, Sales2, and Sales3, or Tax1997, Tax1998, and Tax1999.

You decide to search for only those files beginning with "e" and ending with "n" because you know those are the first and last letters of Einstein's name, although you aren't sure what's in between. To perform this search, you use "e*n" as your search string. Try this search now.

To locate files using the asterisk wildcard:

1. Click the **Named** box.

2. Type **e*n** and then click the **Find Now** button. Find locates files whose names start with "e" followed by any number of characters and then the letter "n."

3. If necessary, scroll through the Find window to view all of the Results list. See Figure 6-9.

Figure 6-9	SEARCHING WITH THE ASTERISK WILDCARD

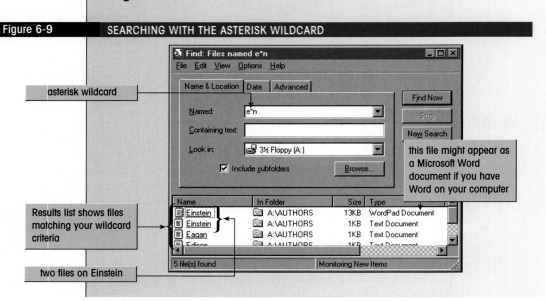

You make a mental note that there are files on Einstein that might be appropriate for the Atomic Energy symposium.

Finding a Text String in a File

You've found a file on Einstein, and now you wonder if there might be files specifically on atomic energy. You search for files named "atomic" or "energy" but don't find any. You know, however, that this doesn't necessarily mean there are no quotes on atomic energy within the files. A very useful feature of the Windows 98 Find utility is its ability to search for a word or phrase within a file. To use this feature, you enter a text string in the Containing text box on the Name & Location tab. A **text string** is a series of characters, such as a word or a phrase. Find searches through the entire text of every file to find the specified text string.

When you use the text string feature of the Find utility, you can specify whether your search is case-sensitive. For example, if you wanted to find a letter you wrote to Brenda Wolf, you could enter "Wolf" as your text string, and then choose the Case Sensitive command on the Options menu to locate only files containing Wolf with an initial capital letter. The Case Sensitive option affects only the case of letters in the Containing text box—not those in the Named box on the Name & Location tab.

You decide to search for the text string "atomic energy" in hopes that you might find files containing quotations Carolyn could use in writing the Atomic Energy symposium speech. Remember that now you are looking for a string within a file's contents, not within a file's name. Find will locate only files that contain all words you typed, in the order you entered them.

To look for the text string "atomic energy" within a file:

1. Delete the contents of the Named box.

2. Click the **Containing text** box.

3. Type **atomic energy**, but don't click **Find Now** yet. Because you aren't sure what case the quote might be in, you want to make sure Find isn't set to perform case-sensitive searches.

4. Click **Options** on the menu bar, and then make sure **Case Sensitive** is not checked. If it is, click it to remove the check mark. Otherwise Find might not locate the file if the case of the search string is not all lowercase.

5. Click the **Find Now** button. Find locates one file, as shown in Figure 6-10.

   TROUBLE? Don't worry if Find takes longer than usual. Searching for file contents, even on a 3½-inch disk, is time-consuming.

   TROUBLE? If Find did not locate any file, check to make sure you typed the text string "atomic energy" correctly and that drive A is selected.

Figure 6-10   **SEARCHING FOR TEXT IN A FILE**

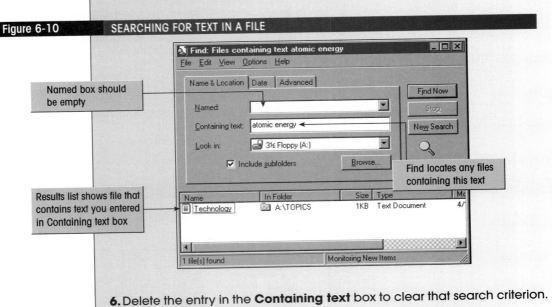

Named box should be empty

Find locates any files containing this text

Results list shows file that contains text you entered in Containing text box

6. Delete the entry in the **Containing text** box to clear that search criterion.

If you use the Containing text option on a hard disk, be prepared to wait, because searching file contents one file at a time is time-consuming. If you can narrow the search range using other criteria so that Find searches fewer files, for example by specifying a folder rather than an entire drive, you will speed things up.

Searching for Files in a Specific Folder

The more you can limit the number of files Find has to search, the more quickly it will locate all the files that meet your criteria. Find can search all drives and folders available to your computer or, as you saw when you selected the drive containing your Student Disk, it can search only a single drive. You can also narrow your search by specifying a specific folder, on your own computer or on a shared network computer.

You report to Carolyn that you've found files containing quotations on atomic energy and on Albert Einstein. She suggests that you now spend some time looking for any material you want, just to get a better feel for the disk's contents. You noticed there was a Comedy folder, and you wonder whether it might contain any quotes by Woody Allen, one of the Senator's favorite celebrities. Hoping for really quick results, you decide to tell Find to search only that folder.

To specify the Comedy folder, you navigate a folder tree similar to the one in Windows Explorer.

To search the Comedy folder on drive A for files that contain the string "woody allen":

1. Click the **Browse** button. A list of devices, drives, and folders appears.

2. Click ⊞ next to 💾 for drive A. The folders on drive A appear. See Figure 6-11.

   TROUBLE? Your list of devices, drives, and folders might look different, depending on your computer's drives and network.

Figure 6-11   SELECTING A FOLDER

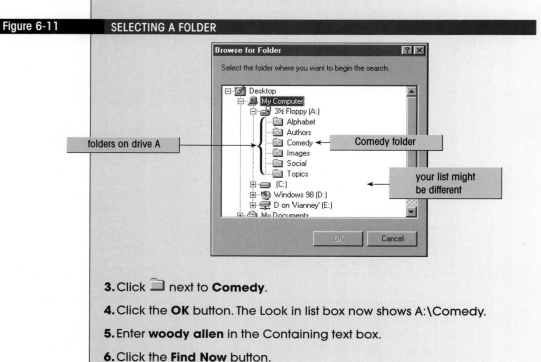

folders on drive A

Comedy folder

your list might be different

3. Click 📁 next to **Comedy**.

4. Click the **OK** button. The Look in list box now shows A:\Comedy.

5. Enter **woody allen** in the Containing text box.

6. Click the **Find Now** button.

This search procedure tells Find to look only in the Comedy folder on drive A and to include any subfolders the Comedy folder might contain as Find searches for files whose contents include the string "woody allen." Find locates two such files.

Clearing a Search

When you've completed a search, you need to remember to clear the criterion so it won't affect your next search (unless you want to use it as one of several criteria in a subsequent search). So far, you've been deleting your criteria whenever you enter new criteria, but you can also clear all search criteria at once using the New Search button. You don't want to limit subsequent searches to just the Comedy folder, so you will use the New Search button to clear it and any other criteria. There is a drawback to using the New Search button, however—if you want to search your Student Disk any further, you must reset the Look in list box to drive A.

To clear all criteria:

1. Click the **New Search** button.

2. Click the **OK** button to acknowledge the message that this will clear your current search. Find returns all settings to their defaults.

The Find: All Files dialog box now displays the default settings.

Working with the Results List

Up until now, the Results lists that you've examined have been short and manageable. When your search yields a large number of files, you can adjust the Results list to display the information in a more suitable and organized format.

You wonder whether there is a way to find quotations by author. You decide to search the disk for any files or folders that contain the term "author."

To search for files and folders named "author" on drive A:

1. Click the **Look in** list arrow and then click **3½ Floppy (A:)**.

2. Type **author** in the Named box.

3. Click the **Find Now** button. The Results list displays all files and folders that have the word "author" located anywhere in their filenames. There are 28 such files.

You display files in the Results list the same way you do in My Computer or Windows Explorer. You can view the files in the list by Large Icons, Small Icons, List, or Details, and you can resize columns by dragging their borders. Details view, the default view, is probably the most useful view because it gives you all the information you need, to verify that you've found the file you want. In Details view, Find shows you the name, location, size, type, and date modified of each file. Just as in My Computer and Windows Explorer, you can sort the files in the Results list by any of these criteria.

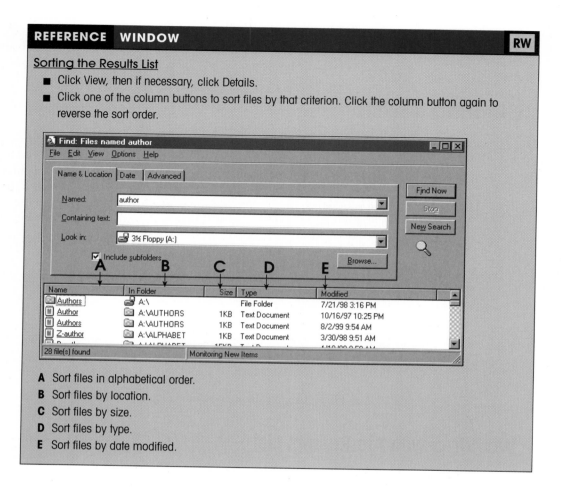

REFERENCE WINDOW   RW

Sorting the Results List
■ Click View, then if necessary, click Details.
■ Click one of the column buttons to sort files by that criterion. Click the column button again to reverse the sort order.

A   Sort files in alphabetical order.
B   Sort files by location.
C   Sort files by size.
D   Sort files by type.
E   Sort files by date modified.

You see files whose names suggest that they contain quotations from authors, labeled by last name. Is there a file for every letter of the alphabet? You can sort the files by name to find out.

To sort the files by name:

1. Maximize the Find window to view all five columns: Name, In Folder, Size, Type, and Modified.

2. Click the **Name** button, as shown in Figure 6-12, to arrange the files in ascending alphabetical order by name.

   TROUBLE? If your files are already arranged in alphabetical order, Step 1 will place them in descending order. Click the Name button again.

3. Scroll down the Results list and observe that there are files for most letters of the alphabet.

Figure 6-12	SORTING THE RESULTS LIST

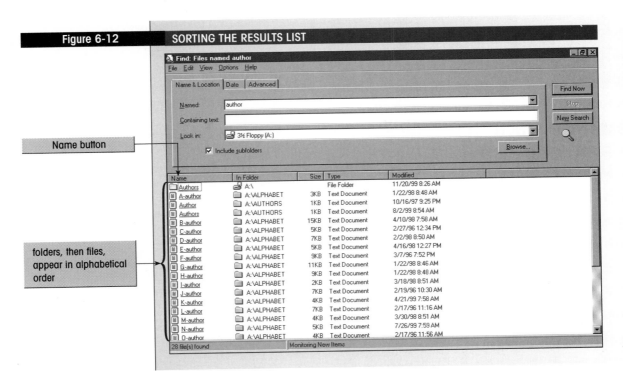

Name button

folders, then files, appear in alphabetical order

If you wanted to find quotations by a given author, you could try the file for the author's last name, located in the Alphabet folder. What else can you learn from the Results list? The Type column shows that the first item on the list is a folder and that the rest of the files are text documents. All the files are small (under 16 KB), and you could sort the files by date modified, to observe that these files were developed in the years between 1996–1999.

The judicious use of search strings has taught you a lot about the files in the quotations archives disk. In Session 6.2 you'll learn how to use additional criteria, such as date, type, and size.

To close Find:

1. Click the Find **Close** button ☒ .

QUICK CHECK

1. To search for a file only on drive A, what do you do?

2. True or False: You can type uppercase or lowercase letters when searching for a filename.

3. True or False: The Results list displays only the files whose names exactly match the search string you entered.

4. What is a wildcard? What is the difference between the asterisk wildcard and the question mark wildcard?

5. How do you display the files in the Results list in alphabetical order?

<table>
<tr><td>

SESSION 6.2

</td><td>

In this session, you will work with file date, type, and size as your search criteria, and then you'll combine these criteria for more effective searches. You'll examine the Documents menu to explore another way of locating a file. Finally, you'll use **Quick View**, a utility that lets you look at the contents of files without actually opening them.

</td></tr>
</table>

Descriptive Search Criteria

In Session 6.1 you searched for files with particular filenames or text strings on the quotations archive disk. When you don't know the filename, you can locate a file using criteria other than the filename or exact contents—criteria such as size, date, and type—using the other tabs in the Find window. These criteria are "descriptive" in that they help you identify files that share common characteristics. You can answer questions such as: Are any files more than a few years old? What files were created using a certain program? What files are larger or smaller than a specified size? You enter the characteristic you want to study, and then Find lists all files that share that characteristic, such as all files created after 1998, all Microsoft Word files, or all files larger than 50 KB.

You can use these descriptive search criteria on their own or in combination with filenames and text strings. The specifications you select on any one tab are added to any criteria you specify on the other tabs.

To prepare to search for files on the quotations archive disk:

1. Make sure your Student Disk is in the drive.

2. Click the **Start** button ⊞Start, point to **Find**, and then click **Files or Folders**.

3. If necessary, click the **Look in** list arrow, and then click the drive containing your Student Disk.

Finding a File by Date

In your new job as research assistant, you want to know when the previous aide collected the files. To search for files by date, you can use the Date tab. Searching for files by date is also useful when you want a file that you know you were working with on a given date but you can't remember where you stored it.

You decide to see how many files were created in the years 1994 and 1995, because you know the aide devoted a lot of time in those years developing the quotations archive. You'd like to see whether there are any files that haven't changed since then. You'll need to change the Date setting from its default of All files.

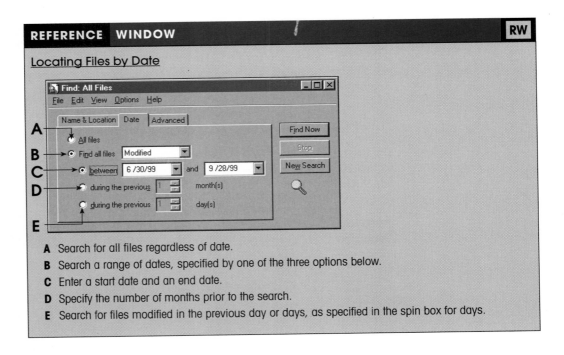

REFERENCE WINDOW   **RW**

Locating Files by Date

A Search for all files regardless of date.
B Search a range of dates, specified by one of the three options below.
C Enter a start date and an end date.
D Specify the number of months prior to the search.
E Search for files modified in the previous day or days, as specified in the spin box for days.

To search for files created between 1994 and 1995:

1. Click the **Date** tab.

2. Click the **between** option button.

3. Click the start date list arrow to open a calendar, and then press and hold down the back arrow until you locate January 1994. Then click **January 1**. See Figure 6-13.

| Figure 6-13 | SELECTING A START DATE |

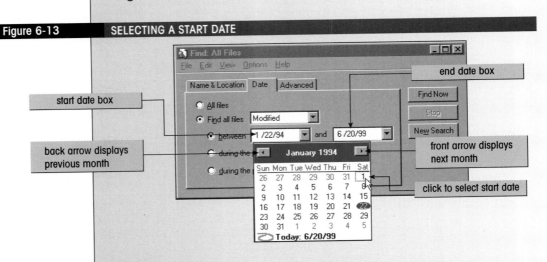

4. Click the end date list arrow to open its calendar, and then select **December 31, 1995** in the same way.

5. Click the **Find Now** button. There is only one file in that range of dates. Apparently most of the files created in 1994 and 1995 have since been updated.

6. Click the **All files** option button to return the date criterion to its default.

It might have occurred to you that you could get information about file dates more quickly by opening Explorer or My Computer and sorting the files by date. You'd be right, if the files were all in one folder. However, when the files are scattered among multiple folders, Find can display files from any of those folders that meet your date criteria, whereas Explorer and My Computer can display the contents of only one folder at a time.

Finding a File by Type

You decide you'd like to get an overview of the types of files on the quotations archive disk, to see whether you have the necessary software on your computer to open them. The Advanced tab of the Find utility lets you specify file type and file size as your search criteria.

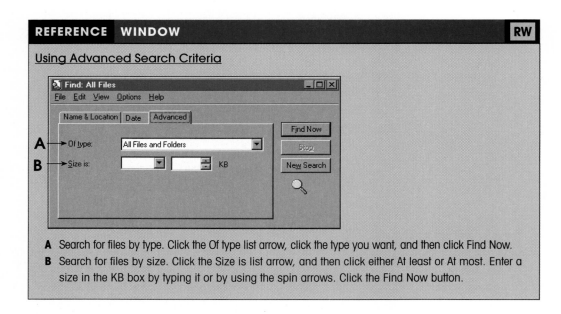

REFERENCE WINDOW   **RW**

Using Advanced Search Criteria

A   Search for files by type. Click the Of type list arrow, click the type you want, and then click Find Now.

B   Search for files by size. Click the Size is list arrow, and then click either At least or At most. Enter a size in the KB box by typing it or by using the spin arrows. Click the Find Now button.

You can look for files by their general file type or by the program that created them. The list of file types from which you can choose includes text files, sound files, movie clips, bitmaps, Word documents, Access databases, Web documents, and so on, depending on the resources on your computer.

You already know there are lots of text files, but you'd like to know how many. You also wonder whether there are any sound files that the Senator might be able to use in a multimedia presentation. You decide to use file type criteria to answer these questions.

To view files by type:

1. Click the **Advanced** tab.

2. Click the **Of type** list arrow, and then scroll down the alphabetical list to locate "Text Document."

3. Click **Text Document**, and then click the **Find Now** button. The status bar reports that there are 92 text files on your disk.

   TROUBLE? If your list is much shorter, you might have forgotten to return the Date setting back to All files. Forgetting to reset criteria to their original settings can confuse your search efforts.

AU clip

4. Next you want to look for sound files. Click the **Of type** list arrow. Scroll to and then click **Sound Clip**. Click the **Find Now** button. There are two such files.

5. Return the type to its default setting: click the **Of type** list arrow, scroll to the top, and then click **All Files and Folders**.

Finding a File by Size

In searching for files by type, you found two sound files. You know these files are usually bigger than text files or word-processed documents. If you are short on disk space, you'll want to identify the largest files so you can move them to free up space. You can find this information by looking for a file by its size. You specify either "at least" or "at most" and then pick the number of kilobytes you want. If disk space is a problem, you might want to look for all files that are at least 25 KB in size. Try that search now.

To search for files by size:

1. Click the **Size is** list arrow, and then click **At least**.

2. Click the **KB** box, and then type **25**. (You could also use the spin arrows to select a number.)

3. Click the **Find Now** button. The Results list shows six such files. You can sort these files to more easily identify the largest.

4. Click the **Size** button twice to sort the files by size, with the largest files first. Not surprisingly, the largest files are the two sound files. See Figure 6-14.

| Figure 6-14 | SEARCHING FOR FILES BY SIZE |

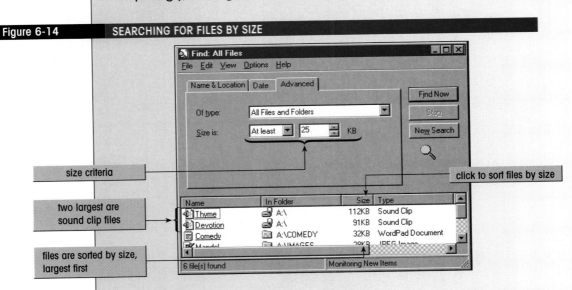

size criteria

click to sort files by size

two largest are sound clip files

files are sorted by size, largest first

5. Click the **Size is** list arrow, and then click the blank entry at the top of the list so that the Size is box is empty.

TROUBLE? Don't worry that 25 KB still appears in the spin box. Find ignores the entry for future searches because the Size is box is blank.

Deleting a File from Your Student Disk Using the Results List

When you ask Carolyn about the sound files, she tells you she has copies of them, so you decide to delete them from the quotations archive disk because they take up so much room, and you only need one copy. In Find you can use many of the My Computer and Windows Explorer file manipulation techniques that you've already learned, such as file deletion. To delete one or more files, you select the files in the Results list first. You can use the Ctrl key or the Shift key to select more than one file at a time.

To delete the sound files:

1. Select the **Thyme** file in the Results list.

2. Press and hold down **Ctrl**, and then select the **Devotion** file. Both Thyme and Devotion are selected.

3. Right-click either selected file, and then click **Delete**. Click **Yes** if you are asked if you are sure. The files are deleted from your quotations archive disk.

Finding a File Using Multiple Criteria

Carolyn stops by your office and informs you that, because Stanton College is a women's college, Senator Bernstein might be interested in having a quote on leadership by a woman. She asks if you could find such a quote. If you specify multiple criteria, such as a likely filename and a likely text string, you might be able to pinpoint one.

You remember that there are files on the archive disk whose filenames contain the search string "women." You guess that the speech probably used the word "leader," so you could specify the root "leader" as your text string. Find uses all the criteria you enter, on any of the tabs, to perform the search.

To find a file with multiple criteria:

1. Click the **Name & Location** tab.

2. Click the **Named** box, and then type **women**.

3. Click the **Containing text** box, type **leader**, and then click the **Find Now** button. One file matches your criteria. See Figure 6-15.

4. Right-click the **Women** file from the Results list, and then click **Open**. It opens in Notepad. You see a quotation on leaders by Mother Teresa.

5. Close Notepad.

6. Clear the contents of the Named and Containing text boxes.

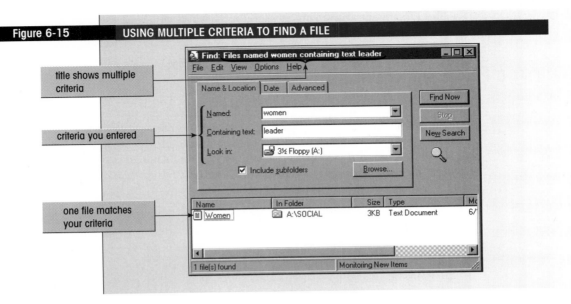

| Figure 6-15 | USING MULTIPLE CRITERIA TO FIND A FILE |

title shows multiple criteria

criteria you entered

one file matches your criteria

Opening Recent Documents

So far in this tutorial you have used Find to locate files. There is another way to locate a file you've worked on recently. You can view a list of recently opened documents, using the Documents command on the Start menu. If you click one of the documents on the Documents menu, Windows 98 locates and starts the program that created the document, and then opens the document. Carolyn drops by, and you decide to use the Documents menu to show her the file you just opened.

To view the most recent documents list:

1. Click the **Start** button ![Start].

2. Point to **Documents**. The Documents menu opens. See Figure 6-16.

| Figure 6-16 | OPENING A FILE FROM THE DOCUMENTS LIST |

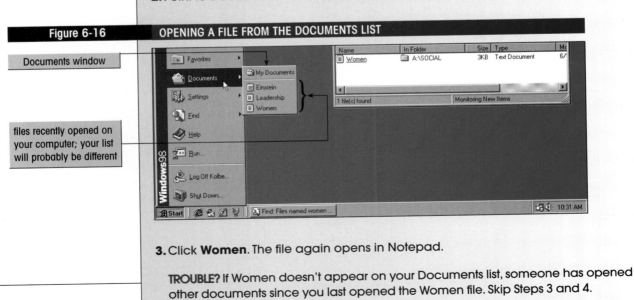

Documents window

files recently opened on your computer; your list will probably be different

3. Click **Women**. The file again opens in Notepad.

   TROUBLE? If Women doesn't appear on your Documents list, someone has opened other documents since you last opened the Women file. Skip Steps 3 and 4.

4. Close Notepad.

The Documents command is useful only when you have recently worked on a file on your own computer. It can be the quickest way to find and open such a file.

Viewing a File Using Quick View

Windows 98 provides a useful utility called Quick View that lets you view a file without starting the program that created it (some programs take a long time to load). Quick View is also useful when you want to view a batch of files quickly. Since Carolyn still seems to be looking for quotations on successful leadership, you decide to search for the text string "success." You can use Quick View to view file contents rather than open each file individually.

REFERENCE WINDOW   **RW**

Viewing Files Using Quick View
- Right-click the file you want to view.
- Click Quick View on the shortcut menu.

Note that Quick View is not included in the typical installation of Windows 98. You'll know if Quick View is installed by looking at a file's shortcut menu.

To check whether Quick View is installed and then to start Quick View:

1. Type **success** in the Containing text box.

2. Click the **Find Now** button, and then click the **Name** button to sort the files alphabetically by filename, so that the file named "Anonymou" is visible at the top of the Results list.

   TROUBLE? If clicking the Name button orders the files in descending alphabetical order, click the Name button again.

3. Right-click **Anonymou**, and then look at the shortcut menu that opens. If Quick View is installed, it appears as an option. See Figure 6-17.

   TROUBLE? If Quick View does not appear as an option, as shown in Figure 6-17, then Quick View is not installed on your computer. Check with your instructor or technical support person for directions, and if you can't install Quick View, skip Step 4 and read through the rest of this section. If you are using your own computer and you have the installation disk, insert it. Open the Add/Remove Programs Properties window from Control Panel or from the Windows 98 CD-ROM window. Click the Windows Setup tab, click Accessories, and then click Details. Scroll down the Components list, and then click Quick View. Click the OK button twice, and then close the Add/Remove Programs Properties dialog box.

| Figure 6-17 | OPENING A FILE'S SHORTCUT MENU |

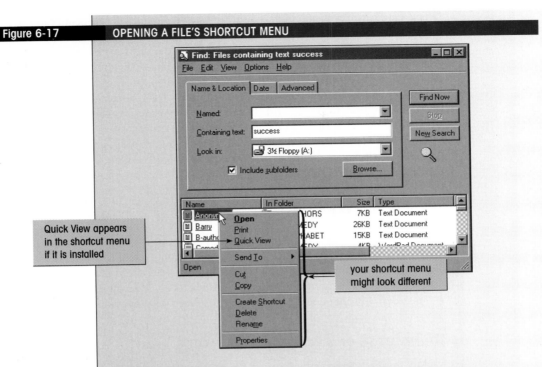

Quick View appears in the shortcut menu if it is installed

your shortcut menu might look different

4. Click **Quick View**. The Quick View window opens. See Figure 6-18.

TROUBLE? If your document appears as a page, click View, and then click Page View to remove the check mark.

TROUBLE? If your font size is different, don't worry. You'll learn how to increase or decrease font size in the next section.

| Figure 6-18 | QUICK VIEW WINDOW |

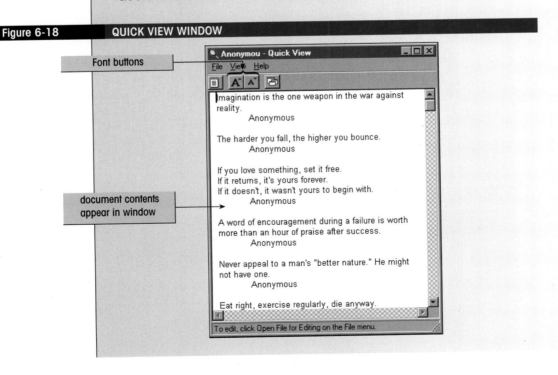

Font buttons

document contents appear in window

Quick View displays the contents of a file in the document window, either in Page or Normal view. **Page view** displays the document in pages. In Page view, if the document is more than one page, page arrows appear in the upper-right corner. **Normal view**, as shown in Figure 6-18, displays the text as a continuous document and supplies scroll bars you can use to view it.

The degree of accuracy with which Quick View displays your documents depends on the type of file you are viewing. If you are viewing a word-processed document, for example, Quick View doesn't duplicate your document's fonts and keeps formatting to a minimum (bold and italic only; no lines or bullets). If there are objects such as graphics or charts in the text document, Quick View represents them with shaded boxes. If you are viewing a document such as a bitmap image or a PowerPoint slide presentation, however, Quick View shows the actual drawing.

Changing the Font Size

Quick View displays documents using a font that is easy to read. The amount of text that appears in the Quick View window depends on the font size of the letters. The larger the letters, the less of the file appears. You might need to adjust font size so that you can read the words more easily. Changing the font size in Quick View does not affect the formatting of the document itself—it only determines how Quick View displays it in the Quick View window.

To increase or decrease font size:

1. Click the **Increase Font Size** button 🅰 several times. The text is easier to read, but fewer quotes fit on the page.

2. Click the **Decrease Font Size** button 🅰 several times. Now more quotations fit on the page, but they are harder to read.

3. Click 🅰 or 🅰 as necessary until the font size is just right for you.

Navigating Quick View Pages

You notice that the fourth quote mentions success, and you decide to scroll through the rest of the document to check whether there are any other quotes Carolyn might want to consider. You can also use your keyboard's navigation keys to move through the document quickly. **Navigation keys** are keys that you press to move through a document, including Page Up, Page Down, Home, End, and the arrow keys →, ←, ↑, ↓. These keys have standard functions in most software packages. Figure 6-19 shows the function of each key, along with a few standard key combinations.

Figure 6-19	NAVIGATION KEYS AND KEY COMBINATIONS
KEY	**FUNCTION**
Page Up	Moves up one screen or page
Page Down	Moves down one screen or page
Home	Moves to the beginning of the current line
End	Moves to the end of the current line
Arrow Keys	Moves through the document one line or one character at a time in the direction of the arrow
Ctrl + Home	Moves to beginning of document
Ctrl + End	Moves to end of document

Try navigating your document in Quick View using the navigation keys.

To navigate in Quick View using the navigation keys:

1. Press **Page Down** two or three times. You move down in the document, one screen at a time.

2. Press **Ctrl + End**. You move to the end of the document.

3. Press **Ctrl + Home**. You move to the beginning of the document.

Dragging a File into Quick View

There are still many interesting files listed in the Find Results list that you've not yet explored. You'd like to take a look at another one—perhaps the Keller one, which has quotes by Helen Keller. Once Quick View is open, the quickest way to look at another of the files in the Results list is to drag the file icon into the Quick View window.

To open additional documents in Quick View:

1. Right-click a blank area of the taskbar, and then click Tile Windows Vertically to arrange the Find and Quick View windows so that they are both visible.

2. Drag the file **Keller** into the Quick View window (scroll the Results list to see it, if necessary). See Figure 6-20. The contents of this file appear.

TROUBLE? If you click the file by mistake and you are using Web style, the file opens. Close the file and then repeat Step 3, but be sure to drag, not click, the file.

Figure 6-20	DRAGGING A FILE INTO QUICK VIEW WINDOW

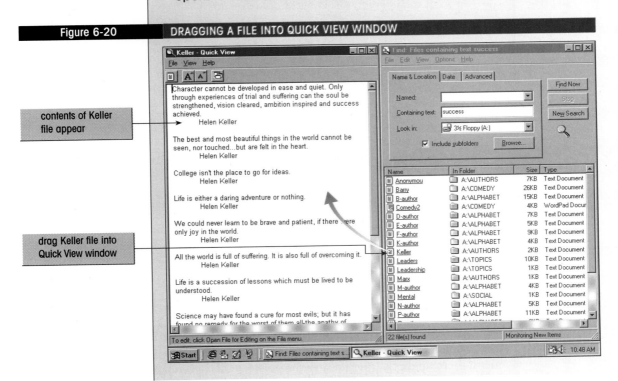

contents of Keller file appear

drag Keller file into Quick View window

After looking at the Keller file in the Quick View window, you decide to print it. You can't print a file directly from Quick View, but you can print from Find, using the Print command on a file's shortcut menu.

To close the Quick View window and print the Keller file from Find:

1. Click the **Close** button ☒ on the Quick View window.

2. Right-click the **Keller** file in the Find window, and then click **Print**. Notepad opens automatically and prints the file and then closes.

3. Click the Find **Close** button ☒.

The Find utility has helped you locate files on your disks that meet one or more criteria. In the next session, you'll expand your search to locate more quotations files on the Internet.

QUICK CHECK

1. If you want the Find utility to display only the bitmapped images on your floppy disk, what tab should you click in Find?

2. If the Results list displays the file you were looking for, how do you open the file for editing?

3. Something seems to be wrong with Notepad. You can see only the first 10 words or so of each paragraph. What should you do?

4. You want to find a file that you know is exactly 48 KB in size. What should you do?

5. Can you use Quick View to view a bitmapped image file, or is it useful only for text files?

6. You can barely read the words in the Quick View window. What button should you click?

SESSION 6.3

In this session, you will learn about searching on the Internet, including searching by query and by subject. You'll learn to search using the Search Explorer bar. Finally, you'll learn to search for people on the Internet.

Searching on the Internet

The Internet has vast resources, but to locate the information you want, you need to search for it. Windows 98 helps you search for information on the Internet with the On the Internet option on the Find menu. When you choose this option, Windows 98 starts the Internet Explorer browser and connects to a search page.

You would like to expand the set of quotations on the quotation archives disk, and you wonder if there might be Internet sites that make quotation collections available. You decide to search the Internet to find out.

To connect to Microsoft's search page:

1. Make sure you are connected to the Internet.

2. Click the **Start** button 🏁Start, and then point to **Find**.

3. Click **On the Internet**. Microsoft's search page opens. See Figure 6-21. Because Microsoft constantly updates this page, it might look different on your computer.

Figure 6-21	MICROSOFT'S SEARCH PAGE

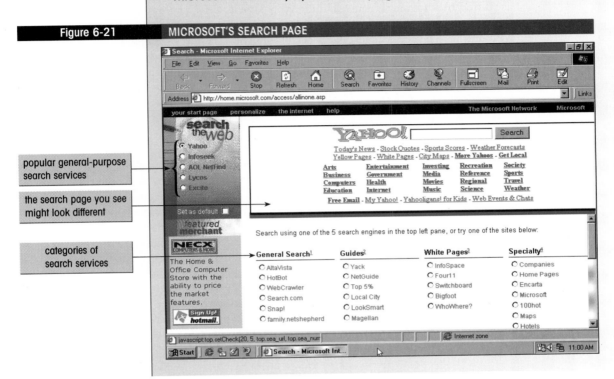

popular general-purpose search services

the search page you see might look different

categories of search services

The Microsoft search page makes available many popular **search services**, software that helps you find information on the Internet. Figure 6-22 describes the categories of search services as they appear on the Microsoft search page shown in Figure 6-21. Remember that because Microsoft updates its search page regularly, your screen might show different categories.

Figure 6-22	SEARCH SERVICE CATEGORIES

SEARCH SERVICE CATEGORY	DESCRIPTION
General Search	General-purpose services that allow you to search the entire Web. Some general search services, such as AltaVista or HotBot, allow you to search every word on every page of the Web.
Guides	Web sites organized by category and/or location
White Pages	Similar to a telephone book, provides names, e-mail and mailing addresses, phone numbers, and so on
Specialty	Services with specific information, such as encyclopedias, hotel listings, or investment information
Business Directories	Similar to a telephone book, provides information about businesses
Newsgroups	Services that allow you to search newsgroup archives. **Newsgroups**, also called **discussion groups**, bring people with common interests together to exchange e-mail messages on a given topic.
International	Provides access to sites in countries and languages around the world

Most general search services employ software that regularly searches through Internet documents and compiles a list of Web pages it locates on the Internet. It organizes and indexes this list by topic. When you use the search service to find Web pages on a specific topic, you use software called a search engine. A **search engine** checks the service's index and provides you with links to all the pages it finds on that topic. Because the Internet is changing so quickly, the indexes change regularly too, so if you don't find the information you want one day, it might be available the next. Moreover, because different search services use different software to compile their Web page indexes, you might get different results for the same search when using two different search services. If you can't find what you want with one search service, such as Yahoo, try another, such as Infoseek.

Most search services allow you to perform two types of searches: searches by query and searches by subject. You'll use Microsoft's search page to try both types of searches.

Searching by Query

A **query** is a request for information. You enter a specific word or phrase, called a **keyword**, into a box, and then click a button, such as Search or Find, that sends your request to the search service. Some search engines allow you to refine your query to get the results you want. For example, if you are looking for information on population statistics, some search engines assume you mean "population" *or* "statistics" and return pages that contain either word. Other search engines assume you mean "population" *and* "statistics" and return only pages with both words. These searches take longer and return fewer pages, but the pages are likely to be more useful. Other search engines assume you mean "population" *and/or* "statistics."

Most search engines allow you to refine your query with symbols called **search operators**, such as plus (which requires a term or phrase), minus (which excludes a term or phrase), and quotation marks (which identify words that must appear together). Figure 6-23 provides examples of how these operators work in the Infoseek search engine; other search engines might work differently. You can check a search engine's online Help to learn how to structure your search query using that search engine.

Figure 6-23	KEYWORD OPERATORS
KEYWORD	**RETURNED PAGES**
population statistics	*population* and/or *statistics*
"population statistics"	the word *population* next to the word *statistics*
+population +statistics	*population* and *statistics* but not necessarily next to each other
+population statistics	*population* but not necessarily *statistics*
+statistics -population	*statistics* but not *population*

Using capital letters for proper names can exclude, for example, pages on the color green when you search for information on Greenpeace.

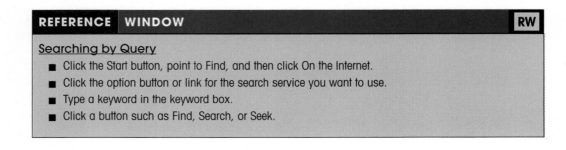

REFERENCE WINDOW   RW

Searching by Query
- Click the Start button, point to Find, and then click On the Internet.
- Click the option button or link for the search service you want to use.
- Type a keyword in the keyword box.
- Click a button such as Find, Search, or Seek.

You want to find information on quotation collections. You decide to use the Infoseek search service with "quotation" as your keyword.

To use the Infoseek search engine to search for quotation collections:

1. Choose **Infoseek** by clicking the appropriate option button or link, or by choosing Infoseek from the drop-down list.

2. In the Infoseek area of the screen, click the box next to the seek button.

3. Type **quotation**, and then click the **seek** button. See Figure 6-24.

Figure 6-24	USING INFOSEEK TO SEARCH FOR A KEYWORD

click a button similar to Seek button

enter keyword in whatever box you see

choose Infoseek from whatever list of search services you see

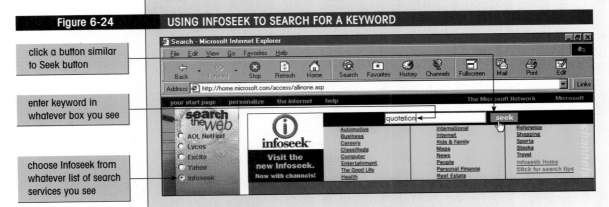

4. If a Security Alert dialog box appears, click **Yes**. After a moment, Infoseek returns a search results page that lists links that match your search criteria.

5. Scroll down the search results page past "related topics" until you see applicable links. See Figure 6-25. The list of links you see will probably be different, and you might see only links, without descriptions.

Figure 6-25	SEARCH RESULTS PAGE

descriptions might not appear on your results page

links to pages that meet your search criteria

this page looks promising

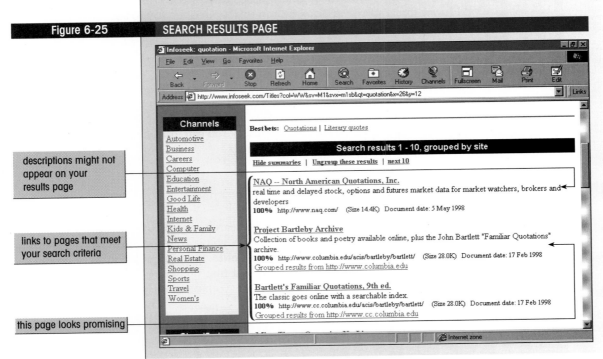

6. On the search results page, click the quotation link that looks most promising. In Figure 6-25, there is a link to a stock quotations service, which obviously is not what you want, but there are other links that look as if they target quotation collections.

7. Follow the links until you locate a collection of quotations. Figure 6-26 shows a typical quotation collection page.

| Figure 6-26 | PAGE ON QUOTATIONS |

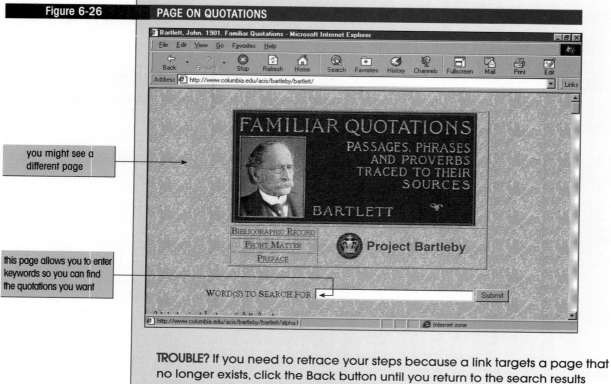

you might see a different page

this page allows you to enter keywords so you can find the quotations you want

TROUBLE? If you need to retrace your steps because a link targets a page that no longer exists, click the Back button until you return to the search results page, and then repeat Steps 6 and 7 with a different link.

8. Click the **Back** button to return to the search page.

Most search results pages show only the first 10 or 20 links; to see the next set of links you need to scroll to locate a link such as Next, Next 10, or Next 20. Some services also rate pages by usefulness, scoring on a 100-point scale. You can learn about a search service's features by connecting directly to the search service.

Searching by Subject

When you search by query, you are asking the search engine to locate information on the topic you specify. In a **subject search**, however, you search for information by browsing through a hierarchy of topics, called a **subject guide**. Subject guides are created and maintained by the search service. They are organized first by general and then by successively more specific subjects. Most search services allow you to search by query or subject.

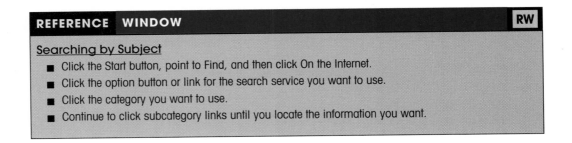

The Yahoo search engine offers one of the most popular subject guides; you decide to use it to locate additional information on quotations.

To search the Yahoo subject guide for quotation collections:

1. Click the **Start** button 🏁 Start , point to **Find**, and then click **On the Internet** to return to Microsoft's search page.

2. If necessary, click the **Yahoo** option button or **Yahoo** link. The subject guide categories appear below the keyword box. See Figure 6-27.

Figure 6-27	SUBJECT GUIDE

Yahoo subject guide categories

Yahoo is selected

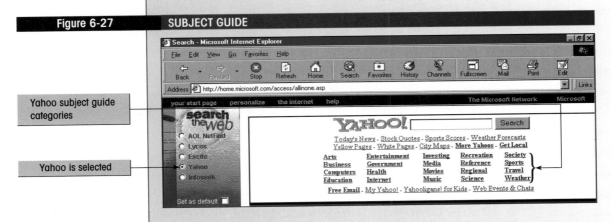

3. Since the Reference category is most likely to have information on quotations, click **Reference**. Yahoo displays all its Reference categories; scroll down to see them if necessary. If you are using a different search service, look for a similar category.

4. Click **Quotations**, as shown in Figure 6-28.

5. In the category list that appears, click one of the Quotations categories that interests you, and continue clicking relevant links until you locate a quotation collection.

Figure 6-28

REFERENCE SUBCATEGORIES

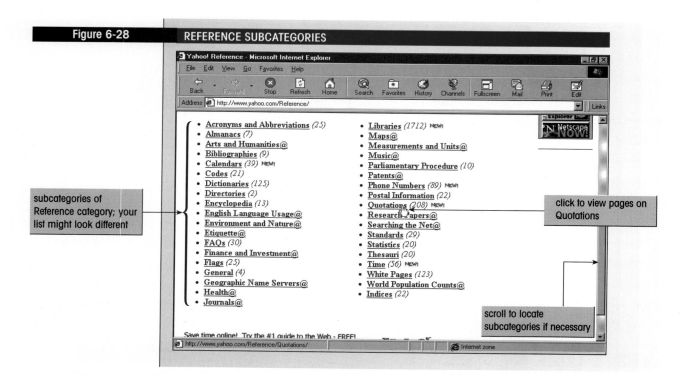

subcategories of Reference category; your list might look different

click to view pages on Quotations

scroll to locate subcategories if necessary

Searching with the Search Explorer Bar

The Start menu gives you access to the Microsoft search page, but Windows 98 gives you another tool for searching the Internet: the Search Explorer bar. You can display the Search Explorer bar in My Computer, Windows Explorer, Internet Explorer, or any folder or device window. The Search Explorer bar makes the same search services available as Microsoft's search page.

To search for quotations using the Search Explorer bar:

1. Close Internet Explorer, and then open the Windows Explorer window and maximize it if necessary.

2. Click **View**, point to **Explorer Bar**, and then click **Search**. The Search Explorer bar appears. See Figure 6-29. A default search service is selected for you; yours might be different from the one in Figure 6-29. You can usually search by query or subject guide; subjects usually appear below the keyword box.

   TROUBLE? If a security warning appears, click No to continue.

3. Type **quotation** in the keyword box.

4. Click the corresponding search button, such as Find, Search, or Seek. Click **Yes** if a Security Alert dialog box appears. The search results appear on the Search Explorer bar below the keyword box.

5. Scroll down the Search Explorer bar until you see the search results.

6. Click one of the quotations links and continue following links until you reach a quotation collection.

7. Close the Exploring window.

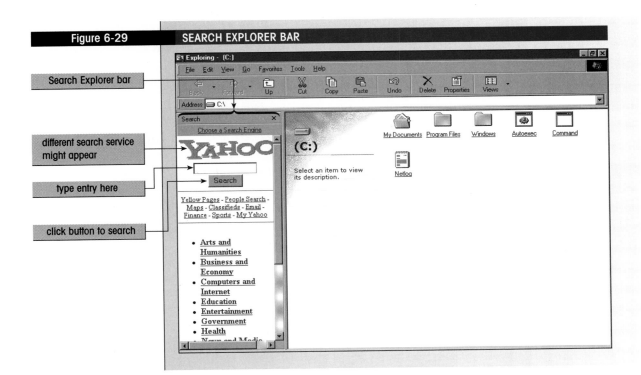

| Figure 6-29 | SEARCH EXPLORER BAR |

Search Explorer bar

different search service
might appear

type entry here

click button to search

There are many quotation collections on the Web—some have search engines built into them that make it even easier to locate a specific quote. You tell Carolyn that if she isn't satisfied with what you've found on the quotations archive disk, you can easily expand your search to include quotation collections on the Web.

Searching for People

Windows 98 also includes an option on the Find menu, Find People, that helps you search for information about specific people. Similar to a telephone book, the Find People option locates information such as a person's mailing or e-mail address or phone number. The Find People dialog box allows you to choose from a variety of people search services, ranging from your computer's local Address Book (a Windows 98 feature that comes with the Internet Explorer suite and allows you to maintain a list of contacts) to Internet people search services such as Bigfoot and SwitchBoard. You enter a name, and the search service returns a list of people with that name. For common names the list is very long; for some names no information is available.

Over the last week Carolyn has asked you to find contact information for some of the sources she's using in preparing Senator Bernstein's Atomic Energy Symposium speech. You've managed to do so by searching through journal articles written by the sources, but you wonder if the Internet might give you an alternate method of finding information about people. You decide to see if you can locate information on yourself, using the SwitchBoard people search service.

To find information about a person:

1. Click the **Start** button ![Start], point to **Find**, and then click **People**.

2. Click the **Look in** list arrow and then click **SwitchBoard**.

3. Type your name in the Name box, first name first, such as Maria Taylor.

4. Click the **Find Now** button. If SwitchBoard has any address information on people with your name, it appears in a list, as shown in Figure 6-30. If SwitchBoard wasn't able to find the information you requested, try using a friend's name, your instructor's name, or a more common name.

TROUBLE? If an error message appears, your Internet connection might be too slow to retrieve the list of names or the Find People service you selected might be busy. Try with a different service, different name, or try again later.

Figure 6-30	SEARCHING FOR PEOPLE

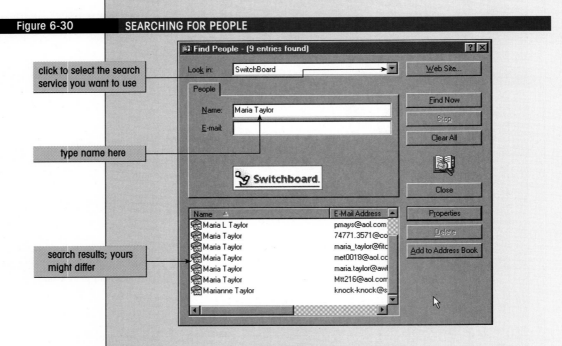

click to select the search service you want to use

type name here

search results; yours might differ

5. Close the Find People dialog box, and disconnect from the Internet, if necessary.

You're confident that you can use Windows 98 and the search services it makes available to find just about any information Carolyn needs. With the Find options built into the Start menu and Explorer windows, it's easy to locate what you need, quickly.

QUICK CHECK

1. What kind of software searches through Internet documents and compiles a list of Web pages it locates on the Internet?

2. True or False: If you don't find information using Yahoo, it's pointless to try to find the same information using Infoseek.

3. What is the difference between a query search and a subject search?

4. If you are using Infoseek and you want information on the dog Toto in the *Wizard of Oz*, but you don't want any pages on the rock band Toto, what search operators can you use?

5. How can you use Windows 98 to find an e-mail address for your state's governor?

TUTORIAL ASSIGNMENTS

1. **Using a Search String to Find a File** The governor has asked Senator Bernstein to represent the state in upcoming meetings with representatives of Taiwan, for the purpose of setting up a student exchange program. In any international exchange, language is always an issue. You remember a very funny story about the translation of an ad for Coca-Cola into another language. Might that anecdote be somewhere on the quotations archive disk?

   a. To find out, start Find and enter likely search strings into the Named box. Make sure you select drive A. If you're having trouble locating a file, try using just part of the search string.

   b. Once you find a file you think looks promising, open it from Find.

   c. When you've found what you want, select the text, click Edit, and then click Copy. You'll paste the text into a new document. Click File, click New (click No if asked if you want to save your changes), click Edit, click Paste, and type your name in the document you just created. At the end of the document, write a few sentences describing the search string you used and the name of the file you located. Print the document, and then close Notepad and Find.

2. **Learning More About Files** On a sheet of paper, write the answers to the following questions about the files on the Student Disk. You can answer all the questions by examining the filenames.

   a. How many files are there with the search string "comedy" in the filename?

   b. How many files and folders in total are on the disk? Use Find to answer this question. What did you do to find the answer? (*Hint*: you can find the answer to this question with a single search.)

   c. Which letters of the alphabet are missing in the filenames of the alphabetically organized Author files?

   d. How many files are there on friendship? What search string did you use to find this answer?

3. **Using Wildcards** What search strings could you use to produce the following Results lists? Write the search strings on a piece of paper. Use a wildcard for each one. For example, a Results list of Budget1996.xls, Budget1997.xls, and Budget1998.xls could come from the search string "Budget199?.xls".

   a. Comedy1.doc, Comedy2.doc, Comedy3.doc

   b. Social.txt, Society.txt, Socratic Method.txt

   c. PhotoWorks, Network, Files for Work

4. **Searching for Files by Date** You can answer these questions about the Student Disk by using the Date tab. Write the answers on a sheet of paper. Return all settings to their defaults when you are done.

   a. What files did Carolyn's previous aide modify on April 2, 1997?

   b. Over what period of time did Carolyn's previous aide modify all author files in the Alphabet folder?

   c. What is the oldest file on the Student Disk?

5. **Locating Files by Size** How many files of 1 KB or less are on the Student Disk? How many files of 15 KB or more? Return this setting to its default when you are done.

6. **Locating Files by Contents** You have always enjoyed Dave Barry's columns. Search the contents of the files on the Student Disk to see how many of them contain the text string "barry", and then record that number. Write down the name of the file that looks as if it contains the most Dave Barry quotations. Open the file from Find. When you are done, delete the criteria you entered.

7. **Experimenting with Search Criteria** You look over Senator Bernstein's speech topics for the next several months and decide to search for appropriate quotations. For each speech topic, write down the criteria you used to locate a file, and then write down the file location as displayed in the In Folder column of the Results list. If you find more than one file, write down the first one in the list.

   a. Senator Bernstein has been invited to give the toast at a football brunch hosted by the President of Riverside College.

   b. The family of a deceased friend has asked Senator Bernstein if she'd like to contribute any thoughts to a written memorial.

   c. Senator Bernstein is co-chairing this year's Renaissance Festival downtown. The Festival will feature outdoor performances of three of Shakespeare's plays, including a performance by the Young Shakespearians Guild, a troupe of children under age 18. She's promised to give the opening remarks at the Festival.

Explore

8. **Opening Files from Find** You learned how to open a text document from Find in Session 6.2. You can open other types of files the same way, as long as your computer contains the application that created the file.

   a. Use Quick Format in Windows Explorer to format your Student Disk, and then make a new Student Disk for this tutorial as described in the beginning of Session 6.1.

   b. Search for Sound Clip files on your Student Disk. Right-click one of them, and click Play, then click the Play button ▶. What did you hear? Click the Close button when the sound file is done playing. If you don't hear anything, your computer might not have speakers, or they might be off.

   c. Search for Video Clip files on your computer's hard drive. If you find any, right-click one of them, click Play, and then click the Play button ▶. Describe what you see. Click the Close button when the video clip is done playing.

9. **Searching and Viewing File Contents** Use Quick View to find the answers to the questions below. You will probably need to search for a text string in the file's contents using the Name and Location tab. If Quick View isn't installed on your computer, open the files from Find to find the answers. For each answer, write the name of the file you used to find the answer. (*Hint*: Once you've located and opened the file, you can either scroll through it to find the answer, or, if the file is a long one, open it in Notepad, click Search on the Notepad menu bar, and then click Find. Type the text string in the Find what box, and then click the Find Next button.)

   a. What did Elsa Einstein think about her husband Albert's theory of relativity?

   b. Do you think cartoonist Jim Borgman is an optimist or a pessimist? Why?

   c. What was Helen Keller's opinion of college?

   d. How many children did Erma Bombeck recommend that one have? (Look carefully at the filenames in the Results list so you don't open more files than necessary.)

   e. What did Elbert Hubbard have to say about books? (Look carefully at the filenames in the Results list so you don't open more files than necessary.)

10. **Locating Information on the Internet** Carolyn asks that you help locate information on Taiwan for Senator Bernstein's upcoming participation in establishing a student exchange program.

    a. Use the Yahoo search service subject guide to locate information on transportation in Taiwan. Write down the subject guide links you navigated to locate information. (*Hint*: Start with Regional.)

    b. Write down the URL of a page on transportation in Taiwan.

    c. Locate a Web page for one of Taiwan's universities. Write down the name of the university and the URL of its Web page

11. **Locating People** Use three different people search services to locate the e-mail address of the president of your university. Were you able to find it in any of them? Did the search services have e-mail addresses for other people with the same name?

PROJECTS

1. On which drive is your Windows folder? Specify My Computer in the Look in list, and then search for "Windows" in the Named box. Write the answer on a piece of paper. If there are too many files in the Results list, sort the files by name so folders appear at the top.

2. Can you locate the e-mail address of the President of the United States? (*Hint:* Because of the President's job position, the e-mail address will end with ".gov".)

3. Specify the following search strings in the Named box, and, searching your Student Disk, examine the Results list for each search string very carefully. What generalizations about wildcards can you make from your observations?

   men

   men.*

   men.

   men*.*

   men?

   men?.*

4. You can use Find to learn about the files on your hard drive. Record how many files of each of the following type exist on your hard drive. Return the file type to its default of All Files and Folders when you are done.
   a. Application. Write down the names of five application files in the Windows folder of your hard drive.
   b. Bitmap Image. What folders on your hard drive seem to store the most bitmapped images?
   c. Screen Saver. Write down the locations of some of the screen savers on your hard drive.
   d. Text Document. Once the Results list shows all the text documents on your hard drive, order them by Name. Are there any files named Readme? Write down the locations of two of them. Software programs often come with a Readme text file that lists known software problems and answers to common questions.

5. Write down the names of 10 documents recently accessed on the hard disk.

Explore

6. You can use the Find Computer dialog box to locate computers on a network. If you are on a network, click Find, and then click Computer. Your instructor will give you the name of a computer for which to search on your network. Enter this name in the Named box, and then click the Find Now button. Once Find has located the computer, open it from the Results list. Make a hard copy of the window that opens and submit it to your instructor.

7. Use the Internet search tools to find information on the city where you live, such as a Chamber of Commerce page or a local news service page. Print the first page of the information you located, and write the URL on the page.

QUICK CHECK ANSWERS

Session 6.1

1. Click the Look in list arrow and then click 3½ Floppy (A:).

2. True

3. False

4. A wildcard is a symbol that stands in place of one or more characters. The asterisk wildcard substitutes for any number of characters; the question mark for only one.

5. Click the Name button in Details view.

Session 6.2

1. Advanced

2. Right-click it, then click Open; or in Web style, click it; or in Classic style, click it then press Enter.

3. Click Edit then click WordWrap.

4. On the Advanced tab, click Size is list arrow, click at least, then type 48.

5. You can display bitmapped images.

6. Increase Font Size

Session 6.3

1. Search engine

2. False

3. A query search allows you to search by keyword. In a subject search, you search through predefined categories of information.

4. +Toto+Oz

5. With the Find People option

WORKING WITH GRAPHICS

Creating Advertisement Graphics at Kiana Ski Shop

CASE

Kiana Ski Shop

Cross-country ski enthusiast Joe Nitka owns Kiana Ski Shop in the heart of the northern Wisconsin Chequamegon National Forest, near the site of the world-class Birkebeiner cross-country ski race. Joe is one of the local promoters of the race. He gathers and releases information on lodging and transportation for competitors, the media, and spectators. An avid cross-country skier yourself, you volunteer to help Joe create his Birkebeiner promotions to make them look more professional. Currently Joe types race information on a typewriter, copies it on colored paper, and distributes these flyers to interested parties. You tell him his promotions would capture more attention if they included a few graphics, such as a skier or a picture of the race logo.

Joe agrees, and says he could photocopy some drawings from a clip art collection of images and pictures at the library. You tell him there are advantages to using a computer instead: computer graphics can be resized more easily, pasted seamlessly into a word-processed document, and edited. You think you can find some eye-catching graphic images on the Internet that you can customize, or you could even create a graphic or two from scratch. Joe is interested, and explains that his first priority is the announcement that he'll send to local motel and hotel owners, asking if they'd like to advertise their services in his promotions.

You spend a little time on the Internet before Joe arrives, and you find a graphic file called Sports that includes several sports-related images. When Joe arrives, you explain that if you decide to use computer graphics, you'll need to make sure they are not copyrighted. Only graphics that are in the public domain may be downloaded and used freely.

SESSION 7.1

In this session, you will open a graphic in the Windows 98 graphics accessory, Paint. You will crop a portion of the graphic and save it in a new file, then edit the graphic to meet your needs and save it in a monochrome and color bitmapped graphic format. For this tutorial you will need a blank 3½-inch disk.

Preparing Your Student Disks

Before you can begin working, you need to bring a blank 3½-inch disk to the computer lab to create a Student Disk containing the sample files you will work with in this tutorial. In the computer lab, you will make your Student Disk, using the NP on Microsoft Windows 98 menu. If you are using your own computer, however, the NP on Microsoft Windows 98 menu will not be available. Before you proceed, refer to the Read This Before You Begin page for instructions on obtaining the files necessary for your Student Disk.

To make your Student Disk:

1. Write "Disk 5—Windows 98 Tutorial 7 Student Disk" on the label of a blank, formatted 3½-inch floppy disk. Insert your Student Disk into drive A.

   TROUBLE? If your 3½-inch disk drive is B, place your formatted disk in that drive instead, and for the rest of this tutorial substitute drive B wherever you see drive A.

2. Point to the **Start** button ⊞Start, point to **Programs**, point to **NP on Microsoft Windows 98-Level III**, and then click **Disk 5 (Tutorial 7)**. When you are prompted to insert your disk in the drive, click the **OK** button, and wait as the files you need are copied to your Student Disk.

3. Close all the open windows on your screen.

Starting Paint

Joe comments how great it is that you can draw things on your computer. You tell him that drawings on a computer are called **graphic images** or **graphics**. Some graphics are created using a **scanner**, which converts an existing paper image into an electronic file that you can open and work with on your computer. You can also create a graphic from scratch using a **graphics program**, software that includes drawing and graphic editing tools. The Windows 98 Accessories group includes a basic graphics program called **Paint**, which lets you create, edit, and manipulate graphics. Graphics come in two fundamental types: bitmapped and vector. A **bitmapped graphic** is made up of small dots, whereas a **vector graphic** is created by mathematical formulas that are used to draw the shapes. Computer graphics can come in either graphic type, although vector graphics are more precise because of their mathematical nature. Many software packages come with collections of graphics called **clip art**. Clip art images are usually in vector format because this allows them to be more easily manipulated. Paint, however, does not handle vector graphic formats. Because the Sports graphic you found is a bitmapped graphic, for Joe's purpose Paint will work fine. In this session you'll work with an existing graphic, and in Session 7.2 you'll create one from scratch.

You decide to start Paint and introduce Joe to the Windows 98 graphics tools.

To start Paint:

1. Click the **Start** button ![Start].

2. Point to **Programs** and then point to **Accessories**. The Accessories menu opens.

3. Click **Paint**. The Paint window opens. See Figure 7-1.

   TROUBLE? If you can't see the entire window, resize it until you can, or maximize it.

Figure 7-1	PAINT WINDOW

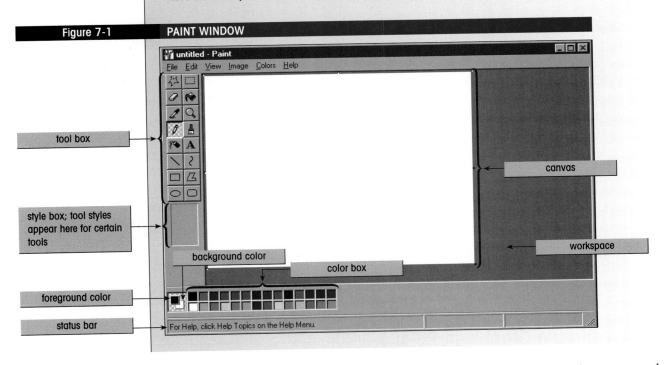

Within the Paint window is a blank white area like an artist's canvas, where you work with your graphic. At the bottom of the window is the color box, which displays available colors or shades for the foreground and background of your graphic. To the left of the color box are two additional overlapping boxes, the top for the foreground color and the bottom for the background color of any object you might draw. The status bar at the bottom of the window provides information about the location of the pointer.

To the left of the canvas is the **tool box**, a collection of tools that you use to draw and edit graphics. The tools all work the same way: You click a tool, the pointer changes to a shape representing the tool, and then you either click or drag on the canvas to draw with the tool. Some of the tools offer different widths or shapes, which are depicted in a style box that appears below the tool box, as you'll see in Session 7.2.

Figure 7-2 shows the available tools, along with the pointer shape that appears when you use the tool.

You'll work with some of the editing tools in this session, with the drawing tools in Session 7.2, and with the color and text tools in Session 7.3.

Figure 7-2	PAINT TOOLS		
TOOL	**BUTTON**	**DESCRIPTION**	**POINTER**
Free-Form Select		Select a free-form portion of a graphic	
Select		Select a rectangular portion of a graphic	
Eraser/Color Eraser		Erase a portion of a graphic	
Fill With Color		Fill an enclosed area with the current color	
Pick Color		Pick up an exsisting color in the graphic	
Magnifier		Change the magnification	
Pencil		Draw a free-form line or draw one pixel at a time	
Brush		Draw using a brush in a variety of widths	
Airbrush		Draw using an airbrush in a varity of widths	
Text		Insert text into a graphic	
Line		Draw a line	
Curve		Draw a curve	
Rectangle		Draw a rectangle or square	
Polygon		Draw a polygon	
Ellipse		Draw an ellipse or circle	
Rounded Rectangle		Draw a rectangle or square with rounded corners	

Opening a Graphic in Paint

Joe wants to take a look at the Sports graphic to see if there is anything that might work for his announcement. To open an existing graphic in Paint, you use the Open command on the File menu. The Sports graphic is located on your Student Disk.

To open the Sports graphic:

1. Click **File** and then click **Open**.

2. Click the **Look in** list arrow, and then click the drive containing your Student Disk.

3. Click **Sports** and then click the **Open** button.

TROUBLE? If Sports appears as Sports.bmp, your computer is set to display file extensions as part of the filename. Click Sports.bmp, click Open, and then continue with Step 4.

4. If necessary, scroll to the bottom of the graphic and to the right side. See Figure 7-3. The Sports graphic contains a number of sporting figures.

TROUBLE? If you can't see the entire graphic image, resize the Paint window as necessary.

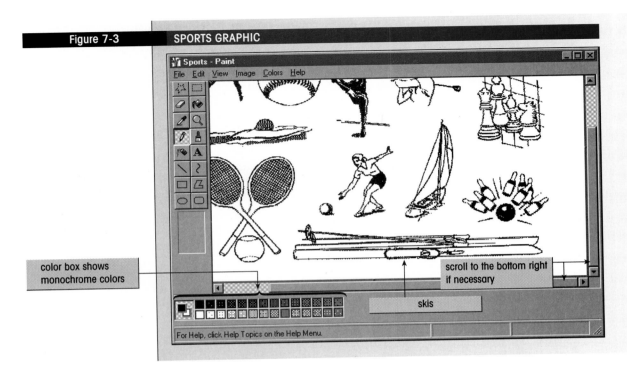

Figure 7-3 **SPORTS GRAPHIC**

color box shows monochrome colors

scroll to the bottom right if necessary

skis

Note the color box at the bottom of the Paint window. It no longer offers the array of colors in Figure 7-1. You tell Joe that the Sports graphic is a **monochrome graphic**, that is, a graphic with only two colors—black and white—available to it. Notice that the color box includes only black, white, and patterns of black and white that give the illusion of gray shading.

Cropping a Portion of a Graphic

Looking over the graphic, Joe notices the pair of skis at the bottom. He thinks the skis alone would look great at the bottom of the announcement. You tell Joe you can capture just that portion of the graphic by **cropping**, or cutting out, everything around it. To crop a graphic, you use either the Select tool or the Free-Form Select tool. With the **Select tool**, you draw a rectangle, called a selection box, around the area you want to crop. With the **Free-Form Select tool**, you draw any shaped line around the area. Once you have selected the graphic you need, you save that selection to a separate file. The separate file contains only the cropped area—in Joe's case, the pair of skis.

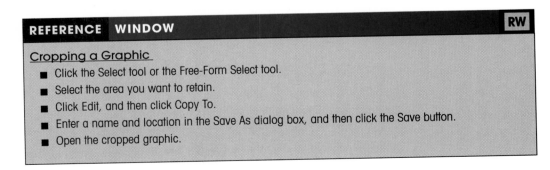

REFERENCE WINDOW **RW**

Cropping a Graphic
- Click the Select tool or the Free-Form Select tool.
- Select the area you want to retain.
- Click Edit, and then click Copy To.
- Enter a name and location in the Save As dialog box, and then click the Save button.
- Open the cropped graphic.

In this section, you'll use the Select tool because it's easier to manipulate than the Free-Form Select tool. However, because the sailboat and the bowling ball images are so close to the skis, when you crop you will inadvertently include portions of those graphics. Don't worry; in the next section you'll learn how to erase parts of a graphic that you don't want. In the Tutorial Assignments, you'll have an opportunity to use the Free-Form Select tool to avoid the extra step of erasing. You're ready to select the skis.

To select the skis:

1. Locate and click the **Select** button 🔲 in the tool box.

2. Move the pointer over the canvas. The pointer looks like ┼ .

3. Next, you need to drag a selection box around the pair of skis. To do this, point to the white space to the upper left of the skis. Press the left mouse button and hold it down while you drag to the lower-right corner of the skis. As you drag, a selection box appears. See Figure 7-4.

   TROUBLE? If you release the mouse button too early, or if your selection box doesn't include the entire pair of skis, click an area of the canvas outside the selection box and repeat Step 3.

| Figure 7-4 | SELECTING AN AREA TO CROP |

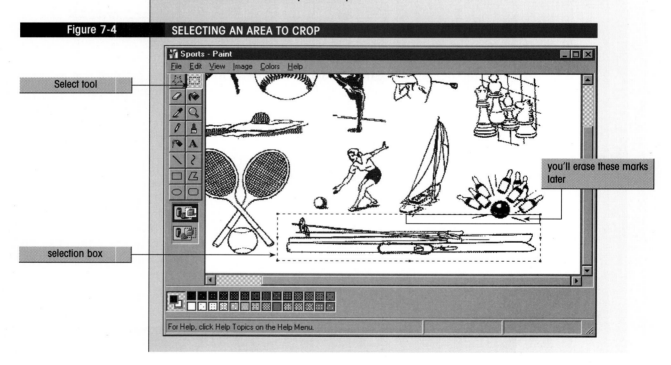

Select tool

selection box

you'll erase these marks later

Now that the skis are selected, you can use the Copy To command to save the selected area to a new file.

To save the selected area to a new file:

1. Click **Edit** and then click **Copy To**.

2. Type **Skis** in the File name box. Make sure the Save in box shows your Student Disk. Notice that the file type is a Monochrome Bitmap because this is a monochrome graphic. You'll learn more about the Paint file types later in this session.

3. Click the **Save** button. The file is saved on your Student Disk with the filename Skis.

The Sports graphic is still open in Paint, and the Skis graphic is in a separate file. In Paint, you can work with only one graphic file at a time. If you try to open another graphic or create a new graphic, Paint closes the current one, prompting you to save it if necessary. If you want two Paint graphics open at the same time, you must start a separate Paint session, so that there are actually two Paint windows open with one graphic in each. You don't need the Sports graphic for now, so you'll simply open the Skis graphic and let Paint close the Sports graphic.

To open the Skis graphic:

1. Click **File** and then click **Open**.

2. Click **Skis** and then click the **Open** button. If Paint asks if you want to save the changes to Sports, click the **No** button. The Skis graphic opens. See Figure 7-5.

| Figure 7-5 | SKIS GRAPHIC, CROPPED FROM SPORTS GRAPHIC |

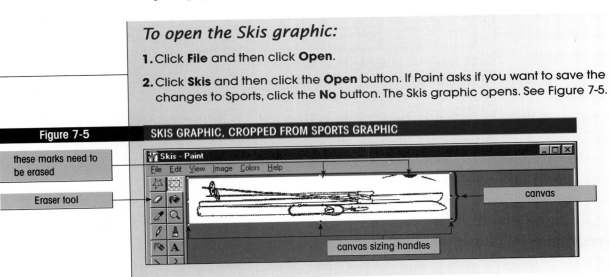

Notice that the canvas now takes up only a small portion of the Paint document window. The canvas **sizing handles**, the small boxes shown in Figure 7-5, allow you to resize the graphic if necessary.

Erasing Parts of a Graphic

Joe notices the portions of the sailboat and bowling ball graphics at the top of the Skis graphic. You tell him it's easy to erase unneeded portions of a graphic. You use the **Eraser/Color Eraser tool**, which erases the area over which you drag the pointer. If you erase more than you intended, you can use the **Undo** command on the Edit menu, which reverses one or more of your last three actions, depending on how many times you click Undo (up to three times).

To erase the portions of the graphic that you don't want:

1. Click the **Eraser/Color Eraser** tool. When you move the pointer over the graphic, it changes to a ☐ shape.

2. Drag the pointer ☐ over the areas at the top of the Skis graphic to erase them. As you drag, the unwanted black marks disappear. See Figure 7-6.

    TROUBLE? If the black marks aren't disappearing, make sure you press and hold the mouse button while you move the Eraser pointer over the black marks.

    TROUBLE? If you erase a portion of the graphic that you wanted to keep, click Edit, and then click Undo.

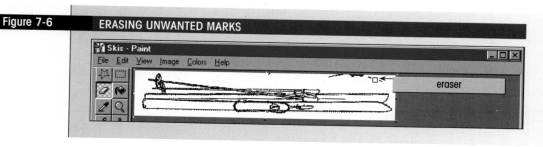

Figure 7-6   ERASING UNWANTED MARKS

Now the graphic looks just the way you want. You tell Joe that he can use a word processor to create his announcement and insert the graphic directly into the word-processed document. But that's a project for another day. You decide to save the Skis graphic.

To save the Skis graphic

1. Click **File** and then click **Save**.

Because the graphic is black and white, Joe could print it and reproduce it inexpensively, using a simple photocopier.

Bitmapped Graphics

Joe wonders how easy it would be to add color to the Skis graphic, if he decides to create an announcement in full color. You tell him you'd have to change the file type from Monochrome Bitmap to one of the color bitmapped graphic types. Joe asks you to explain.

You tell Joe that a computer screen is a gridwork of small dots of light called **pixels**, which is short for "picture elements." The pixels form images on the screen by displaying different colors, much like a television set. Buttons on the taskbar, for example, are formed by the pixels shown in Figure 7-7.

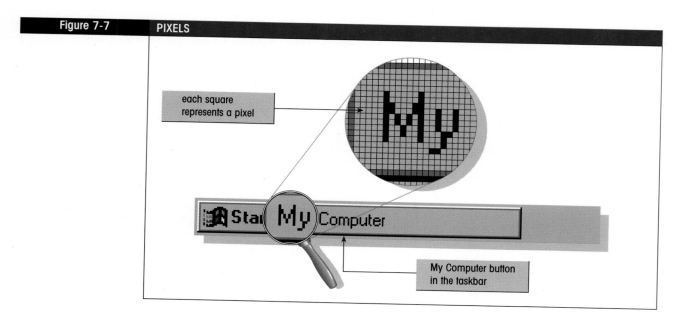

Figure 7-7   PIXELS

each square represents a pixel

My Computer button in the taskbar

Each pixel has a color, and the individual colored pixels form the graphics you see on your screen. To understand how a graphic can be created from pixels, imagine a piece of graph paper where each square represents a pixel. To draw a straight line, you color in a row of squares, or, to draw a circle you fill in the squares as best you can to approximate the curve, as shown in Figure 7-8. In this drawing, every pixel within the circle's border is black, and every pixel not in the circle is white. Your computer uses 0's and 1's as a code for the color of each pixel. Each 0 or 1 is called a **bit**. To determine the color of each pixel in a drawing that is only black and white, you need only one bit, because a bit can "take on" a value of either 0 or 1—that is, it can be either off or on, either black or white.

Figure 7-8	BITS DETERMINE PIXEL COLOR

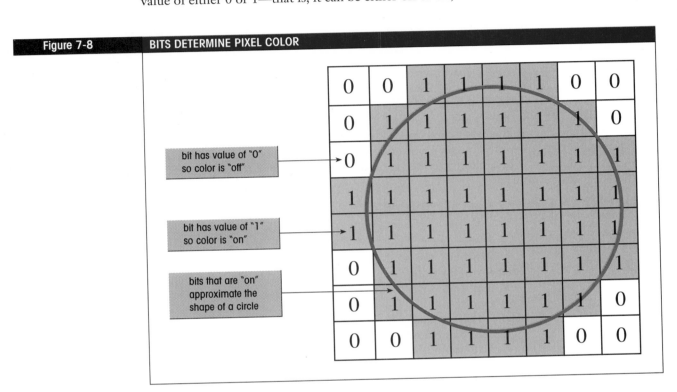

bit has value of "0" so color is "off"

bit has value of "1" so color is "on"

bits that are "on" approximate the shape of a circle

A 1-bit graphic, where each pixel is described by a single bit, is also known as a **monochrome bitmap**. The Skis image is such a graphic. If your graphic contains more colors, the computer needs to use more bits for the code. For example, to code the colors black, white, blue, and red, you would need two bits—00 for black, 01 for white, 10 for red, and 11 for blue. There are four bitmap types available in Paint: 1-bit, 4-bit, 8-bit, and 24-bit. The more bits you use, the more colors are available.

Your computer maps, or assigns, a color to each code, hence the term "bitmap." A sequence of four zeros, 0000, might mean "black"; a sequence of four ones, 1111, might mean "white." The sequence 1000 might mean "blue." With 4 bits there are 16 available colors, so in Paint a graphic that uses 4 bits is saved in the **16 Color Bitmap** file type. The other file types are Monochrome Bitmap, 256 Color Bitmap, and 24-bit Bitmap. The **256 Color Bitmap** type uses sequences of 8 bits to represent 256 colors. Similarly, the **24-bit Bitmap** type uses sequences of 24 bits to represent 16.7 million colors—useful for working with color photos. Figure 7-9 summarizes the bitmap file types that Paint allows, the number of bits per pixel, the number of distinct colors each type can display, and the size of a file that starts out as a 4 KB monochrome bitmap and then is saved in each type.

Figure 7-9	PAINT FILE FORMATS		
FILE TYPE	**NUMBER OF BITS**	**NUMBER OF COLORS**	**SAMPLE FILE SIZE**
Monochrome	1	2	4 KB
16 Color Bitmap	4	16	13 KB
256 Color Bitmap	8	256	27 KB
24-bit Bitmap	24	16.7 million	77 KB

Note that as the number of bits increases, so does the number of available colors. This increases the size of the file. Therefore, you might not want to select a bitmap type with more colors than you need. For a simple black-and-white graphic, monochrome is the best choice.

By default, Paint stores its graphics with the .bmp file extension—the standard Windows 98 file format for bitmapped graphics. However, if you have Microsoft Office installed, you can also choose to save your file as a GIF or JPEG image. These two image types are often used for graphics placed on Web pages. If you want Paint to work with graphics that have other file extensions, or if you do not have Microsoft Office, you need to use a software program called a **graphics converter** to change the file to a format that Paint can work with.

Resizing Bitmapped Graphics

Joe comments that he's heard people complain about how bitmapped graphics can look rough around the edges. You agree. If the bitmapped graphic is sized correctly it looks fine, but if you try to resize it you might have problems. A bitmapped graphic is defined by pixels, but you can't change the size of an individual pixel. When you try to enlarge a bitmapped graphic, Paint duplicates the pixels to approximate the original shape as best it can—often resulting in jagged edges. On the other hand, when you shrink a bitmapped graphic, Paint removes pixels, and the drawing loses detail. In either case, you distort the original graphic. Sometimes the resized bitmapped graphic will look fine, as when there are many straight lines, but just as often the resized graphic's image quality suffers. For example, if you were to enlarge the Skis graphic, the result might look like Figure 7-10.

How do you get around this problem? In Paint, there is no easy solution to resizing graphics, because they are all bitmapped. If your work with graphics requires resizing—for example, if you want a graphic that will look good on a small business card and a large poster—vector graphics are a better choice. Because vector graphics are mathematically based, you can resize them as necessary without sacrificing image quality. You will need to buy a graphics program that allows you to work with vector graphics, however.

Figure 7-10   **SKIS GRAPHIC AS IT LOOKS WHEN ENLARGED**

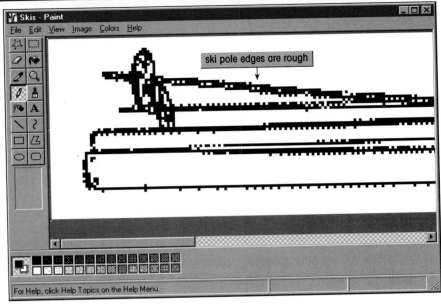

Saving a Paint Graphic

Joe decides he would like you to save the Skis graphic in a color file type so he can experiment later with adding color.

When you save a graphic in a different file type in Paint, the graphic's appearance doesn't change. The pixels that were black stay black, and those that were white stay white. However, the number of bits that defines each color changes, and so the file changes in size. When you are ready to color the graphic, you'll find a new set of colors available to you. Instead of the black, white, and pattern boxes that you see now in the color box, you will see colors. You decide to save the Skis graphic as a 256 Color Bitmap, because this format provides a wide array of colors but doesn't take up as much space as the 24-bit Bitmap format.

To save the graphic file as a 256 Color Bitmap:

1. Click **File** and then click **Save As**.

2. Click the **Save as type** list arrow, and then click **256 Color Bitmap**.

3. Type **Skis256** in the File name box.

4. Make sure the Save in list box specifies your Student Disk.

5. Click the **Save** button.

The monochrome graphic closes. Paint now offers an array of colors in the color box. You decide to show Joe how the 256-color format affects the size of the graphics file.

To view the size of the graphics files:

1. Minimize the Paint window.

2. If necessary, open **My Computer**.

3. Open the **3½ Floppy (A:)** window.

4. Click **View** and then click **Details** to view file sizes and compare the relative sizes of the Skis graphic and the Skis256 graphic. The Skis256 graphic is much larger.

You tell Joe that if he wants to come back another time and add color to the Skis graphic, that's fine with you. But for now, you're ready for a break.

To finish the session:

1. Click the **Close** button ☒ to close the floppy drive window.

2. Right-click the **Skis256 - Paint** button on the taskbar, and then click **Close**.

3. Close any other open windows on the desktop.

QUICK CHECK

1. Describe how you save a portion of a graphic to a separate file.

2. How do you resize the canvas?

3. True or False: You can open only one graphic in Paint at a time.

4. The small dots on your screen are called _____.

5. Why do color graphics use more file space than monochrome graphics?

6. If you have a graphic in a file format that Paint doesn't support, what can you do to open the file in Paint?

SESSION 7.2

In this session, you will learn to edit an existing graphic and draw new graphics with the collection of drawing tools in Paint. You'll use the Pencil, Line, Brush, and Ellipse tools, and you'll look at options for flipping, rotating, sizing, and stretching your graphics. You'll learn techniques that make drawing easier, such as controlling the magnification, editing one pixel at a time, using the grid and a thumbnail, and copying and pasting parts of a graphic.

Drawing with the Pencil Tool

Joe drops by a few days after your initial computer session, with a problem: The Skis graphic isn't right for the Birkebeiner announcement because it shows a downhill ski, not a cross-country ski. The bindings for the two ski types are different, as shown in Figure 7-11.

Figure 7-11	PROBLEM WITH THE SKIS GRAPHIC

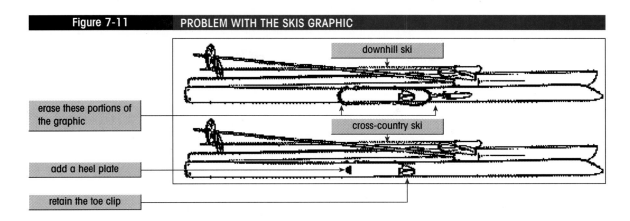

downhill ski

erase these portions of the graphic

cross-country ski

add a heel plate

retain the toe clip

You tell Joe you can fix this problem by erasing unwanted portions and then using the **Pencil tool**, which draws free-form dots or lines. Once you have selected the Pencil tool, you click the canvas to draw pixel-size dots, or you drag over the canvas to draw a line that is one pixel wide. You decide to show Joe these two methods of drawing with the Pencil tool before you fix the Skis graphic.

To experiment with the Pencil tool:

1. Make sure your Student Disk is in drive A, and then start Paint. Paint opens to an empty canvas.

2. If necessary, click the **Pencil** tool, [pencil icon] and then move the pointer onto the canvas. The pointer looks like a ∂ shape.

3. Hold the mouse button down and drag ∂ over the canvas. Your pointer leaves a trail as you drag it. See Figure 7-12. Practice drawing lines with the Pencil tool until you feel comfortable with its operation.

Figure 7-12	DRAWING WITH THE PENCIL TOOL

Pencil tool

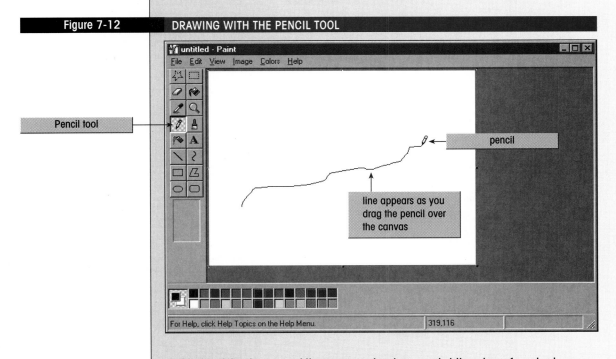

pencil

line appears as you drag the pencil over the canvas

4. Click a blank area of the canvas to draw a dot the size of a pixel.

Now that you've shown Joe how easy it is to draw lines or dots with the Pencil tool, you are ready to edit the Skis graphic. You first must erase the parts of the binding that are for downhill skis, and then you must add a heel plate for the cross-country ski binding.

Changing View Options

The changes you need to make to the Skis graphic require careful erasing and redrawing—a task made easier when the view is magnified. The **Magnifier tool** allows you to view a graphic at a number of different magnification levels. The default magnification is 100%, also called **Normal view**. If you click the Magnifier tool and then click the graphic, Paint displays it at 400%. You can select a different magnification, using the box that appears below the tool box when you click 🔍: 1x (Normal view), 2x (200% magnification), 6x (600% magnification), and 8x (800% magnification). The **Custom Zoom dialog box** adds the 400% zoom option. Increasing the magnification is called **zooming in**.

If you are magnifying the view to edit a few pixels at a time, the grid can help you navigate. The **grid** is a checkerboard background like a piece of graph paper, where each square represents a pixel. The grid guides your drawing so your lines are straight and your shapes are precise.

REFERENCE WINDOW | **RW**

Magnifying a Graphic
- To zoom in, click the Magnifier tool, and then click the graphic to zoom to the default magnification of 400%, or click one of the magnifications in the box below the tool box.
- To view gridlines, switch to a magnified view, click View, point to Zoom, and then click Show Grid.
- To view a portion of the magnified graphic in Normal view, switch to a magnified view, click View, point to Zoom, and then click Show Thumbnail.

You decide to work with the monochrome Skis graphic because Joe's Birkebeiner announcement will be in black and white, not color. You need to open the Skis graphic, zoom in to the highest magnification, and then show the grid so you can more easily edit the graphic. So that your Skis graphic will match the one shown in the figures, you'll open a copy of the graphic, stored on your Student Disk as Skis2, and save it with the name Skis, replacing the original graphic.

To change the view for editing:

1. Click **File**, click **Open**, and then locate and open the **Skis2** file on your Student Disk. Click **No** when you are prompted to save changes to the untitled graphic you were just working with.

2. Click **File** and then click **Save As**. Make sure the Save in box displays the drive containing your Student Disk and that the Save as type box shows Monochrome Bitmap. Enter **Skis** in the File name box, and then click the **Save** button. Click **Yes** when you are asked whether you want to replace the existing file.

3. Click the **Magnifier** tool 🔍 and move the pointer over the canvas. The pointer changes to 🔍, and a box appears that shows the portion of the graphic Paint will magnify.

4. Click the far left side of the graphic to use the default 400% magnification.

5. Click **View**, point to **Zoom**, and then click **Show Grid**. You can see the individual pixels. See Figure 7-13. The boxes are too small to work with easily, so you decide to use the Custom dialog box to zoom in even more.

TROUBLE? If your graphic shows a different portion of the skis, scroll all the way to the left. Resize your Paint window as necessary to view the same portion as in Figure 7-13.

Figure 7-13	GRID IN A MAGNIFIED VIEW

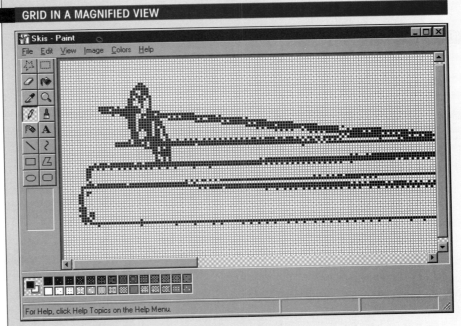

6. Click **View**, point to **Zoom**, and then click **Custom**. The Custom Zoom dialog box opens. See Figure 7-14.

Figure 7-14	CHOOSING A DIFFERENT MAGNIFICATION

current magnification is 400%

7. Click the **800%** option button, and then click the **OK** button. Now the boxes are larger, and you'll have no problem editing individual pixels.

When you're zoomed in this closely, you sometimes lose sight of the picture's appearance. You can view a **thumbnail**, a small box that shows in Normal view the area you're zooming in on. Thumbnails are especially handy for editing. You decide to view a thumbnail of the area you're working on.

To view a thumbnail:

1. Click **View** and then point to **Zoom**.

  TROUBLE? If the thumbnail already appears, skip Steps 1 and 2.

2. Click **Show Thumbnail**. A thumbnail of the area you're examining appears on the Paint window. See Figure 7-15.

  TROUBLE? If the thumbnail appears in a different area of the Paint window and it obscures an area you want to examine, drag it out of the way.

Figure 7-15	VIEWING A THUMBNAIL OF THE MAGNIFIED AREA

thumbnail of magnified area

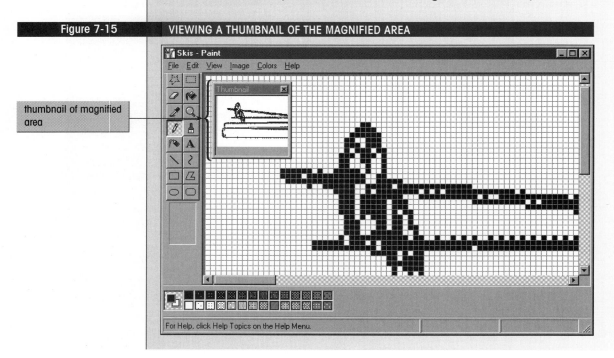

With the grid on, you can see each pixel, and you are viewing a thumbnail so you can see how your changes affect the larger picture. You're ready to start editing!

Erasing in a Magnified View

Once you are zoomed in, you can erase unwanted portions of the graphic a few pixels at a time. You need to erase the portions of the binding that are for downhill skis. To erase, you drag the Eraser tool over the appropriate pixels. The Eraser tool comes in several different sizes; select the size according to the number of pixels you need to erase. The largest size lets you erase large sections of a graphic in 10 × 10 boxes (100 pixels at a time). The smallest size lets you erase in 4 × 4 boxes (16 pixels at a time). There is no way to erase one pixel at a time using the Eraser tool. You can, however, use the Pencil tool to accomplish the same purpose: choose white as your drawing color, and then any pixel you click will turn white.

To erase the parts of the ski binding you don't need:

1. Scroll until you see the binding. Watch the thumbnail to see where the binding is located, and click the **Eraser** tool ⬜.

TROUBLE? If the thumbnail is in the way, drag it to the lower-right corner of the screen. Resize the window as necessary.

2. Click the **smallest box** in the Eraser tool styles box. See Figure 7-16.

| Figure 7-16 | SELECTING THE SMALLEST SIZE OF THE ERASER TOOL |

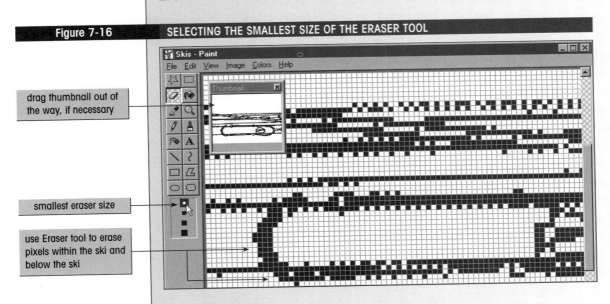

drag thumbnail out of the way, if necessary

smallest eraser size

use Eraser tool to erase pixels within the ski and below the ski

3. Drag the **Eraser** tool over the pixels inside the ski and below the ski, as shown in Figure 7-17. Scroll as necessary to complete the erasures. The pixels that you should erase are shown in red in Figure 7-17.

TROUBLE? If you erased an area you didn't want to erase, click Edit, and then click Undo. If you need to start over, do so without saving your changes.

| Figure 7-17 | PIXELS THAT NEED TO BE ERASED |

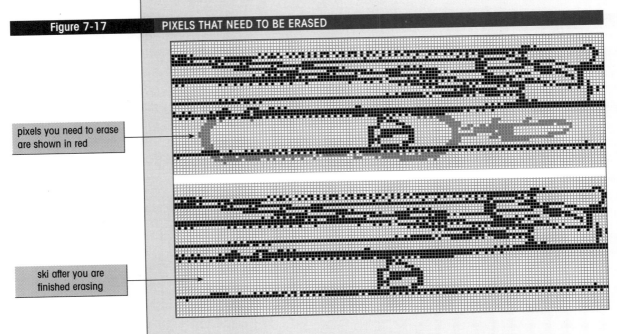

pixels you need to erase are shown in red

ski after you are finished erasing

4. Click the **Magnifier** tool , and then click **1x** to return to Normal view.

In Normal view you can see how your erasures have changed the look of the ski. It looks good.

Drawing in a Magnified View

You are now ready to draw the heel plate, which has a trapezoidal shape. You'll use the Pencil tool to draw it a few pixels at a time.

You've already seen how to use the thumbnail to "locate" yourself in the Paint window. Paint offers one other feature to help you control your location as you draw. The **pixel coordinates** in the status bar specify the exact location of the pointer on the canvas, relative to the pixels on your screen. Paint displays the pixel coordinates in an (*x,y*) format (*x* representing the horizontal location and *y* the vertical location). Pixel coordinates of 138,25, for example, indicate that the pointer is 138 pixels from the *left* edge of the screen and 25 pixels from the *top*. The next set of steps uses pixel coordinates to help you add the heel plate in just the right location.

You'll use the Magnifier tool to zoom back in, this time to only 600%, because the work isn't as meticulous. A lower magnification lets you view a little more of your graphic.

To create the heel plate:

1. Click the **Magnifier** tool 🔍, and then click the **6x** magnification option in the box below the tool box.

2. Scroll to the binding area of the ski.

3. Click the **Pencil** tool ✏️, and then position the pointer at pixel coordinate **155,57**. See Figure 7-18 for the location of this pixel.

4. Click both the **155,57** pixel and the **155,58** pixel. Then drag to fill in the rest of the pixels shown in Figure 7-18. When your screen looks like Figure 7-18, view the skis in Normal view.

   TROUBLE? If you draw in an area you didn't intend to, click Edit, and then click Undo.

Figure 7-18	USING PIXEL COORDINATES TO DRAW THE HEEL PLATE

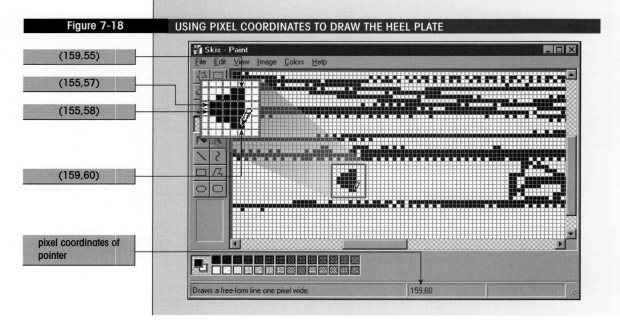

(159,55)

(155,57)

(155,58)

(159,60)

pixel coordinates of pointer

5. Click the **Magnifier** tool 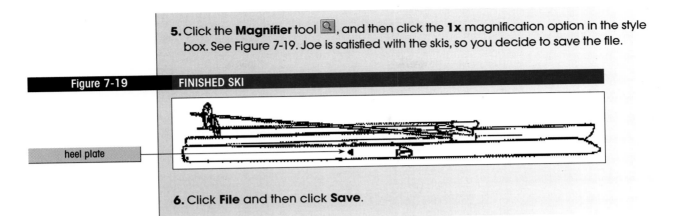, and then click the **1x** magnification option in the style box. See Figure 7-19. Joe is satisfied with the skis, so you decide to save the file.

| Figure 7-19 | FINISHED SKI |

heel plate

6. Click **File** and then click **Save**.

Drawing with the Brush Tool

Joe sees how easy it is to draw and asks about creating some new graphics that he could use for advertising Kiana Ski Shop. You've already saved the Skis graphic, so you have three choices for creating a new graphic: You can erase the contents of the canvas, using the Eraser tool, and then save the file under a different filename; you can choose Clear Image from the Image menu to clear the canvas and then save the file under a different filename; or you can choose New from the File menu to open a new file. You decide to use the third option.

To create a new file:

1. Click **File** and then click **New**. An empty canvas opens.

Joe sketches a few ideas, and you decide to draw the sketch in Figure 7-20.

| Figure 7-20 | IDEA FOR A KIANA GRAPHIC |

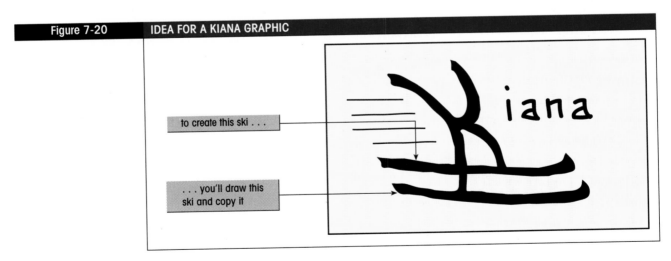

to create this ski . . .

. . . you'll draw this ski and copy it

To create this graphic, you explain to Joe, you can use the **Brush tool**. Unlike the Pencil tool, the Brush tool offers a variety of widths and different brush styles to draw with. To create the skis, you can use an angular style brush. To create the letter "K" you can use a rounded brush. You can add the other letters with the Text tool, which you'll learn to use in Session 7.3. First you're going to show Joe how to use the Brush tool.

To draw with the Brush tool:

1. Click the **Brush** tool ▣. Notice the brush styles in the style box. The current brush style is highlighted.

2. Drag the brush pointer over the canvas. A thick rounded line appears.

3. Now try a different brush style. Click the leftmost **angular line** brush style in the third row, as shown in Figure 7-21, and then drag the brush pointer over the screen. You create a line like the one in Figure 7-21.

| Figure 7-21 | BRUSH STYLES |

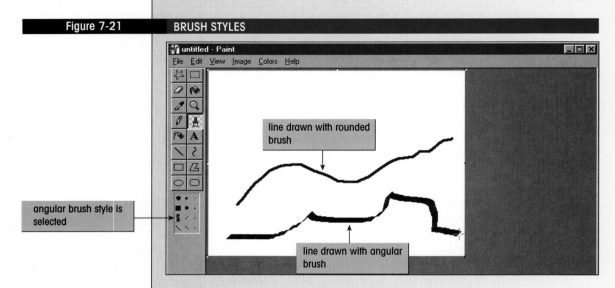

line drawn with rounded brush

angular brush style is selected

line drawn with angular brush

4. Drag the brush pointer around a little corner and then draw a straight horizontal line, as in Figure 7-22. Don't worry about being too accurate with this drawing because you're going to erase it shortly anyway.

| Figure 7-22 | DRAWING A SKI, USING THE ANGULAR BRUSH |

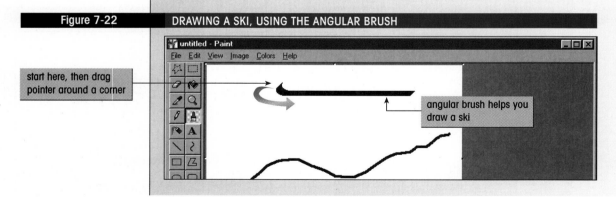

start here, then drag pointer around a corner

angular brush helps you draw a ski

Now that you have an idea of how the brush tools work, you can clear the screen and try drawing the real ski. This time, rather than using the New command, you'll use the Image menu's **Clear Image** command, which erases the entire image all at once and lets you start over with an empty canvas.

To clear the graphic and then draw the ski:

1. Click **Image** and then click **Clear Image**. Your drawings disappear as the canvas is cleared.

2. Now try drawing the ski. This time try to make it look like the ski in Figure 7-22. Click **Undo** if you aren't satisfied, and try again.

   TROUBLE? If you have a difficult time holding the mouse steady to draw the straight line, you could try controlling the pointer with the arrow keys rather than the mouse. Use the MouseKeys option available through the Accessibility Options dialog box. You could also try drawing just one section of the ski at a time.

Copying, Pasting, and Moving a Portion of a Graphic

Once you have drawn a satisfactory ski, you want to draw a second ski that has the same size and shape as the first ski. To ensure a consistent look, you can make a copy of the first ski and then paste it on the graphic as the second ski. To copy a portion of a graphic, you select it, and then you choose the Copy command on the Edit menu. Your selection is copied into memory. You can then use the Edit menu's Paste command to paste the copy into the graphic, where it "floats" in the upper-left corner of the canvas.

REFERENCE   WINDOW   **RW**

Copying, Cutting, and Pasting Graphics
- Click the Select or Free-Form Select tool.
- Drag a selection box around the area you want to copy or cut.
- Click Edit, and then click Copy or Cut.
- Click Paste. The selection appears in the upper-left corner of the canvas.
- Drag the selection to the new location, and then click outside the selection box to anchor the selection into place.

You are ready to copy the first ski, paste it, and then move it just above the existing ski. So that your drawing will match the one shown in the figures, you'll open a copy of the drawing of the ski, which is stored on your Student Disk in the Brush file. You'll then save this file with the name Kiana.

To copy and paste the first ski and then position it:

1. Click **File**, click **Open**, and then locate and open the **Brush** file on your Student Disk. Click **No** if you are prompted to save changes to the untitled graphic you were just working with.

2. Click **File** and then click **Save As**. Make sure the Save in box displays the drive containing your Student Disk and that the Save as type box shows 256 Color Bitmap. Type **Kiana** in the File name box, and then click the **Save** button.

3. Click the **Select** tool .

4. Draw a selection box around the ski.

5. Click **Edit** and then click **Copy**. The ski is copied into memory.

6. Click **Edit** and then click **Paste**. The ski appears in the upper-left corner of the Paint window.

7. Place the pointer over the pasted ski. Make sure the pointer looks like ✛.

8. Drag the ski down and slightly to the right. See Figure 7-23.

TROUBLE? If you want to reposition the second ski after you release the mouse button, repeat Steps 7 and 8.

TROUBLE? If the ski does not move when you drag it, but the selection box changes size, you might have pointed at a sizing handle. Click Edit, and then click Undo. Make sure the pointer looks like ✛ before you start to drag. Then repeat Steps 7 and 8.

| Figure 7-23 | MOVING THE PASTED SKI |

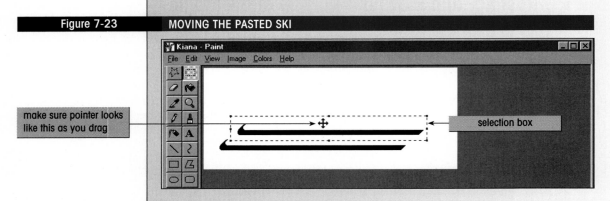

make sure pointer looks like this as you drag

selection box

9. Once the pasted ski is positioned correctly, click a blank area of the canvas outside the selection box. The ski is anchored into place.

Flipping a Graphic

When you and Joe look at the skis, you decide you want them to point in the other direction. You can flip a graphic using the **Flip/Rotate** option on the Image menu. This option lets you reverse a graphic or rotate it by a specified number of degrees.

To flip the skis so they point in the other direction:

1. Click **Image** and then click **Flip/Rotate**. The Flip and Rotate dialog box opens. See Figure 7-24.

| Figure 7-24 | FLIP AND ROTATE DIALOG BOX |

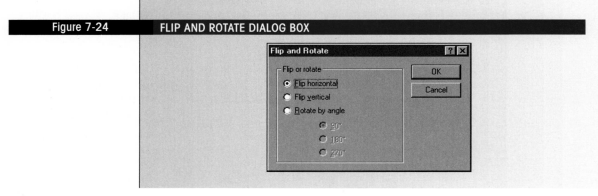

2. Click the **Flip horizontal** option button, if it isn't already selected. This tells Paint to flip the graphic horizontally.

3. Click the **OK** button. The skis now point in the other direction.

4. Click **File** and then click **Save** to save the graphic.

Now you're ready to create the letter "K." You think you can create the look you want by using the rounded brush style, which is in the first row of brush styles.

To create the letter K:

1. Click the **Brush** tool 🖌, and then click the **largest circle** in the top row of brush styles.

2. Draw the letter K so it looks like a skier. Follow the steps shown in Figure 7-25.

TROUBLE? If you make a mistake, use the Undo command or erase what you've drawn and start over.

Figure 7-25	DRAWING THE LETTER K

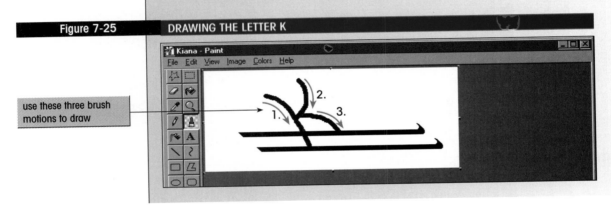

use these three brush motions to draw

Drawing a Straight Line

Now you want to make the K look as if it's moving. The **Line** option lets you draw straight lines, which you can place in your graphic to give the illusion of movement. You can create a horizontal, vertical, or diagonal line by pressing Shift while you drag the Line pointer in one of those directions. You can, of course, draw a line using the Pencil tool, but it's difficult to keep the line straight. You are going to draw a single line behind the K, and then you'll copy it and paste it a few times to add several "movement" lines.

To add straight lines to your drawing:

1. Click the **Line** tool ◥. Notice that you can draw lines in several different line widths. You want the narrowest line (the default).

2. Press **Shift** and hold it down while you draw a horizontal line behind the K, as shown in Figure 7-26.

Figure 7-26 | **DRAWING A STRAIGHT LINE WITH THE LINE TOOL**

line you drew

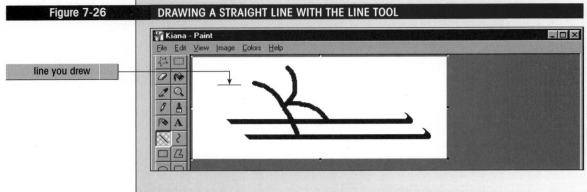

3. Release the mouse button and then release the **Shift key**. The line is perfectly straight. You can copy and paste this line several times to create several speed lines that are all the same size.

4. Click the **Select** tool ⬚, and then draw a selection box around the line you just drew. Keep the selection box as close to the line as possible to avoid copying the surrounding white space.

5. Click **Edit**, click **Copy**, click **Edit**, and then click **Paste**. Move the line you just pasted so that it is below and slightly to the right of the original line.

6. Click **Edit**, and then click **Paste** twice more to add two more straight lines, moving both pasted lines until they match the positions of those shown in Figure 7-27.

7. Click a blank area of the canvas to anchor the last line into place.

Stretching a Graphic

As a final touch, you decide to stretch the graphic to see if that effect enhances the illusion of movement. You can stretch a graphic either horizontally or vertically using the **Stretch/Skew** option on the Image menu. You specify a percentage, and Paint expands or contracts the graphic by that percentage in the direction (horizontal or vertical) that you specify.

To stretch the Skis graphic:

1. Click **Image** and then click **Stretch/Skew**.

2. If necessary, click the **Horizontal** percentage box in the Stretch pane.

3. Replace the default value of 100% with **140%**.

4. Click the **OK** button. The graphic is stretched in the horizontal direction. Your graphic now looks like Figure 7-27.

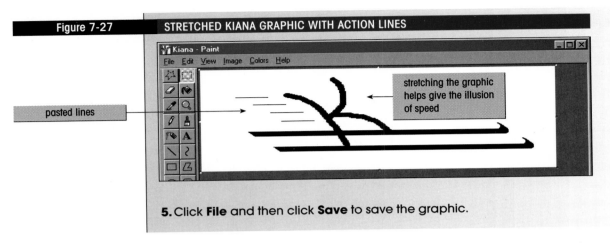

Figure 7-27   **STRETCHED KIANA GRAPHIC WITH ACTION LINES**

pasted lines

stretching the graphic helps give the illusion of speed

5. Click **File** and then click **Save** to save the graphic.

You'll add the text to the Kiana graphic in the Tutorial Assignments at the end of this tutorial.

Creating Shapes

Joe suggests that you next create a scenic image, such as a few mountains on a sunny day. You tell him that's a job for one or more of the shape tools—Line, Curve, Rectangle, Polygon, Ellipse, and Rounded Rectangle. These tools let you draw predetermined shapes. When you click one of the shape tools, a collection of options appears below the tool box. You can choose the shape as an outline, a filled shape with a border, or a filled shape without a border. See Figure 7-28.

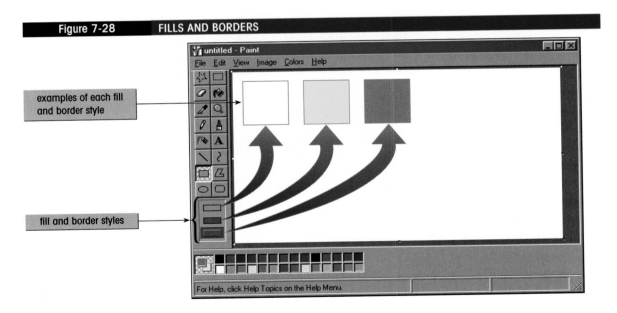

Figure 7-28   **FILLS AND BORDERS**

examples of each fill and border style

fill and border styles

For Help, click Help Topics on the Help Menu.

You'll learn later how to control the colors of the border and the fill for these shapes.

Joe quickly sketches what he'd like to see, as shown in Figure 7-29, and asks if you can draw it.

| Figure 7-29 | IDEA FOR A SCENIC GRAPHIC |

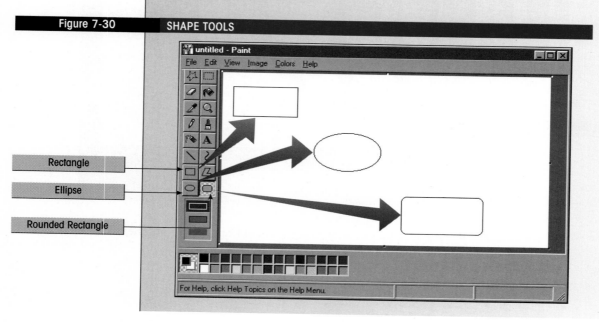

It's Ski Time!

To create the mountains, you can use the Line tool, which you've already used, and to create the sun you can use the Ellipse tool. Once you have drawn the shapes, you will color them and add text in Session 7.3.

You want to start by giving Joe a quick overview of the shapes you can draw.

To draw with a variety of the Paint shapes:

1. Click **File** and then click **New** to open a new canvas. Click **Yes** if prompted to save changes.

2. Click the **Rectangle** tool, and then drag a rectangle.

3. Click the **Ellipse** tool, and then drag an ellipse.

4. Click the **Rounded Rectangle**, and then drag a rounded rectangle. Compare your screen to Figure 7-30.

   TROUBLE? If your screen doesn't look like Figure 7-30, don't worry. These shapes are just for experimenting.

| Figure 7-30 | SHAPE TOOLS |

Rectangle
Ellipse
Rounded Rectangle

Now you're ready to create the new graphic. To save you time in this session, the mountains have already been drawn for you. They are stored in a file named Mountain. All you need to do is add the sun. In the same way the Shift key helped you draw a straight horizontal line, it also helps you draw a perfect circle when the Ellipse tool is selected. Likewise, if you use Shift with the Rectangle tool, you can draw a perfect square. When you draw a shape, you can use the **sizing coordinates**, immediately to the right of the pixel coordinates, to control the size of the shape you are dragging. For example, when you draw a circle, you might start at pixel coordinates 15,15 and drag with sizing coordinates of 30 × 30—so your circle has a 30-pixel diameter.

To open the Mountain file and add the sun:

1. Click **File**, click **Open**, and then locate and open the **Mountain** file on your Student Disk. Click the **No** button if you are prompted to save changes.

2. Click **File**, click **Save As**, and then change the name to **Mountain and Sun**, so your changes won't affect the original file. Click the **Save** button.

3. Click the **Ellipse** tool.

4. Press **Shift**, and then drag a circle starting at pixel coordinates **15,15**. Drag to sizing coordinates of **30 × 30**, and then release the mouse button and the Shift key. See Figure 7-31.

Figure 7-31	DRAWING A CIRCLE

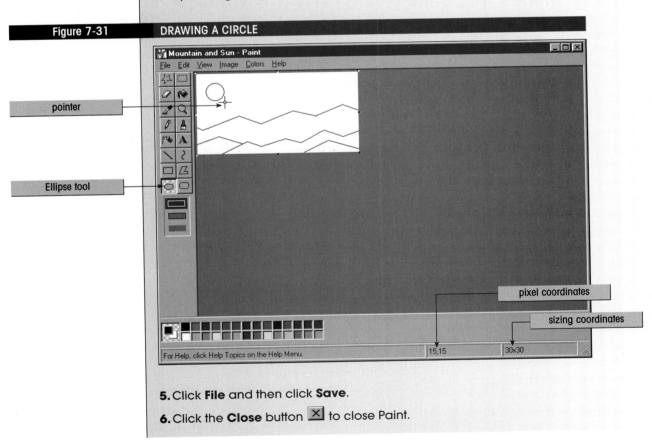

5. Click **File** and then click **Save**.

6. Click the **Close** button ☒ to close Paint.

Joe now has three graphics to choose from: the Skis graphic, the Kiana graphic, and the Mountain and Sun graphic. You remind him that you still plan to add text and color to two of these graphics. You'll work with text and color in Session 7.3.

QUICK CHECK

1. How wide a line do you draw with the Pencil tool, in pixels?

2. When you view the grid, what does each box represent?

3. What option can you use to view the magnified portion of your graphic in Normal view while retaining the magnification on the canvas?

4. Name three ways to clear a canvas.

5. How do you draw a perfect circle?

6. What is the diameter of a circle drawn to 50×50 sizing coordinates?

SESSION 7.3

In this session, you will work with color and text. You'll begin by filling enclosed areas with color, using the Fill With Color tool, and then you'll paint with the Airbrush and work with background and foreground colors. Finally, you'll add text with the Text tool and format it using the Fonts toolbar.

Filling an Area with Color

Joe isn't sure when he'll be able to afford full-color printing, but he is interested to see what effect color has on his graphics. You can add color to a graphic in one of two ways: choosing colors as you draw, or coloring in shapes after you have finished drawing them. You decide to color the Mountain and Sun graphic, whose shapes are already in place. You'll learn to choose colors as you draw later in this session.

REFERENCE WINDOW   **RW**

Filling an Area with Color
- Click the Fill With Color tool.
- Click the color box color you want.
- Click inside the border of the area you want to color. Make sure the tip of the paint pouring out of the bucket is within the border.

In the Mountain and Sun graphic, the shapes you want to color are already in place. You click a color in the color box, and then click an enclosed area in the graphic with the Fill With Color pointer ✏. The area within the borders of the enclosure fills with color. When you use the Fill With Color tool, make sure the area you click is a fully enclosed space. If there are any openings, color "spills out" of the boundaries you are trying to color.

You want to color each mountain range a different color to give the impression of distance and shadow. You decide to use a mix of blues and purples.

To fill the Mountain and Sun graphic with color:

1. Start Paint, and make sure your Student Disk is in drive A.

2. Click **File**, click **Open**, and then locate and open the **Mountain and Sun** file on your Student Disk.

3. Click the **Fill With Color** tool [icon]. The pointer changes to [icon]. You'll color each layer of mountains a different color.

4. Click the **dark blue** color in the top row, seventh from the left.

   TROUBLE? This color might appear purple on your monitor. Make sure it is the seventh from the left in the top row.

5. Click inside the border of the **top mountain range** with the Fill With Color pointer [icon]. The mountain range turns blue. See Figure 7-32.

   TROUBLE? If the sky turns blue instead of the mountain range, you clicked the sky instead of the mountain range. You must click the area to be colored with the active part of the Fill With Color pointer, which is the tip of the paint pouring out of the can. Click Edit, click Undo, and then repeat Step 5, and make sure the tip of the paint is within the border of the mountain range.

Figure 7-32	FILLING FIRST MOUNTAIN RANGE WITH COLOR

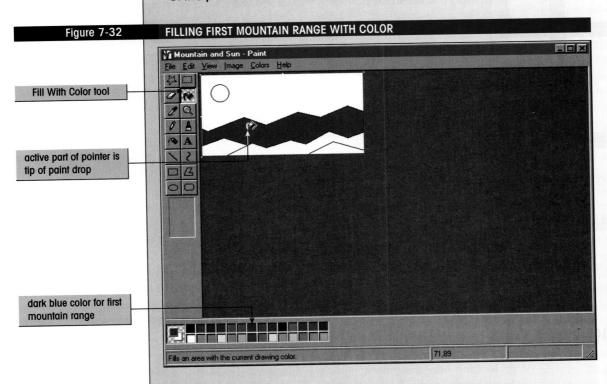

Fill With Color tool

active part of pointer is tip of paint drop

dark blue color for first mountain range

6. Click the **purple color** in the top row, eighth from the left, and then click the front-left mountain range to color it purple.

7. Click the **bright blue** color in the bottom row, seventh from the left, and then click the middle mountain range.

8. Click the **periwinkle** color in the bottom row, third from the right, and then click the right mountain range.

9. Finally, click the **yellow** color in the bottom row, fourth from the left, and then click the sun.

As you've already seen, you can color an enclosed area using the Fill With Color tool. When you filled in the mountain ranges earlier with this tool, you clicked an area with the *left* mouse button, and Paint then applied the foreground color to the area. You can apply the background color by clicking the area with the *right* mouse button. Notice that this is different from drawing a shape from scratch—in that case, the foreground color determines the border, and the background color determines the fill. When you use the Fill With Color tool on *an already existing shape*, you are working only with the fill, and you can switch between foreground and background colors using the left or right mouse button. You decide to change the fill color back to yellow.

To select a new background color and use it to fill a shape:

1. Right-click the yellow color in the bottom row, fourth from the left, to set the background color to yellow.

2. Click the **Fill With Color** tool, and then right-click the **sun**. The fill color of the sun changes to yellow, the background color you just set. This sun, yellow with a brown border, looks good.

It can be confusing that foreground and background colors take on different roles, depending on whether you're drawing an object from scratch, using a shape tool, or coloring in an object using the Fill With Color tool. Just remember that for drawing an object from scratch, the foreground color is the border, and the background color is the fill. When you are coloring an object with the Fill With Color tool, Paint uses the foreground color if you left-click and the background color if you right-click.

You and Joe are satisfied with the coloring of the Mountain graphic. Now you're ready to add the text.

Using the Text Tool

Joe had written the phrase "It's Ski Time!" on his sketch. To add words to the graphic, you use the **Text tool**. To add text to a graphic, you first create a selection box using the Text tool, and then you type your text in this box. If your text exceeds the length and width of the selection box, you can drag the sizing handles to enlarge the selection box.

REFERENCE WINDOW   RW

Adding Text to a Graphic
- Click the Text tool, and then drag a selection box on the canvas.
- Click View, and then click Text Toolbar if the Fonts toolbar does not appear.
- Use the Fonts toolbar to select a font, font size, or attributes (bold, italic, or underline).
- Type the text in the selection box, resizing the selection box if necessary using the sizing handles.
- Adjust the font, font size, or attributes (bold, italic, or underline), and resize the selection box as necessary.
- Click outside the selection box.

You decide to type "It's Ski Time!" just to the right of the sun in the Mountain and Sun graphic, and you decide that the text should appear in the same shade of dark blue you used in the first range of mountains.

To select the text color and create the selection box:

1. Click the **dark blue** color in the top row, seventh from the left, with the left mouse button.

2. Click the **white** color in the bottom row, farthest to the left, with the right mouse button.

3. Click the **Text** tool [A].

4. Create a selection box by dragging from pixel coordinates 54,15 to a size of 185 × 30. Make sure you don't make the box any larger than this or it will obscure the mountains. After you've created the selection box, the Fonts toolbar appears.

TROUBLE? If the Fonts toolbar does not appear, click View. Notice that the Fonts toolbar appears as "Text Toolbar" on the View menu. Click Text Toolbar.

Any letters you type into the selection box will appear with the **font**—or typeface—style, size, and attributes shown in the Fonts toolbar. The font size of the letters is measured in **points**, where a single point is ½ inch. Thus a 1-inch tall character would be 72 points, and a ½-inch tall character would be 36 points. **Attributes** are characteristics of the font, including bold, italic, and underline. You can change the font, font size, and the font attributes using the Fonts toolbar before you type, after you type, or as you edit the text. Once you are satisfied with the text and its appearance, you click outside the selection box. The selection box disappears, and the text is "anchored" into place, becoming a part of the bitmapped graphic. Once text is anchored in a graphic, you can change the font or its attributes only by deleting the text and starting over with the Text tool.

You decide to use an Arial 12-point font. **Arial** is the name of a common font that comes with Windows 98.

To choose the Arial 12-point font and insert the text:

1. Click the **Fonts** list arrow. The list of fonts available on your computer opens. See Figure 7-36. Your list will probably be different.

Figure 7-36	FONT LIST

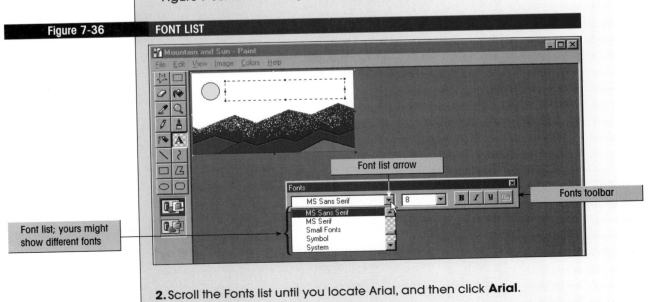

2. Scroll the Fonts list until you locate Arial, and then click **Arial**.

TROUBLE? If your Arial font appears multiple times with a number of different styles, scroll to the top of the list to locate Arial without any style variations.

3. Click the **Font Size** list arrow, and then click **12**. Make sure the Bold and Italic buttons are not selected; if they are, click them to deselect them.

4. Click inside the selection box.

5. Type **It's Ski Time!** Your text appears in the selection box in the Arial 12-point font. See Figure 7-37.

TROUBLE? If nothing appears when you type, it's possible that you clicked the color white with the left mouse button instead of the right mouse button, in the previous set of steps. White text will not appear against a white background. Make sure the foreground color is dark blue and the background color is white.

Figure 7-37	ADDING TEXT USING THE TEXT TOOL

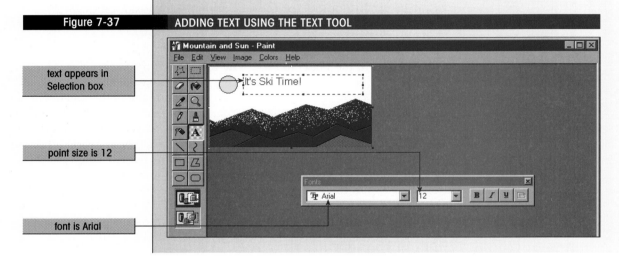

text appears in Selection box

point size is 12

font is Arial

Joe would like to use a more interesting font. You decide to experiment with several fonts, sizes, and attributes to find the look you want. Windows 98 comes with a standard set of fonts, including Arial and Times New Roman, but most users add fonts so they can format text in a variety of styles. The fonts that appear on your computer will most likely differ from those shown in the figures.

To experiment with the font:

1. Click the **Font** list arrow.

2. Scroll the Font list until you locate Times New Roman, and then click **Times New Roman**.

   TROUBLE? If your Times New Roman font appears multiple times with a number of different styles, click any one of the Times New Roman fonts, such as Times New Roman (Baltic).

3. Click the **Bold** button to see how the text looks in bold format.

4. Click the **Italic** button. You like the look of both bold and italic, though you'd like to keep looking at other font styles.

5. Continue to select different fonts and attributes, as shown in Figure 7-38.

TROUBLE? If you can't find the fonts shown in Figure 7-38, experiment with fonts available on your computer. Although Windows 98 comes with a few fonts, your computer lab manager might have added more fonts to your computer

Figure 7-38	EXPERIMENTING WITH DIFFERENT FONTS

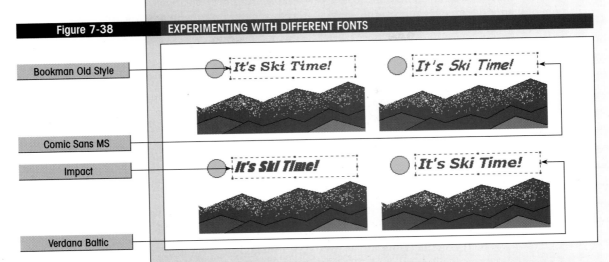

Bookman Old Style

Comic Sans MS

Impact

Verdana Baltic

6. Joe likes bold and italic Verdana Baltic best. Click **Verdana Baltic** if you have it, using both the Bold and Italic attributes. Otherwise click one of your favorites. (You can also leave it as Times New Roman, which is a font that is installed with Windows 98, so every computer should have it.)

7. Now enlarge the font to make the text more visible. Click the **Font Size** list arrow, and then click **16**.

   TROUBLE? If you are using a font that is especially large, 16 points might cause some of the letters to disappear. Repeat Step 7, but this time pick a smaller point size.

8. Click a blank area of the canvas outside the selection box to accept this style of text. The selection box and Fonts toolbar disappear, and the text is anchored into place. See Figure 7-39.

Figure 7-39	COMPLETED GRAPHIC WITH TEXT

It's Ski Time!

9. Click **File**, and then click **Save** to save the Mountain and Sun graphic.

10. Click the Paint **Close** button ☒.

Joe has enjoyed watching you work with the Paint program. Although he recognizes that these graphics do not match the quality of those you could create with a full-featured graphics program such as CorelDraw, he is, nevertheless, impressed with Paint's versatility and ease of use. Now that he has a few usable graphics, he looks forward to creating more announcements and promotional materials for the Birkebeiner ski race.

QUICK CHECK

1. To change a shape's fill color, you use the _____ tool.

2. What does it mean to say that a font is "10 points"?

3. What font attributes can you work with in Paint?

4. You just opened a graphic containing text, and you'd like to change the font of the text. Describe your options.

5. When you draw an object from scratch, the foreground color controls an object's _____, whereas the background color controls its _____.

6. If you select the Fill With Color tool and then right-click an enclosed area, which color is applied, the foreground or the background?

TUTORIAL ASSIGNMENTS

1. **Cropping a Graphic** Joe is also the coordinator for a university students' bowling league, and he asks you to help create a graphic for an informational promotion he is preparing.

   a. Open the Sports graphic in Paint.
   b. Use the Select tool to select the bowling ball hitting the bowling pins in the lower-right corner of the Sports graphic.
   c. Use the Copy To option to save the cropped graphic to your Student Disk as a monochrome graphic with the name Bowling Ball.
   d. Open the Bowling Ball graphic and, if necessary, erase any portions of it that aren't part of the graphic.
   e. Save the graphic.

Explore

2. **Cropping a Graphic with the Free-Form Select Tool** You're helping design league jackets for the Community Tennis League. You want to crop the tennis rackets in the lower-left corner of the Sports graphic. In Session 7.1, you used the Select tool to crop part of a graphic, but the selection box included portions of other images that you then had to erase. You can avoid this extra step by using the Free-Form Select tool. With the Free-Form Select tool, you can draw a line of any shape around the area you want to crop.

   a. Open the Sports graphic.
   b. Use the Free-Form Select tool to draw around the tennis rackets in the lower-left corner of the Sports graphic. Notice that when you are done drawing around the rackets, a selection box appears, similar to the selection box you used with the Select tool. However, Paint erases any areas in the box that were not included when you used the Free-Form Select tool.
   c. Save the cropped graphic to your Student Disk as a monochrome graphic with the name Tennis Rackets.

d. Open the Tennis Rackets graphic and ensure that you didn't include any unwanted portions of the Sports graphic.

e. Save the Tennis Rackets graphic.

3. **Drawing in Color** One of the Birkebeiner participants was in the most recent Winter Olympics, and one of Joe's promotions highlights the fact that the Birkebeiner attracts top-notch competitors. Joe asks you to create a graphic of the Olympic rings that he can use. The top three rings are blue, black, and red. The bottom two rings are yellow and green. Save the file on your Student Disk as a 256 Color Bitmap graphic with the name Rings. Here are some tricks you can use to make this assignment easier:

■ Use Shift to draw perfect circles.

■ Use the sizing coordinates to ensure that each circle is the same size (such as 30 × 30).

■ Draw each new circle in a blank area of the canvas, and then use the Select tool to select the circle and drag it into place.

■ Use the pixel coordinates to ensure that you place all rings in each row on the same level.

Figure 7-40 shows such a drawing.

Figure 7-40

4. **Adding Text to the Kiana Graphic** You and Joe decide to finish the Kiana graphic. You need to add the rest of the word "Kiana." First open the Kiana file that you created earlier in this tutorial and saved on your Student Disk. Save the file as Kiana2.

a. Use the Text tool to insert a selection box, and then type the letters "iana" and select a font and font size that you like.

b. Use the Fill With Color tool to fill each letter with a different color.

c. Make the graphic take up less room on your disk by selecting the entire drawing and dragging it up to the corner of the canvas. Then resize the canvas to fit the drawing.

Explore

d. Give the graphic a background color that complements the letter colors. Compare your figure to Figure 7-41.

e. Save and print your graphic.

Figure 7-41

Explore

5. **Editing Graphic Images** Joe would like his promotions to look more professional, and he asks if you could connect to the Internet and locate another ski graphic for him. He'd like the graphic to have the word "Birkebeiner" on it.

  a. Connect to the Internet and use Yahoo's subject guide to search for Web pages that make graphic images available. (*Hint*: Try the Computers and Internet category, and the Graphics subcategory.)

  b. Once you have located a graphics page, search for a Sports category and locate a skier graphic. It must have a format that Paint supports: bmp, or, if you have Microsoft Office, gif, or jpeg. If you can't find a graphic image on the Internet, use the Skis graphic you used in this tutorial, and save it as "Skier."

  c. Download the Skier graphic to your Student Disk with the name "Skier."

  d. Open the Skier graphic in Paint, and add the word "Birkebeiner" to the graphic. (*Hint*: If there is no blank area in which to add this word, resize the canvas as necessary.)

  e. Save the graphic.

PROJECTS

1. You work for Jensen Telecommunications. Jensen is hosting an engineering conference to share ideas on making high-speed fiber-optic data lines available to homes. You're helping host the conference banquet, and you'd like to create a classy design to imprint on the cocktail napkins and coasters. Use the Brush tool to draw the graphic, as shown in Steps a through f, and then save it as a Monochrome Bitmap graphic.

  a. Create a vertical line as shown, using the largest angular brush style in the third row.

  b. Copy the vertical line and paste it as shown.

  c. Draw the horizontal line to hook up with the vertical line.

  d. Copy the horizontal line and paste it on top.

  e. Copy a short section of the horizontal line and paste it in the middle.

  f. Save the image as "Letter J" on your Student Disk.

2. You work for a commercial graphics design company, Ace Design Group (ADG). ADG has just landed a contract to create a new font style for the posters and materials of the American Statistical Association's annual conference. Your boss has asked you to start drafting possible designs for the new font style. You decide to use Paint to create a few sample letters, specifically, an uppercase and lowercase "a" and "f." You'll probably want to use a combination of drawing tools for this assignment. You'll almost certainly need to zoom in and edit, using the grid, to ensure consistency from letter to letter. The previous project showed you how to go about drawing a letter. When you are finished drafting a few ideas for a new letter design, save your file as Fonts using the monochrome Bitmap file type and print it.

3. You're preparing a flyer for a Sailing Club, and you need a graphic that shows a sailboat. You plan to print your flyer in color, so you need a graphic with color.

  a. Open the Sports graphic and copy the sailboat image to a new file named "Sailboat" on your Student Disk. Save the file as a 256 Color Bitmap image.

  b. Use the Fill With Color tool to color the sails of the sailboat red.

  c. Add the words "Time to Sail!" on the sailboat graphic.

  d. Save the graphic on your Student Disk.

4. You coordinate the Chess Club at Stanton Junior High. You want to create a simple graphic for a tournament brochure. Use the Rectangle tool and your copy and pasting skills to create the chessboard in the following Steps a through f.

   a. Use the Rectangle tool in combination with the Shift key to create a perfect square with dragging coordinates of 35 × 35. Don't forget to use the Shift key.

   b. Copy the square, and then paste it and drag it so that the edges overlap. Do this three times to create the first four squares.

   c. Copy the four squares, and then paste that image and drag it to the right of the first four squares.

   d. Copy those eight squares, and then paste that image and drag it to the right of the existing eight squares.

   e. Copy those 16 squares, and paste and drag them three times to create the rest of the chessboard.

   f. Save the images as Chess on your Student Disk using the 256 Color Bitmap file type.

5. You just completed the Chess graphic in Project 4. You now want to add text and color.

   a. Color in every other square, using the Fill With Color tool, to create a chessboard.
   b. Add the words "Stanton Chess Club" to the top of the chessboard. Choose a font style and size that complement the colors and board you drew.
   c. Add the word "Tournament" below the chessboard.

Explore

   d. Now use the Select tool to select just the word "Tournament." Then rotate the word and drag it to the right side of the chessboard, as shown in Figure 7-42. Using the Flip/Rotate command on the Image menu, click Rotate by angle, and then click 270. Your graphic should look like Figure 7-42, but will vary depending on the font you chose.
   e. Print the graphic, and then save it on your Student Disk as "Chess with Text."

Figure 7-42

QUICK CHECK ANSWERS

Session 7.1

1. Select the portion you want to save, click Edit, then click Copy To, enter a name and location in the Save As dialog box, then click the Save button.

2. Drag the sizing handle.

3. True

4. Pixels

5. Color graphics require more bits to define the colors.

6. Convert it to a format Paint does support, using a graphics converter.

Session 7.2

1. A single pixel

2. A single pixel

3. Thumbnail

4. The Eraser tool, the Clear Image command on the Image menu, or the New command on the File menu

5. Press Shift and use the Ellipse tool.

6. 50 pixels

Session 7.3

1. Fill With Color

2. Its size is $10 \times \frac{1}{2}$ inch.

3. Bold, italic, and underline

4. You must erase or cut the text, then click the Text tool and enter new text with the font you want.

5. Border, fill

6. Background

LABS

Multimedia

OBJECT LINKING AND EMBEDDING

Creating a Multimedia Document for the Jugglers Guild

CASE

Preparing for the Jugglers Guild Convention

The Tenth Annual Jugglers Guild Convention is scheduled for this summer in New Orleans. Maria Arruda, secretary of the Jugglers Guild, is chairing the convention, aided by a committee of which you are a member. Maria has assigned tasks to each committee member—yours is to work on gathering materials that will promote the event. Maria would like you to hire a designer to design a graphics file that can serve as a logo for informational flyers, posters, and convention T-shirts. Maria asks you also to look for an eye-catching video clip that will run on the computer screens used at the convention. A **video clip** is a file that contains a very short movie, either real-life or animated.

You hire a graphic designer to design the logo and a computer animation company to create an animated video clip. Once you receive the disks containing the graphics file and video clip, you give them to Maria so she can evaluate them. The next day she returns the disks and says she likes the logo and the animation, but she'd like feedback from the rest of the committee. She asks you to create a single WordPad document that will contain the graphics file and the video clip, and into which the committee members can add their comments. A document that includes a variety of media, such as text, graphics, and video, is called a **multimedia document**.

Windows 98 provides three ways to combine data from a variety of sources into a single multimedia document: pasting, embedding, and linking. You'll learn about pasting in Session 8.1, embedding in Session 8.2, and linking in Session 8.3. How do you decide which method to use in a given situation? It depends on what you need to do with the information after you've inserted it into the multimedia document—whether you need to use the tools in the program that originally created the data, and whether you are likely to change the data once you've inserted it. As you proceed through these three sessions, notice how the pasting, embedding, and linking techniques offer you different options to meet these needs.

SESSION 8.1

In this session, you will learn how to use the Windows 98 Clipboard to make data from one source available to another document or program, using the Edit commands. You'll also learn how to examine the contents of the Clipboard with Clipboard Viewer.
To perform the steps of this tutorial, you will need one blank 3½-inch disk. To complete the Tutorial Assignments and Projects, you will need a second blank 3½-inch disk.

Creating a WordPad Document

You'll start by creating the WordPad document that will contain the data you want other members of the committee to view. You'll format the document as a memo, beginning with a standard memo heading that includes To, Date, and Subject headings.

To start a new WordPad document:

1. Write "Disk 6—Windows 98 Tutorials 8 & 9 Student Disk" on the label of a blank, formatted 3½-inch disk. Insert your Student Disk into drive A.

2. Point to the **Start** button [Start], point to **Programs**, point to **NP on Microsoft Windows 98 – Level III**, and then click **Disk 6 (Tutorials 8 & 9)**. When you are prompted to insert your disk in the drive, click the **OK** button, and wait as the files you need are copied to your Student Disk.

3. Close all the open windows on your screen.

4. Click the **Start** button, point to **Programs**, point to **Accessories**, and then click **WordPad**.

5. Type the following memo heading into the WordPad document. Press the **Enter** key twice after each line, and **Tab** twice after the first two colons (just press **Tab** once after the SUBJECT colon).

   MEMO

   TO: **Jugglers Guild Convention Committee**

   DATE: **3/18/99**

   SUBJECT: **Tenth Annual Jugglers Guild Convention**

6. Make sure you press Enter twice after typing the SUBJECT line. Click **File**, and then click **Save As** to save the work you've done so far.

7. Type **Feedback** in the File name box.

8. Click the **Save in** list arrow, and then click the drive containing your Student Disk.

9. Click the **Save** button.

The Clipboard

Maria has decided that she wants the committee members to give their feedback on the graphics and video files in a specific way. She drafts a document that outlines the feedback procedure and includes her own feedback. She suggests you insert her document into your Feedback document.

Windows 98 offers several ways to transfer data from one document to another; the most basic technique is **Paste**, whereby you cut or copy data from one document and then paste it into another. This procedure uses the **Clipboard**, an area in your computer's active memory that temporarily stores the data you cut or copy. For example, suppose you had an e-mail message that contained information you wanted to paste into a WordPad document. Figure 8-1 illustrates how you copy the message to the Clipboard and then paste it into your document.

Figure 8-1   **USING THE CLIPBOARD**

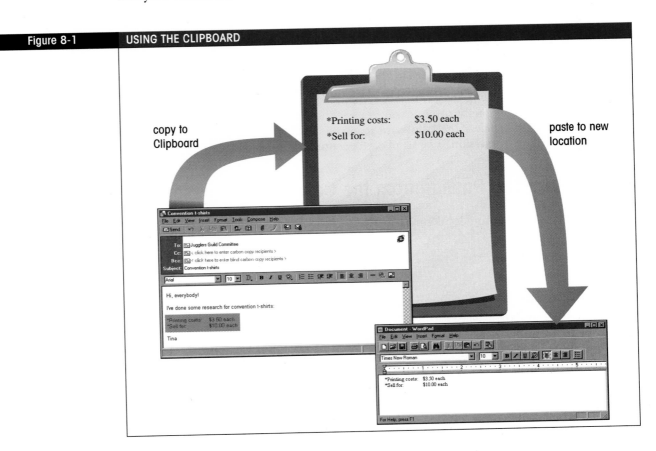

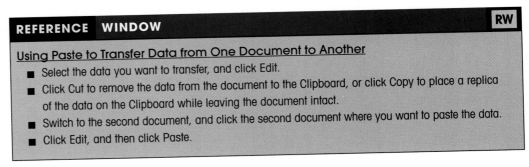

REFERENCE   WINDOW   **RW**

Using Paste to Transfer Data from One Document to Another
- Select the data you want to transfer, and click Edit.
- Click Cut to remove the data from the document to the Clipboard, or click Copy to place a replica of the data on the Clipboard while leaving the document intact.
- Switch to the second document, and click the second document where you want to paste the data.
- Click Edit, and then click Paste.

The Clipboard is part of the operating system and is available in most Windows programs through standard Cut, Copy, and Paste commands. Figure 8-2 shows the equivalent keyboard methods you can use to cut, copy, and paste data within a document or from one document to another.

Figure 8-2	CUT AND PASTE OPTIONS		
OPERATION	**MENU COMMAND**	**TOOLBAR BUTTON**	**KEYBOARD SHORTCUT**
Cut	Edit, then Cut	✂	Ctrl+X
Copy	Edit, then Copy	📋	Ctrl+C
Paste	Edit, then Paste	📋	Ctrl+V

When you paste data from the Clipboard into a document, you do not remove the data from the Clipboard; you can continue to paste the data as many times as you want, into as many documents as you want. The Clipboard stores the data until you cut or copy new data, since the Clipboard can hold only one piece of data at a time.

If the Clipboard contains a large amount of data when you close a program, Windows 98 might prompt you to clear the Clipboard contents to free your system's memory. You can clear the Clipboard manually, using the Clipboard Viewer, as you'll see at the end of this session. The Clipboard's contents are also cleared when you shut down your computer.

Copying and Pasting from the Calculator Accessory

You decide to open Maria's document to see what it contains.

To open Maria's document:

1. Open the document named **Maria** from your Student Disk in WordPad. Because you can open only one document at a time in WordPad, the Feedback document closes. Figure 8-3 shows Maria's document.

   TROUBLE? If you are asked if you want to save changes, click Yes only if you are sure the document contains the memo heading. Otherwise click No.

Figure 8-3	MARIA'S DOCUMENT

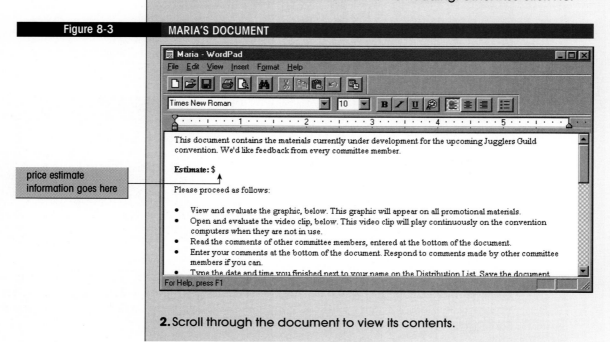

price estimate information goes here

2. Scroll through the document to view its contents.

You see that Maria has left room to insert both the graphic and the video clip. Then you notice she left room for a price estimate at the top. You've received quotes from the two vendors: $235 for the graphic and $390 for the video clip. The graphic design vendor is also offering a 12% discount if you print your convention materials there. You want to inform the committee members of these quotes, so you decide to use the Windows 98 Calculator to calculate the total. The **Calculator** is a Windows 98 accessory that looks and functions just like a hand-held calculator. It can appear in two views: **Standard** view, which provides basic arithmetic operations, or **Scientific** view, which includes a variety of algebraic, trigonometric, and statistical functions.

You are less likely to make a mistake entering the total into your document if you use the Clipboard to copy the data from the Calculator to your document, instead of typing it. The Calculator includes a Copy command that copies the current entry to the Clipboard. You can transfer the answer to any program that offers Clipboard access.

To calculate the total, you multiply 235 by .88 to calculate the price of the graphic discounted by 12%, and then add 390.

To open the Calculator and copy the total to Maria's document:

1. Click **Start**, point to **Programs**, point to **Accessories**, and then click **Calculator**. See Figure 8-4.

   TROUBLE? If your Calculator window appears twice this size, your Calculator opened in Scientific view. You can perform the calculations in Scientific or Standard view.

Figure 8-4   **CALCULATOR ACCESSORY**

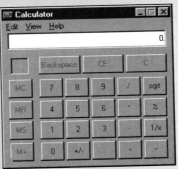

2. Click the buttons ⊟, ⑧, ⑧, ✕, ②, ③, ⑤, ⊞, ③, ⑨, ⓪, ⊜ to calculate the total of 596.8.

3. Click **Edit**, and then click **Copy**. With the Calculator, you don't have to highlight the data you want to copy. Even though the text does not appear highlighted, the Calculator automatically copies the entry in the results box. Notice that when you copy, the information is not removed from the program. You have simply placed a copy of it on the Clipboard.

4. Click the **Close** button ☒ to close the Calculator.

The Clipboard now contains the value 596.8. You need to paste this value into Maria's document.

To paste the total into Maria's document:

1. Click and then scroll to the top of Maria's document, and click to the right of the $ next to the boldface **Estimate**: heading.

2. Click the **Paste** button 📋. See Figure 8-5.

   TROUBLE? If the Paste button doesn't appear, click View, and then click Toolbar.

| Figure 8-5 | PASTING THE CALCULATED ESTIMATE |

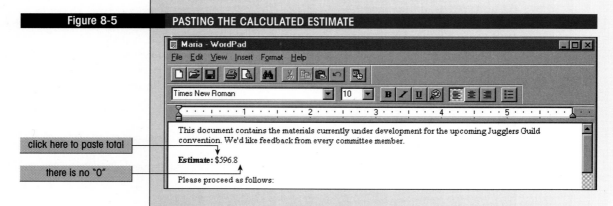

3. Notice that there is no "0" in the cents position of the total estimate. Type **0** to complete the currency format.

Cutting and Pasting Between Two WordPad Documents

The next step in your project is to move the information from Maria's document to your document. This time, rather than copying the information over, you decide to cut it from Maria's document and paste it into yours. When you copied, the information remained in the source program, as you saw with the Calculator accessory. However, when you cut, you permanently remove the information from the original program.

To cut the contents from Maria's document and move it to the Clipboard:

1. Click **Edit**, and then click **Select All**. The entire document is selected.

2. Click the **Cut** button ✂. Windows 98 removes the selected material from Maria's document and places it on the Clipboard.

The Clipboard now contains the data from Maria's document. It will stay there until you copy or cut something else, until you manually clear the Clipboard, or until you shut down your computer. You can now open your Feedback document and insert the contents of the Clipboard.

To insert the contents of the Clipboard into your Feedback document:

1. Click **File**, and then click **A:\Feedback**, which appears near the bottom of the File menu.

TROUBLE? If A:\Feedback does not appear, and you have left the computer since you were working with the Feedback document in the WordPad window, other files opened more recently might appear at the bottom of the File menu. If this is the case, open the Feedback file using the Open dialog box.

2. Click **No** when WordPad prompts you to save changes to Maria's document; you don't need to save changes because you won't be using this document again.

3. Click at the end of your Feedback document. The insertion point appears where you click. Any text you type or paste will appear at the insertion point.

TROUBLE? If the insertion point appears at the end of the last line, press Enter so the graphic doesn't appear on the same line as the text.

4. Click the **Paste** button 📋 to paste the information from Maria's document into your Feedback document.

5. Scroll back to the top of the document. See Figure 8-6.

| Figure 8-6 | FEEDBACK DOCUMENT WITH PASTED INFORMATION |

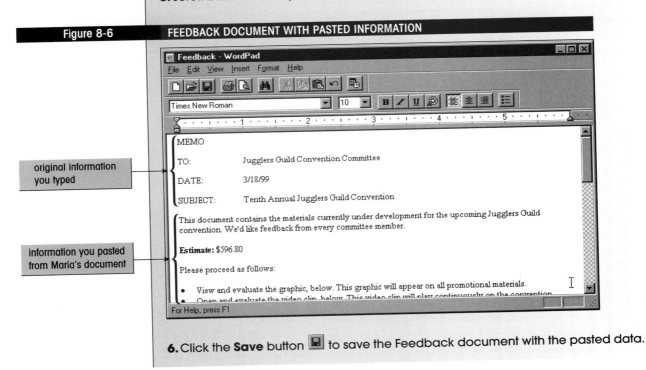

original information you typed

information you pasted from Maria's document

6. Click the **Save** button 💾 to save the Feedback document with the pasted data.

Viewing Clipboard Contents

The Clipboard still contains the text of Maria's document. Remember that when you choose Paste, you are simply pasting a copy of the Clipboard contents into your document. The contents remain on the Clipboard in your computer's memory. If you need to free up memory, you can clear the contents of the Clipboard using a Windows 98 accessory called Clipboard Viewer. **Clipboard Viewer** lets you examine, save, and delete the contents of the Clipboard.

You decide to open Clipboard Viewer and delete its contents to free up memory. In reality, the amount of text you cut from Maria's document does not take up that much memory, but in practice you might find that cutting or copying graphics or large quantities of data could cause memory problems if your computer is low on memory.

To view and clear the contents of the Clipboard:

1. Click the **Start** button, point to **Programs**, point to **Accessories**, and then point to **System Tools**. Look at the System Tools menu to see whether Clipboard Viewer is installed.

   TROUBLE? If Clipboard Viewer does not appear, then you cannot complete this session until Clipboard Viewer is installed. Check with your instructor or technical support person for assistance. If you are using your own computer and you have the installation disks, insert the installation CD-ROM. Click Add/Remove Software, and on the Windows Setup tab, click System Tools, click the Details button, place a check mark in the Clipboard Viewer check box, and then click OK twice. Close the Windows 98 CD-ROM window and repeat Step 1. If you still can't install Clipboard Viewer, read to the end of this section without doing the steps.

2. Click **Clipboard Viewer**. The Clipboard Viewer window opens. The text you cut from Maria's document appears. See Figure 8-7.

| Figure 8-7 | CLIPBOARD VIEWER |

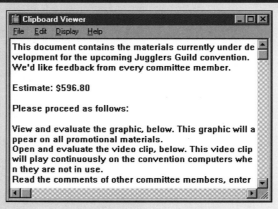

3. Click **Edit**, click **Delete** to clear the contents, and then click **Yes** when you are asked if you are sure.

4. Click the **Close** button ☒ to close Clipboard Viewer.

5. Click the **Close** button ☒ to close WordPad.

QUICK CHECK

1. What is the Clipboard?

2. What happens to the selected text in the original document when you cut it? When you copy it?

3. What keyboard shortcuts can you use to cut, copy, and paste?

4. True or False: Once you paste the contents of the Clipboard into a document, it is no longer available to be pasted into other documents.

5. How do you clear the contents of the Clipboard? Why would you want to do this?

6. Why would you use the Copy and Paste commands to transfer answers from the Calculator or similar programs into other documents?

SESSION 8.2

In this session, you'll learn how object linking and embedding (OLE) extends your ability to transfer data between files. You'll focus on embedding: you'll learn to embed a graphic object, change its size, and edit the embedded object. Then you'll display the embedded object as an icon, change its name, and change the icon that represents it.

Object Linking and Embedding (OLE)

So far you have pasted text into your WordPad document, first from the Calculator accessory and then from another WordPad document. The text you pasted actually became part of the Feedback document, and you could work with it in the same way you work with text you typed in—using the tools provided with WordPad. However, a multimedia document like the one you're creating can contain data from many different sources—graphics from Paint, charts from a spreadsheet, sounds from an audio file—as well as text.

In your multimedia document, how can you work with data that comes from programs with different tools? For example, your WordPad document offers only text-editing tools. If you place a Paint graphic in this document, you can't use the WordPad tools to edit that graphic. Windows 98 provides the tools you need through a process called **object linking and embedding**, or **OLE** (pronounced "oh LAY"). OLE lets you insert an object into a document and access tools to manipulate the object. An **object** is a unit of data, such as a graphic, a sound clip, or text.

With OLE, you place objects into documents using either of two methods: you embed them or you link them. In this session, you'll learn how to embed objects, and in Session 8.3 you'll learn how to link objects.

To understand both embedding and linking, you need to know the terms listed in Figure 8-8.

Figure 8-8	OLE TERMS
TERM	**DEFINITION**
source program	The program that created the original object
source file	The file that contains the original object
destination program	The program that created the document into which you are inserting the OLE object
destination file	The file into which you are inserting the OLE object

Figure 8-9 applies the terms in Figure 8-8 to the document Maria wants you to create. Paint and Media Player are the source programs, and the Pins graphic and Video video clip are the source files. WordPad is the destination program, and Feedback is the destination file.

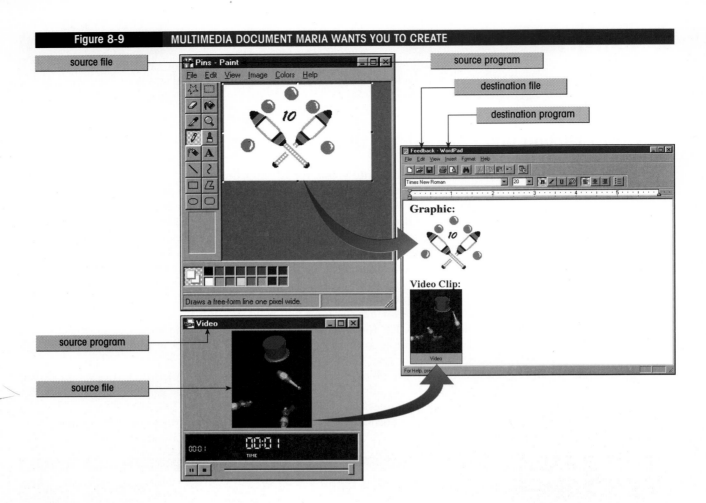

Figure 8-9   MULTIMEDIA DOCUMENT MARIA WANTS YOU TO CREATE

Embedding an Object Using Paste

You are ready to place the graphic into the Feedback document, but you want to retain the ability to work with the graphic with tools from the program that originally created it—in this case, Paint. When you want to be able to use the tools from the source program within the destination file, you should embed the object into the destination file. **Embedding** places a copy of an object into a document and "remembers" which program created the object, although it doesn't remember the name of the source file. Compare this technique to copying, which simply places the copy of the data in the new program with no reference to its source. There are several ways to embed an object. If both the source and destination programs feature OLE technology, you can simply paste the object from one to the other. Many of the programs designed for Windows 98 feature OLE.

The graphic provided by the graphic design company is called Pins. You want to embed a copy of this graphic into the Feedback document.

To copy the Pins graphic to the Clipboard:

1. Click the **Start** button, point to **Programs**, point to **Accessories**, and then click **Paint**.

2. Open the **Pins** graphic from your Student Disk.

3. Click **Edit**, and then click **Select All**. A selection box appears around the graphic.

4. Click **Edit**, and then click **Copy**. Windows 98 copies the graphic to the Clipboard.

5. Click the **Close** button to close Paint.

The graphic is now copied to the Clipboard. To embed it, you open the Feedback document in WordPad and then use WordPad's Paste command.

To embed the Pins graphic into the Feedback document:

1. Start WordPad and open the **Feedback** document from your Student Disk.

2. Scroll the **Feedback** document until you locate the boldface **Graphic**: heading.

3. Click the blank line two lines below the **Graphic**: heading.

4. Click the **Paste** button . The Pins graphic is embedded in the Feedback document, and it appears in a selection box. See Figure 8-10.

Figure 8-10	EMBEDDED OBJECT

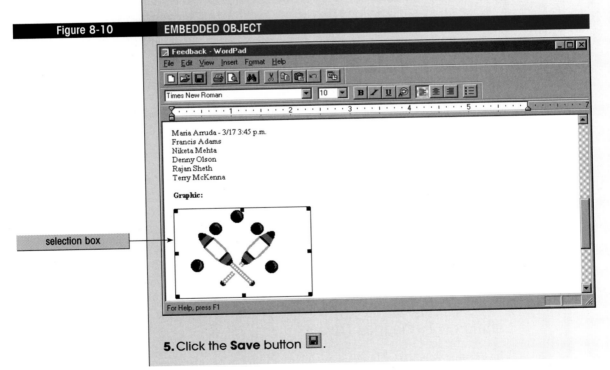

selection box

5. Click the **Save** button .

It can be confusing that the Paste command seems to function differently with different objects. In Session 8.1, Paste simply pasted text, but here Paste embeds an object. How can you tell what Paste is doing? There are no hard-and-fast rules for how each program takes advantage of the OLE technology, although the following generalization can be helpful: When you use Paste to transfer the same type of data from one document to another (as it did when you transferred text into WordPad), Paste inserts the data without embedding. However, when you are transferring a different type of data from one document to another, and both the source and destination programs use OLE, Paste usually, but not always, embeds the data. When you copy and paste between Windows 98 programs, it's a good idea to examine what you've pasted so you can see how the program uses the Paste command.

One clue is that if a selection box appears when you click the pasted data, it is embedded, and you can edit the data with the tools from the source program.

Changing the Size of an Embedded Object

As you examine the embedded graphic, you wonder if it might be easier to evaluate the image if it were a little bigger.

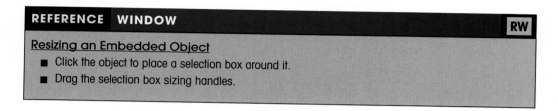

REFERENCE WINDOW   RW

Resizing an Embedded Object
- Click the object to place a selection box around it.
- Drag the selection box sizing handles.

To enlarge the embedded graphic:

1. Drag the lower-right sizing handle down and to the right. The pointer changes to ↘ when you point at the sizing handle. The embedded object is enlarged. See Figure 8-11.

Figure 8-11   ENLARGING THE EMBEDDED PAINT OBJECT

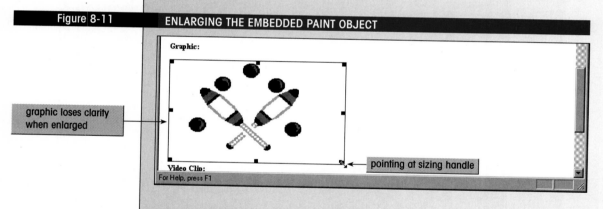

graphic loses clarity when enlarged

pointing at sizing handle

2. You realize that the enlarged graphic is less sharp, so you decide to leave it in its original size. Click **Edit**, and then click **Undo** to undo your last action.

Editing an Embedded Object

The graphic is in place, but you decide that before the other committee members see it, you want to enhance it by adding color, since you noticed Maria's comment about the lack of color. You can edit an embedded object using the source program's editing tools. The ability to edit an object that has been embedded into a different program's document is called **in-place editing**—it gives you access to the source program's tools without making you leave the destination program. In-place editing is a valuable Windows 98 data-transfer feature, because it brings the tools you need to work with your document right to you, rather than making you get them.

When you use in-place editing, you sometimes might momentarily forget which program you are using. In that case, remember that the title bar identifies the program that contains your destination document, whereas the menus and toolbars identify the program you're using to edit the OLE object.

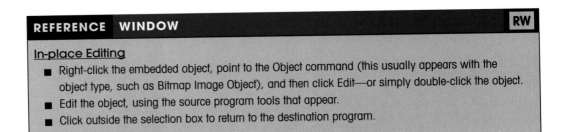

REFERENCE   WINDOW   **RW**

In-place Editing
- Right-click the embedded object, point to the Object command (this usually appears with the object type, such as Bitmap Image Object), and then click Edit—or simply double-click the object.
- Edit the object, using the source program tools that appear.
- Click outside the selection box to return to the destination program.

To edit the Pins graphic within the WordPad document:

1. Right-click the **Pins** graphic to open its menu, and then point to **Bitmap Image Object**.

2. Click **Edit**. The graphic appears inside a selection box, the Paint tools appear, and the menu bar changes to the Paint menus, but the title bar identifies that you are still in WordPad. See Figure 8-12.

| Figure 8-12 | USING IN-PLACE EDITING |

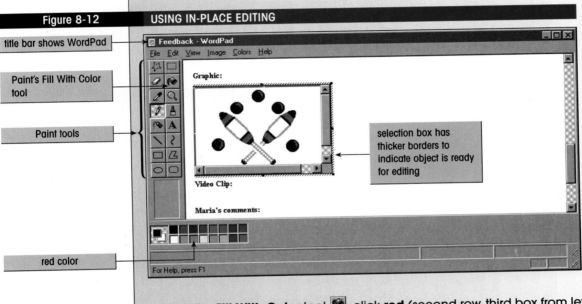

title bar shows WordPad

Paint's Fill With Color tool

Paint tools

selection box has thicker borders to indicate object is ready for editing

red color

3. Click the **Fill With Color** tool ![tool], click **red** (second row, third box from left in the Color box), and then click the farthest ball on the left. The ball turns red. Click each ball, one at a time, to color them red.

   TROUBLE? If you mistakenly click an area outside one of the balls, click Edit, click Undo, and then click the ball again.

   TROUBLE? If you can't see the entire image within the selection box, scroll to the right until you can.

4. Click outside the selection box in the WordPad document. The WordPad menus and window reappear.

5. Click the **Save** button ![save] to save the Feedback document with the edited embedded Pins graphic.

As you'll see in Session 8.3, one of the important features that distinguish embedding from linking is that *when you edit an embedded object, the source file is not affected*. You are accessing only the tools that created the object, not the original file. You can verify that the original graphic remains unchanged by opening the original Pins graphic in Paint.

To see that the original Pins graphic has not changed:

1. Click the **Start** button, point to **Programs**, point to **Accessories**, and then click **Paint**.

2. Click **File**, and then click **A:\Pins** near the bottom of the File menu. Notice that the original Pins graphic has not changed.

3. Click the **Close** button ▣ to close Paint.

Embedding an Object Using Insert Object

To paste an object into a different document, the object must be open and displayed on the screen so you can copy or cut it to the Clipboard. Most Windows programs that offer OLE technology also offer the **Insert Object** command, which lets you embed an object without having to open it and copy it to the Clipboard.

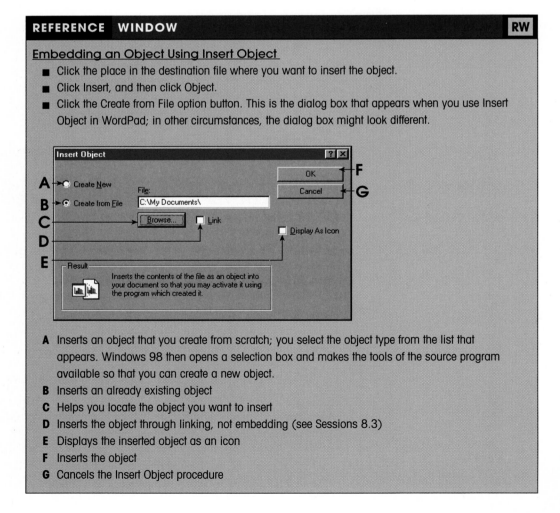

REFERENCE WINDOW   **RW**

Embedding an Object Using Insert Object
- Click the place in the destination file where you want to insert the object.
- Click Insert, and then click Object.
- Click the Create from File option button. This is the dialog box that appears when you use Insert Object in WordPad; in other circumstances, the dialog box might look different.

A Inserts an object that you create from scratch; you select the object type from the list that appears. Windows 98 then opens a selection box and makes the tools of the source program available so that you can create a new object.

B Inserts an already existing object

C Helps you locate the object you want to insert

D Inserts the object through linking, not embedding (see Sessions 8.3)

E Displays the inserted object as an icon

F Inserts the object

G Cancels the Insert Object procedure

Insert Object embeds the entire file, without giving you the option to embed just a part of it, such as a single paragraph of text or a single table or chart. As you'll see shortly, to embed a part of a file, you must use Paste Special.

When you talked to the graphic designer on the phone the other day, you mentioned that it might be nice to include the number "10" in the graphic, for 10th anniversary. The designer has just delivered a new disk with the revised file, called Pins10. You decide to embed Pins10 into the Feedback document, using Insert Object.

To embed an object using the Insert Object command:

1. Scroll down the **Feedback** document until you see the boldface Video Clip: heading.

2. Click to the left of the Video Clip: heading until the insertion point appears.

3. Press the **Enter** key twice to add two new lines, and then press **Up Arrow** twice.

4. Click **Insert**, and then click **Object**.

5. Click the **Create from File** option button.

6. Click the **Browse** button, and then locate and click the **Pins10** file on your Student Disk.

7. Click the **Insert** button. The filename is inserted into the File box.

8. Verify that the Link and Display As Icon check boxes are not selected. See Figure 8-13.

| Figure 8-13 | INSERT OBJECT DIALOG BOX |

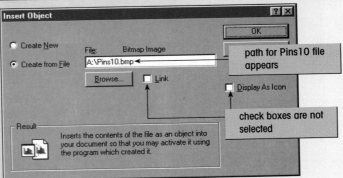

9. Click the **OK** button in the Insert Object dialog box. The object appears in the Feedback document.

Controlling an OLE Object's Appearance

When you place a graphic image in a document, your computer might take longer to display the document than if it contained only text. For example, when you scroll up and down the Feedback document, depending on the speed of your computer and the size of the graphics, it may take significantly longer to "redraw" the graphics as you scroll. For this reason, some users prefer to use the ability of Windows 98 to display OLE objects as icons, especially during the draft phases of creating a multimedia document. Like most Windows 98 objects, your embedded object has a property sheet that lets you work with the object. You decide to display the first graphic you embedded, the red Pins graphic, as an icon.

To display the embedded Pins graphic as an icon:

1. Scroll up the **Feedback** document so you can see the first graphic you embedded, the Pins graphic.

2. Right-click the **Pins** graphic, and then click **Object Properties**.

3. Click the **View** tab.

4. Click the **Display as icon** option button, and then click the **OK** button. An icon appears that represents the graphic. See Figure 8-14.

| Figure 8-14 | DISPLAYING AN OBJECT AS AN ICON |

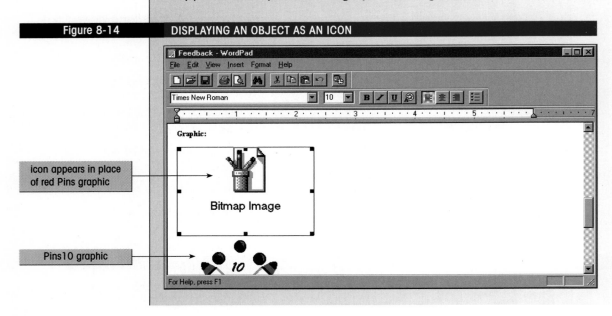

icon appears in place of red Pins graphic

Pins10 graphic

Changing the Display Icon

Because you changed the graphic to an icon, and so can no longer identify the contents of the embedded object, you decide to change the label of the icon to make it more descriptive. You can change the icon label using the embedded object's property sheet.

To change the label of the icon:

1. Right-click the icon representing the embedded Pins graphic.

2. Click **Object Properties**.

3. Click the **View** tab.

4. Click the **Change Icon** button.

5. Delete the contents of the Label box, and then type **Pins Graphic**. See Figure 8-15.

| Figure 8-15 | **CHANGE ICON DIALOG BOX** |

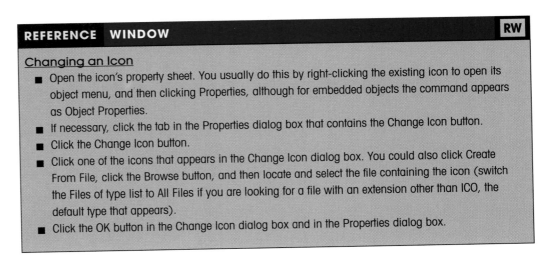

If your multimedia document includes icons in its final form, you might not like the look of the icons Windows 98 chooses to represent your embedded objects. You can change the icon representing the embedded object, using the property sheet. Incidentally, you can use this method to change the appearance of many icons, including some icons on the desktop.

REFERENCE WINDOW   **RW**

Changing an Icon
- Open the icon's property sheet. You usually do this by right-clicking the existing icon to open its object menu, and then clicking Properties, although for embedded objects the command appears as Object Properties.
- If necessary, click the tab in the Properties dialog box that contains the Change Icon button.
- Click the Change Icon button.
- Click one of the icons that appears in the Change Icon dialog box. You could also click Create From File, click the Browse button, and then locate and select the file containing the icon (switch the Files of type list to All Files if you are looking for a file with an extension other than ICO, the default type that appears).
- Click the OK button in the Change Icon dialog box and in the Properties dialog box.

You decide to change the icon representing the Pins graphic to a more descriptive icon. Your Student Disk contains a bitmap graphics file called Icon that you will use as the icon.

To change the appearance of the icon:

1. In the Change Icon dialog box, which should still be open, click the **From File** option button, and then click the **Browse** button.
2. Click the **Look in** list arrow, and then click the drive containing your Student Disk.
3. Click the **Files of type** list arrow, and then click **All Files**.
4. Click **Icon** (the name of the file you'll use to represent the icon), and then click the **Open** button.

5. Click the **OK** button in the Change Icon dialog box, and then click the **OK** button in the Bitmap Image Properties dialog box. The new icon appears. Click outside the selection box. See Figure 8-16.

TROUBLE? Windows 98 can be a little unpredictable when you change an icon in a document. If the new icon doesn't appear, wait a few seconds, then scroll up the document until the original icon is no longer visible on the screen. Then scroll back down. This forces Windows 98 to display the correct icon.

Figure 8-16	NEW ICON FOR EMBEDDED OBJECT

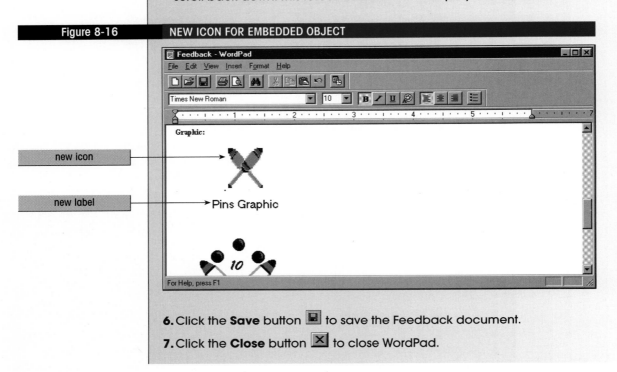

new icon

new label

6. Click the **Save** button 🔲 to save the Feedback document.

7. Click the **Close** button ✖ to close WordPad.

You could reduce the size of the icon image to take up even less space; in this example, it's not much smaller than the original graphic. However, displaying objects as icons is a good skill to remember if your computer is low on memory and you are working with a document with multiple embedded objects.

Paste Special

When you want to embed only a portion of a file, such as a single chart without the worksheet from Microsoft Excel, you can't use Insert Object, because Insert Object inserts an entire file. Although you can use Paste in some circumstances, you have more control over the embedding process when you use **Paste Special**, a command on the Edit menu of programs that support OLE. Figure 8-17 shows the Paste Special dialog box as it appears when you embed an Excel chart into a Word document. This dialog box appears when you select a chart in Excel, copy it, switch to Word, and then choose Paste Special on the Edit menu.

Paste Special sometimes gives you more than one embedding option. In this example, you can embed the object either as a chart or as a bitmap image. If you choose the latter, the Excel tools are no longer available to you, and the chart is inserted as a graphic image.

Figure 8-17	PASTE SPECIAL DIALOG BOX

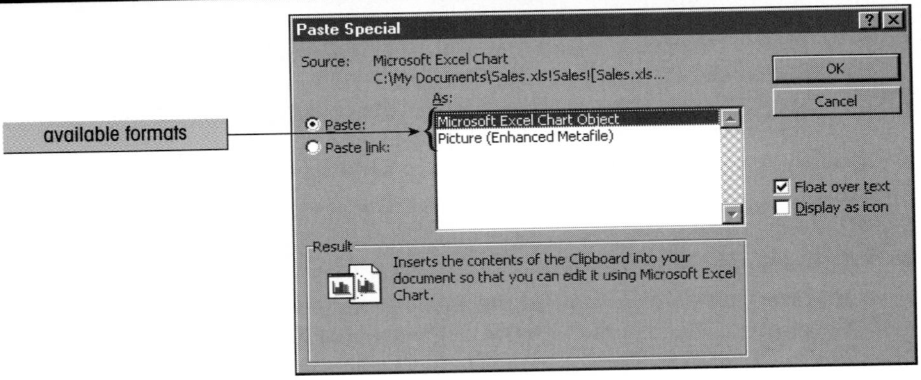

available formats

Paste Special   ? ×

Source: Microsoft Excel Chart
C:\My Documents\Sales.xls!Sales![Sales.xls...

As:

○ Paste: Microsoft Excel Chart Object
○ Paste link: Picture (Enhanced Metafile)

OK

Cancel

☑ Float over text
☐ Display as icon

Result
Inserts the contents of the Clipboard into your document so that you can edit it using Microsoft Excel Chart.

REFERENCE WINDOW   RW

Methods of Embedding

- **Paste or Paste Special** Using Paste Special allows you to embed the objects in specialized formats. Open the source file, select the object you want to embed, click Edit, and then click Copy. Then open the destination file, click Edit, and then click Paste or Paste Special. If you choose Paste Special, select the file format option you want to use, and then click the OK button.
- **Insert Object** This method is faster than Paste when you are embedding an entire file, because you don't need to open the source file first. If you need to embed an entire file, such as a graphic image or video clip, click Insert, click Object, and then click Create from File. Locate the file you want to embed, and then click the OK button.

Be aware that there are programs that feature neither OLE nor Clipboard. You then must depend on the data transfer commands within those programs, commands that often appear on the File menu as Import or Export. When you attempt to transfer data from other programs and it doesn't seem to be working as you expect, the first thing you should suspect is that your program doesn't feature OLE.

QUICK CHECK

1. What is OLE?

2. You just embedded text from a WordPad document into a PowerPoint presentation. Identify the source program and the destination program.

3. Name two ways to embed an object with OLE. Under what circumstances might you use these different methods?

4. What is in-place editing?

5. True or False: You can use the Clipboard to transfer data between any two programs.

SESSION 8.3

In this session, you will link a new version of the Pins graphic into your Feedback document. Then you'll work with the original file to see how linking lets you update the linked information in the source document. You'll learn how to delete OLE objects from your document. Then you'll link a video clip into the Feedback document and work with the Windows 98 Media Player.

Linking

The graphic designer you have been working with has supplied you with another new version of the Pins graphic, called Pins2, that makes better use of color. You want the committee members to see this new version. But what if the graphic designer calls again with an even newer version? You don't want to have to re-embed the graphic every time you receive a new version. Therefore, you decide to link the Pins2 graphic into your Feedback document rather than embed it.

Linking is another way to insert information into a document, but with linking you insert a *representation* of the object. When you edit a linked object, you are editing the *original* object, the source file itself, whether you are in the source or destination file. For example, if you change the color of the balls in a linked object, you are changing the color of the ball in the source file itself. Notice how this differs from embedding. With embedding you place a *copy* of the object into the destination file; it does not connect to the source file, so any changes you make to the embedded object are not reflected in the source file. With linking, however, you maintain a connection between the source file and the destination file, and a change to one object changes the other object. See Figure 8-18.

Figure 8-18	LINKING VS. EMBEDDING

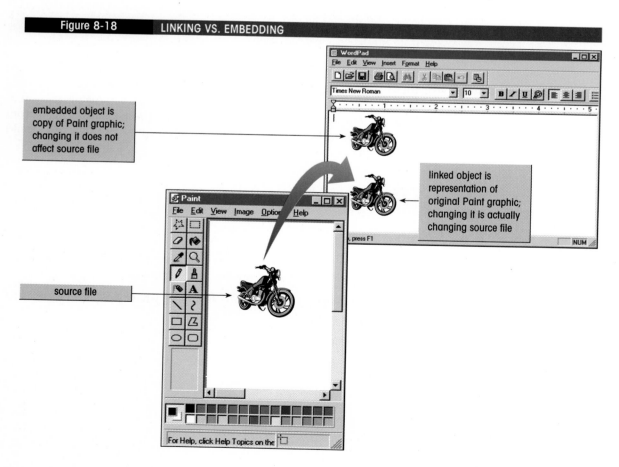

embedded object is copy of Paint graphic; changing it does not affect source file

linked object is representation of original Paint graphic; changing it is actually changing source file

source file

You link an object when you want only one copy of the object to exist. For example, you might want to use an object in several documents. When you update the object, all the documents use the updated version. When you give someone a document that contains links, make sure to include the source files. Note also that links target specific locations on a disk, so if you move the linked object source, the destination document will no longer be able to display it (although you can update a link by right-clicking it, clicking Object Properties, clicking Link, and then clicking Change Source).

Linking a Graphic File to a WordPad Document

You want only one version of the Pins graphic to be in use, so you decide to link Pins2 to the Feedback document. As with embedding, you can use Insert Object, Paste, or Paste Special to link objects. Insert Object allows you to insert an entire file, while Paste Special allows you to insert a portion of a file.

REFERENCE WINDOW   **RW**

Linking an Object
- To use Insert Object, click the location in the destination file where you want to insert the object. Then click Insert, click Object, and then click Create from File. Next click Browse, locate and select the file, click the Link check box, and then click the OK button twice.
- To use Paste Special, first open the source file and highlight the information you want to insert. Click Edit, and then click Copy. Next open the destination file and click the location where you want to insert the object. Click Edit, click Paste Special, click Paste Link, and then click the OK button. Note that Paste Special does not always allow you to paste with a link.

You'll use Insert Object to link the Pins2 graphic because you want to link the entire file, not just a portion of it.

To insert the Pins2 graphic as a linked object:

1. Start WordPad, and then open **Feedback** from your Student Disk.
2. Scroll down the **Feedback** document below the two embedded objects. Click to the left of the **Video Clip**: heading, press the **Enter** key twice to insert two new lines, and then press **Up Arrow** twice.
3. Click **Insert**, and then click **Object**.
4. Click the **Create from File** option button, click the **Browse** button, click the **Look in** list arrow, click the drive containing your Student Disk, and then click **Pins2**.
5. Click the **Insert** button.
6. Check the **Link** check box to place a check mark in it, and then click the **OK** button. The multicolored Pins2 graphic appears in the Feedback document.

Arranging Windows Using Tile and Cascade

You like the look of the color graphic, but you think it would look better if all the balls were one color. You decide to edit the source file, Pins2, in Paint, but you want to see the effect on your WordPad document at the same time. You could resize and drag the windows into place, or you could use the Tile or Cascade commands on the taskbar menu. The **Tile** command arranges all open windows so that they are all visible. You can tile vertically (side by side) or horizontally (one above the other). The **Cascade** command arranges all open windows so that they overlap each other and all their title bars are visible. Figure 8-19 shows these two arrangements.

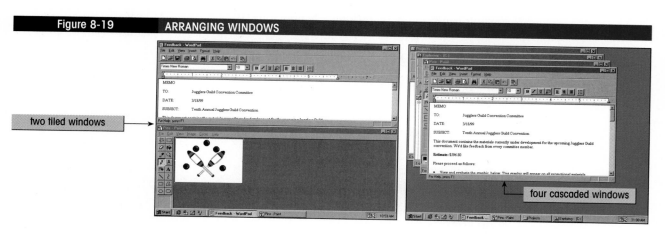

| Figure 8-19 | ARRANGING WINDOWS |

two tiled windows

four cascaded windows

Tiling is useful when you have just a few open windows, whereas cascading is useful when you have many open windows. Arranging windows can be helpful when you work with data transfer, because you are often working with more than one open program, and you want to see what's happening in the open programs at the same time. You decide to vertically tile the WordPad and Paint windows.

To open and tile the Paint and WordPad windows:

1. Click the **Start** button, point to **Programs**, point to **Accessories**, and then click **Paint**.

2. Open the **Pins2** file from your Student Disk in Paint. This is the file you just linked to the Feedback document.

3. Right-click a blank area of the taskbar to open the taskbar menu. See Figure 8-20.

   TROUBLE? If program buttons fill your taskbar, right-click the space between two program buttons until your menu looks like that in Figure 8-20.

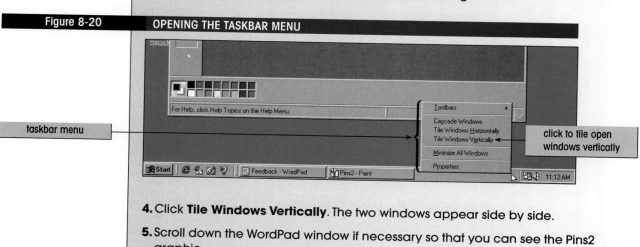

| Figure 8-20 | OPENING THE TASKBAR MENU |

taskbar menu

click to tile open windows vertically

4. Click **Tile Windows Vertically**. The two windows appear side by side.

5. Scroll down the WordPad window if necessary so that you can see the Pins2 graphic.

Editing a Linked Object in the Source Program

The object you just inserted is linked, so you can change it in either the source or destination file, and your changes will be stored in the original file. You decide to color the balls red in the original Pins2 file.

> ### To edit the Pins2 graphic in Paint:
>
> 1. Click the **Fill With Color** tool 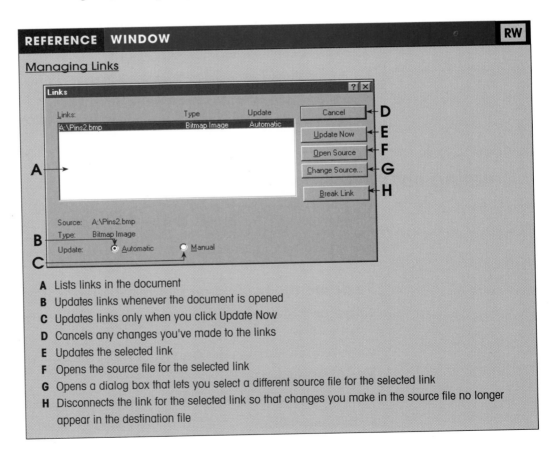 in Paint.
>
> 2. Click the **red** box (in second row, third box from left in Color box), and then click each of the four balls that aren't already red. All five balls should be red when you finish.
>
> 3. Click **File**, and then click **Save** in Paint.

Updating a Linked Object

If the destination file is closed when you change the source file, any linked objects will usually update automatically the next time you open the file, or you'll be given the option to update the links when you next open the file. If the destination file is open when you change the source file, you have to update it manually, using the Links command. This opens the Links dialog box, which gives you control over the links in your document.

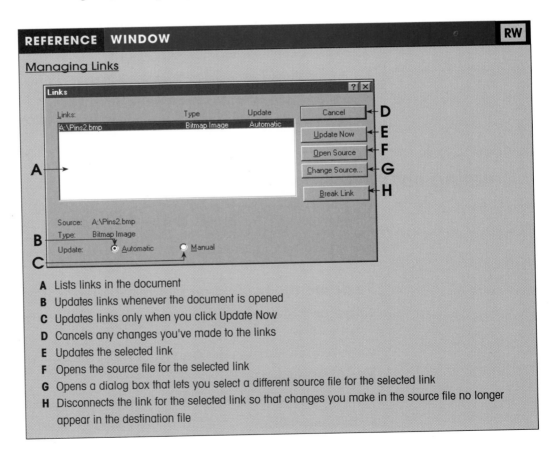

REFERENCE   WINDOW   **RW**

Managing Links

Links

Links:	Type	Update
A:\Pins2.bmp	Bitmap Image	Automatic

Cancel — D
Update Now — E
Open Source — F
Change Source... — G
Break Link — H

Source: A:\Pins2.bmp
Type: Bitmap Image
Update: ● Automatic   ○ Manual

A
B
C

A Lists links in the document
B Updates links whenever the document is opened
C Updates links only when you click Update Now
D Cancels any changes you've made to the links
E Updates the selected link
F Opens the source file for the selected link
G Opens a dialog box that lets you select a different source file for the selected link
H Disconnects the link for the selected link so that changes you make in the source file no longer appear in the destination file

You decide to update the link between the Pins2 source file and the Feedback destination file so you can verify that the changes take place.

To update the link in the WordPad document:

1. Click the **Pins2** graphic in the WordPad window.

2. Click **Edit**, and then click **Links**. A dialog box displays all links in the current document. Click the link that represents the connection between the linked object in the destination file and the source file. See Figure 8-21.

Figure 8-21   **LINKS DIALOG BOX**

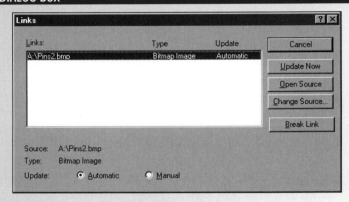

3. Click the **Update Now** button. The graphic is updated. (Move the Links dialog box if you can't see the change.)

4. Click the **Close** button ☒ to close the Links dialog box.

5. Click the **Close** button to close Paint.

6. Maximize the WordPad window.

Deleting an OLE Object

As you look over your document, you notice that you have now inserted three graphic objects into the Feedback document. The first two are both older versions of the graphic. You decide you don't need to include them in the Feedback document, so you delete them.

To delete the two old embedded graphics, Pins and Pins10:

1. Scroll up the **Feedback** document until you see the icon representing the first Pins graphic.

2. Click the icon labeled **Pins Graphic**. A selection box appears.

3. Press the **Delete** key.

4. Click the **Pins10** graphic (the monochrome one). A selection box appears.

5. Press the **Delete** key.

6. Delete the two blank lines below the boldface **Graphic:** heading.

Regardless of how your object uses OLE technology, you delete it the same way. You've completed the graphics portion of your Feedback document.

Linking and Playing a Video Clip

Now you turn your attention to the next object you want to show to the committee members: the video clip. You decide to link the video clip to your Feedback document so that if the computer animation vendor sends you an updated file, you won't have to reinsert the file. You can link a video clip in the same way you linked a graphic, using Insert Object, since you are linking an entire file and not just a portion of a file.

To link a video clip to a document:

1. Scroll the **Feedback** document until you locate the boldface **Video Clip**: heading.
2. Click the line above the boldface **Maria's comments:** heading.
3. Click **Insert**, and then click **Object**.
4. Click the **Create from File** option button.
5. Click the **Browse** button.
6. If necessary, click the **Look in** list arrow, and then click the drive containing your Student Disk.
7. Click **Video**, and then click the **Insert** button.
8. Click the **Link** check box to place a check mark in it, and then click the **OK** button.

The video clip looks like a graphic object, but of course it isn't. You can play the video clip by double-clicking it or by right-clicking it and using the Play Linked Video Clip Object command. Because it is a linked object using OLE technology, you don't have to leave WordPad or start a separate program to play it.

To play the video clip:

1. Right-click the video clip, and then point to **Linked Video Clip Object**.

   TROUBLE? If this appears as "Linked Media Clip Object," click that instead.

   TROUBLE? If a message appears warning you that Windows 98 couldn't launch the server application, ask your instructor or lab manager to install the multimedia accessories.

2. Click **Play**. The video clip plays in a small window. See Figure 8-22. It might play once very quickly and then stop, perhaps even before it appears to reach the end, or it might play continuously. You'll learn momentarily how to control the way the video clip plays.

   TROUBLE? If your clip plays very choppily, your computer might not have sufficient memory to play it smoothly.

3. If necessary, click the video clip window's **Close** button .

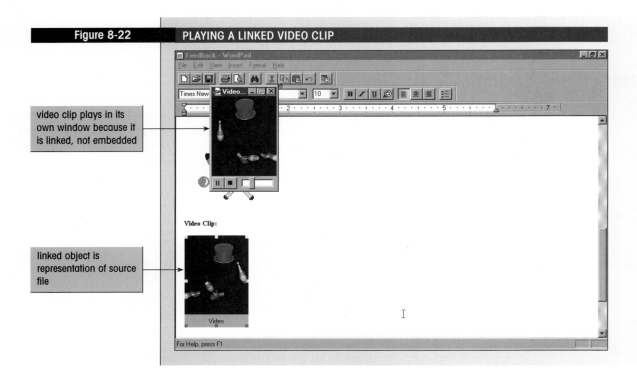

Figure 8-22   PLAYING A LINKED VIDEO CLIP

video clip plays in its own window because it is linked, not embedded

linked object is representation of source file

You've now inserted the video clip into the Feedback document. However, you'd like to refine the way it plays.

Windows 98 Multimedia

The window that opened when you played the video clip was part of the Windows 98 **Media Player**, one of the accessories Windows 98 provides that handle multimedia files. The Windows 98 multimedia accessories, listed in Figure 8-23 and available on the Entertainment submenu of the Accessories menu, let you create, edit, and play multimedia clips. Some of the accessories, such as NetShow, are not included in a normal installation, and others, such as DVD Player, won't appear if you don't have the appropriate hardware. You can install them from the CD-ROM Multimedia section.

Figure 8-23   MULTIMEDIA ACCESSORIES

ACCESSORY	DESCRIPTION
ActiveMovie Control	An Internet Explorer component that enhances the playing of audio and video files on a Web page
CD Player	Plays music CDs
DVD Player	Plays DVD discs or regular CDs from a DVD drive
Media Player	Plays audio and video clips
NetShow	Plays audio and video across the Internet, playing immediately without having to wait for the entire file to download
Sound Recorder	Records and plays audio files
Multimedia Sound Schemes	Provides different sounds that you can attach to Windows 98 events (such as exiting a program)
Volume Control	Adjusts your speaker volume

Multimedia clips can use sound, video, or both. To play a clip that uses sound, you need a sound card and speakers. If your computer doesn't have these hardware devices, you can still hear sounds through your computer's internal speaker—such as the "beeps" you hear when the computer alerts you to something. The internal speaker, however, is inadequate for playing most sound files.

The **Sound Recorder** accessory uses the **WAV** (which is short for waveform-audio) file format to store and record sounds as realistically as possible. The Media Player accessory, on the other hand, uses the **MIDI** (short for Musical Instrument Digital Interface) format. MIDI files use artificial, synthesized sounds to mimic a real sound and hence are usually much smaller than WAV files. Although you can't use MIDI files to store voices, you can use them very effectively to store the synthesized sounds of special MIDI instruments.

To play a video clip, you don't need a sound card or speakers, but the quality of the video will depend on your computer's video card capabilities and on its speed and memory capacity. You use the Media Player accessory to play ActiveMovie files or video clips in the **AVI** (short for Audio-Video Interleaved) format. This format is sometimes called "Video for Windows." AVI files can contain both images and sound (of course, if you want to hear the sound you'll need a sound card and speakers). Media Player lets you scroll back and forth through a video clip, but you cannot use Media Player to edit the clip itself.

ActiveMovie plays many existing file types, including MPEG audio and video, AVI video, WAV audio, MIDI audio, and QuickTime video.

Using **Media Player**

When you played the Juggler video clip, it might have played only once and then stopped, or it might have played continually. You want to control the way it plays. To do this, you need to start Media Player and edit the video's settings. Media Player plays a video one frame at a time, just as a filmstrip is shown. A slider appears that shows you which frame is appearing at any given moment, so you can move forward or backward through individual frames. Media Player also includes a set of buttons that resemble the buttons on a cassette tape player or a VCR, as described in Figure 8-24.

Figure 8-24		MEDIA PLAYER BUTTONS
BUTTON	**NAME**	**DESCRIPTION**
▶	Play	Plays the multimedia clip. Turns into the Pause button when multimedia clip is playing
❚❚	Pause	Play button turns into Pause button when multimedia clip is playing; pauses clip
■	Stop	Stops the clip at its current frame or track
⏏	Eject	Appears only when you are playing a clip off a CD-ROM; ejects the CD
⏮	Previous Mark	Moves to the previous mark (like a track on a CD)
⏪	Rewind	Moves backward in increments as you click
⏩	Fast Forward	Moves forward in increments as you click
⏭	Next Mark	Moves to the next mark (like a track on a CD)
⏫	Start Selection	Starts the selection (if you select just a few frames to play)
⏬	End Selection	Ends the selection (if you select just a few frames to play)

You decide you want to make sure the video plays continually. You can either start Media Player from the Start menu and then open the video clip source file, or you can start Media Player from within the Feedback document by opening the video clip for editing.

To make changes to the video clip's settings:

1. Right-click the video clip, point to **Linked Video Clip Object**, and then click **Edit**. Media Player opens. See Figure 8-25.

Figure 8-25	MEDIA PLAYER

slider

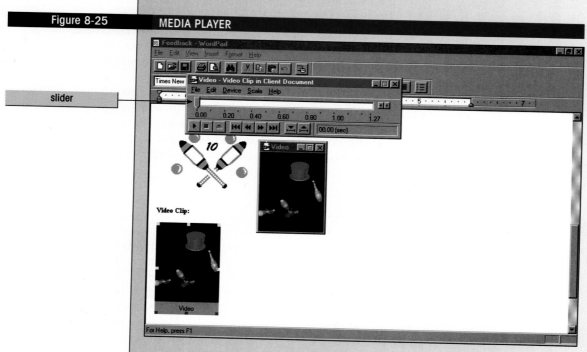

2. Click **Edit**, and then click **Options**. First see how the video plays when it is not set on Auto Repeat.

3. If necessary, click the **Auto Repeat** check box to deselect it, and then click the **OK** button.

    TROUBLE? If Auto Repeat is already deselected, skip Step 3. See Figure 8-26.

Figure 8-26	MEDIA PLAYER OPTIONS

clip plays repeatedly when check box is selected

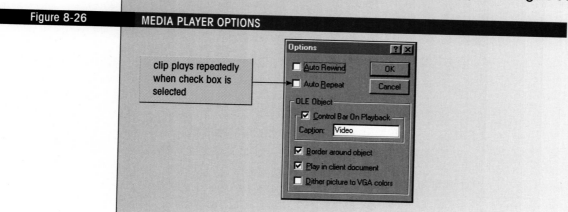

4. Click the **Play** ▶ button. The video clip plays once and then stops.

5. Click **Edit**, click **Options**, click the **Auto Repeat** check box to select it, and then click the **OK** button.

6. Click the **Play** button ▶. The video clip plays over and over. Notice the slider as it moves through the frames of the video clip.

7. Click the **Close** button ✕ to close Media Player. Click **Yes** to save changes to the video clip.

   TROUBLE? If you close the video clip window instead of the Media Player window, close Media Player.

The Feedback document now contains no embedded objects and two linked objects: the graphic and the video clip. You can send the document, along with the two source files, to the committee members for their feedback. They can easily view both objects and can then add their comments to the bottom of the document.

To save your work and close all open windows:

1. Click the **Save** button 🖫 to save your Feedback document.

2. Click the **Close** button ✕, to close WordPad.

Your final version of the Feedback document used only linking, not embedding, because you decided that both objects were likely to undergo further revision, and you wanted to be able to easily update the document without having to reinsert the objects. As you created the Feedback document, however, you used several different methods to exchange information between documents. As with other aspects of Windows 98, the focus is on the document, not on the program that created it. You create a document by bringing in tools from other programs without even being aware that you are doing so. Many people see this focus on the document as the future of personal computing.

QUICK CHECK

1. What is the difference between linking and embedding?

2. If you want to share a document that contains embedded objects with another person, do you need to include the source files? Explain why or why not.

3. When you use the Insert Object method to insert an object into a document, do you first need to open the source file?

4. What's the difference between the appearance of tiling and cascading windows?

5. True or False: Media Player plays only video, not audio, clips.

6. Describe these three file types: WAV, MIDI, and AVI.

TUTORIAL ASSIGNMENTS

1. **Copying and Pasting Text** A friend of yours owns a small tailor shop and wants to advertise his services in the Yellow Pages. He wants feedback from his employees and friends on his advertisement and wonders if you'd share Maria's feedback process with him. You write him a note and then paste in the steps to your process.

   a. Start WordPad, and then open Maria from your Student Disk.
   b. Highlight the bulleted list, and then copy it to the Clipboard.
   c. Open Tailor from your Student Disk, and scroll to the boldface Follow this Procedure: heading. Add a few blank lines below the heading, and then paste the copied information. Replace the name "Jan" with your name.
   d. Print and save Tailor, and then close WordPad.

2. **Pasting Text into Paint** In this tutorial, you pasted a Paint graphic into WordPad. Now you'll try pasting in the other direction. You are designing a banner that announces the names of incumbent officers up for reelection for the Jugglers Guild. You have created a Paint graphic called Election. You want to insert the names of the five officers into that graphic.

   a. Start Paint and open the Election graphic from your Student Disk.
   b. Start WordPad, open Maria, and copy the last five names (not including Maria Arruda) in the Distribution List to the Clipboard. These are the five officers up for reelection.
   c. Close WordPad. Paste the names into the Election graphic. Click Yes if Paint asks if you want to enlarge the bitmap.
   d. Drag the pasted names so they are centered below the heading.
   e. Print and save the Election graphic, and then close Paint. Now experiment with the pasted information. Are you able to use the source program tools from within Paint?
   f. On your printout, write a paragraph answering the following questions: Is the text you just pasted inserted as an embedded object into the Paint graphic? How can you tell? How does the process you just completed differ from the way you pasted a Paint graphic into a WordPad document in Session 8.2?

3. **Linking and Editing a Graphic** You are a clown named Chester, and you are attending the juggling convention. You want to distribute a flyer at the convention that advertises your clowning services. You have created the flyer in the WordPad document named Clowning, and you want to link a graphic file into that document.

   a. Open the WordPad document named Clowning.
   b. Use Insert Object to insert the graphic named Chester into the bottom of the Clowning document. Make sure you insert the object with a link.
   c. After you've inserted the Chester graphic, open it for editing by right-clicking the object, pointing to Linked Bitmap Image Object, and then clicking Edit. Change Chester's hair color to brown. Close Paint, saving the changes to Chester, and then return to the WordPad document.
   d. Update the link, if necessary, and then print and save the Clowning document. On the printout, write a paragraph about how editing a linked object from the destination document differs from editing an embedded object.

Explore

4. **Using Sound Recorder** If you have a microphone, a sound card, and speakers, you can create your own sound file, using the Sound Recorder accessory that comes with Windows 98. You want to send a colleague an electronic "Happy Birthday" message, so you decide to sing the Happy Birthday song into the microphone, save it as a sound file, and then embed it into a message.

   a. Click the Start button, point to Programs, point to Accessories, point to Entertainment, and then click Sound Recorder.
   b. Click the Record button on the far right of Sound Recorder.

c. Sing Happy Birthday into the microphone. (Sing just the first few words to keep the size of the audio clip small.) Click the Stop button when you are finished singing.

d. Save the document as Happy Birthday on a new, blank, formatted disk—not your Student Disk. Label this disk "OLE Disk." (You need a second disk because if you complete all the Tutorial Assignments and Projects, you won't have room on your Student Disk.)

e. Play the Happy Birthday sound file.

f. Compose a Happy Birthday message in WordPad, and embed the Happy Birthday sound file into this message.

g. Print the message and save it as Birthday Message. Hand in the printout to your instructor. If you have access to e-mail and you know how to send a file, you could send the WordPad file to a friend who's celebrating a birthday.

PROJECTS

1. You work for the Internal Revenue Service and have been using Notepad to draft a brochure to inform taxpayers about online tax filing. Notepad, however, does not offer any text-formatting options, and you'd like to format your document. You decide to move the text into a WordPad document.

a. Start Notepad, and then open IRS from your Student Disk.

b. Start WordPad, and then open New from your Student Disk.

c. In Notepad, select and then copy the entire document. Close Notepad.

d. In the WordPad window, click below the Online Tax Filing heading, and then paste the text. Type your name at the top of the document.

e. Print and save the WordPad document.

2. You are a member of the Tokunta Construction company. You are developing a training manual for new employees. You need to link a graphic that illustrates a construction principle, but you want to display it as an icon.

a. Open the House document in WordPad from your Student Disk.

b. Use Insert Object to insert the House graphic at the end of the document. Make sure you link the graphic.

c. Change the graphic display so that it displays an icon.

d. Change the icon to the Tools icon on your Student Disk.

e. Change the caption of the icon to Cantilever.

f. Print and save the House document.

3. Your Student Disk includes a sound file of J. F. Kennedy's "Ask not what your country..." speech. You'd like to link this sound file to a WordPad document that you are creating for a linguistics class, in which you are studying American accents. Kennedy's sound clip exemplifies a Boston accent.

a. Create a new WordPad document and type "Linguistics, Bostonian accent" at the beginning. Save the document as Linguistics on your Student Disk, using WordPad or Word. Make sure you type your name.

Explore

b. Use the Insert Object method to insert the Kennedy sound file into your document. Make sure you insert it with a link.

c. You'll be able to complete this task only if you have a sound card and speakers. Use the linked object's menu to first play the object and then open it for editing. When you open it for editing, what accessory does Windows 98 use?

4. You work at CarpetMaster, a company that specializes in residential and commercial carpet cleaning and restoration. A customer wants an estimate for repair costs for an Oriental rug that was damaged in a recent fire. You need to draw a rectangle in Paint that proportionally approximates the carpet size and indicate the area that you'll be repairing. Then you need to embed that graphic into a WordPad document that gives the estimate.

   a. Create a Paint graphic that shows the carpet and the damaged area. Save this graphic as Carpet on your OLE Disk (the one you created in Tutorial Assignment 4)—not your Student Disk. Close Paint. Figure 8-27 shows an example of a graphic with the marked portion of damaged carpet.

Figure 8-27

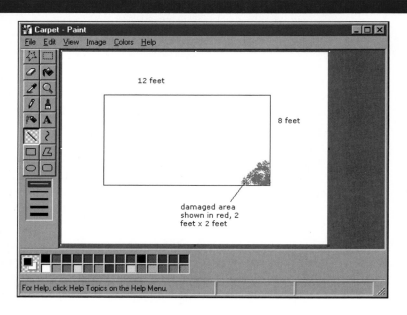

   b. Create a WordPad document that uses appropriate language for an estimate and includes a description of the necessary repairs. Save the document as CarpetMaster Estimate.

Explore

   c. Open Calculator and calculate 6.5 hours at $47/hr. Paste this amount into the WordPad document.
   d. Use Insert Object to embed the Paint graphic in the WordPad document.
   e. Print and save the WordPad document.

5. **Transferring Data Between Other Programs** If you have access to other software programs, such as a word processor, a spreadsheet program, or a database program, experiment with the data transfer operations available in those programs. Create new documents in these programs, add sample data, and then save the documents on your disk. Then try to copy and paste data between the programs. Next try embedding and linking. Write a short essay that answers the following questions:

   a. What programs did you test? In what situations were you able to copy and paste?
   b. In what situations did Paste embed the data? In what situations did Paste simply transfer the data without embedding?
   c. In what situations were you able to do in-place editing?
   d. Were there any situations in which you were unable to link?
   e. Based on your experiments, what conclusions can you draw about whether or not your programs feature OLE?

6. **Creating a New Embedded Object** You own Circle K Ranch, a working ranch that welcomes families, summer campers, and groups for weekly stays, so they can experience life on a ranch. You are working on a flyer that you will mail to former clients and travel agents.

   a. Create a WordPad document called Flyer on your OLE disk. Write a brief description of the ranch. Mention that you are working on the summer schedule and that people should make their reservations as soon as possible.

   b. Use Calculator to calculate this year's weekly rate. You need to earn $15,000 this summer from your visitor income, to make an acceptable profit. There are 12 weeks in the summer, and you have room for eight guests each week. To calculate a room charge per person per week, you click 15000 / 12 / 8 = on the Calculator keypad. Paste the Calculator results into your document.

   c. Use Insert Object to create a new bitmapped image in your advertisement. The Create New option button should be selected, with an object type of Bitmap Image. Create a small Paint graphic that shows a letter K in an interesting font with a circle around it.

   d. Print and save the flyer as Circle K on your OLE Disk (the one you created in Tutorial Assignment 4)—not your Student Disk.

LAB ASSIGNMENTS

Multimedia brings together text, graphics, sound, animation, video, and photo images. In this Lab you will learn how to apply multimedia and then have the chance to see what it might be like to design some aspects of multimedia projects. See the Read This Before You Begin page for information on installing and starting the Lab.

1. Click the Steps button to learn about multimedia development. As you work through the Steps, answer all of the Quick Check questions that appear. After you complete the Steps, you will see a Quick Check report. Follow the instructions on the screen to print this report.

2. How many videos are included in the Multimedia Mission Log? The image on the Mission Profile page is a vector drawing. What happens when you enlarge it?

3. Listen to the sound track on Day 4. Is this a WAV file or a MIDI file? Why do you think so? Is this a synthesized or a digitized sound? Listen to the sound track on the first page. Can you tell if this is a WAV file or a MIDI file?

4. Suppose you were hired as a multimedia designer for a multimedia series on targeting fourth- and fifth-grade students. Describe the changes you would make to the Multimedia Mission Log so it would be suitable for these students. Also, include a sketch showing a screen from your revised design.

5. The Multimedia Mission Log does not contain any hyperlinks. Suppose that you were hired to revise the design of this product and to add hyperlinks. Provide a list of five specific instances where you would use hyperlinks and indicate what sort of information each would link to.

6. Multimedia can be effectively applied to projects such as encyclopedias, atlases, and animated storybooks; to computer-based training for foreign languages, first aid, or software applications; for games and sports simulations; for business presentations; for personal albums, scrapbooks, and baby books; for product catalogs and Web pages.

7. Suppose you were hired to create one of these projects. Write a one-paragraph description of the project you would be creating. Describe some of the multimedia elements you would include. For each of these elements, indicate its source and whether you would need to obtain permission for its use. Finally, sketch a screen or two showing your completed project.

QUICK CHECK ANSWERS

Session 8.1

1. An area in your computer's memory that stores data you cut or copy

2. When you cut selected text, it is removed from the original document to the Clipboard. When you copy it, a replica of the data is moved to the Clipboard, but the original document remains intact.

3. Ctrl+X to cut, Ctrl+C to copy, Ctrl+V to paste

4. False

5. Open Clipboard Viewer, click Edit, then click Delete. Clearing Clipboard contents frees up memory.

6. It is more accurate than typing.

Session 8.2

1. Object linking and embedding—a technology that allows you to transfer data from one program to another and retain the ability to access tools from the original program

2. WordPad is the source program; PowerPoint is the destination program.

3. Paste, Paste Special, or Insert Object. Paste allows you to embed a selected portion of a file, Paste Special allows you to embed a selected portion with more control, and Insert Object allows you to embed an entire file without having to open it first.

4. Editing an embedded object using the source program tools without ever leaving the destination document

5. False; older programs might not support Clipboard technology.

Session 8.3

1. Linking places a representation of the source file, whereas embedding places a copy of the source file, into the destination document.

2. No. Embedded objects have been copied into the document.

3. No.

4. Tiling arranges open windows so they are all visible. Cascading overlaps open windows so their title bars are visible.

5. False

6. The WAV format records and stores sounds as realistically as possible. The MIDI format uses artificial sounds to mimic real sounds. The AVI format is the Windows video clip format.

In this tutorial you will:

- Print a document to the active printer and to a different printer

- Work with a printer's print queue to pause, remove, and reorder print jobs

- Examine serial, parallel, and USB ports for connecting devices to a computer

- Use the Add Printer Wizard

- Use the Print Troubleshooter

- Explore Plug and Play

- Open the Fonts window to examine fonts installed on your computer

- Get system information with the System Information utility

HARDWARE, PRINTERS, AND FONTS

Installing and Troubleshooting a Printer at Chan & Associates

CASE

Chan & Associates

You are continuing to help plan the Tenth Annual Jugglers Guild Convention. You and other committee members have been designing materials ranging from convention schedules and announcements to souvenir T-shirts. You'd like to print some of these documents so you can send them to other members of the Guild. One of the other committee members, Wai Chan, owns a small desktop publishing company, Chan & Associates. He tells you that he recently ordered a color printer that should be arriving on Friday. He suggests that if you're free this weekend, you could help him install the color printer—and then you could use it to print some of your documents in color.

When you arrive at Wai's office on Saturday, he's already there, finishing up some paperwork. You ask if you could use his monochrome printer to get started while he finishes up. You'd like to print the Pins graphic, which is black and white. He tells you to go ahead, and so you decide to spend a little time familiarizing yourself with Windows 98 printing techniques, so that when the new color printer is installed you'll know how to select and use it.

SESSION 9.1

In this session, you will print a document to an existing printer and work with the Windows 98 print queue to control print jobs. You will inspect a printer's property sheet and learn how Windows 98 handles the installation of hardware devices. *You might not be able to perform all the procedures in this tutorial if you are working in a computer lab. The steps in this tutorial include notes to alert you when this might be the case. When you can't perform a procedure, take special note of the information outside of the steps that will help you learn about the procedure.*

Printing a Document

You have probably printed documents many times in Windows 98 without giving much thought to what goes on behind the scenes, even if you noticed signs that Windows 98 was processing your print request. You might have noticed a dialog box that tells you your document is printing, or you might have seen icons that look like printers appear and then disappear in the taskbar. You might even have heard your hard drive spinning for a second or two when you printed a large document. Let's "look under the hood" and see what Windows 98 is doing with all that activity.

To print a document in Windows 98, you can drag a document icon onto a printer icon in Windows Explorer or on the desktop, or you can use a program's Print button 🖨. When you need more control over the printing process, however, you use the Print command on a program's File menu to open the Print dialog box, where you have more options. Regardless of which method you use to make the print request, Windows 98 processes your request the same way, as shown in Figure 9-1.

Figure 9-1	PRINTING A DOCUMENT

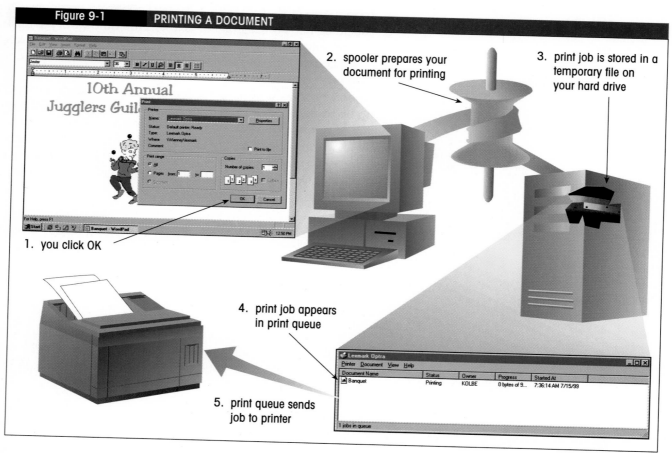

2. spooler prepares your document for printing

3. print job is stored in a temporary file on your hard drive

1. you click OK

4. print job appears in print queue

5. print queue sends job to printer

First, Windows 98 uses print spooling to quickly prepare your document for printing. **Print spooling** inserts the electronic codes that control your particular printer, such as the code to move down to the next line or to eject a page. As Windows 98 is spooling, it might display a dialog box such as the one shown in Figure 9-2.

Figure 9-2	DIALOG BOX THAT APPEARS DURING PRINT SPOOLING

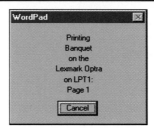

While the document is being spooled, you can click Cancel to cancel printing. Once print spooling is complete, the document, complete with the electronic codes inserted by the spooling process, is stored as a temporary file on your computer's hard disk. These temporary files are sometimes referred to as "print jobs." Once a print job is created, you can continue working on other documents—your document will print while you do other computing tasks. By sending print jobs to your computer's hard disk rather than storing them in memory, spooling frees your computer's resources.

Print jobs are managed by a print queue. A **print queue** is a file that keeps track of the order in which print jobs were submitted and usually prints the jobs in this order. When the printer has finished with one job, the print queue sends the next job. You can control the print queue for a particular printer by opening its print queue window. Figure 9-3 shows the print queue for a printer that is used by several computers on a network. This is the situation you are likely to encounter in a computer lab—many computers using the same printer. You'll learn more about network printers in the network tutorial.

Figure 9-3	PRINT QUEUE WINDOW

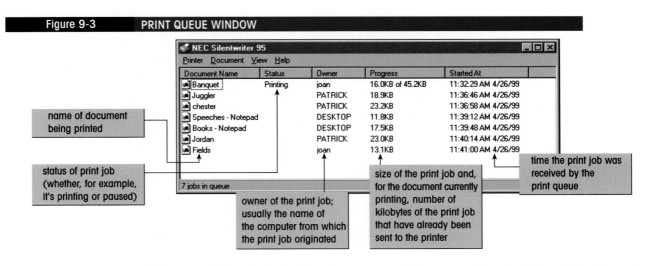

The print job listed first in the print queue typically goes to the printer first. Once the entire job is transferred into the printer's temporary memory, it disappears from the print queue.

The print queue also gives you some control over print jobs waiting to be printed. For example, you can pause or cancel print jobs or change their order. You can do this for all jobs, using the Printer menu, or for just one print job, using the Document menu. If you are on a network, you are likely to have limited control over print jobs. See the "Using the Print Queue" reference window for information on what options usually are available in the print queue window. Although you can open the print queue even when there aren't any print jobs in it, most of the time you'll need to open it only when you are printing something.

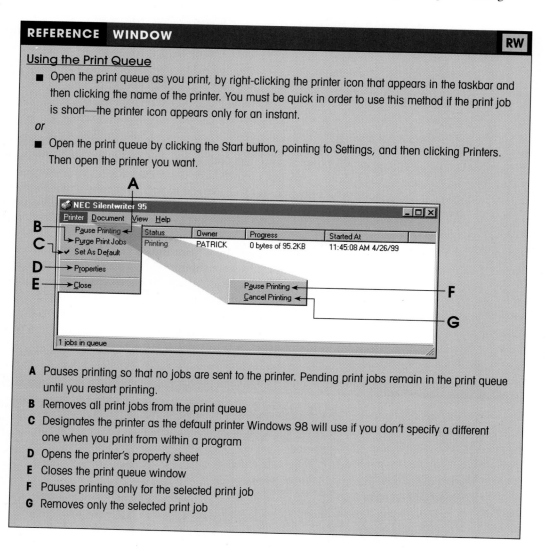

REFERENCE WINDOW | RW

Using the Print Queue

- Open the print queue as you print, by right-clicking the printer icon that appears in the taskbar and then clicking the name of the printer. You must be quick in order to use this method if the print job is short—the printer icon appears only for an instant.

or

- Open the print queue by clicking the Start button, pointing to Settings, and then clicking Printers. Then open the printer you want.

A Pauses printing so that no jobs are sent to the printer. Pending print jobs remain in the print queue until you restart printing.

B Removes all print jobs from the print queue

C Designates the printer as the default printer Windows 98 will use if you don't specify a different one when you print from within a program

D Opens the printer's property sheet

E Closes the print queue window

F Pauses printing only for the selected print job

G Removes only the selected print job

You decide to print your Pins graphic by opening it in Paint and printing it on Wai's printer, a monochrome Lexmark Optra. If you are working in a computer lab where many computers use the same printer and where there are other students using this book, you might have a hard time telling which Pins print job is yours. For this reason, you should rename your Pins graphic before you print. You'll begin by making a new Student Disk in case the one you used in Tutorial 8 no longer contains the necessary files. You can use your original Student Disk if you don't need it any more, or you can use a new, blank disk.

To open and rename the Pins graphic:

1. Format your disk so that it contains no files.

2. Click the **Start** button, point to **Programs**, point to **NP on Microsoft Windows 98 – Level III**, and then click **Disk 6 (Tutorials 8 & 9)**. Place your Student Disk in the appropriate drive.

3. When a message box opens, click the **OK** button. Wait while the program copies the practice files to your formatted disk. When all the files have been copied, the program closes. If necessary, close any open windows.

4. Start Paint, and then open the **Pins** graphic on your Student Disk.

5. If you are in a lab and need to be able to identify your printout, use the Paint Text tool to add your name to a corner of the graphic.

6. Click **File**, and then click **Save As**.

7. Click the **File name** box, and then type your name after the word Pins so the name of the file becomes, for example, Pins Laura Smith.

8. Click the **Save** button.

Now you'll be able to identify your job in the print queue window. You are ready to open the print queue for your computer's default printer (the one currently handling your print jobs) so you can have more control over your print jobs.

To open the print queue for your computer's default printer:

1. Click **File**, and then click **Print**. The Print dialog box opens. In Figure 9-4, Wai's Lexmark Optra is the default printer. On your screen you will see the name of the printer Windows 98 will use to print your graphic.

Figure 9-4   **PRINT DIALOG BOX**

name of default printer on Wai's computer

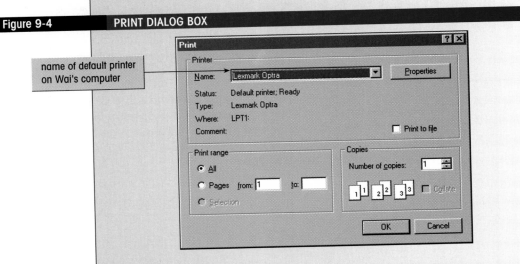

2. Now open the print queue for your computer's default printer. Click the **Start** button, point to **Settings**, and then click **Printers**. Figure 9-5 shows the Printers window on Wai's computer.

TROUBLE? If your window looks different, change the view settings as needed.

Figure 9-5   **PRINTERS WINDOW**

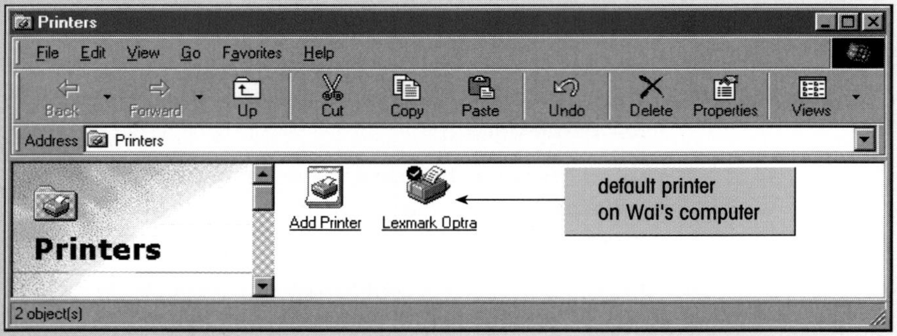

3. Locate your computer's default printer in the Printers window, identified by ⬤. This is the printer you saw in the Print dialog box in Step 1.

4. Click the name of the default printer to open its print queue. Your print queue might be empty, or, if the printer is a network printer, it might show other documents being printed.

   TROUBLE? If you are not using Web style, click the printer, and then press Enter.

5. Switch to the Printers window, and then close the Printers window.

6. Right-click an open area on the **taskbar**, and then click **Tile Windows Horizontally** so you can see the Print dialog box and the print queue window at the same time.

Now you are ready to print your document.

To see what happens on the spooler and queue:

1. Click the **Print** dialog box to activate it.

2. Compare the printer name that appears in the Name box with the one in the title bar of the print queue window. They should match exactly. See Figure 9-6.

   TROUBLE? If the printer in the Name box is not the same as the printer in the title bar of the print queue window, you might have opened the wrong print queue. Reopen the Printers window, and this time make sure you open the correct print queue window, identified by its title. Don't worry if the windows are placed slightly differently on your screen.

Figure 9-6 DEFAULT PRINTER

print queue window

name in print queue title bar matches default printer in Name box; yours might be different

print dialog box

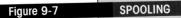

3. Click the **OK** button in the Print dialog box. As Windows 98 spools your print job, the dialog box shown in Figure 9-7 appears.

TROUBLE? If you don't notice this dialog box as you print, don't worry. Your computer might process print jobs so quickly that you don't notice it. It's also possible that when you tiled the windows, part of Paint was moved off the screen, and the dialog box might actually appear off-screen.

TROUBLE? If a "User intervention required" message appears, there is a problem with the network printer, which can be fixed only on the computer that manages that printer. Ask your technical support person for assistance.

Figure 9-7 SPOOLING

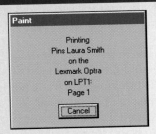

4. Locate the place on your screen—pointed out in Figure 9-8—where the printer icon appears once the document is spooled, and notice when the icon appears. The print job appears in the print queue window at the same time.

Figure 9-8	PRINT JOB APPEARS ON TASKBAR AND PRINT QUEUE

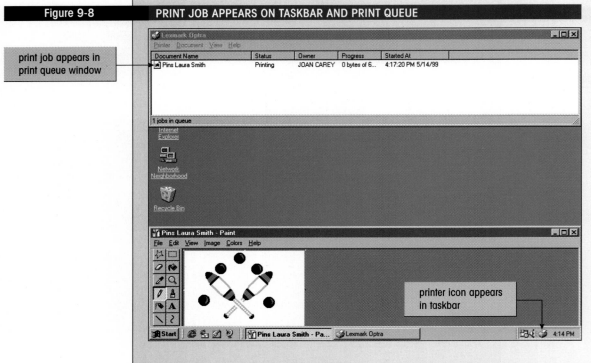

print job appears in print queue window

printer icon appears in taskbar

TROUBLE? If you didn't notice the icon in the taskbar, don't worry. When you are printing a very small document such as the Pins graphic, the icon appears only momentarily and then disappears when Windows 98 has sent the document to your printer.

5. Watch as your print job disappears from the print queue window—this means it has been sent successfully to the printer.

Pausing One or All Print Jobs

On occasion you might want to delay your computer from sending jobs to the printer. For example, if you want to use a specific letterhead for a print job, you have to change the paper in the printer before you print a job. Windows 98 lets you pause one or all documents in the print queue.

If you want to pause the entire queue, you select the Pause Printing command from the Printer menu. This tells Windows 98 to stop sending jobs to the printer. Once you restart printing, the print queue starts sending all print jobs in the order shown in the queue. If you want to pause a specific print job, you select the Pause Printing command from the Document menu. Pausing a single print job halts your job while allowing other print jobs in the queue to print. However, if you are printing to a network printer, you probably cannot pause printing at all because, by pausing, you might pause not only your print jobs, but everyone else's.

Wai tells you he's almost ready to start installing the color printer. When you tell him you're experimenting with the print queue, he suggests you pause printing so you can learn how to manage print jobs in the print queue—a skill that comes in handy when you need more control over your print queue.

To pause printing:

1. Click **Printer** on the print queue window menu bar.

2. Click **Pause Printing**. The word "Paused" appears in the title bar.

   TROUBLE? If you are on a network you might not be able to pause printing, and will get a message similar to "you do not have permission to modify the settings for this printer." Skip Step 2, close the Printer menu, and then skip the next set of steps on paused printing.

Now that printing is paused, you can print your document and watch it move into the print queue and then pause.

To print the document with paused printing:

1. Click **File** on the Paint menu bar, and then click **Print**.

2. Click the **OK** button. Watch the print queue window as your document appears. As before, the printer icon appears in the taskbar, but if printing is paused, the title bar shows "Paused," and the print job is not sent to the printer but remains in the print queue (stored temporarily on the hard disk).

Removing Print Jobs from the Print Queue

Suppose you started to print a document, but then noticed a typo on the screen. You might want to remove the job from the print queue to prevent it from printing. You can prevent Windows 98 from sending a print job to the printer by deleting the job from the print queue.

REFERENCE WINDOW   **RW**

Removing Print Jobs from the Print Queue
- To remove all jobs, click Printer, and then click Purge Print Documents.
- To remove a single job, click the job in the print queue, and then either press the Delete key or click Document and then click Cancel Printing.

After you attempt to remove a job, you might discover that all or part of the document prints anyway. If this happens, Windows 98 had already sent part of the job—maybe even all of it—to the printer before you sent the cancel command. Your printer has memory too, and removing print jobs from the Windows 98 print queue does not affect the parts of a print job already in the printer's memory. You can clear your printer's memory by resetting your printer. How you do this depends on what type of printer you have, but some printers have a Reset button.

Because you have already printed the Pins graphic once, you decide to remove it from the print queue.

To remove a print job from the print queue:

1. Right-click the **Pins** print job in the print queue. (Remember this print job appears with your name, such as Pins Laura Smith.)

   TROUBLE? If you weren't able to pause printing in the previous section because you are printing to a network printer, try printing and pausing the individual document here. The document might print so quickly that you don't have time to select and then delete it, but don't worry; just read through the steps and study the figures.

2. Click **Cancel Printing**.

3. Click **Printer**, and then click **Pause Printing** to remove the check mark and return the print queue settings to their original state.

4. Click the **Close** button ⊠ to close the print queue, and then close Paint.

Managing Print Jobs in the Print Queue

Suppose you were working under a deadline and you needed to give your print job top priority over the jobs already in the print queue. You can rearrange the print queue order by dragging one or more print jobs to a different place in the print queue list, as shown in Figure 9-9.

| Figure 9-9 | REARRANGING PRINT JOBS |

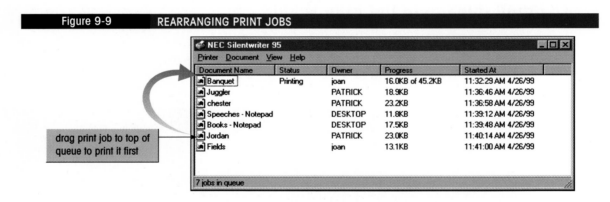

drag print job to top of queue to print it first

In Figure 9-9, a user on a computer named Patrick (Patrick here is the name of the computer, identified in the Owner column) needs the hard copy of the Jordan document immediately, so he drags it to the top of the queue. To give his print job precedence over other print jobs in the queue, his computer has to be set so that he has the authority to override the jobs of other computers on the network. In many network situations, the only computer that can control the order of the print jobs is the one that administers the print server.

Opening a Printer's Property Sheet

Wai wants to install his new printer, but he asks you to help him by first reviewing the properties of the printer already installed. This information will guide him in making changes to his system as he installs the second printer. A printer is a **hardware device**, a physical component of a computer system. Other hardware devices include scanners, speakers, CD-ROM drives, and so on. As with objects on the desktop, hardware devices have property sheets that display the properties, or characteristics, of the device. You can use a device's property sheet to learn about the device and to change the device's settings.

To view the property sheet for your printer:

1. Click the **Start** button, point to **Settings**, and then click **Printers**. The **Printers** window opens.

2. Right-click the icon for your printer, and then click **Properties** from the menu.

   TROUBLE? Your computer might list several printers. Use the default printer.

3. Click the **Details** sheet tab to display the Details property sheet for your printer. See Figure 9-10.

| Figure 9-10 | DETAILS PROPERTY SHEET FOR DEFAULT PRINTER |

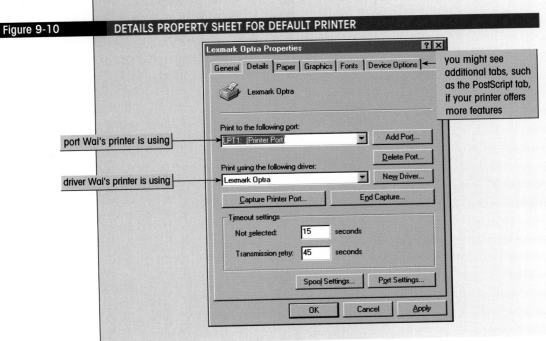

port Wai's printer is using

driver Wai's printer is using

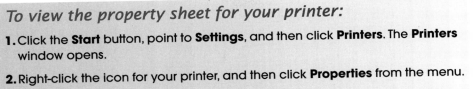

you might see additional tabs, such as the PostScript tab, if your printer offers more features

The Details property sheet shows several important pieces of information about how Wai's existing printer is connected to his computer. As you read through the next sections, refer to this property sheet on your own computer to learn more about how it is configured.

Installing a Hardware Device

How you install hardware devices depends on whether your computer system uses the most recent Windows 98 technology. Hardware devices can be **internal**, located on the inside of your computer, or **external**, attached to the computer on the outside. To connect internal devices, you must remove the chassis and fit the device into a slot in your computer. To connect an external device to a computer, you plug a cable into a socket, called a **port**, on the computer. See Figure 9-11.

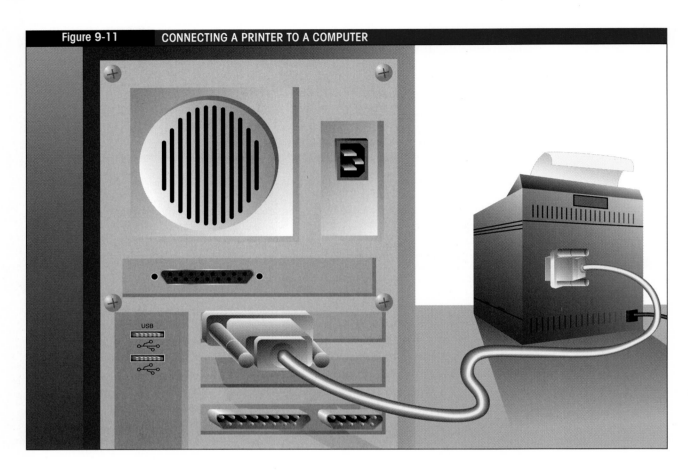

Figure 9-11   CONNECTING A PRINTER TO A COMPUTER

Systems built prior to the release of Windows 98 usually require three steps to install any hardware device:

1. Check your existing configuration so you can see what ports are available and what information you will need to install the device—as you just did when checking Wai's existing printer's property sheet.

2. Connect the device to the computer. If the device is external, you usually plug in a cable. If the device is internal (like most disk drives, modems, or CD-ROM drives), you shut down and unplug the computer first, then you remove the chassis and fit the device into your computer. Although installing internal devices is not difficult, it can be intimidating to new users, so you might want an experienced friend or a professional to help you.

3. Install the software that enables your new device to communicate with your computer, and then make any changes to your existing setup to accommodate the new device.

Systems built to take advantage of Windows 98 technology allow you to skip most of the traditional hardware installation procedures—often you can simply plug the device in, and Windows 98 takes care of the rest.

Serial and Parallel Ports

A computer usually has several different port types; you can plug a printer into a serial or parallel port, or, if it takes advantage of new Windows 98 technology, into a USB port, as described in the next section. A **serial port** transfers data 1 bit at a time, whereas a **parallel port** transmits data 8 bits at a time. A computer can contain up to four different serial ports, although most computers have only two. They are called COM1, COM2, COM3, and COM4 (COM stands for "communications"). A serial port is usually used for an external modem or mouse, although it can be used for some printers. Parallel ports are named LPT1, LPT2, and LPT3 (LPT stands for "line print terminal"). They are usually reserved for printers, and most computers have only one parallel port. In the property sheet shown in Figure 9-10, the printer is currently attached to the parallel port LPT1. Wai tells you that he'll add a second parallel port to his computer for the new printer.

The Details property sheet also gives you information on the driver that is installed for your printer. A **driver** is a file with program code that enables Windows 98 to communicate with, and control the operation of, a hardware device. When Windows 98 spools a document for printing, it is using information provided by the driver to insert the appropriate electronic codes. Wai's monochrome printer uses a Lexmark Optra driver.

Universal Serial Bus Ports

The Windows 98 operating system supports USB ports in addition to serial and parallel ports. **USB**, short for **Universal Serial Bus**, is a new high-speed technology that facilitates the connection of external devices, such as joysticks, scanners, keyboards, video conferencing cameras, speakers, modems, and printers, to a computer. To use USB technology, your computer must have a USB port, and the device you install must have a **USB connector**, a small, rectangular plug. You simply plug the USB connector into the USB port, and the computer will recognize the device and will allow you to use it immediately. USB-compatible computers thus work more like stereo systems, in that you don't have to completely disassemble the unit to add a component.

Owners of new computers that take advantage of USB technology no longer have to worry about which ports to use. Any USB device can use any USB port, interchangeably and in any order. You can "daisy chain" up to 127 devices together, plugging one device into another, or you can connect multiple devices to a single inexpensive hub. Data is transferred through a USB 10 times faster than, for example, through a serial port. For many USB devices, power is supplied via the port, so there is no need for extra power cables. Older computers can have a plethora of connectors—a keyboard connector, a mouse port, a parallel port, a joystick port, two audio ports, and two serial ports. USB computers replace this proliferation of ports with one standardized plug and port combination.

If you are purchasing a new computer or additional hardware for your computer, make sure the new computer has at least two USB ports, one for the printer and one for the keyboard, so other devices can connect into either the printer or the keyboard. Make sure any additional hardware you purchase has its own USB port.

Plug and Play

Hardware devices that work best with Windows 98 support Plug and Play technology. **Plug and Play**, or **PnP** for short, means that you can "plug" a device into your computer and immediately begin to "play" with it, avoiding the frustrations involved with setting up your system to work with the new device. When you add a Plug and Play device, Windows 98 recognizes and configures the new device without your needing to do anything, whereas for non-Plug and Play devices you must use one of the installation Wizards to install a new device on your system.

When you plug a new Plug and Play hardware device into your computer, Windows 98 checks and corrects your computer's settings "behind the scenes" (including IRQs, I/O addresses, DMA channels, and memory addresses—the jargon alone is enough to frustrate a new user) to make sure your new device doesn't cause any problems. To take advantage of Plug and Play, the device you are adding needs to meet a set of standards—not all devices do. For example, devices that you installed on your system many years ago, called **legacy devices**, came out before the Plug and Play standards were available. Thus, if your system has a modem you bought several years before Windows 98 was released, that modem is considered a legacy device. Windows 98 has added features to accommodate legacy devices, but to use the full power of Plug and Play, the device must be new enough to meet the new specifications. Most Plug and Play devices will advertise this fact. USB devices, for example, are all Plug and Play compatible.

Now that you have examined your computer's printer configuration, you can close the property sheet. You'll install the new printer in Session 9.2.

To close the Printer property sheet and the Printers window:

1. Click the **Cancel** button to close the Printers property sheet without making any changes.

2. Close any open windows.

QUICK CHECK

1. When you print a document, where does the printer icon appear?

2. How does Windows 98 prevent print jobs from using up your computer's memory?

3. You just started printing a 35-page term paper from your word processor. Suddenly you remember you forgot to add page numbers. You hate to waste paper, so you want to stop the job from printing. What should you do?

4. You've attempted to remove a job from the print queue, but part of it prints anyway. What happened?

5. How can you give your print job top priority among all the jobs in the print queue?

6. A file that enables a hardware device to communicate with your operating system is called a _____.

SESSION 9.2

In this session, you will learn how to install a printer, print a document to a different printer, and troubleshoot problems that arise as you print. You'll also learn how Windows 98 manages fonts. Finally, you'll learn how to locate information about your computer's system. Even though you probably won't be able to install a new printer in a computer lab, you can read through the steps, even performing many of them, to learn how it's done.

Using the Add Printer Wizard

Wai plans on purchasing a new computer with USB ports within the next year, but since his current computer is several years old, it does not have a USB port, and Wai must install his printer on a parallel port. Once the new printer is attached to Wai's computer, he tells you to install the software that will allow his computer to communicate with the new printer. Windows 98 has greatly simplified this process by providing hardware installation wizards. The Add Printer Wizard helps you install your printer's driver software and configure your printer so that it doesn't conflict with the other devices on your computer.

Although you aren't likely to be able to install a new printer in your computer's lab, you can still do many of the steps in this session. The steps tell you specifically when you should cancel the procedure. If you were really installing a new printer, you would need to have the Windows 98 installation disks or CD-ROM handy, so Windows 98 could access installation data.

Now that the second printer is physically attached to Wai's computer, you decide to use the Windows 98 Add Printer Wizard to complete the installation process.

To start the Windows 98 Add Printer Wizard:

1. Open the Printers window, and then click the **Add Printer** icon. The Add Printer Wizard opens a dialog box that tells you about the installation process.

   TROUBLE? If you are using Classic style, click the Add Printer icon and then press Enter to open the Add Printer Wizard.

   TROUBLE? If you are worried that you haven't actually physically installed a new printer and should therefore not be going through these steps, don't worry. You can go through the steps in the Add Printer Wizard until Windows 98 prompts you for the installation disk. Then you'll need to cancel the procedure, as instructed in the steps.

2. Click the **Next** button to open the Add Printer Wizard dialog box shown in Figure 9-12.

   TROUBLE? If this dialog box does not appear, there are no network printers available to your computer. Proceed to Step 4.

Figure 9-12 **ADD PRINTER WIZARD DIALOG BOX**

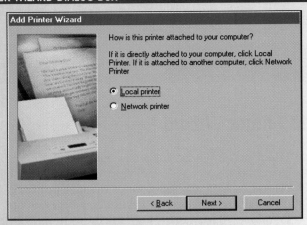

3. Click the **Local printer** option button, and then click the **Next** button.

4. Now you must enter the make and model of your new printer. Drag the vertical scrollbar down the Manufacturers list, and then click the **HP** manufacturer entry.

5. Drag the vertical scrollbar down the Printers list, and then click the entry for the **HP DeskJet 870Cse**. See Figure 9-13.

Figure 9-13 **SELECTING A MANUFACTURER AND PRINTER**

Add Printer Wizard

Click the manufacturer and model of your printer. If your printer came with an installation disk, click Have Disk. If your printer is not listed, consult your printer documentation for a compatible printer.

Manufacturers:	Printers:
Generic	HP DeskJet 855Cse
Gestetner	HP DeskJet 855Cxi
Hermes	HP DeskJet 870C
HP	HP DeskJet 870Cse
IBM	HP DeskJet 870Cxi
Kodak	HP DeskJet 1200C (MS)
Kyocera	HP DeskJet 1200C/PS

HP is manufacturer

HP DeskJet 870Cse is printer

Have Disk...

< Back   Next >   Cancel

6. Click the **Next** button.

7. Click **LPT2**, the port that Wai wants to use, and then click the **Next** button.

   TROUBLE? If LPT2 doesn't appear, your computer might not have a second parallel port. Click LPT1, or one of the COM ports instead. You'll be canceling the procedure at the end anyway, so it doesn't matter if these ports are already in use.

You have now given Windows 98 enough information to install the driver for the new printer. However, the Wizard still prompts you with additional questions. The next dialog box allows you to specify a name for the new printer. This is the name that will appear in the Printers window when you are finished with the installation. The name you enter could be the printer model (the default) or it could be a description of the printer's function (such as Marketing Printer). You decide to enter a name describing the printer's function. Next, you have to decide whether this printer will be the default printer on your system. The **default printer** is the printer that has been designated to handle all printing, unless you specify a different printer from within a program. Wai tells you he does not want to install the color printer as the default, because he won't use it as often as he uses his monochrome printer.

To name the printer and indicate that it is not the default:

1. Type **Color Printer** in the Printer name text box.

2. Verify that the **No** option button is selected so that this printer will not be the default printer on your system. See Figure 9-14.

Figure 9-14	NAMING THE PRINTER

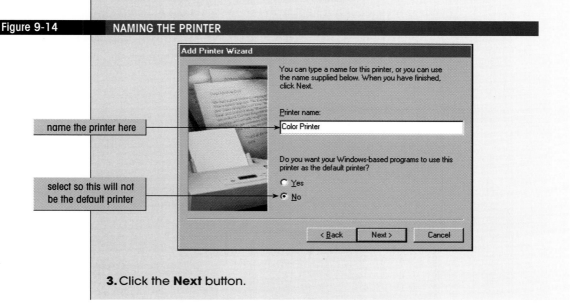

name the printer here

select so this will not
be the default printer

3. Click the **Next** button.

Now the Add Printer Wizard asks you whether you want to print a test page to verify that the installation was completed properly. If you decide against printing a test page, you can always print one later by clicking the Print Test Page button on the General page of the printer's property sheet. Because you are not actually installing this printer, the steps direct you to click No. Windows 98 will prompt you to insert the disk that contains the printer driver for the new printer. If this were your computer and your printer, you would click the OK button to finish the installation, but in the steps you will cancel the procedure. In the rest of this tutorial, you will learn what would have happened if you had actually installed the DeskJet printer.

To cancel the installation of a new printer:

1. Click the **No** option button to prevent printing a test page.

2. Click the **Cancel** button to cancel the Add Printer Wizard.

3. Close the Printers window.

Installing New or Rare Printers

The last thing the Add Printer Wizard asked you to do was to insert the installation disk so it could locate the driver for the printer you specified earlier in the Wizard steps. The drivers for some printers, however, are not on the Windows 98 installation disk and are not included in the list of printers provided by the Add Printer Wizard. This can occur either when your printer is so new that its drivers were not available when Windows 98 released its installation disks or when your printer is so rare that Microsoft didn't include it in the Wizard list. Most manufacturers include a disk that contains the driver along with the printer.

Using Have Disk

If your printer does not appear in the Wizard's list of printers, you will need to install the driver from the disk that came with your printer. You can usually install the driver from within the Add Printer Wizard by clicking the Have Disk button when the Wizard asks for your printer model, and by inserting the disk containing the driver when prompted. See Figure 9-15.

Figure 9-15	USING HAVE DISK

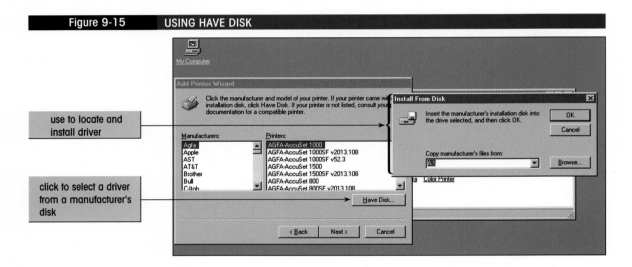

use to locate and install driver

click to select a driver from a manufacturer's disk

Manufacturers are constantly updating and improving their printer drivers. Some of these changes are made to remove bugs; others are made to increase printing speed. You can check with your manufacturer or with Microsoft to see whether a new version of your printer driver has been released. Many manufacturers make their new drivers available on their electronic bulletin boards or World Wide Web pages.

Using Windows Update

Updated drivers are also available via the Windows Update option on the Start menu. When you choose this option, you connect to a Web page maintained by Microsoft that scans your system and alerts you if your system has old drivers. The Windows Update feature then gives you the option to update your drivers automatically. You should only use this feature if you have your own computer. When you select Windows Update from the Start menu, directions appear on the screen that prompt you through the update procedure.

Printing **a Document to a Different Printer**

Windows 98 will print your document to the default printer unless you specify a different printer from within a program. The printer you specified then becomes the active printer. Depending on what program you are using, it is possible that when you open that document again, the program will remember which printer you chose and might display that printer instead of the default printer.

REFERENCE   WINDOW   **RW**

Printing to a Different Printer
- Open the document you want to print within the program that created it.
- Click File, and then click Print.
- Click the Name list arrow.
- Click the name of the printer to which you want to print.
- Click the OK button.

Wai has more than one printer now. He still wants his monochrome printer as his default printer, but sometimes he'll want to print to the color printer. Wai is eager to see how that printer handles color print jobs. You tell him you were hoping to print Pins2, the full-color graphic, so he tells you to print it on his new printer.

To print a document on a different printer:

1. Open **Pins2** from the Student Disk you used in Session 9.1, in Paint. Resize the Paint window if necessary.

2. Click **File**, and then click **Print**.

3. Click the **Name** list arrow.

4. Click the printer you want to use. Wai wants to use the one named "Color Printer." See Figure 9-16.

TROUBLE? You won't see "Color Printer" in the Printer box, because you didn't actually install that printer. If you don't see more than one printer on the list, there are no other printers available to your computer. Leave the default printer selected, and then continue with Step 5. If there is more than one printer listed, ask your instructor or technical support person which printer you should use.

| Figure 9-16 | PRINTING TO A DIFFERENT PRINTER |

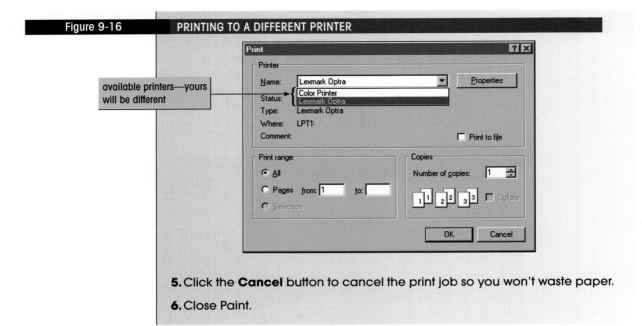

available printers—yours will be different

5. Click the **Cancel** button to cancel the print job so you won't waste paper.

6. Close Paint.

Changing the Default Printer

When you went through the installation procedure, you had the opportunity to select the printer you were installing as the default printer. Windows 98 would print all documents to that printer. Just now, you saw how to print to a printer other than the default printer. Suppose, however, that Wai decides he wants his color printer to be the default printer. He can designate the color printer as the default printer by opening the print queue for that printer. He then would click Printer on the menu bar and choose Set As Default. See Figure 9-17.

| Figure 9-17 | SPECIFYING A DEFAULT PRINTER |

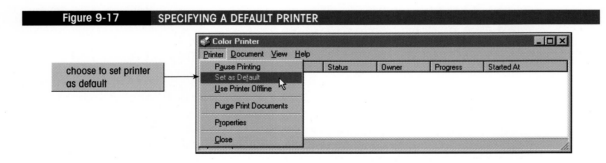

choose to set printer as default

You won't change the default printer in this tutorial.

Using the Print Troubleshooter

Printers, like all devices, do not always work properly. On occasion you might have problems printing a document; or if the document does print, it might not print correctly. Windows 98 provides help in the form of a Print Troubleshooter that you can use to diagnose and correct printing problems. **Troubleshooters** are a part of the Windows 98 online Help system. They ask you questions about the problem, and you answer these questions by selecting one of the options that appear in the Troubleshooter dialog box. As you go through the Troubleshooter to test different solutions, Windows 98 gives you immediate access to the tools you need, such as a property sheet or an accessory. The Troubleshooter does not always successfully pinpoint the source of your problem, but it is an excellent place to start trying to find a solution.

You and Wai are finished installing the color printer on Wai's computer. The Pins2 printout looks great, and Wai asks you if you have any other documents to print in color. You tell him that Celia Koch, the committee member in charge of the convention banquet, sent you an announcement for the banquet. Because this is a festive occasion, Celia would like the announcement printed in color. She gave you a disk with the WordPad file, Banquet, and a black and white printout, as shown in Figure 9-18.

Figure 9-18	BANQUET DOCUMENT

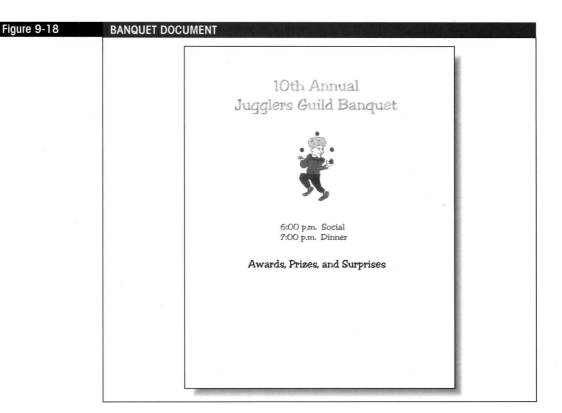

You decide to open the file and print it on Wai's color printer.

To open WordPad and view the Banquet document:

1. Click the **Start** button, point to **Programs**, point to **Accessories**, and then click **WordPad**.

2. Open and then print the **Banquet** file from your Student Disk. As you compare your screen to the printout, you realize something has gone wrong. The printout in Figure 9-19 is different from the printout in Figure 9-18.

   TROUBLE? If the file you opened looks identical to Figure 9-18, then your computer does not have the same problem as Wai's. You can follow the rest of the steps in this section, but keep in mind that in your case the problem you are solving doesn't actually exist.

Figure 9-19 | **BANQUET DOCUMENT PRINTED INCORRECTLY**

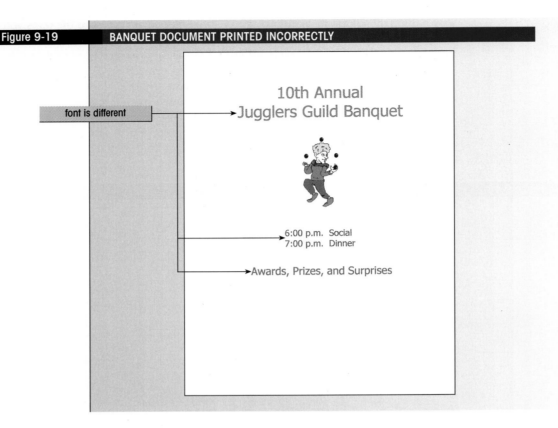

font is different

10th Annual
Jugglers Guild Banquet

6:00 p.m. Social
7:00 p.m. Dinner

Awards, Prizes, and Surprises

The font used to announce the banquet has been replaced by a different font. For some reason, your computer has substituted the incorrect font. You worry that something is wrong with Wai's printer, so you decide to use the Print Troubleshooter to see if you can figure out what happened.

To use the Print Troubleshooter:

1. Click the **Start** button, and then click **Help**.

2. Click the **Contents** tab.

3. Click **Troubleshooting**.

4. Click **Windows 98 Troubleshooters**.

5. Click **Print**.

6. Click the button to the left of the third option, "Fonts are missing or do not appear as they do on the screen." See Figure 9-20.

Figure 9-20   USING THE PRINT TROUBLESHOOTER

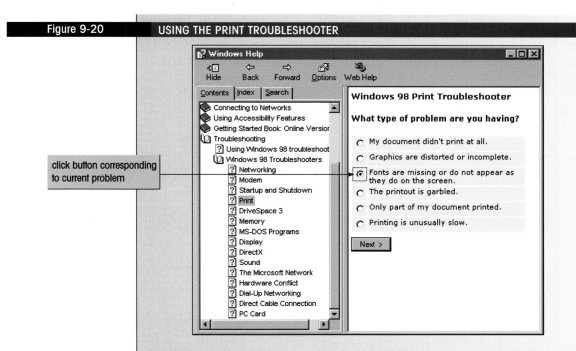

click button corresponding
to current problem

7. Click the **Next** button. The Troubleshooter displays the information shown in Figure 9-21. The Troubleshooter suggests that the problem might be occurring with TrueType fonts. What does this mean? After reading the Troubleshooter, you decide to find out.

Figure 9-21   OPTIONS IN THE PRINT TROUBLESHOOTER

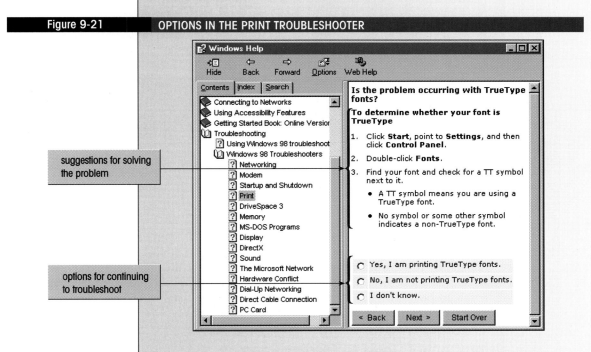

suggestions for solving
the problem

options for continuing
to troubleshoot

8. Click the **I don't know** button, and then click **Next**. The information suggests that you examine the Fonts window, so you'll do this next.

9. Close Windows Help.

Working with Fonts

When the fonts in a document do not appear as you expect, the problem could be that part of the document was formatted with a font that isn't actually installed on your computer. You can find this out by first checking which font Windows 98 expects to find, and then checking whether that font is actually installed on your computer. If it isn't, you might need to choose a different font for that section of the document.

In WordPad, you can assign a different font to any part of your document: to a section, a paragraph, a sentence, a word, or even a character. To see which font a particular section uses, you click anywhere within that section and then look at what font appears in the Font box in the WordPad toolbar.

To open the Banquet document in WordPad and open the Font list:

1. Make sure the banquet document is open in WordPad.

2. Click anywhere in the title of the document (depending on the size of your WordPad window, the title might take up two or three lines), which contains the text "10th Annual Jugglers Guild Banquet." The insertion point moves to the location you clicked.

3. Look at the Font box on the toolbar. The font name that appears is Jester.

4. Click the **Font** list arrow to view all the available fonts.

   TROUBLE? If the Format bar doesn't appear, click View, and then click Format Bar.

5. Scroll the Font list and notice that Jester does not appear. See Figure 9-22.

Figure 9-22	FONT LIST

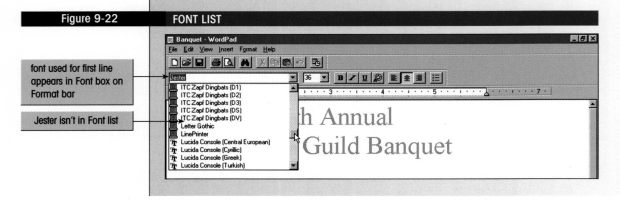

font used for first line appears in Font box on Format bar

Jester isn't in Font list

Apparently this document uses a font named Jester for the document's title. You've never heard of this font before. The fact that the font does not appear in the Font list suggests that there is a problem with this font or that it is not actually installed on your computer. You can find out which is the case by opening the Fonts window.

Using Control Panel to Display Fonts

From the Control Panel you can open the Fonts window, which manages the fonts installed on your computer. From the Fonts window, you can open fonts to look at their style and print a test to see how your printer produces the font. You can also install new fonts or delete unneeded ones.

The Control Panel Fonts window shows many more fonts than appear in a program's Font list because there are many fonts that Windows 98 needs but that are not available to programs.

To view the fonts installed on your computer:

1. Click the **Start** button, point to **Settings**, and then click **Control Panel**.

2. Click the **Fonts** icon. Windows 98 opens the Fonts window displayed in Figure 9-23.

   TROUBLE? If your fonts are listed differently, don't worry.

Figure 9-23   FONTS WINDOW

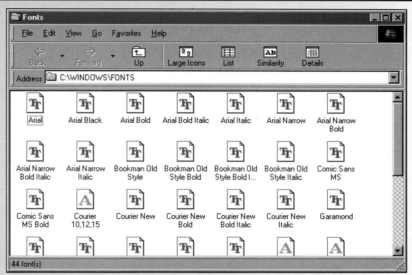

3. To display more details about your fonts, click **View**, and then click **Details**.

4. Scroll down the list of fonts to see which fonts are installed on your computer. The Jester font does not appear. See Figure 9-24.

   TROUBLE? If Jester does appear, it is already installed on your computer. Read through the rest of the section to see what you would do if it weren't installed on your computer.

Figure 9-24   **VIEWING FONT DETAILS**

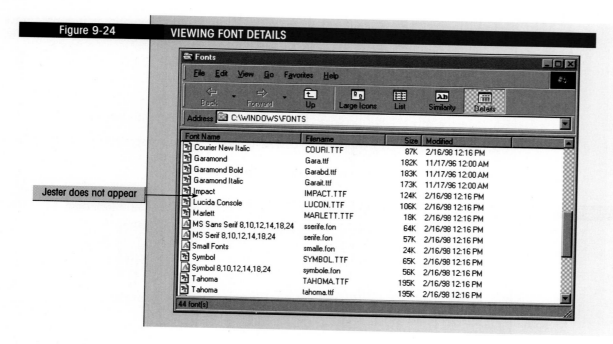

Jester does not appear

You believe you have pinpointed the problem: the reason your document didn't look right in WordPad is that the Banquet document used a font that was not installed on your computer. WordPad was able to display the name of the font in the Font box, but when Windows 98 tried to display the font, it didn't have the actual font file. In this case, it was forced to substitute a different font. You have two options: you can either try to locate and install Jester, or you can review the fonts that are available and choose one to use in your document. The Fonts window can help you with either option.

Font Types

In Details view, the Control Panel Fonts window shows you both the name of the font and its filename. A **font file** contains the information Windows 98 needs to display the font on your monitor or print the font on your printer. The Control Panel Fonts window displays all the font files installed on your computer. A font file's name is not necessarily the same as the name of the font itself, as you can see from Figure 9-24. The Garamond Bold font, for example, is stored in a file named Garabd.ttf. To understand which fonts are available in the Fonts window and how you can use these fonts, you need to know a little bit about which font types you can use with Windows 98. Figure 9-25 describes the font types you are likely to encounter.

Figure 9-25	FONT TYPES
FONT TYPE	**DESCRIPTION**
Printer fonts	Fonts built into your printer. These are not stored in files on your computer and therefore do not appear in the Fonts window.
Screen fonts	Fonts used by your computer monitor to display the text that appears in dialog boxes, menus, buttons, icons, and other parts of the interface. Screen fonts are also used when you preview how your document will look when printed. When you create a document in a Windows 98 program, you choose a font and Windows 98 tries to match a screen font to it. However, screen fonts do not always perfectly match up with the fonts your printer uses. In some cases this causes your documents to print in ways slightly different from what you expect.
TrueType fonts	Fonts that are capable of both being displayed on your monitor and being printed on your printer with minimal or no change in appearance. Windows 98 includes many of these fonts, and you will probably prefer to use them because there is no guesswork involved in how the printout will compare with what you see on the monitor. You can also **scale** a TrueType font—you can enlarge or shrink it without its losing its shape and appearance. You can also rotate a TrueType font, enabling you to print your text upside down or at different angles.
Postscript fonts	Fonts developed by a company called Adobe that are described by a special language called **Postscript**, which produces fonts and graphics. You can scale and rotate Postscript fonts, but they require an extra software utility called the **Adobe Type Manager** to be converted into a form that can be displayed on a computer monitor (something Windows 98 can do automatically with TrueType fonts).

You probably noticed as you scrolled through the Fonts window that there are two different kinds of icons that represent fonts: 🖳 and 🅰. The first icon represents TrueType fonts, whereas the other icon represents screen fonts. The filenames for TrueType fonts end with the .ttf file extension, whereas screen font filenames end with .fon, as you can see if your computer's view options are set to display file extensions.

Some fonts use more than one file. For example, Times New Roman uses four files: Times.ttf, Timesbd.ttf, Timesbi.ttf, and Timesi.ttf—Times New Roman, Times New Roman Bold, Times New Roman Bold Italic, and Times New Roman Italic, respectively. When you choose an attribute such as bold or italic from within a program you are actually choosing an alternate file (although this is not the case with underlining). If you're interested in viewing only the font names and not these variations, you can use the Hide Variations command on the View menu. The Fonts window then hides the font variations, reducing the number of fonts you have to scroll through to find a font you want to use.

Font files are widely available. Windows 98 is shipped with 16 different TrueType fonts. Many programs, such as Microsoft Office, include fonts, and you can also find them on the Internet or in font collections you can buy on disk or CD-ROM.

Opening a Font

For the Banquet document, you want to use only a TrueType font because those fonts give you the most flexibility, so you decide to search for a font that you might be able to use instead of Jester. You can open a font in the Fonts window to see its characteristics and how it will look in a variety of sizes. One of the fonts that comes with Windows 98 is Comic Sans MS. Perhaps this font will look good on the Banquet announcement.

To open the Comic Sans MS font:

1. Locate and then right-click the **Comic Sans MS** font icon.

   TROUBLE? If the Comic Sans MS font does not appear in your Fonts window, choose a different font to complete these steps.

2. Click **Open**. Windows 98 opens a window that displays the font in different sizes, along with information about the font and its creator at the top of the window.

3. Maximize the Comic Sans MS window. See Figure 9-26.

Figure 9-26	OPENING A FONT

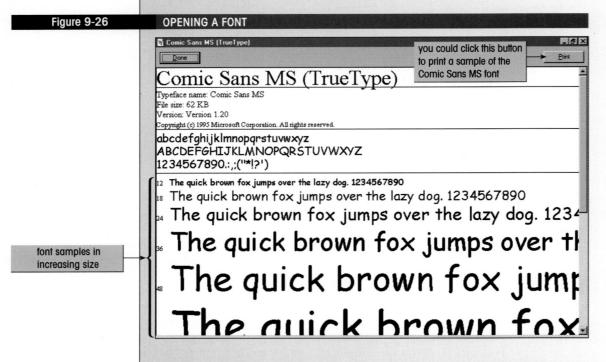

4. Click the **Done** button to close the Comic Sans MS window. Now return to the Fonts window.

Installing a Font

If you can locate the font file Jester.ttf, then you are in luck and you can install it. The document should then print correctly. You can often find font files on the Web.

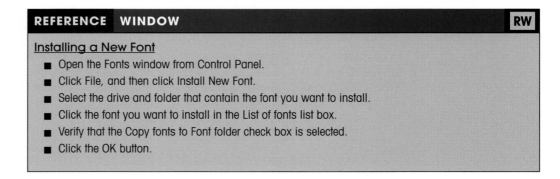

REFERENCE WINDOW RW

Installing a New Font
- Open the Fonts window from Control Panel.
- Click File, and then click Install New Font.
- Select the drive and folder that contain the font you want to install.
- Click the font you want to install in the List of fonts list box.
- Verify that the Copy fonts to Font folder check box is selected.
- Click the OK button.

Your Student Disk does not actually have a font on it, so in this tutorial you won't actually install a font, though you can open the Add Fonts dialog box to see how you would install a new font if you had one.

To open the Add Fonts dialog box:

1. Click **File**, and then click **Install New Font**. The Add Fonts dialog box opens. See Figure 9-27. If you needed to install a font, you would select the drive and folder containing the font. It would then appear in the List of fonts box. You would click it, and then click the OK button.

Figure 9-27	INSTALLING A FONT

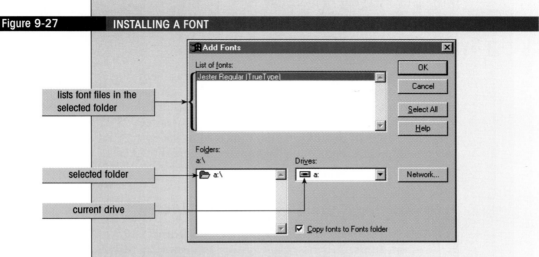

2. Click the **Cancel** button to close the Add Fonts dialog box without installing a font, and then close all open windows.

When you install Jester on Wai's computer, you find that the problem is solved. The Banquet document now prints correctly.

Deleting a Font

Many users collect fonts to give their documents variety. Once you start adding fonts, though, especially if you purchase them in batches, you might find that you have many that you don't use very often. Fonts take up valuable disk space, so you should periodically review your fonts and delete those you don't need.

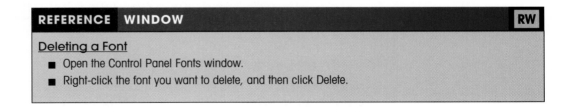

REFERENCE WINDOW   **RW**

Deleting a Font
- Open the Control Panel Fonts window.
- Right-click the font you want to delete, and then click Delete.

You need to be careful when you delete fonts, however. A document might use a font you deleted, and then, as you saw in this tutorial, that document would no longer print correctly. You also should not delete fonts with the 🅰 icon unless you are sure you understand what you are doing, because you might inadvertently delete a font that Windows 98 needs to display objects on the screen. If you are working in a computer lab, it is unlikely you will be able to delete fonts.

You reflect on how easy it was to install and work with Wai's new printer—and how quickly you solved the font problem. Here's one interesting thing to note about the font problem you encountered—if Celia had been using a word-processing program, such as Microsoft Word, she might not have needed to include the font file for the Jester font. Many programs allow you to embed the fonts you are using into the document, so anyone with whom you share the document will be able to view and print the document without needing to install one or more font files.

Checking System Information

Computer users sometimes encounter problems with their computers that even the Troubleshooters can't solve. When the problem seems to involve hardware or system settings, computer users can get help from the System Information accessory, which makes system information readily accessible and provides several system tools that can help solve problems. Much of the information displayed in the System Information window is useful only to computer experts, but all computer owners should be aware of the type of information it provides.

To view the System Information window:

1. Click the **Start** button ![Start], point to **Programs**, point to **Accessories**, point to **System Tools**, and then click **System Information**. The Microsoft System Information window opens, as shown in Figure 9-28.

Figure 9-28	SYSTEM INFORMATION WINDOW

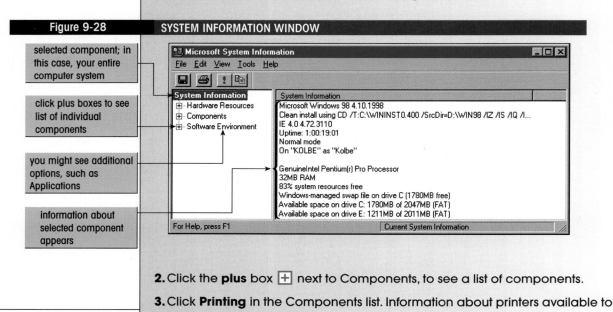

selected component; in this case, your entire computer system

click plus boxes to see list of individual components

you might see additional options, such as Applications

information about selected component appears

2. Click the **plus** box ⊞ next to Components, to see a list of components.

3. Click **Printing** in the Components list. Information about printers available to your computer appears.

4. Close the Microsoft System Information window.

When all attempts to solve a problem fail, computer owners can get help from the manufacturers of the hardware and software installed on the computer. Most hardware and software companies have **technical support staff**, employees who have been trained to help computer users solve computer problems over the phone. Technical support staff are in a sense "working in the dark" because they are not sitting in front of the ailing computer. The System Information window often contains information that can help them solve the problem, so computer owners can speed up a technical support call by being aware of this window and knowing how to navigate it.

QUICK CHECK

1. If Windows 98 doesn't seem to be able to locate the driver for a printer you just bought, what should you do?

2. How do you access the Windows 98 Troubleshooters?

3. How can you tell which font a paragraph in a WordPad document is using?

4. Is the name of a font necessarily the same as its filename?

5. What are some of the advantages of using a TrueType font?

6. If you are having a computer problem and you call your technical support person, and she requests information on your system, how can you find this information?

TUTORIAL ASSIGNMENTS

1. **Exploring Your Printer**   Open the Print dialog box (you can open it from WordPad or Paint), then answer the following questions on a piece of paper. When you are finished, close the Print dialog box.

   a. What is the name of your printer?
   b. What is your printer's type?
   c. Where is your printer connected? Do you see a port name or something else?
   d. Are there any other printers available from your computer? What are their names?

2. **Exploring Your Printer's Properties**   Open the Printers window, then open your printer's property sheet. Answer the following questions on a sheet of paper.

   a. What port is your printer connected to?
   b. What driver does your printer use?
   c. Click the Paper tab, and then describe how your printer processes paper when printing. For example, what paper size does it use? Where is the paper located? How many copies does it print?

3. **Installing a Printer**   You just purchased a NEC Silentwriter 97 printer that you want to install as your default printer. You plan to install it locally on LPT1. You plan to name it Sales Printer. Go through the Add Printer Wizard and write down the options you chose for each dialog box.

Explore

4. **Providing Printer Technical Support**   You are installing Windows 98 on several computers in your office. Afterwards, you receive a phone call from a fellow employee. Printing is unusually slow for him. Using the Printer Troubleshooter, try to determine an explanation for his problem. Write your answer on a piece of paper.

5. **Previewing a Font's Appearance in WordPad**   You can preview the way a font will appear in WordPad without opening the Fonts window in Control Panel. Try picking a different font to replace the Jester font used in the Banquet document. To preview different fonts from within WordPad:

   a. Start WordPad and open the Banquet document from your Student Disk.
   b. Select the title, "10th Annual Jugglers Guild Banquet."
   c. Click Format, and then click Font. The Font dialog box opens.
   d. Select a different font from the Fonts list. Notice the Sample box. Figure 9-29 shows the Font dialog box as it looks when you select the Stencil font. If you don't see a sample in the Sample box, check with your technical support person for assistance.

Figure 9-29

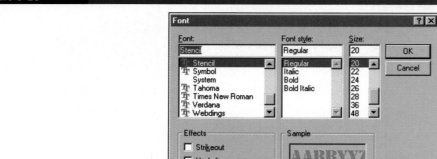

e. Go through the list of fonts and pick out the font that you think looks appropriate for the announcement, and then click the OK button.

f. Print a copy of the revised announcement to hand in to your instructor. Write the name of the font you chose on the printout. Close the Banquet document without saving your changes.

Explore

6. **Changing a Screen Font on your Desktop**   In this tutorial, you saw that Windows 98 uses screen fonts to display the text in dialog boxes, title bars, and other elements on the screen. You can choose a different screen font for your desktop objects. You can use any screen font or TrueType font, allowing you a wide range of desktop appearances. Use the property sheet for the desktop display and change the font style for the icon titles.

a. Right-click a blank area of the desktop and click Properties from the menu.

b. Click the Appearance property sheet tab.

c. Choose Icon from the Item list.

d. Write down the font and size values entered in the Font and Size boxes for the Icon item.

e. Click the Font list arrow and choose the Comic Sans MS font (or a different font if that font is not available).

f. Change the Font size to 8.

g. Click the OK button.

h. Press the PrintScreen key.

i. Open a WordPad document and paste the image of the desktop into a blank document. Type your name and section number at the top of the page.

j. Print the document to hand in to your instructor. Close WordPad without saving the document.

k. Make sure to reopen the Appearance property sheet and restore the Icon font type and size to their original settings.

Explore

7. **Installing a Font**   You want to use a different font for Celia's Banquet document title. There are many free fonts available on the Web.

a. If you have an Internet connection, connect to the Web and search for the string "font" or "freeware font."

b. Connect to any pages that look promising. Graphics collection pages are promising candidates.

c. Search through the fonts you find and download one for use in your Banquet document. Save it on your Student Disk.

d. Install the font you found, using the Fonts window and the Install New Font option.

e. Open the Banquet document and change the font for the title of the flyer to the font you downloaded.

f. Print the document with the new font. You don't need to save changes to the Banquet document.

g. Delete the font from the Fonts window when you are finished.

PROJECTS

1. You work for Jacobson & Sons, a meat processing company. You just started printing one hundred copies of your bratwurst order forms. Suddenly your boss knocks on the door and tells you he's on the phone with a local deli. He needs you to print a copy of the sales contract you have been negotiating with the deli. He asks you to slide it under his office door the second it's done printing. Write the steps you could take to print this document immediately. There are several ways to do this; just describe one way.

2. You work for a commercial graphics company. Your supervisor wants you to produce sheets of TrueType fonts styles so that users can refer to a book of styles when designing documents. You can open each font from the Fonts window as you did in this tutorial, and then click the Print button to print that font. Create sheets for the following fonts (substitute different ones if you can't find one or more of these):

   a. Arial
   b. Brush Script MT Italic
   c. Comic Sans MS
   d. Monotype Sorts

3. You are creating a manuscript for a publishing house. You want to use a font in your manuscript that is similar to the Times New Roman font, but that is not Times New Roman. Windows 98 allows you to list fonts by similarity. Use the View options in the Fonts window to list the fonts that are either very similar or fairly similar to Times New Roman.

   a. Open the Fonts window through the Windows 98 Control Panel.
   b. Click View, and then click List Fonts By Similarity.
   c. Choose Times New Roman from the List Fonts by Similarity to list.
   d. Remove the font variations from the Fonts window, using the Hide Variations option on the View menu.
   e. Write down the list of fonts that are either very similar or fairly similar to Times New Roman, and hand in the list to your instructor. If there are more than 10 such fonts listed, just write the first 10.
   f. Close the Fonts window and the Control Panel.

4. When you purchase hardware devices, it is helpful to know what port types you have on your computer. Open the Microsoft System Information window, choose Components, and then choose Ports. Click the Basic Information option button, and then observe the number of ports you have. Write down the number and kind (for example, COM or LPT). Close the Microsoft System Information window when you are finished.

QUICK CHECK ANSWERS

Session 9.1

1. Taskbar

2. By storing them on the hard drive instead of in your computer's memory

3. Open the print queue, select the print job, then click Cancel Printing from the Document menu

4. That part of the print job had already been sent to the printer.

5. Drag it to the top of the print queue.

6. Driver

Session 9.2

1. Use the disk that came with the printer.

2. From online Help

3. Click the paragraph, then look at the name that appears in the Font box.

4. No

5. It looks the same on the screen as it does when you print it, and you can scale it without losing quality.

6. Open the Microsoft System Information window.

OBJECTIVES

In this tutorial you will:

- Get an overview of networks and network terminology

- View your network using Network Neighborhood

- View your network's properties and identify your computer on the network

- Consider network security and access rights issues

- Log on to a workstation and a server

- Change your password

- View the servers to which you are attached

- Log off from a server and a workstation

- Access network resources, including folders and printers

- Map a drive and troubleshoot network problems

NETWORK NEIGHBORHOOD

Exploring Network Resources at Millennium Real Estate

CASE

Millennium Real Estate

You are a real estate agent who recently joined Millennium Real Estate Company, a small firm comprised of a real estate division and a land development division. Millennium rents an office suite in Hilldale Mall. Recently, Millennium connected all their computers together to form a network. A **network** is a collection of computers and other hardware devices linked together so that they can exchange data and share hardware and software resources.

Networks offer a company such as Millennium many advantages. Groups of computers on the network can use the same printer, so Millennium doesn't have to purchase a printer for each computer. Networks facilitate group projects, because one person can save a document in a folder that other users on other computers can access using the network. A network also improves communication in a company because coworkers can easily share news and information.

Joan Alvarez, the company's owner, wants you to learn to use the Millennium network effectively, and she would like you to spend the next several hours exploring it. She decides to start you off by giving you an overview of the basic concepts of networking. Once you have been introduced to fundamentals, Joan will show you how to use Windows 98 to be productive on the company's network. You will share an office with Anjali Kolbe, one of the Millennium agents, so Joan decides to use the computer in Anjali's office to show you how to use the network.

SESSION 10.1

In this session, you will explore the basic concepts of how a network operates. Then you will learn about some of the Windows 98 tools that help you understand and work with your network. Because every network is different, some of the topics in this tutorial will not apply to your network. If this is the case, you should still review those tasks to further your understanding of the networking capabilities of Windows 98.

Network Concepts

Joan begins her overview by discussing the fundamentals of networks and network terminology. She believes that, armed with these fundamentals, you will be better equipped to use the network effectively.

Each device on a network is called a **node**. Nodes are typically connected to each other by means of network cabling, although connections can also be established using phone lines, satellites, and infrared signals. If the network nodes are close together, as they would be in a computer lab or the Millennium office suite, the network is called a **local area network**, or **LAN**. Figure 10-1 shows a typical LAN.

Figure 10-1   A LOCAL AREA NETWORK

cable connects nodes on the network

printer can be made available to all computers on the network

each computer on the network is a node

If the nodes are spread out over a wider area, such as across a state or nation, the network is often called a **wide area network**, or **WAN**. For example, an insurance company with offices in many large cities might be on a WAN, so that an office in Detroit can access information about a client whose insurance history is located on a computer in the San Antonio branch of the company. A WAN might use satellite connections to exchange data among the nodes.

Individual networks can also be connected together to share information. A **domain** is the label given to a network so that it can be recognized by other networks. The term **subnet** is also used to describe a network existing within a larger network. Just as information can be shared between nodes in a network, so too can information be shared between computers in different domains. The biggest and most famous example of this is the Internet, which is sometimes referred to as a "network of networks." With Internet access, a computer in one domain can communicate with a computer in a different domain, if a path connects the two networks and these two networks communicate using the same standards and conventions that the Internet uses.

Because Millennium's computers are located in the same building, they are configured as a local area network. There are two models people follow to set up LANs: the hierarchical model and the peer-to-peer model.

Hierarchical Client/Server Network

In the **hierarchical model**, often called the **client/server model**, computers called **servers** provide access to resources such as files, software, and hardware devices. A computer that uses these resources is called a **workstation** or **client**. Figure 10-2 illustrates the hierarchical model.

Figure 10-2	HIERARCHICAL NETWORK MODEL

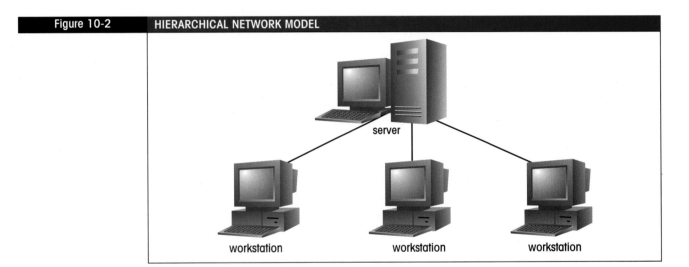

Servers offer many resources to the network. For example, a server might store a database, making it accessible to many workstations. A server might also handle electronic mail, faxes, or printing for a network. If a network is large, it often has several servers, with each server dedicated to the needs of a separate group of users or to a specific task. Most university networks use a hierarchical model, with students, faculty, and staff using workstations to access files and resources stored on servers across campus. A network operating system is usually installed and maintained by an individual called the **network administrator**. The administrator is ultimately responsible for how you interact with the network.

A hierarchical network requires special software on the server. This software, called a **network operating system**, manages the operations of the entire network. In addition, client software must be installed on each workstation so that it can communicate with the server. Although Windows 98 does not provide the network operating system software to allow your computer to act as a network server in the hierarchical model, it does provide the client software so your computer can work with a server using network operating systems such as Novell NetWare, Windows NT, IBM OS/2 LAN, and Banyan Vines.

Peer-to-Peer Network

A second kind of network model is based on the peer-to-peer model. In the **peer-to-peer model**, a network does not require a server dedicated to managing network resources. Instead, nodes on a peer-to-peer network can act as both clients and servers, with each node sharing its resources with other nodes on the network. Figure 10-3 shows the layout of a peer-to-peer network.

Figure 10-3	PEER-TO-PEER NETWORK MODEL

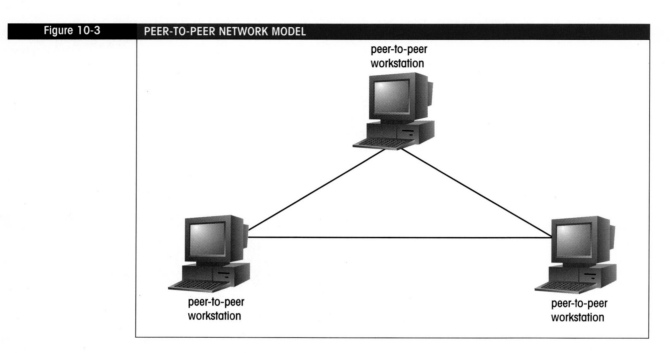

In a peer-to-peer network, the network administrator often organizes nodes into workgroups. A **workgroup** is a group of computers that performs common tasks or belongs to users who share common duties and interests. A network administrator for a business, for example, might organize computers used by the office staff into an Office workgroup and computers used by upper management into a Management workgroup. Organizing the network in this fashion makes it easier for the network administrator to manage the differing needs of each group.

An advantage of the peer-to-peer model for Windows 98 users is that the network can be set up without purchasing any additional software. Everything needed to create a peer-to-peer network is built into the Windows 98 operating system. One problem, however, with peer-to-peer networks is that performance of individual nodes can deteriorate as they manage tasks for other computers as well as performing their own duties. Moreover, a peer-to-peer network does not have the same extensive network management features offered by network operating systems under the hierarchical model. For these reasons, peer-to-peer networks are usually used for smaller networks with just a few nodes, as is the case at Millennium.

Each network is different. The network administrator tries to create a network structure that best meets the needs of the users, sometimes including elements from both the hierarchical and peer-to-peer models. How a user interacts with the network can also vary from network to network. In some cases the network administrator will limit your ability to work on the network, whereas other administrators will give users great flexibility in sharing and accessing network resources. Joan wants you to understand that what you see on the Millennium peer-to-peer network might not necessarily apply to other networks you encounter.

To view network identification information:

1. Click the **Identification** tab. This property sheet displays the name, workgroup, and description of your computer. See Figure 10-10. Yours will probably be different—and you might have no workgroup assignment.

Figure 10-10	IDENTIFYING A COMPUTER ON A NETWORK

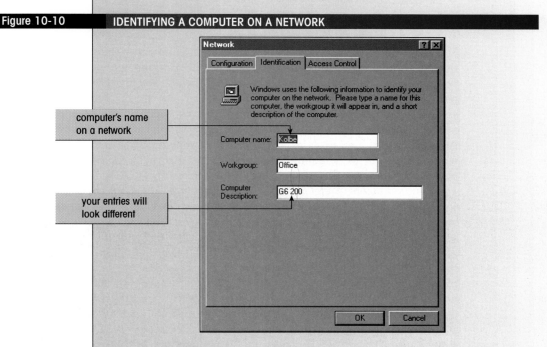

computer's name on a network

your entries will look different

2. Click the **Cancel** button to close the Network property sheet without saving any changes you might have inadvertently made.

QUICK CHECK

1. What is a network?

2. Define the following terms:

    a. node

    b. LAN

    c. WAN

    d. server

    e. client

3. Name the two types of network models, then briefly describe each.

4. Name three tasks a network server might have to perform.

5. What are the four components needed to set up a Windows 98 machine to work on a network?

6. What is a communications protocol? Give an example of a communications protocol and describe what it is used for.

SESSION 10.2

In this session, you will learn how to log on to your network and how Windows 98 manages access to different network resources with user accounts and access rights. You'll learn how passwords work and how to create a secure password.

Network **Security and Access Rights**

You mention to Joan that when you were at the university there were a number of things that, as a student, you were "blocked out" of doing on the network. Joan replies that similar restrictions are in place on the Millennium network. She explains that these restrictions are part of an overall plan for maintaining security on the Millennium network. **Network security** involves the control of two aspects of a network: the people who can access the network and the actions they're allowed to perform on the network once they're connected. At Millennium, Joan explains, the network administrator wants to make sure that the network is used only by Millennium employees and that each employee has access only to those parts of the network that apply to his or her job.

Measures taken to ensure network security vary for different networks. If you have a small network set up in your home, you probably don't need to have a sophisticated security system controlling who has access to the network. You are there to monitor the situation, and you have other means of controlling who gets into your home. However, the network requirements for a small business might be different. A small business might want to have security measures in place to control who gets access to the network; once employees receive authorization, however, they might have free access to all network resources.

A large network with hundreds of people working on different projects involving confidential information is another matter. For example, a university network server that stores, among other things, student grades and records needs tight security over who can access the system and what information they can view once they get access. Likewise, a network at a hospital must have rigorous restrictions in place to limit access to patient data, to ensure the integrity of the doctor-patient relationship.

Network administrators don't just need to restrict access to data; they also need to restrict access to hardware. For example, the graphic arts department on campus might have purchased an expensive high-quality color laser printer, and they don't want students from other departments using it. The network administrator might therefore limit access to that printer to students and faculty in the graphic arts department.

Network administrators control who gets on the network—and what users are allowed to do once they are connected—through network accounts and access rights. A **network account** is the collection of information about you and the work you do on the network. Before you can use the network, the network administrator creates an account for you that identifies you as an authorized user of the network. In a network that has several different servers, you might have several network accounts. For example, a student who is getting an engineering degree but is taking a class in the art department might have two network accounts, one in each department.

Network administrators limit access to network data, software, and hardware through the use of user IDs and passwords. Your **user ID**, or **username**, identifies you to other users on the network. A user ID might be your first name, or a number such as 445228, or a word such as Agent. On some systems, user IDs are limited to eight characters and exclude spaces or special symbols.

Along with your user ID, you enter your password. Your **password** is a string of symbols, letters, and numbers, known only to you and the network administrator, that shows you are the legitimate user of the account. Passwords are a security device to prevent other people who might know your user ID from using your account. Once you have entered both the user ID and password, the server checks to see if these are valid before allowing you network access.

Once you're connected to the network, your ability to use network resources is controlled by a set of guidelines, set up by the network administrator. The ability to use a resource is called an **access right**. Access rights can be limited to **read-only access**, which allows you to view the contents of a file but not to edit or delete the file. This might occur if you were a physician who needs to be able to review patient records stored on a hospital network database. Your network administrator might grant you read-only access so that you could view the files without accidentally changing or deleting a record. In other situations you might need **read and write** access, which allows you to view and edit files but not delete them, or **full access**, which gives you the ability to view, edit, and delete a file. Read and write access is often granted on networks where your files are stored in folders located on a network server.

Network **Logons**

The process of accessing your account is called **logging on** or **logging in**. When you first start a network computer, you are prompted for your user ID and password in a dialog box called a **logon dialog box**. The appearance of the logon dialog box varies, depending on the operating system used by your network. Figure 10-11 shows a sample logon dialog box for Windows 98.

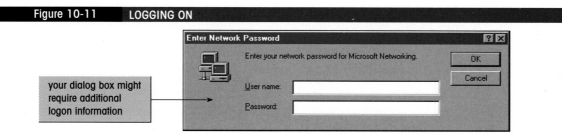

| Figure 10-11 | LOGGING ON |

your dialog box might require additional logon information

Completing this dialog box allows you to access the Windows 98 operating system after entering your user ID and password.

The Windows 98 logon dialog box also can be used in situations where a single workstation is shared by several people. Windows 98 allows each user to customize the desktop, storing the desktop each user designs in a file called a **user profile**. Logging on to Windows 98 accesses your user profile and loads the settings for your customized desktop. Not every network will have the Windows 98 user profiles feature installed.

Logging on to a Windows NT Domain

If your computer is on a Windows NT network, you see a dialog box similar to that shown in Figure 10-11, but in addition to the user ID and password, you specify a domain name or the name of the server that maintains the list of authorized users on the network. This server is called a **login server**, and like other workstations and servers on the network, it has a name. Once you click OK, the login server checks your user ID and password and confirms that you are a legitimate network user. The Windows 98 desktop appears, and you are logged on.

Logging on to a NetWare Tree

If your computer is on a NetWare network, the NetWare dialog box you see is similar to the one in Figure 10-11, but you are also prompted for your **Novell Directory Services (NDS) tree name**, a name your network administrator assigns that allows you to access the NetWare network. Once you've entered this information and closed the dialog box, NetWare looks up that information in its database to confirm that you are a legitimate user. The Windows 98 desktop appears, and you are logged on.

Attaching to a Server

Usually when you log on to a Windows NT domain or a NetWare tree, you are automatically attached to all servers for which your account allows access. However, sometimes you need to **attach to**, or access, a server for which you do not automatically have access. For example, you might regularly log on to one server, but occasionally need access to a database located on another network server.

To attach to such a server, you open Network Neighborhood and then open the icon for that server. Depending on whether it is a Windows NT server, a NetWare server, or another user's computer on a peer-to-peer network, there will be a different result. Windows NT will determine if you are allowed access, and if you are, will automatically connect you. NetWare will prompt you to enter your user ID and password in an Attach As dialog box. A computer participating in peer-to-peer sharing could do either, depending on how that computer's files are shared.

Password Protection

You have already seen how network administrators enforce network security through the use of user IDs and passwords. Joan emphasizes that keeping your password secret helps maintain the security of a network and its resources. If you are allowed to create your own password for your account, you should keep the following principles in mind:

- Do not use fewer than seven characters in your password.
- Do not use your name, birth date, nickname, or any word that an unauthorized user might be able to guess.
- Try to include numbers or special symbols (!@#%&*) in your password, because they make it harder for other users to guess your password.
- Never write down your password where others can see it or share your password with other users.

You also should change your password every few months. On some networks this is a requirement, and the network administrator will set up an automatic prompt that appears when you are supposed to change your password. In the process of changing your password, you will be prompted to enter your old password and then to enter your new password twice. You enter the new password twice to reduce the possibility of a typing error.

REFERENCE WINDOW   **RW**

Changing Your Windows 98 Password
- Click the Start button, point to Settings, and then click Control Panel.
- Open the Passwords window.
- Click the Change Windows Password button.
- Type your current password in the Old password box.
- Type your new password twice: once in the New password box and once in the Confirm new password box.
- Click the OK button to save the new password.
- Close the Windows 98 Control Panel.

Joan tells you that password protection is one of Millennium's network security measures, and you will be required to change your password every two months. Joan suggests that you review the dialog box you will use to do this.

If you are in a university computer lab, you might not be able to change your password. You should ask your instructor or network administrator about your network's policies for changing passwords. In the next set of steps, you will be directed to click the Cancel button to prevent you from making any changes to your current password. If you are using a Windows NT network, a message might inform you that you can change other passwords to match your Windows password so that you don't have to enter multiple passwords. If you choose to do so, you can click the Microsoft Networking check box. If you are using a NetWare network, you need to right-click your NDS tree in Network Neighborhood and choose Change Password. You could change your password to match your Windows 98 password.

To review the techniques for changing your Windows 98 password:

1. Click the **Start** button ⊞Start, point to **Settings**, and then click **Control Panel**.

2. Click the **Passwords** icon. The Passwords Properties dialog box opens. See Figure 10-12.

| Figure 10-12 | PASSWORDS PROPERTIES SHEET |

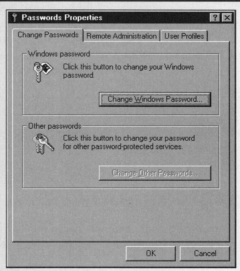

3. Click the **Change Windows Password** button. The Change Windows Password dialog box opens. See Figure 10-13.

   TROUBLE? If this button is unavailable, close the Passwords Properties dialog box and read through the rest of the steps.

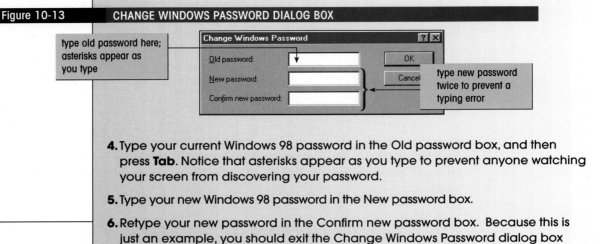

Figure 10-13   CHANGE WINDOWS PASSWORD DIALOG BOX

type old password here; asterisks appear as you type

type new password twice to prevent a typing error

4. Type your current Windows 98 password in the Old password box, and then press **Tab**. Notice that asterisks appear as you type to prevent anyone watching your screen from discovering your password.

5. Type your new Windows 98 password in the New password box.

6. Retype your new password in the Confirm new password box. Because this is just an example, you should exit the Change Windows Password dialog box without saving your changes.

7. Click the **Cancel** button.

8. Click the **Cancel** button to close the Passwords Properties dialog box, and then close Control Panel.

To change your password for a network account, you might be required to send a command to the appropriate network server. How you change your password depends on your access rights and the procedures used on your network. If you need to change your password and don't know how, talk with your technical support person or your instructor.

Logging off

When you're done using a workstation, you should log off. **Logging off** is the process of closing your account on the server. Some servers allow only a limited number of users on at any given time, and network administrators want to avoid tying up servers with nonactive users.

Logging off from Windows 98

When you are finished working on your workstation, you should log off not only from all your network accounts but also from your workstation account. Depending on your network, your network administrator might want you to leave the computer on for those following you to use, so make sure you understand the procedures in your computer lab before you follow any of the instructions here.

There might be several options available to you when you are ready to stop working with Windows 98 on your workstation. You can:

■ **Log off your account:** This option, accessed by the Log Off command on the Start menu, leaves the Windows 98 operating system loaded, but closes any active programs or network accounts. The logon dialog box appears. Network administrators whose workstations are shared among several users often request that you use this option for shutting down your account.

■ **Shut down:** This option, accessed by the Shut Down command on the Start menu, unloads the Windows 98 operating system. The next user will have to restart the workstation and reload the Windows 98 operating system. You should check with your instructor to see whether this option is allowed on your network. Many network administrators request users not to shut down individual workstations.

■ **Restart:** This option, accessed by the Shut Down command on the Start menu, shuts down and then reloads the Windows 98 operating system. The next user will have to enter his or her user ID and password in the logon dialog box before using the computer. You might also see the Restart in DOS option, which allows you to restart your computer without loading the Windows 98 operating system.

If your hardware supports Standby mode, you will also see the Standby option.

You should talk to your instructor or network administrator to determine which of these options you should select when you're finished working with Windows 98. At Millennium, the network administrator prefers the first option: that you log off from your account but keep the Windows 98 operating system loaded. Joan shows you how to log off from Windows 98 using this option.

To log off from your account:

1. Click the **Start** button ![Start].

2. Click the **Log Off** command, which appears as "Log Off (*Your Name*)" where (*Your Name*) is the name given to your account. See Figure 10-14.

Figure 10-14	LOGGING OFF

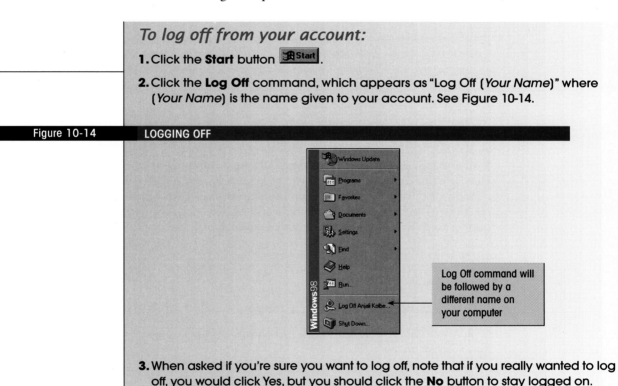

Log Off command will be followed by a different name on your computer

3. When asked if you're sure you want to log off, note that if you really wanted to log off, you would click Yes, but you should click the **No** button to stay logged on.

Logging Off from a Network Server

When you are attached to a server for which you are not automatically logged on, you might want to detach from that server without exiting Windows. You can right-click the server in Network Neighborhood and then choose the Log Off command. You can log off from a server at any time during your Windows 98 session without affecting your accounts on other servers.

Joan emphasizes that you should remember to log off from your account when you're done working. If you leave the workstation running, still connected to your network accounts, other users could access your work.

QUICK CHECK

1. Network security involves what two aspects of a network?

2. Give four guidelines you should follow in choosing a password.

3. What information do you need before logging on to an account on a NetWare network?

4. How would you change your Windows 98 password?

5. When you log off from your workstation account, which option leaves Windows 98 loaded for the next user?

SESSION 10.3

In this session, you will learn how to access the resources on your network. You will access a folder on the network using Windows Explorer and will share a folder of your own with the network. Then you will explore different ways to represent the location of files on the network to your applications. You'll learn how to access a network printer. Finally, you'll learn about the Windows 98 Network Troubleshooter, which can help you diagnose and fix a problem if the network is not working the way you expect.

Using Network Resources

Joan wants to show you some of the available resources on the Millennium servers. You can view a list of the resources a server makes available through the Network Neighborhood window or through Windows Explorer. Joan decides to use Explorer because it gives a better view of the structure of the network. She is logged on to the Kolbe computer and decides to show you the network services available on the computer named Joan.

To view available resources on a network server using Windows Explorer:

1. Click the **Start** button, point to **Programs**, and then click **Windows Explorer**.

2. If necessary, scroll down the All Folders list until you see the Network Neighborhood 🖳 icon.

3. If necessary, click the plus box ⊞ to the left of the Network Neighborhood icon to display the list of servers in your workgroup.

4. Click the server icon 🖳 representing one of the servers you're logged on to. If you aren't sure what servers you are logged on to, ask your technical support person. Joan clicks the icon for the server named Joan so she can show you what resources are available on her computer. The resources offered by that server appear in the right pane. Windows Explorer shows that two folders—clients and listings—are made available to the network by the Joan node, as well as a printer named "hp." See Figure 10-15.

TROUBLE? If you don't immediately see a network server that you have access to, you will have to look for servers elsewhere in the network. To do so, click the Entire Network icon 🌐 to display a list of additional servers and examine those. If you still cannot find a server you can use, talk to your instructor or network administrator.

TROUBLE? You might have to enter a password before you can view the resources shared by a server. If you have trouble accessing the server, talk to your instructor or network administrator.

Figure 10-15   SERVER RESOURCES

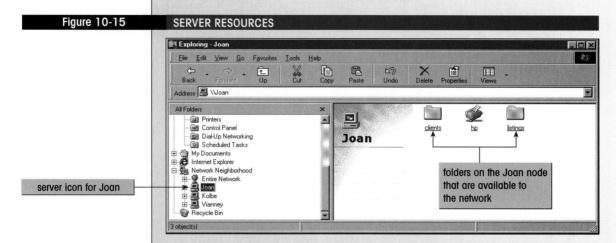

server icon for Joan

5. Leave the Windows Explorer window open. Notice what resources you have access to, such as printers and network folders.

Folders placed on servers and made available to the network are called **network folders**. Folders on your own computer are called **local folders**. You can work with the files in a network folder using the same techniques you apply to files in your local folders. For example, you could click one of the files, and Windows 98 would open the file in the appropriate software program. However, remember that you might not have the same access rights for files on the network server as you do with your own files. You might not be able to move, modify, or delete files, or you might need to enter a password before you are allowed to manipulate network folders and files.

Windows 98 uses two methods to control access to network resources: share-level access control and user-level access control. With **share-level access control**, you need to enter a specific password for each network resource. Share-level access control is used primarily in peer-to-peer networks in which there is no dedicated server that maintains a list of legitimate users for each resource. If the network is designed around the hierarchical model, access to resources is determined by **user-level access control** in which only certain users have access to a resource. For added security, some networks employ both techniques. Figure 10-16 demonstrates the difference between the two methods.

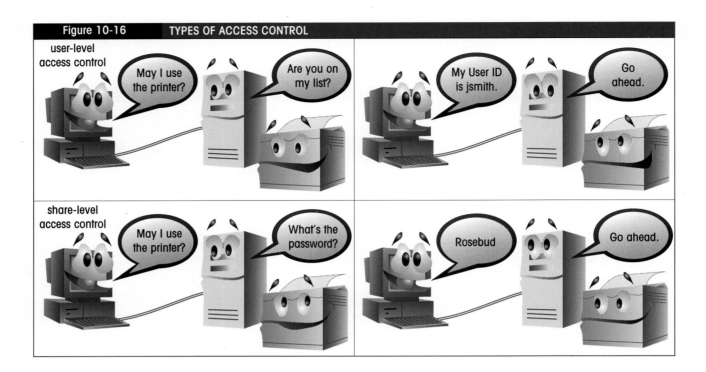

Figure 10-16 — TYPES OF ACCESS CONTROL

Drive Mapping

Newer software programs allow you to access files located on a network through Network Neighborhood, but to make a network file available to an older software program, you must use drive mapping. **Drive mapping** represents a network folder with a single drive letter. Your software recognizes the drive letter and gives you access to the files the folder contains. Even for newer software programs drive mapping is useful because it gives you a more direct route to network files—the drive letter appears in Windows Explorer on the same level as your own local drives; you don't need to open Network Neighborhood and the appropriate server to locate the folder and the files it contains. In Figure 10-17, the mapped drive named Clients on 'Joan' (mapped as drive E) is accessible to the Kolbe computer at the same level as Kolbe's drive C. Without drive mapping, a user would have to open Network Neighborhood, open the Joan server, and then click the Clients folder—a more circuitous route.

Figure 10-17	DRIVE MAPPING

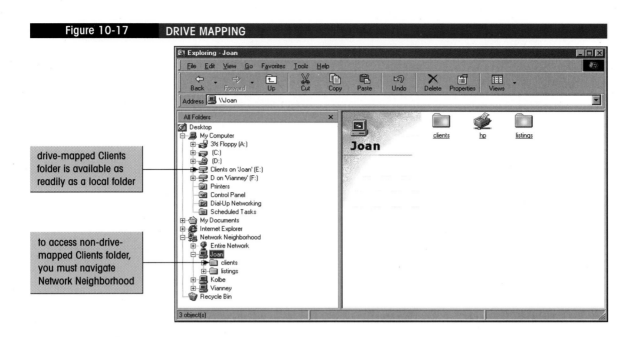

drive-mapped Clients folder is available as readily as a local folder

to access non-drive-mapped Clients folder, you must navigate Network Neighborhood

Sharing a Folder

You ask Joan how the procedure of drive mapping works. She explains that first the owner of the folder must share it, or make it available to the network. Since the Clients folder is on the node named Joan, it must be shared from that computer. Joan leads you into her office to see how sharing works, so that if, for example, you add a hard drive to your computer, you can share it with the Millennium network. In a school lab you are unlikely to be able to share a drive, so if necessary, read through these steps without performing them.

To share a folder:

1. From Windows Explorer, right-click the folder or device you want to share. You can only share folders and devices, not single files. Only share folders and devices you want to make available to the network.

2. Click **Sharing**. The property sheet for the folder or device opens to the Sharing tab.

   TROUBLE? If the Sharing option doesn't appear, or if you get an error message, you are not allowed to share folders on your network.

3. Click the **Shared As** option button and then enter a share name for the folder in the Share Name box. On Joan's computer, she shared the Clients folder with the name "clients."

4. Click the **Access Type** option button for the type of access you want to grant: read-only, full, or password-dependent. Joan has granted full access to the Clients folder.

5. Enter a password if you want to assign one. See Figure 10-18.

Figure 10-18   SHARING THE CLIENTS FOLDER ON JOAN'S COMPUTER

share name is 'clients'

full access is granted to users

users must enter a password, represented by asterisks, to use the shared folder

Clients Properties

General | Sharing

○ Not Shared
● Shared As:
   Share Name: clients
   Comment:

Access Type:
   ○ Read-Only
   ● Full
   ○ Depends on Password

Passwords:
   Read-Only Password:
   Full Access Password: ******

OK   Cancel   Apply

6. Click the **OK** button.

Once a drive or folder is shared, any computer on the network that has permission can access it.

Mapping a Network Folder

Once a folder has been shared on the network, you can use drive mapping to make it accessible to the programs on your computer. Whether or not a network user decides to use drive mapping depends on the level of convenient access the user wants to establish. Anjali Kolbe uses drive mapping so she can access the Clients folder from her older software programs and so she won't have to navigate Network Neighborhood to locate it every time she wants to use its contents. When you map a drive, the Map Network Drive dialog box shows the location of the drive you are going to map. This location is called the file's **pathname**. Windows 98 pathnames follow the **universal naming convention**, or **UNC**, an accepted set of rules for expressing pathnames, including those for network folders. The general form is *server**sharename*, where *sharename* is the name you used when sharing the folder.

To map a network folder to the drive letter:

1. In Windows Explorer, navigate Network Neighborhood to locate the network folder you want to map.

2. Right-click the icon representing the network folder you want to map to a drive letter.

3. Click **Map Network Drive** from the menu.

TROUBLE? Your network administrator might not have given you the ability to do drive mapping on your computer. If that is the case, the option will be unavailable. Review the steps listed here, but do not actually complete them.

4. Click the **Drive** list arrow, and then click the drive letter you want to use for the network folder. In Figure 10-19, the pathname \\Joan\clients, where Joan is the server name and clients is the folder, is mapped to the drive letter E.

4. Click **Windows 98 Troubleshooters**.

5. Click **Networking**.

6. Click the third option, **I am unable to share files or printers**. See Figure 10-24.

Figure 10-24	NETWORK TROUBLESHOOTER

Networking
Troubleshooter

click to see suggestions
for sharing problems

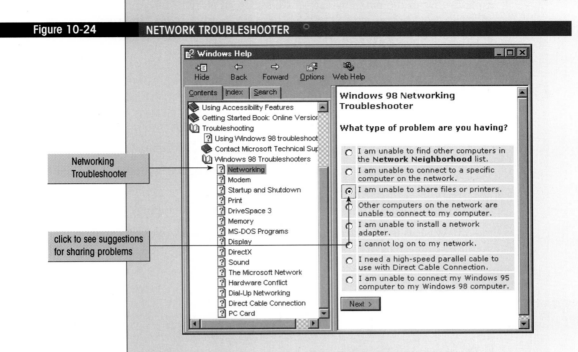

7. Click the **Next** button. The Troubleshooter displays the information shown in Figure 10-25. According to the Network Troubleshooter, one reason that you might not be able to share files is that you don't have the appropriate network software installed. The Troubleshooter walks you through the steps of installing the network software.

Figure 10-25	SHARING SOLUTIONS

one possible solution;
scroll to see more

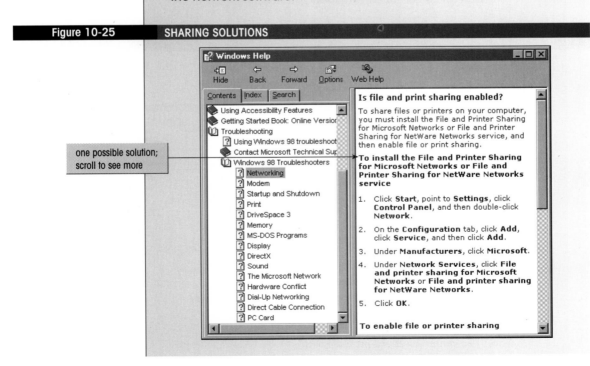

8. Close Help.

As Joan concludes your training on using the Millennium network with Windows 98, she explains that in the next few days she'll set up an account for you on the Kolbe workstation and will provide you with your own user ID and password. She then reminds you of the importance of keeping your password secret so unauthorized users can't access your account.

QUICK CHECK

1. What is a local folder and what is a network folder?

2. What is share-level access control? In which network model would it usually be used?

3. What is user-level access control? In which network model would it most likely be used?

4. Under what circumstances must you use drive mapping?

5. What is the pathname for a printer named Work that is located on the Millennium network server?

TUTORIAL ASSIGNMENTS

1. **Diagramming Your Network** One way to understand your network is to sketch a diagram of the network layout. Figure 10-26 shows a sample schematic drawing. Create a schematic drawing of the network you use. Identify the servers and the resources they share. If there is a large number of workstations on your network, show only a few of them, identifying them by their node names. Talk to your technical support person or instructor to get the information you need.

Figure 10-26

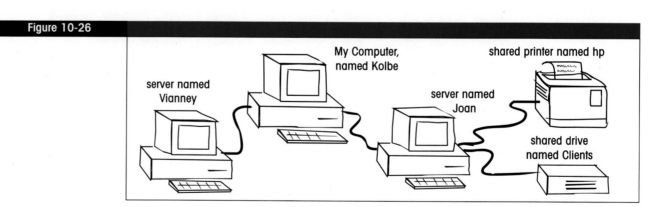

2. **Reporting Your Network Configuration** Write a description of your network. Include the following information in your report:
   a. The number of nodes on the network
   b. The network model (peer-to-peer, hierarchical, or mixed)
   c. The network operating system
   d. The network standard
   e. The communications protocol used

3. **Password Protection** Part of creating good passwords is understanding how password protection can be overcome by people trying to break into a system. Use the Internet or your library to learn the methods used to bypass password protection. Write a one-page report summarizing these techniques and include some suggestions for ways to protect yourself against them.

4. **Transferring a File from the Network Folder** (*Note to Instructor*: You must place a file onto a network server which your students can retrieve in order to complete Tutorial Assignment 4.) Your instructor has placed a file on a network folder. With the filename and name of the folder given to you by your instructor, use Windows Explorer to copy the file to your Student Disk. Enter your name into the document and then print a copy of the file's contents.

5. **Mapping a Network Folder to a Drive Letter** (*Note to Instructor*: For students to complete this assignment, you must indicate to which folder they should apply drive mapping.) You can map network folders from within the Network Neighborhood window. Open the Network Neighborhood window and select the network folder indicated by your instructor. Map the folder to the driver letter U. Open the My Computer window on your desktop to verify that the network folder has been mapped to drive U. Print an image of the My Computer window. Remove the drive mapping.

PROJECTS

Explore

1. One of the uses of a network server is electronic mail. Servers that handle electronic mail are called "mail servers." Find out which server handles your mail messages, and then investigate the properties of that server to answer the following questions about your mail server:

   a. Which server handles your mail messages?
   b. In which network folder are mail messages stored?
   c. Which client program do you use to retrieve your mail messages from the server?

Explore

2. (*Note to Instructor*: If the network your students work on is not connected to the Internet, they will not be able to complete parts a and b of Project 2.) Many university computers are now connected to the Internet. The Internet uses the TCP/IP communications protocol. Try to discover whether your computer has the TCP/IP protocol component installed. Prove your findings by creating a printout of the Network Properties dialog box for your computer, opened to the Configuration tab. Examine the properties for the TCP/IP protocol component and answer the following questions:

   a. What is your computer's IP address? (This is the address that other Internet nodes use to uniquely identify your computer.)
   b. What is the domain for your node? (*Hint*: Look in the DNS Configuration property sheet in the TCP/IP Properties dialog box. The domain is the name for your network.)

Explore

3. (*Note to Instructor*: For your students to complete this project, you must give them the name of the server to find.) You can use the Windows 98 Find command to find network servers as well as files. To access the Find Computer command, click the Start button, point to the Find command, and then click Computer to open the Find Computer dialog box. Enter the name of the network server given to you by your instructor, and click the Find Now button. Print the Find Computer window.

4. A friend is having trouble using the network. She is trying to locate the network server, but she can't find it when she looks through the Network Neighborhood window. Nor does it appear when she uses the Find Computer command. Use the Network Troubleshooter to explain one possible reason for this problem.

QUICK | CHECK ANSWERS

Session 10.1

1. A collection of computers and other hardware devices linked together so that they can exchange data and share hardware and software resources

2. Node: a device on a network; LAN: local area network, a network in which the nodes are located close together; WAN: A network in which the nodes are spread out over a wide area such as a state or nation; server: a computer that provides access to its resources to other computers; client: a computer that uses the resources of a server

3. The hierarchical model in which servers provide resources to the network, and clients use those resources; the peer-to-peer model, in which each computer can act as both client and server

4. Store a database, handle electronic mail, manage printing, etc.

5. Adapter, client, protocol, and service

6. A communications protocol determines how computers recognize each other on the network and what rules they use to transfer data. TCP/IP is used on the Internet. IPX/SPX is used in NetWare networks. NetBEUI is used in a Windows NT network.

Session 10.2

1. Do not use fewer than seven characters in your password; do not use a word that someone might be able to guess; include numbers or special symbols; never write down your password or share it with others.

2. The network you are primarily using whenever you log on to a network

3. Your user ID, password, and the name of your login server

4. Click the Passwords icon in the Control Panel, click Change Windows Password, enter your old and new passwords, and then click OK.

5. The Log Off option leaves Windows 98 loaded, and the Restart option reloads Windows 98.

Session 10.3

1. A local folder is a folder on your computer, whereas a network folder is located on a network computer other than your own.

2. Share-level access control controls access to network resources through the use of a password. It is most often used on peer-to-peer networks.

3. User-level access control controls access to network resources through a list of approved users. It is most often used on hierarchical networks.

4. When you work with older software programs and when you want direct access to network folders without having to navigate Network Neighborhood

5. \\Millennium\Work

OBJECTIVES

In this tutorial you will:

- Remove unneeded files using the Disk Cleanup accessory

- Restore a deleted file from the Recycle Bin

- Scan a disk for errors using the ScanDisk accessory

- Defragment a disk using the Disk Defragmenter accessory

- Schedule disk maintenance tasks with the Maintenance Wizard and check the schedule with Task Scheduler

- Create a startup disk

- Place a folder on your computer's hard drive and back it up using Backup

- Restore a backed up file

LABS

Defragmentation and Disk Operations

Data Backup

DISK MAINTENANCE

Maintaining Disks at Arboretum Energy

CASE

Arboretum Energy

After working for a utility company for a number of years, you recently started your own business, Arboretum Energy. Arboretum sells products designed to conserve energy and lower utility bills, such as specialized lightbulbs that use a fraction of the energy of normal lightbulbs, or meters for dehumidifiers that shut them down when they are not needed. You purchased a Windows 98 computer to help run your business, and you've decided to attend a three-day seminar to orient yourself to the operating system.

The third day of the seminar covers disk maintenance. Your instructor, Pete Laska, explains that **disk maintenance** involves checking your disks regularly for errors and ensuring that the data on the disks is efficiently stored and protected. Windows 98 provides several accessories that help you maintain the data on your disks. Pete says that today you will learn about removing unneeded files, restoring deleted files, scanning your disk for errors, defragmenting your disk to improve its efficiency, scheduling maintenance tasks, and backing up your data.

Pete explains that the Windows 98 disk maintenance accessories are most often used to maintain hard disks, which usually contain permanent data and are expensive to replace. Three-and-a-half-inch disks, on the other hand, usually are used for temporary data storage, and if they are damaged they can be replaced easily and inexpensively. For the purposes of the seminar, however, Pete explains that you will practice disk maintenance techniques on 3½-inch disks rather than hard disks, because access to the hard disks on the seminar lab computers is limited, and disk maintenance procedures take much longer on a hard disk than on a 3½-inch disk.

SESSION 11.1

In this session, you will learn how to improve the performance of your disks. You might not be able to perform all the steps in this tutorial in your computer lab, so the steps include notes at points where that might be the case. Take special note of the information outside of the steps, because it will help you learn about procedures even when you can't perform them.

For this session you will need your Student Disk (the same one you used in Tutorials 8 and 9) and an additional blank 3½-inch disk, if you want to create a startup disk. For Session 11.2 you will need an additional blank 3½-inch disk to use as a backup disk. In the tutorial assignments you will need an additional blank disk to explore file fragmentation.

Windows 98 **Disk Maintenance Accessories**

Pete begins by telling you that disk maintenance is a critical part of owning a computer. Individuals and businesses are relying more and more on computers and the data they contain. If a computer's hard disk fails, it can be disastrous for some businesses. Backing up data is the primary way to prevent such a disaster, as you'll see in Session 11.2. But Windows 98 helps you prevent disk failure from occurring in the first place by providing some valuable disk maintenance accessories. In this tutorial, you'll learn about the disk maintenance accessories listed in Figure 11-1.

Figure 11-1	DISK MAINTENANCE ACCESSORIES
ACCESSORY	**PURPOSE**
Backup	Creates a backup copy of your files
Disk Cleanup	Deletes unnecessary files to free disk space
Disk Defragmenter	Rearranges the way files are stored on your disk to ensure that your programs run as quickly as possible
Maintenance Wizard	Schedules disk maintenance tasks
ScanDisk	Checks files and folders for errors and repairs some problems
Task Scheduler	Manages scheduled tasks

Disk maintenance accessories are available on the Tools tab of the disk's property sheet (accessible by right-clicking the disk in My Computer and then clicking Properties) or via the System Tools submenu of the Accessories menu.

Pete explains that if you have your own computer or are responsible for maintaining other people's computers, you should use these accessories as part of a scheduled comprehensive disk maintenance plan. You should begin a "cycle" of disk maintenance with a "spring cleaning," in which you delete old or unneeded files and scan for **viruses**, programs that run on your computer and disrupt its operations. A virus can "infect" your computer if you execute a program that has a virus attached to it. There are numerous software products on the market designed to protect your computer from viruses by performing regular scans for known viruses, but Windows 98 does not include a virus accessory. If you own your own computer, you should purchase a virus checker and use it regularly as part of your disk maintenance plan.

Once you have ensured that your computer is free from viruses, you then scan each disk on your computer to locate and repair errors. Then you defragment each disk so that the files it contains are organized most efficiently. Finally, you back up all the files on your computer. How often such a cycle should occur depends on how much you use your computer. If you are responsible for maintaining a computer that is used all day long, you might want to run these maintenance procedures on a weekly or even daily basis. If, on the other hand, you use your computer more infrequently—for example, if it is a home computer that you use only for correspondence, games, and maintaining your checkbook—you might only need to run disk maintenance procedures once every month or so.

Removing **Unneeded Files**

When you work with programs and files in Windows 98, unnecessary files tend to accumulate. The Disk Cleanup accessory helps you free up disk space by getting rid of these files. When you start Disk Cleanup, it displays a list of check boxes corresponding to the types of unnecessary files it located on the disk you are cleaning. See Figure 11-2. When you start Disk Cleanup, you might not see all the options on this list. What you see depends on what files Disk Cleanup finds on your disk.

Figure 11-2	DISK CLEANUP OPTIONS
CATEGORY	**DESCRIPTION**
Temporary Setup files	Temporary files created when you install a program—some programs delete these files when they are no longer needed; others leave them on your hard drive
Temporary Internet files	Web pages stored on your hard disk for quick viewing, stored in the Temporary Internet Files folder
Downloaded program files	Program files downloaded automatically from the Internet when you view certain Web pages
Recycle Bin	Files you deleted from your computer, which are stored in the Recycle Bin until you delete them
Old ScanDisk files	Files created by ScanDisk when it locates corrupted data
Temporary files	Files generated by programs to be used temporarily; usually these are deleted when you close the program, but if the program isn't shut down properly the temporary files remain on your disk
Windows 98 uninstall information	Files from a previous version of Windows—these appear only if Windows 98 was installed on a computer that used an older version of Windows; they can be safely deleted if you don't intend to revert to the original version
Non-critical files	Files that are seldom used, such as screen savers or Help files, or files that are useless, such as zero-byte files or lost clusters—this appears only if you have Windows 98 Plus! installed

You can also use the More Options tab of Disk Cleanup to delete optional Windows components or installed programs that you do not use. The Settings tab allows you to schedule Disk Cleanup to run whenever the drive is running low on disk space.

Pete wants you to see how Disk Cleanup works, but explains that you won't be able to clean up the hard drives on seminar computers, so you'll close Disk Cleanup without executing the cleanup.

To start Disk Cleanup:

1. Click the **Start** button ![Start], point to **Programs**, point to **Accessories**, point to **System Tools**, and then click **Disk Cleanup**.

2. Click the **Drives** list arrow, click **(C:)**, and then click the **OK** button. Disk Cleanup calculates how much space you'll be able to clean up and then displays the dialog box shown in Figure 11-3.

   TROUBLE? If drive C doesn't appear or you receive an error message, you don't have permission to clean up drive C. Acknowledge the message, then close any open windows and read through the rest of this section without performing the steps.

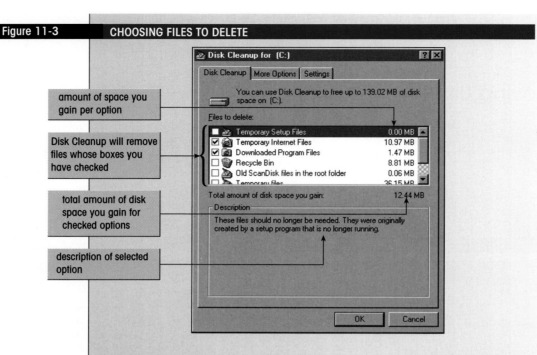

Figure 11-3   CHOOSING FILES TO DELETE

amount of space you gain per option

Disk Cleanup will remove files whose boxes you have checked

total amount of disk space you gain for checked options

description of selected option

3. Notice the amount of disk space you can save, then check the boxes corresponding to the files you want to delete.

4. Click the **Cancel** button. If you are using your own computer and want to clean up your disk, you could click the OK button and then the Yes button to confirm.

Restoring a Deleted File

Deleting a file is a two-step process. First, you delete the file using an application such as Windows Explorer. The file no longer appears when you view the contents of the folder or device from which you deleted it. However, Windows 98 has not actually removed it from the disk. Instead, it remains on the disk, and the information about its original location is stored in the Recycle Bin. To delete a file completely from your hard drive, you must empty the Recycle Bin by right-clicking its icon 🗑 in Windows Explorer or the desktop and then clicking Empty Recycle Bin. Emptying the Recycle Bin frees disk space, but do not choose this option unless you are absolutely sure you will no longer need the files stored in the Recycle Bin.

If you have deleted a file but not emptied the Recycle Bin, you can restore the file to its original location by opening the Recycle Bin and choosing the Restore command. Note, however, that you cannot restore files you deleted from a floppy disk or from a network drive, because these are not stored in the local drive's Recycle Bin. Once you empty the Recycle Bin, it is almost impossible to recover the file.

REFERENCE   WINDOW   **RW**

Restoring a File Deleted from a Local Drive
- Open the Recycle Bin from the desktop or from Windows Explorer.
- Right-click the file you want to restore, then click Restore.

Pete asks you to test this feature by creating a folder on the hard drive, creating a file in that folder, deleting the file, and then restoring it from the Recycle Bin.

To restore a file from the Recycle Bin:

1. Open Windows Explorer, click the drive C device icon 🖳 if necessary, click **File**, point to **New**, click **Folder**, and then type **Seminar** as the new folder name.

   TROUBLE? If your hard disk already has a folder named Seminar, give your folder a different name, such as your last name. Then substitute the name you gave your folder for the Seminar folder throughout the rest of this tutorial.

2. Open the Seminar folder, click **File**, point to **New**, click **Text Document**, and then type **Test1** as the filename.

   TROUBLE? If your computer is set to display file extensions, Windows 98 warns you that the file might become unstable if you change the file extension. If this occurs, type Test1.txt as the filename.

3. Open the Test1 file and type your name in it, then close Notepad and click the **Yes** button to save changes. You have now created a file in the Seminar folder on drive C. You will now delete it so that you can practice how to restore it from the Recycle Bin.

4. Right-click the **Test1** icon, and then click **Delete**. Click **Yes** when asked if you want to send Test1 to the Recycle Bin. The Seminar folder is now empty, but the file is still available in the Recycle Bin.

5. If necessary, scroll down the All Folders Explorer bar, and then click the **Recycle Bin** icon 🗑 . The contents of the Recycle Bin appear in the right pane.

   TROUBLE? If your computer is set to show all files, you might see a Recycled folder on drive C with the same icon as the Recycle Bin on the desktop. Make sure you click the Recycle Bin icon shown in Figure 11-4, not the Recycled folder on drive C.

6. Click **View**, and then click **Details** to view file details. See Figure 11-4.

   TROUBLE? If your Details window looks slightly different, don't worry. You might just have different settings.

Figure 11-4	RECYCLE BIN CONTENTS

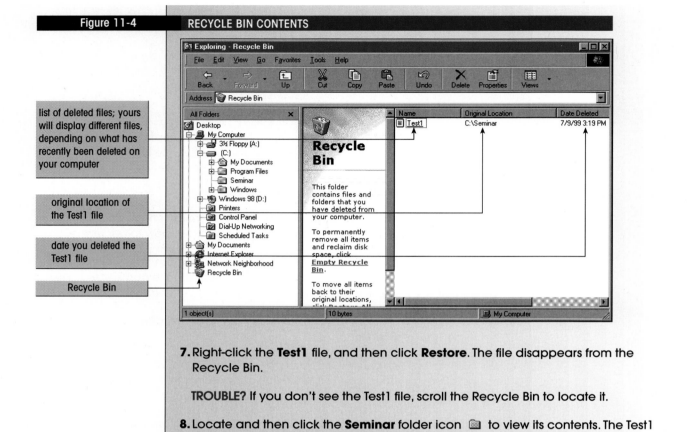

list of deleted files; yours will display different files, depending on what has recently been deleted on your computer

original location of the Test1 file

date you deleted the Test1 file

Recycle Bin

7. Right-click the **Test1** file, and then click **Restore**. The file disappears from the Recycle Bin.

   TROUBLE? If you don't see the Test1 file, scroll the Recycle Bin to locate it.

8. Locate and then click the **Seminar** folder icon 📁 to view its contents. The Test1 document has been restored to its original location.

9. Close Windows Explorer, and leave the Seminar folder on drive C for now; you'll use it again in Session 11.2.

Note that you can delete and restore folders in the same way you delete and restore files.

Scanning a Disk for Errors

Sections of the magnetic surface of a disk sometimes get damaged. Regularly scanning your disks for errors can be an effective way to head off potential problems that would make data inaccessible. The Windows 98 ScanDisk accessory not only locates errors on a disk but also attempts to repair them, or at least mark the defective portions of the disk so that the operating system won't attempt to store data there.

To understand what errors ScanDisk is looking for and how it repairs them, you need to learn a little bit about the structure of a disk. When you format a disk such as a 3½-inch disk, a formatting program divides the disk into storage compartments. First it creates a series of rings, called **tracks**, around the circumference of the disk. Then it divides the tracks into equal parts, like pieces of pie, to form **sectors**, as shown in Figure 11-5.

Figure 11-5	A FORMATTED DISK

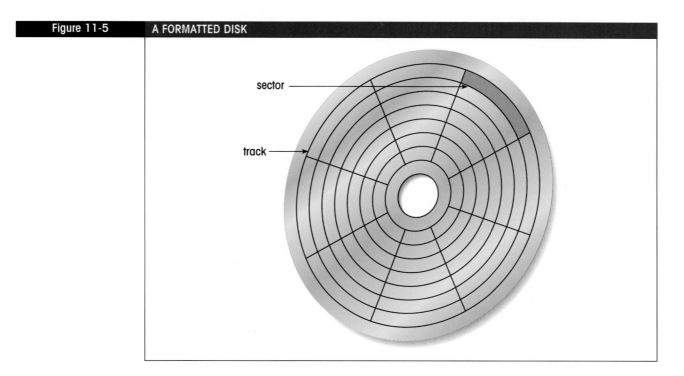

The number of sectors and tracks depends on the size of the disk. A high-density disk, such as your Student Disk, stores data on both sides of the disk. Each side has 80 tracks, and each track is divided into 18 sectors. Each sector can hold 512 bytes, for a total of 1,474,560 bytes or 1.44 MB (a megabyte is 1024 × 1024 bytes).

Although the physical surface of a disk is made of tracks and sectors, a file is stored in clusters. A **cluster**, also called an **allocation unit**, is one or more sectors of storage space— it represents the minimum amount of space that an operating system reserves when saving the contents of a file to a disk. Most files are larger than 512 bytes. Therefore, a file might be stored in more than one cluster. Figure 11-6 shows a file that takes up four clusters on an otherwise empty disk.

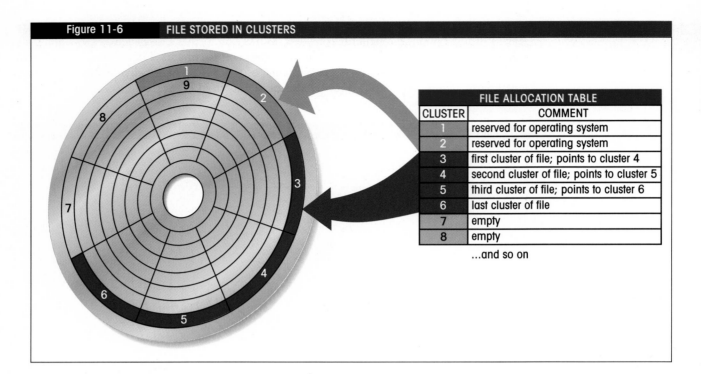

Figure 11-6   FILE STORED IN CLUSTERS

Each cluster is identified by a unique number; the first two clusters, shown in yellow, are reserved by the operating system. Windows 98 maintains a **file allocation table** (or **FAT**) on each disk that lists the clusters on the disk and records the status of each cluster: whether it is occupied (and by which file), available, or defective. Each cluster in a file "remembers" its order in the chain of clusters—and each cluster points to the next one until the last cluster, which marks the end of the file.

One of the other seminar attendees tells Pete she's seen FAT mentioned in advertisements for Windows 98 as "FAT32" and she wondered what that meant. Pete explains that previous versions of Windows used FAT to manage the data on a disk, but FAT could only work with hard drives smaller than 2 GB in size. Windows 98 improves on the older version of FAT (now referred to as **FAT16**) with a new version called **FAT32**. FAT32 uses disk space much more efficiently than FAT16 and can access hard drives up to 2 terabytes in size (a terabyte is 1,000,000,000,000 bytes). Older computers that upgraded to Windows 98 might still use FAT16, but if Windows 98 was installed new on your computer, it probably uses FAT32. Pete explains that if you are using an older computer, you can convert a FAT16 drive to FAT32 using the Drive Converter accessory on the System Tools submenu of the Accessories menu, but that once you convert a drive to FAT32 you can't convert it back without reformatting it. Hence Drive Converter won't be covered during the seminar.

When you use ScanDisk to check your disk, you can specify whether you want it to check the physical surface of the disk, the files, or both the surface and the files. ScanDisk checks the disk surface by looking for damaged sectors. If it finds any, it marks those sectors and prevents data from being stored there. A damaged sector is called a **bad sector**.

ScanDisk checks the files on a disk by comparing the clusters on the disk to the FAT. It looks specifically for lost clusters and cross-linked files. A **lost cluster** is a cluster that contains data that the FAT can't match to a file. If your computer suffers a power surge, a power failure, or any problem that locks it up, the operating system might lose one or more clusters from a file that was open when the problem occurred, and you might lose the data stored in those clusters. The presence of lost clusters on a disk is not damaging, but lost clusters do take up valuable space, and if there are too many of them, the disorder of clusters on your disk might lead to further errors. ScanDisk identifies lost clusters and either deletes them or saves them to a new file. Although sometimes you recover lost data from such a file, more often you won't be able to do much with the file and should simply delete it. Figure 11-7 shows how ScanDisk repairs lost cluster problems on a 3½-inch disk.

Figure 11-7	REPAIRING LOST CLUSTERS

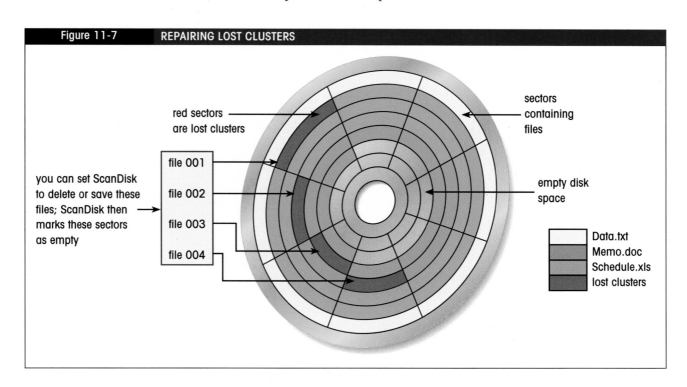

ScanDisk also checks for cross-linked files. A **cross-linked file** contains at least one cluster that has been allocated to more than one file in the FAT. Like lost clusters, cross-linked files can result from an abrupt termination of a program. Because a cluster should be occupied by data coming from only one file, the FAT becomes confused about which clusters belong to which files. You can tell ScanDisk how you want it to handle such a file—by deleting it, copying it, or ignoring it. If you want to maintain the integrity of your files, it's best to allow ScanDisk to copy each file to a new location on the disk and remove the original files so they are no longer cross-linked. This procedure often saves both files, although you might lose a portion of one of the files where the cross-link occurred.

REFERENCE WINDOW RW

Using ScanDisk

- Click the Start button, point to Programs, point to Accessories, point to System Tools, and then click ScanDisk.
- Click the disk you want to scan and the type of test you want to perform.
- Click the Start button.

ScanDisk - [C:]

Select the drive(s) you want to check for errors:

A → 3½ Floppy (A:)
    [C:]

Type of test

B → ⚪ Standard
      (checks files and folders for errors)
C → ⚫ Thorough
      (performs Standard test and scans disk surface for errors)   Options... ← H

D → ☑ Automatically fix errors

    Start   Close   Advanced...
     ↑   ↑   ↑
     E   F   G

A Lists drives that can contain disks available for scanning—does not include CD-ROM drives or network drives
B Checks only the file and folder structure for errors
C Checks the file and folder structure and the disk's physical surface for errors; click Options to specify which parts of the disk's physical surface to scan
D Automatically repairs errors it finds; click Advanced to specify how ScanDisk should fix the errors
E Starts scanning the disk
F Closes ScanDisk without initiating a scan
G Lets you specify whether to display a scan summary or log file, how ScanDisk should fix cross-linked files and lost clusters, and whether it should check invalid filenames and dates
H Lets you specify which parts of the disk's physical surface to scan—system and data, system only, data only—and lets you specify repair options

Pete announces that the first thing he wants you to do is scan your disk for errors. He reminds you that although you'll be performing the scan on a 3½-inch disk, this procedure is most useful for maintaining a hard disk.

To start ScanDisk:

1. Close all open programs—if a program is in use while a disk is being scanned, you could lose data.

2. Place your Student Disk in the appropriate drive. Use the Student Disk you used for Tutorials 8 and 9.

3. Click the **Start** button, point to **Programs**, point to **Accessories**, and then point to **System Tools**.

4. Click **ScanDisk**. The ScanDisk dialog box opens. See Figure 11-8.

TROUBLE? If ScanDisk does not appear as an option on the menu, then you cannot complete this session until ScanDisk is installed. Check with your instructor or technical support person for directions.

TROUBLE? If ScanDisk warns you that it can't start until you specify a drive, follow the instructions in the dialog box and choose drive A when directed. If you still have problems running ScanDisk, check with your instructor.

| Figure 11-8 | SCAN DISK DIALOG BOX |

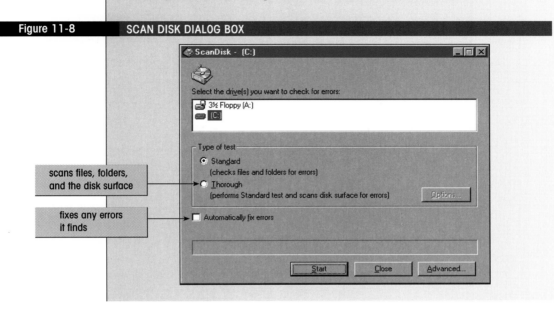

scans files, folders, and the disk surface

fixes any errors it finds

Two test-type options appear: Standard and Thorough. You look at the options, and decide to perform a Thorough test so ScanDisk will check both the files and the surface of the disk. Pete tells you that you should always try to use the Thorough scan unless you're in a hurry. A Standard scan is quicker—and useful when you want to make sure the file structure and filenames are okay, but you aren't worried about the disk surface.

To scan your Student Disk for errors:

1. Click **3½ Floppy (A:)**.

2. If necessary, click the **Thorough** option button.

3. If necessary, click the **Automatically fix errors** check box so it is selected.

4. Click the **Start** button. ScanDisk displays a status bar that tells you which particular cluster is currently being examined.

5. Watch for the ScanDisk Results dialog box to appear when the process, which might take several minutes, is complete. This dialog box reports errors and disk status. See Figure 11-9.

TROUBLE? If the ScanDisk Results dialog box does not appear, a previous user might have changed the ScanDisk settings so no summary would appear. Click the Advanced button to open the ScanDisk Advanced Options dialog box, then click Always in the Display summary area. Click the OK button, and repeat Steps 1–5.

Figure 11-9	RESULTS OF DISK SCAN

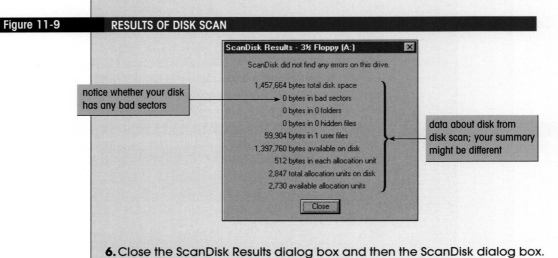

notice whether your disk has any bad sectors

data about disk from disk scan; your summary might be different

6. Close the ScanDisk Results dialog box and then the ScanDisk dialog box.

Scanning a 3½-inch disk takes a few minutes. However, scanning a hard disk could take an hour or more, depending on the disk size and whether you've chosen the Thorough scan option. Your computer might be set up to run ScanDisk automatically if Windows 98 has been improperly shut down. If this is the case, when you next launch Windows 98 you might be asked if you want to run ScanDisk.

Disk Defragmenter

Now that you've corrected any errors on your disk, you can use Disk Defragmenter to improve the disk's performance so that programs start and files open more quickly. When you save a file, Windows 98 puts as much of the file as it can into the first available cluster. If the file won't fit into one cluster, Windows 98 locates the next available cluster and puts more of the file in it. Windows 98 attempts to place files in contiguous clusters whenever possible. The file is saved once Windows 98 has placed all the file data into clusters. In Figure 11-10, you have just saved two files to a new 3½-inch disk: Address and Recipes.

Figure 11-10	DISK WITH TWO FILES

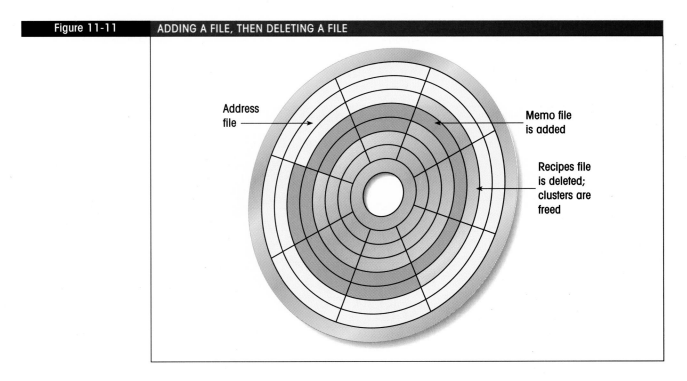

As you create and save new files, more clusters are used. If you delete a file or two, those clusters are freed. In Figure 11-11, you have saved a new file, Memo, and then deleted Recipes.

Figure 11-11	ADDING A FILE, THEN DELETING A FILE

The next time you save a file, Windows 98 searches for the first available cluster, which is now between two files. Figure 11-12 shows what happens when you save a fourth file, Schedule. It is saved to clusters that are not adjacent.

| Figure 11-12 | ADDING A NEW FILE IN FRAGMENTED CLUSTERS |

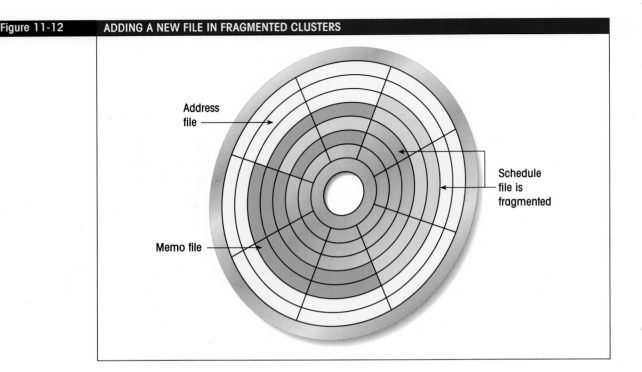

The more files you save and delete, the more scattered the clusters for a file become. A disk that contains whose clusters are not next to each other is said to be **fragmented**. The more fragmented the disk, the longer Windows 98 takes to retrieve the file, and the more likely you are to have problems with the file. Whenever a disk has been used for a long time, it's a good idea to defragment it. Defragmenting rearranges the files on the disk so they each occupy adjacent clusters. Figure 11-13 shows a fragmented disk. When a program tries to access a file on this disk, file retrieval takes longer than necessary because the program must locate clusters that aren't adjacent.

| Figure 11-13 | FRAGMENTED FILES |

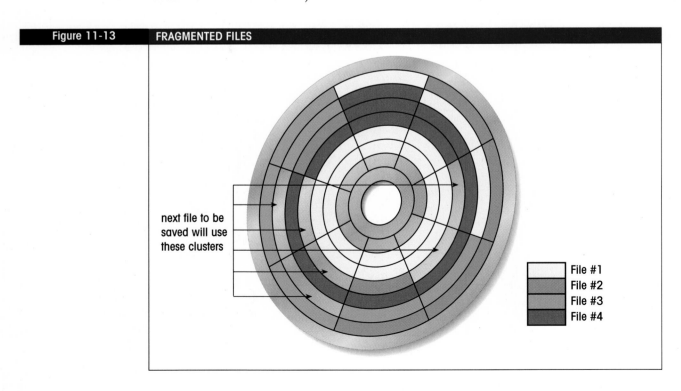

Before you begin defragmenting a disk, make sure your data is backed up. If your computer experiences a power loss while one of its disks is being defragmented, you could lose data.

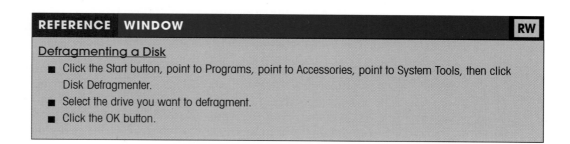

REFERENCE   WINDOW   RW

Defragmenting a Disk

- Click the Start button, point to Programs, point to Accessories, point to System Tools, then click Disk Defragmenter.
- Select the drive you want to defragment.
- Click the OK button.

You're ready to defragment your disk. Pete tells you that he can't guarantee that your disk needs defragmenting. It's possible that you'll go through the defragment procedure but Windows 98 won't have to make any changes because your disk is not fragmented. If this is the case with your disk, you might not be able to perform all the steps in this section.

To start Disk Defragmenter:

1. Close all open programs to prevent loss of data.

2. Click the **Start** button, point to **Programs**, point to **Accessories**, point to **System Tools**, and then click **Disk Defragmenter**.

3. In the Select Drive dialog box, click the drive list arrow, then click **Drive A.**

4. Click the **OK** button. As Disk Defragmenter defragments your Student Disk, a status bar shows the percentage of the disk that has been defragmented so far. See Figure 11-14.

| Figure 11-14 | DEFRAGMENTING DISK IN DRIVE A |

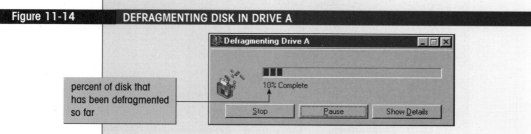

percent of disk that has been defragmented so far

5. When the defragmentation is complete and you are asked if you want to quit Disk Defragmenter, click the **Yes** button.

Scheduling Maintenance Tasks

Performing disk maintenance tasks regularly will help your computer run efficiently. You can schedule Windows 98 to take care of the tasks automatically using the Maintenance Wizard. The Maintenance Wizard schedules and then runs tasks according to your computer's clock (if your computer is on).

To set a maintenance schedule:

1. Click the **Start** button 🟦Start, point to **Programs**, point to **Accessories**, point to **System Tools**, and then click **Maintenance Wizard**. The Maintenance Wizard starts by giving you two options: Express or Custom. Express uses typical settings, while Custom allows you to set your own schedule.

   TROUBLE? If your computer has Maintenance Wizard tasks already set up, a dialog box appears asking whether you want to perform maintenance now or change your maintenance settings or schedule. Click the Change option button and then click OK. When you view Task Scheduler in the next set of steps, do not delete the Maintenance tasks as directed, because they were already running on your computer. It's possible your lab won't allow you to schedule tasks.

2. Click the **Express** option button if necessary, and then click **Next**. You now need to choose the Nights, Days, or Evenings option, whatever best fits your computing schedule. Choose a time when you are not likely to be at the computer so the maintenance procedures won't interfere with your computer time.

3. Click the **Nights** option button, and then click **Next**. The Maintenance Wizard informs you of the tasks it will perform. See Figure 11-15.

Figure 11-15	MAINTENANCE WIZARD SCHEDULED TASKS

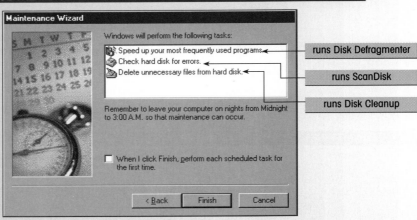

4. In the dialog box shown in Figure 11-15, make sure the **When I click Finish...** check box is not checked.

5. Click the **Finish** button. The Wizard closes. Windows 98 will run the appropriate maintenance procedures at the scheduled time.

You can manage your scheduled tasks using Task Scheduler, which displays all tasks scheduled to run on your computer. You can also use Task Scheduler to schedule new tasks, such as running a virus checker at a regularly scheduled time or connecting to the Internet to download e-mail or updated subscription information.

Pete suggests you open Task Scheduler to view the tasks you just scheduled. He then wants you to delete the tasks because the seminar computers don't need regularly scheduled maintenance tasks.

To delete tasks from Task Scheduler:

1. Click the **Start** button ![Start], point to **Programs**, point to **Accessories**, point to **System Tools**, and then click **Scheduled Tasks**.

2. The Scheduled Tasks window opens, displaying a list of tasks. Click **View**, and then click **Details** to view task details. See Figure 11-16.

| Figure 11-16 | TASKS SCHEDULED ON YOUR COMPUTER |

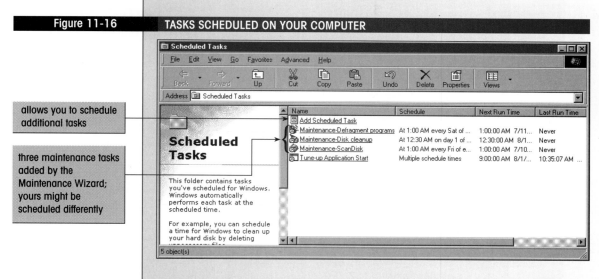

allows you to schedule additional tasks

three maintenance tasks added by the Maintenance Wizard; yours might be scheduled differently

3. If you added the three maintenance tasks in the previous set of steps, delete them from the Scheduled Tasks window by right-clicking them and then clicking **Delete**. If the TROUBLE in the previous set of steps applied to you, do not delete these tasks.

4. Close the Scheduled Tasks window.

Creating a Startup Disk

Even when you regularly perform maintenance tasks, problems can occur on a computer. If your computer's processes are damaged so that your computer no longer starts, you can boot your computer from a **startup disk**, also called a **boot disk**, which contains boot programs and diagnostic programs that help determine the problem and sometimes provide the solution.

When you boot your computer, Windows 98 checks first to see if there is a disk in your floppy drive. If you place a startup disk in your floppy drive, Windows 98 boots from that disk, which allows you to bypass the normal boot routine when it isn't functioning properly. If you mistakenly leave a nonstartup disk in the floppy drive when you shut down your computer, the next time you start it, Windows 98 will attempt to boot from that disk, and a message, "Invalid system disk," will warn you that Windows 98 can't boot from the disk.

To create a startup disk, you need a 3½-inch disk with at least 1.2 MB capacity and the Windows 98 installation CD-ROM. Pete emphasizes that you should always have a startup disk on hand for each computer you own, because startup problems can occur at any time. He explains, however, that you won't be able to create a startup disk from the seminar computers, so you will need to cancel the procedure once you've seen how it works.

To view the Startup Disk accessory:

1. Click the **Start** button ![Start], point to **Settings**, and then click **Control Panel**.

2. Open **Add/Remove Programs**, and then click the **Startup Disk** tab. See Figure 11-17.

Figure 11-17	CREATING A STARTUP DISK

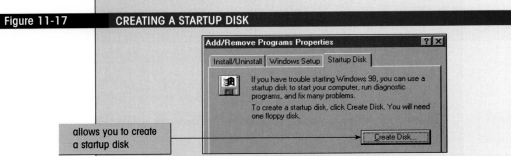

allows you to create a startup disk

3. Click the **Cancel** button, and then close the Control Panel. Or, if you are using your own computer and you don't yet have a Startup Disk, insert a blank disk in the appropriate drive, click the Create Disk button, and follow the directions that appear on the screen. When the procedure is finished, remove the disk and write "(*Computer Name*) Startup Disk" and the date on the disk label, and store it in a safe place.

4. Close all open windows.

You have now performed and scheduled the necessary routine disk maintenance procedures, and you are ready to back up your files. If you are continuing immediately to Session 11.2 or are working on your own computer, leave the Seminar folder you created on the hard disk. You'll work with it in Session 11.2. If you are working in a lab and are not continuing immediately to Session 11.2, you should delete the Seminar folder now, but you'll need to recreate it as directed in Session 11.2.

QUICK CHECK

1. Why are the techniques you are learning in this tutorial especially important for hard disks?

2. A destructive program that runs on your computer to disrupt its operations is called a _____.

3. Why should you regularly defragment your disks?

4. What is a cluster?

5. What is the purpose of the file allocation table?

6. True or False: Windows 98 always stores a file in adjacent clusters.

7. How does a disk become fragmented?

<table>
<tr><td>**SESSION**
11.2</td><td>In this session, you'll learn how to use Backup to protect your data. You'll create and save a "backup job" that specifies what files you want to back up. Next you'll create the "backup" that stores a copy of the files you want to back up. Finally, you'll restore a file from a backup. *For this session you will need a blank 3½-inch disk to use as a backup disk, and you will need access to the folder you created on the hard disk in Session 11.1.*</td></tr>
</table>

Computer **Backups**

Data Backup

No one is safe from computer problems that result in data loss. A power surge, power loss, a failed section of a hard disk, a computer virus—these problems can strike at any time. Rather than risk disaster, you should make copies of your important files regularly. You have already learned how to copy data from one 3½-inch disk to another and how to copy a file from one disk to another. Making a copy of a disk or a file is one way to protect data. Copying a disk or a file is your only choice when you store your data on a 3½-inch disk, as is usually the case in a computer lab, where you usually don't have access to a hard disk.

To protect data on a hard drive, however, you will almost certainly want to use a backup program instead of a copy or disk-copy procedure. A **backup program** copies and then automatically compresses files and folders from a hard disk into a single file. The backup program stores this file on a **backup medium** such as a 3½-inch disk, tape cartridge, Zip drive, or writeable compact disk. Pete explains that such a software program, called **Backup**, comes with Windows 98.

When you back up a set of files with the Windows 98 Backup program, you go through the following steps.

1. You designate the folders and files you want to back up.

2. Backup creates a **backup job**, which lists the files you want to back up and tells your computer how, when, and where to perform the backup.

3. Backup copies the files and folders listed in the backup job, compresses them, and stores them in a single file called a **backup**.

4. Backup stores the backup on the backup medium you specify.

Suppose you store all of your important files in three folders on drive C, named Projects, Accounts, and Clients. Figure 11-18 shows how Backup backs up the files in these folders.

Figure 11-18   BACKING UP DATA

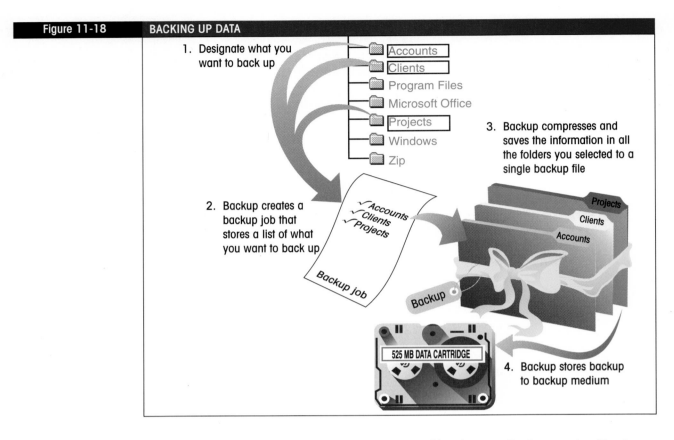

This process is different from simply copying files, because Backup copies files into a single, compressed file, whereas a copy simply duplicates the files. Figure 11-19 points out the differences between copying and backing up, showing why backing up files is a better data-protection method than simply copying files.

Figure 11-19   COPYING VS. BACKING UP FILES

COPY	BACKUP
A copy of a file occupies the same amount of space as the original file. For this reason, making a copy of all the files on a hard disk is impractical.	Because it is compressed, a backup of a file is much smaller than the original file, depending on the file type.
It would take a lot of time and effort to copy all the files on a hard disk to 3½-inch disks—not least because of the time it would take to swap disks in and out of the floppy drive. Copying 800 MB of data would require more than 560 3½-inch disks.	Backups are much quicker. If you have a tape drive, you can back up 800 MB of data to a single tape in a matter of minutes.
Because you can't split a large file over two 3½-inch disks, you must manually break up the file into smaller parts and then copy them to separate 3½-inch disks.	Backup is designed to split files across disks.
Every time you want to back up your data, you must either copy all the files on your disk again or you must painstakingly locate and then copy only those files that have changed.	Backup can automatically detect and back up only those files that have changed since your last backup.
If you do lose data because of a computer failure, there is no easy way to locate a file you need.	The Backup software keeps track of the files you have backed up, and it's very easy to find and recover a file.

Placing Files on the Hard Disk to Back Up

Pete explains that when you are working in a lab, as you are at the seminar, you normally save your data on a 3½-inch disk. To protect data on a 3½-inch disk, you simply copy the disk from My Computer or Windows Explorer, because the Backup accessory is designed to back up the contents of a hard drive (or several hard drives). Because Pete wants you to learn how to perform a real backup, you must first place some data on the hard disk, which you can then back up onto the blank disk you brought to the lab.

Although in this seminar you will simulate backing up files to a 3½-inch disk, in reality using 3½-inch disks as your backup medium is impractical if you have more than just a few files to back up. A more practical solution, if you can afford it, is to invest in a drive such as a tape, Zip, or CD writeable drive that lets you back up your data to larger storage devices.

You will place two new files in the Seminar folder you created in Session 11.1. You will then back up the files in the Seminar folder to your blank disk, which you will name "Backup Disk."

To create new files in the Seminar folder:

1. Open **Windows Explorer**, and then locate and open the Seminar folder on drive C. The Seminar folder should still contain the file Test1 that you created in Session 11.1.

TROUBLE? If the Seminar folder has been deleted, create it again on drive C, and create a new text document named Test1 in the Seminar folder.

TROUBLE? If you are in a computer lab and are not permitted to save files to your computer's hard disk, close Windows Explorer, skip the rest of the steps in this section, and ask your instructor which folder on what drive you should use to back up.

2. With the Seminar folder open, click **File**, point to **New**, and then click **Text Document**. Type **Test2**, then open **Test2** in Notepad, type your name, close Notepad, and save changes.

TROUBLE? If your computer is showing file extensions, type Test2.txt as the filename. Include the file extension for any other files your create.

3. Repeat Step 3, this time creating a text document named **Test3**.

4. Close Windows Explorer.

Backup Strategies

You start the backup process by designating which files and folders you want to back up. In this simulation, the designation is easy: you just tell your backup program to use the Seminar folder. However, Pete explains that in reality, choosing which files you want to back up is a little more complicated because it is part of a larger backup strategy.

A **backup strategy** is a plan you develop to ensure that you have a backup of all the files on your computer in their most current version. The foundation of a backup strategy is a **full backup**, a backup of all the files on your computer. A full backup can contain the Windows 98 program, all your system files, all your program files, and all the data files that existed on the day you performed the backup. Some people don't include their operating system or other software programs in a full backup because they feel they can simply reinstall the software from the original disks. Once you have a full backup, you can perform **partial backups** that back up only the files that have changed since the last time you backed up your data. There are two kinds of partial backups: differential and incremental. In a **differential backup**, the backup program searches for and backs up only those files that have changed since the last full backup. In an **incremental backup**, the backup program searches for and backs up only those files that have changed since the last backup, regardless of whether it was a full or partial backup. Figure 11-20 helps you understand the difference.

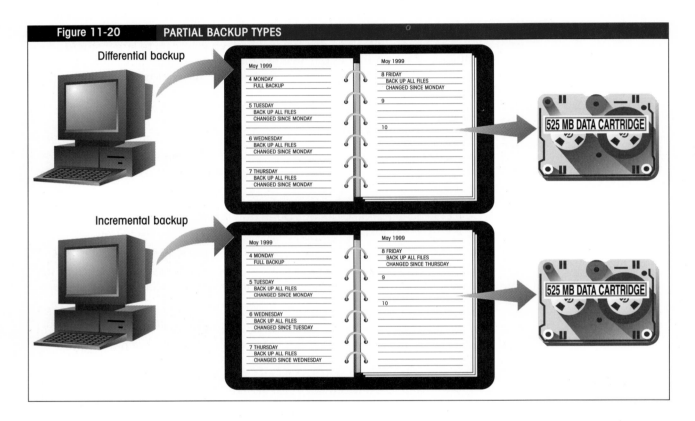

Figure 11-20   PARTIAL BACKUP TYPES

Incremental backups are generally faster and take less space, but restoring from an incremental backup can be slow. Differential backups, on the other hand, are generally slower and require more space, but restoring is quicker.

You might think that to be on the safe side, you should simply perform a full backup every time you back up your data. However, a full backup can take several hours, depending on how many hard disks you have and how big they are. For this reason, most users perform a full backup only once a week or once a month, depending on how substantially their files change from day to day. Many of your files don't change at all over the course of weeks or months. Your program files, for example, change only when you install a new version of software. Some users choose not to back up program files because those files are preserved on the original installation disks.

How often should you perform full and partial backups? It's best to develop a backup strategy based on a schedule. For the user in Figure 11-20, a backup strategy begins with a full backup at the beginning of the week. Then this user performs a partial backup on a daily basis. Perhaps the last thing he or she does before leaving the computer for the evening is run the backup software to back up any files changed during the day.

Some users might want to perform more frequent backups—especially those who can't afford to lose even a few hours' work. They might perform a partial backup more than once a day—at lunch time, after work, and then at midnight, for example. You don't want to overdo it, however. Even a partial backup can slow your productivity, because, even if the backup program is running in the background, it uses system resources. Only you can decide how many times to run a backup. If you can structure it so that your computer runs backups while you are busy doing something else, that's best. The important thing is that you back up your data often enough so that if your computer fails, your backup will contain enough of your data that it wouldn't take you too long to reconstruct the rest.

Backing Up Files in a Folder

In this simulation, you are not going to perform a full backup. Instead, you are going to perform a backup of only one folder: the Seminar folder. There are circumstances in which you might want to back up only the contents of one or several folders. For example, suppose you habitually store all the files you work with on a daily basis in the Seminar folder or the My Documents folder. You might want to back up just that folder. It will speed up the daily backup process considerably if Backup doesn't have to search your entire computer for changed files. Users who perform more than one backup a day might especially profit from searching just a few folders.

Pete says you're ready to start Backup.

To start Backup:

1. Click the **Start** button, point to **Programs**, point to **Accessories**, point to **System Tools**, and then click **Backup**. The Microsoft Backup window opens, shown in Figure 11-21.

   TROUBLE? If a message appears warning you that there is no backup device (other than the floppy drive), click No to acknowledge the message and continue with the steps. This message appears the first time you start Backup, if you don't have a backup device such as a tape or optical drive installed.

   TROUBLE? If Backup does not appear as an option on the menu, then you cannot complete this session until Backup is installed. Check with your instructor or technical support person for directions. If you are using your own computer, insert the installation CD-ROM. The Windows 98 CD-ROM window might open automatically, but if necessary, open Control Panel. Click Add/Remove Programs (or Add/Remove Software), either from the Windows 98 CD-ROM window or from Control Panel. Click the Windows Setup tab, then locate and click System Tools (make sure you don't click the System Tools check box). Click Details, check Backup, and then click OK twice. Restart your computer when directed, then close any open windows and repeat Step 1.

Figure 11-21	MICROSOFT BACKUP WINDOW

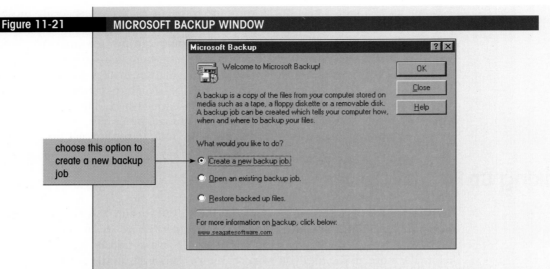

choose this option to create a new backup job

2. If necessary, click the **Create a new backup job** option button, and then click the **OK** button. The Backup Wizard starts, letting you choose whether you want to back up all the files and folders on your local drives or selected files.

3. Click the **Back up selected files, folders and drives** option button, and then click **Next**. The next Backup Wizard dialog box allows you to choose the items you want to back up.

Selecting Files and Folders to Back Up

To select the files or folders you want to back up, you navigate a window similar to Windows Explorer. To include a folder in the backup job, you click the empty box ☐ next to the folder, to place a check mark in it. For example, suppose you had a folder named Contracts that you wanted to back up. You would display the folder in the Folders list and then click its box. See Figure 11-22.

Figure 11-22	SELECTING FILES AND FOLDERS TO BACK UP

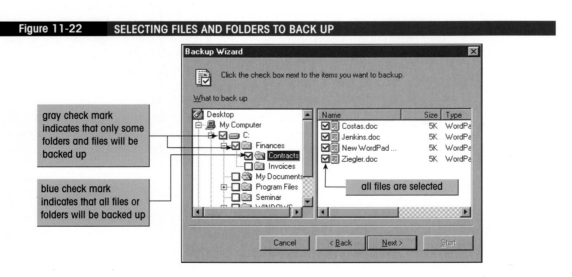

gray check mark indicates that only some folders and files will be backed up

blue check mark indicates that all files or folders will be backed up

all files are selected

Notice that the box next to the Contracts folder is white, whereas the box next to the Finances folder, which contains the Taxes folder, is gray. A blue check mark ☑ indicates that the entire folder or file will be backed up. A gray check mark ☑ indicates that only part of the contents of that folder or drive will be backed up. If you want to include only selected files in a folder, you click the folder's icon in the Folders list and then click the empty boxes just for those files.

You want to select the Seminar folder on drive C to back up.

To select the Seminar folder:

1. Click the **plus** box ⊞ next to the drive C icon 🖾 to display the folders on drive C, and then click the **Seminar** folder icon 🖾 .

2. Click the empty box to the left of the Seminar folder. A blue check mark appears in the box. The Contents list in the right window shows all the files in the Seminar folder, with their check boxes selected with blue check marks. See Figure 11-23.

| Figure 11-23 | SELECTING THE SEMINAR FOLDER FOR BACKING UP |

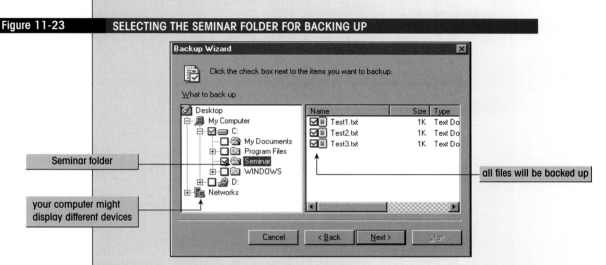

3. Click the **Next** button. Now you need to choose whether to back up all selected files or new and changed files.

4. Click the **New and changed files** option button, and then click the **Next** button. This option will back up all files the first time, and then when you run this backup job again, it will back up only new and changed files in the Seminar folder.

By default, the New and changed files option performs a differential backup, but you can change the backup to incremental from the Backup window. You click the Options button, click the Type tab, choose Incremental backup type, and then click the OK button.

Selecting a Backup Device

Backup displays the next step in the process: selecting the **backup device**, the drive that contains the backup medium. If your computer contains a tape or other backup drive, Backup automatically detects it and displays it in the list box. In this simulation, however, you will store your backup files on your blank disk. Do not use your Student Disk because there might not be enough space.

To select your floppy drive as the destination for the backup and then check your backup:

1. Write **Backup Disk** on the label of your blank 3½-inch disk and insert it into the appropriate drive.

2. Click the **Where to back up** list arrow, if necessary click **File**, and then click the folder button 🖳 . See Figure 11-24.

Figure 11-24	SELECTING A BACKUP DESTINATION

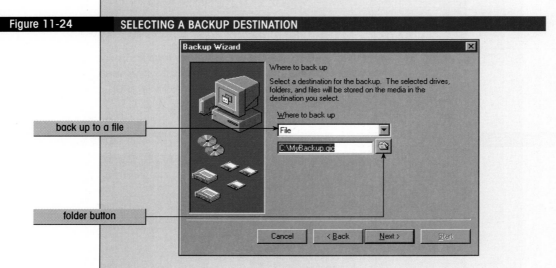

back up to a file

folder button

3. In the Where to back up dialog box, click the **Look in** list arrow, and then click the floppy disk drive containing your backup disk.

4. Make sure the File name box says MyBackup; if it doesn't, type **MyBackup** in the File name box.

5. Click **Open**. Backup will create a backup file named MyBackup.qic on the drive you specified. Click **Next**. Now you can choose whether to compare files and whether to compress data.

6. Make sure both the **Compare** and **Compress** check boxes are selected, and then click **Next**.

Creating a Backup Job

Once you have selected the folders and files you want to back up, designated a backup medium, and checked your backup settings, you can save those backup specifications in a backup job. The backup job not only remembers which files and folders you want to back up, it also stores the settings you've chosen. In the future if you want to back up the Seminar folder again, you can simply open this backup job in the first Backup Wizard window, without having to go through the entire Backup Wizard.

To save your choices to a backup job:

1. Type **Test Backup**. See Figure 11-25.

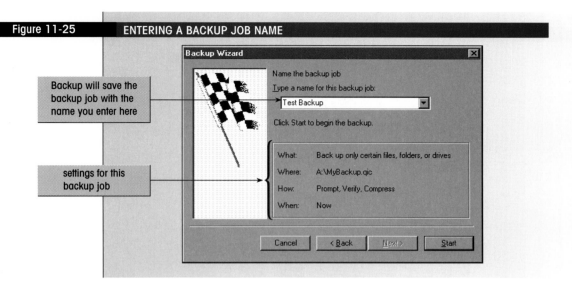

Figure 11-25   ENTERING A BACKUP JOB NAME

Backup will save the backup job with the name you enter here

settings for this backup job

Backup Wizard

Name the backup job

Type a name for this backup job:

Test Backup

Click Start to begin the backup.

What: Back up only certain files, folders, or drives
Where: A:\MyBackup.qic
How: Prompt, Verify, Compress
When: Now

Cancel   < Back   Next >   Start

Backup will store the Test Backup backup job on your hard drive. Remember that you are saving the backup to your Student Disk, but the backup job, the file that specifies the backup settings, is saved on the hard drive.

Creating the Backup

You have now created the backup job; all you need to do is start the backup. When you click Start, Backup will locate the files you've selected, copy them, and compress them into a single compressed file—Test Backup.qic. When Backup is finished, it tells you how many files it backed up and how much space the backup requires.

To back up your selected files:

1. Click **Start** to begin the backup job. The Backup Progress – Test Backup dialog box displays the status of the backup.

   TROUBLE? If a message appears warning you that Test Backup already exists, type your name and then the word "Backup," for example: Kateri Klingele Backup. Then when you see "Test Backup" in the rest of this tutorial, substitute the name you typed.

2. Click the **OK** button when the message "Operation completed" appears. Backup displays a summary of the backup. See Figure 11-26.

Figure 11-26   BACKUP SUMMARY

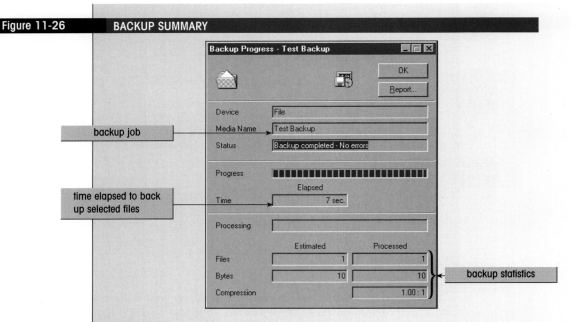

3. Click the **OK** button to return to the Microsoft Backup window, and then click the **Close** button ☒ to close Backup. Your disk now contains a backup of the files in the Seminar folder. If you ever have computer problems, you can rest assured that your data is safe.

Once you have the backup, what should you do with it? Or more appropriately, what should you not do with it? You should not store it near your computer. A fire that destroys your computer will probably destroy your backup as well. If a thief wants your data, it's quicker to steal your backups than your computer. Many computer owners rent safe deposit boxes at banks and store their backups there. Business owners sometimes store their backups off-site at their own homes. Fire is not likely to strike in two locations at once. Backup storage is part of your overall backup strategy. You need to decide how often you will put your backups into storage. Many users maintain two backup tapes: They store the backups for a single week on one tape, then at the end of the week they put the tape into storage. They use the other tape for the following week, and then at the end of the week they swap the tapes.

Restoring Files

Pete tells the class to imagine that disaster has just struck. Your hard disk has failed, and your computer maintenance person believes data recovery is hopeless—you're going to have to reformat your hard disk. "I hope," says your maintenance person, "you made a backup." If you did, then your problem is solved. You simply take the backup out of storage and run the Restore procedure on the backup containing the files you lost.

Pete says that to simulate a file restoration, you'll first delete the entire Seminar folder from your computer's hard disk. In a real-life situation, these files might have been ruined in a power failure, by a disk defect, by a virus, or by some other misfortune.

To delete the Seminar folder from the hard drive:

1. Open **Windows Explorer**, then locate and right-click the Seminar folder icon on drive C.

2. Click **Delete**.

3. Click the **Yes** button if you are prompted to confirm that you want to delete the folder.

4. Close Windows Explorer.

Pete points out that at this point you could recover the folder and its contents from the Recycle Bin, but he asks you to imagine that you emptied the Recycle Bin after deleting the Seminar folder, to free up disk space.

You are ready to use Backup to restore the Seminar folder to your hard disk. You must first identify the backup that contains the Seminar folder. In this simulation, there will be only one backup on your disk: the Seminar folder Backup you created earlier. In real life, there could be multiple backups on your backup disk—especially if you run backup jobs regularly. How you restore data depends on what kind of loss you suffered. If you lost only a single file, you can choose the backup that you made after you changed the file. If the file or folder you want to restore is not in that backup, that means you haven't worked with it since the last backup, in which case you'll have to check another backup. If you have lost all the data on your disk, how you recover it depends on what kind of partial backups you use. If you use incremental backups, you will need to use all the backups you've created since your most recent full backup. You would start by restoring the full backup, and then restoring each backup, one at a time, beginning with the oldest. If you use differential backups, you restore the full backup and then the most recent differential backup.

You are ready to restore the Seminar folder.

To select the backup and check the restore settings:

1. Click the **Start** button, point to **Programs**, point to **Accessories**, point to **System Tools**, and then click **Backup**.

2. Click the **Restore backed up files** option button, and then click **OK**.

3. If necessary, click the **Restore from** list arrow, and then click **File**. The box displays A:\MyBackup.qic.

   TROUBLE? If the box doesn't display the path for your backup, click the folder button, 🗁 then locate and select the drive containing your Backup Disk, and click Open.

4. Click **Next**, then in the Select Backup Sets dialog box, make sure **Test Backup** is selected. See Figure 11-27.

| Figure 11-27 | SELECTING THE BACKUP JOB |

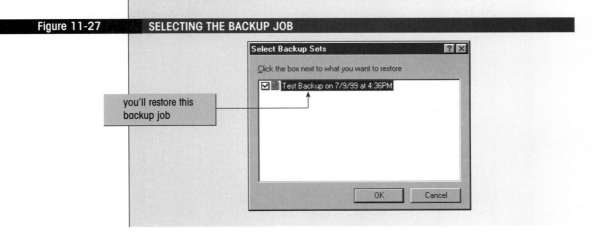

you'll restore this backup job

5. Click the **OK** button.

6. In the Restore Wizard dialog box, click the **plus** box  next to drive C, and then click the empty box ☐ next to the Seminar folder icon 📁 . This tells Backup which folder to restore.

7. Click the **Next** button, make sure the **Where to restore** list box displays Original Location, and then click **Next**. This tells Backup to restore the Seminar folder to its original location. You could select Alternate Location to restore your files to a different location.

8. Now you specify what you want Backup to do if it encounters files with the same name in the location you specified; click the **Do not replace the file on my computer** option button (to prevent writing over important files), and then click the **Start** button.

9. Click the **OK** button when informed that the Test Backup backup job must be available. Backup restores the folder and informs you when the operation is complete.

10. Click the **OK** button to acknowledge the message, then click the **OK** button again to close the Restore Progress dialog box. Finally, click the **Close** button ☒ to close the Backup window.

Now you should check whether the Seminar folder was restored successfully to your hard drive.

To verify that the Seminar folder has been restored:

1. Open **Windows Explorer**, and then locate and open the Seminar folder.

2. Click **View** and then click **Refresh**, then verify that the folder and files have been successfully restored.

3. Delete the Seminar folder to return the hard drive to its original state, and then close Windows Explorer.

Pete ends the seminar by telling you that if you're lucky, you'll never have to use Restore to recover lost data. Then he tells you that Backup is probably one of the most important topics he's covered in the seminar. Practically everyone who has been around computers for very long has a data-loss story to tell. Many computer owners who now have backup drives, such as tape drives or optical disc drives, learned the hard way how important it is to protect data. If you are a computer owner, put a backup strategy planning session at the top of your list, and then stick to your strategy scrupulously. You won't be sorry.

QUICK CHECK

1. How does copying a disk differ from backing up a disk?

2. What is the difference between a backup job and a backup?

3. What is a partial backup? Identify and differentiate between two kinds of partial backups.

4. Why would you use a partial backup rather than perform a full backup?

5. When you select the folders and files to back up, Backup uses colored check marks to indicate which files and folders will be backed up. If a folder has a blue check mark in front of it, will the entire folder be backed up?

TUTORIAL ASSIGNMENTS

1. **Cleaning up a Hard Disk** Upon returning from the seminar to Arboretum Energy, you decide to apply some of the disk maintenance procedures you learned. You decide to use the Disk Cleanup accessory to explore the different types of files that are likely to be cluttering your disks.

   a. First start the Disk Cleanup accessory and select your Student Disk (the same disk you used at the beginning of this tutorial). What check box options appeared in the cleanup list? Why are there fewer than in the list in Figure 11-2?

   b. Close and then restart Disk Cleanup, and this time select drive C. What appears in the cleanup list when you select drive C? Are there more or fewer options than those listed in Figure 11-2? If there are any differences, can you account for them?

   c. Select all the check boxes available for drive C, and record the amount of disk space you could save by running the Disk Cleanup accessory.

   d. If you are using a lab computer, close Disk Cleanup without cleaning up any disks. If you are using your own computer, proceed with the Disk Cleanup procedure to clean up your own hard disk.

2. **Scanning a Floppy Disk** You asked one of your employees to take over disk maintenance tasks at Arboretum Energy, and she tells you one of the backup disks is acting strangely. You decide to scan the disk. Place the Backup Disk you used in Session 11.2 into drive A, then scan this disk. Make sure you perform a Thorough scan and that ScanDisk is set to fix errors automatically. When the scan is complete, paste an image of the ScanDisk Results dialog box into WordPad (using the Print Screen button). In the WordPad document, type your name, and then type a paragraph that interprets the results reported in the ScanDisk Results dialog box. Submit the WordPad document to your instructor.

Explore

3. **Scanning a Hard Disk** If you have your own computer or you have permission from your computer lab's staff to scan a hard drive, you can do this tutorial assignment. Otherwise, ask your instructor about an alternative. Start ScanDisk, then click drive C. Make sure you perform a Thorough scan and that ScanDisk is set to fix errors automatically. Once you start the scan, be prepared to wait a few minutes. Print out the ScanDisk Results dialog box (make sure you include your name on the printout). Write a paragraph on the printout that interprets the results reported in the ScanDisk Results dialog box.

Explore

4. **Viewing the ScanDisk Log File** When you scan a disk, you can have Windows 98 automatically maintain a log file that keeps track of the errors ScanDisk identifies and fixes. This log can be a useful way to keep a history of problems you've had with a disk. Windows 98 automatically saves the log file with the name Scandisk.log in the root directory of drive C.

   a. Place a 3½-inch disk in drive A. Try to use a disk that has not been scanned recently and that has been used frequently. Use your Student Disk if you have no other disk, but recognize that you aren't likely to find any errors because you just scanned this disk in Session 11.1.

   b. Start ScanDisk, specify drive A, and then click the Advanced button. Make sure the Append to log option button is selected, then click the OK button.

   c. Click the Start button.

   d. When the scan is complete, close all open dialog boxes, then start Notepad. Click File, then click Open. Select drive C, then select All files in the Files of type box. Click Scandisk, then click Open.

   e. If a number of scans have taken place on your computer, the log could be quite long. Scroll to the very end of the log file to find the report on your most recent scan.

   f. You should print the contents of this file to turn it in to your instructor, but if the log file is quite long, don't print all of it. If it's longer than a few pages, use your data transfer skills to copy just the results from the most recent scan (at the bottom of the log) into a new Notepad file, and then print that file. You don't have to save the file.

Explore

5. **Defragmenting a Disk** When you defragmented your Student Disk in Session 11.1, it's possible your disk was not badly fragmented. This tutorial assignment gives you a chance to fragment a disk on purpose so that you can then watch Disk Defragmenter reorder the file clusters. The Show Details button appears during the defragmentation process, and you can click this button to watch Disk Defragmenter reorder the clusters.

   a. Make a copy of your Student Disk, and label this disk Fragmented Disk.

   b. Copy files from other disks onto your Fragmented Disk until you have filled the disk completely. Use any files you want—files from a hard disk, files from your Backup Disk, or files from other 3½-inch disks. Once you get an error message that tells you the disk is full, delete a batch of files that were saved to the disk at different times. Then copy another batch of files to the disk until it is again full. Then delete another batch of files saved at different times. Fill the disk one last time.

Explore

   c. Run Disk Defragmenter on your Fragmented Disk, and click the Show Details button as soon as the defragmentation process begins. Continue with the next step, Part d, immediately— while the defragmentation process is going on.

   d. Print an image of the details window that shows the reorganization of the clusters. If the defragmentation process goes so quickly that you can't get an image, just print what you see when the process is complete.

Explore

6. **Scheduling Tasks** You learned at the seminar how to schedule maintenance tasks using the Maintenance Wizard. You'd like to schedule a virus checker on your Arboretum Energy computer. You can use the Task Scheduler accessory to schedule additional tasks. If you have access to a computer with a virus checker, schedule the virus checker so it runs whenever you start your computer. If you don't have a virus checker, choose a different program to schedule.

   a. Open the Scheduled Tasks window, click the Add Scheduled Task button, and then click Next. A list of programs appears. Locate the virus checker program in the Application list, then click Next. If the program doesn't appear in the Application list, click the Browse button and then locate and select the virus checker's executable file. Click Open, and then click Next.
   b. Click the When my computer starts option button, and then click Next.
   c. Make sure the Open advanced properties... check box is not checked, and then click Finish. The task appears in your task scheduler.
   d. Delete the task from the Scheduled Tasks window to return your list of scheduled tasks to its original state.

7. **Performing a Backup** You would like to back up some of the Arboretum Energy files on your hard disk to your Backup Disk. You'll need to create a folder on your hard disk, create some files in the folder, and then back them up.

   a. Open Windows Explorer and create a folder named Arboretum on your hard drive. Create one new Bitmap Image file named Lightbulb and two new Text Document files named Lighting Conservation and Heating Conservation. You don't need to enter any data in these files.
   b. Place your backup disk in the appropriate drive. Start Backup and create a new backup job to back up selected files. Select the Arboretum folder you just created, and choose the New and changed files option.
   c. Select your backup disk as the backup device. Name the backup "Arboretum," and name the backup job "Arboretum Backup Job."
   d. In Windows Explorer, display the contents of your backup disk, showing the Arboretum.qic backup file you just created, and then print the screen (include your name).
   e. Delete the Arboretum folder from your hard disk, and then use the Backup accessory to restore the folder.

PROJECTS

Explore

1. If you have your own computer and it has a tape drive, you can do this project. Otherwise, just read this assignment so you can see how you would back up an entire system. Backing up your full system is an important part of a comprehensive backup strategy, but it can take an hour or more, depending on the speed of your backup drive and the size of your hard disk or disks.

   a. Start Backup and choose the Create a new backup job option.
   b. Choose the Back up My Computer option and the New and changed files option.
   c. When you choose the backup device, make sure you select the backup device on your computer, not a file on a 3½-inch disk.
   d. Name the backup job "My Computer backup."
   e. Follow the prompts that appear on the screen. Be prepared to wait an hour or more for the backup to finish. Print an image of the Backup summary dialog box before you close Backup, and then hand this printout in to your instructor.

2. Ask your instructor for the names of businesses whose systems managers might take a minute with you on the phone to be interviewed. You could also ask your employer. You might ask the systems managers the following questions:

   a. What training did you receive to get this job?
   b. How many computers do you manage? Are they on a network?
   c. What backup media do you use?
   d. How often do you back up the entire system?
   e. How often do you perform partial backups?
   f. Do you perform incremental or differential backups? Explain why you chose to perform this type of partial backup.
   g. Are individual employees responsible for their own backups?
   h. If an employee has a problem with a computer, who is expected to fix the problem?

3. You work at Hal's Food Warehouse in inventory management. You are responsible for backing up the computer system. You performed a full backup on Friday, and then on Monday you worked with a database file named Orders. You performed an incremental backup on Monday evening. On Tuesday you worked with the Orders file again, and on Tuesday evening you performed an incremental backup. When you attempt to open the Orders file Wednesday morning, you receive an error message that says the file cannot be found. How would you restore the file?

4. If you have your own computer, do you use a disk maintenance strategy? If not, now's your chance to implement one. Ask yourself the following questions, and then write a disk maintenance strategy and schedule:

   a. How often do I install different software on my computer?
   b. How often do I work with important files, and how much are they worth to me?
   c. What would I lose if the hard disk drive failed?

5. Research the different types of backup media available, such as tape drives, CD write-able drives, and Zip drives. You can use the Internet or computing trade magazines as sources. Make a chart with four columns: backup medium name (such as tape drive), description of the backup medium (describe tape drives), brand names, and price. (Include both the price of the drive and the disks the drive uses, if applicable.) Then write a paragraph below the chart describing which device you would purchase for your own computer, and why.

LAB ASSIGNMENTS

Defragmentation and Disk Operations

Defragmentation and Disk Operations   In this Lab, you will format a simulated disk, save files, delete files, and undelete files to see how the computer updates the FAT. You will also find out how the files on your disk become fragmented and what a defragmentation utility does to reorganize the clusters on your disk. See the Read This Before You Begin page for instructions on installing and starting the lab.

1. Click the Steps button to learn how the computer updates the FAT when you format a disk and save, delete, and undelete files. As you proceed through the Steps, answer all of the Quick Check questions that appear. After you complete the Steps, you will see a Quick Check Summary Report. Follow the instructions on the screen to print this report.

2. Click the Explore button. Click the Format button to format the simulated disk. Try to save files 1, 2, 3, 4, and 6. Do they all fit on the disk?

3. In Explore, format the simulated disk. Try to save all the files on the disk. What happens?

4. In Explore, format the simulated disk. Save FILE-3, FILE-4, and FILE-6. Next, delete FILE-6. Now, save FILE-5. Try to undelete FILE-6. What happens, and why?

5. In Explore, format the simulated disk. Save and erase files until the files become fragmented. Draw a picture of the disk to show the fragmented files. Indicate which files are in each cluster by using color, crosshatching, or labels. List which files in your drawing are fragmented. Finally, defragment the disk and draw a new picture showing the unfragmented files.

Data Backup

Data Backup   The Data Backup Lab gives you an opportunity to make tape backups on a simulated computer system. Periodically, the hard disk on the simulated computer will fail, which gives you a chance to assess the convenience and efficiency of different backup procedures. See the Read This Before You Begin page for instructions on installing and starting the lab.

1. Click the Steps button to learn how to use the simulation. As you work through the Steps, answer all of the Quick Check questions that appear. After you complete the Steps, you will see a Summary Report of your Quick Check answers. Follow the directions on the screen to print this report.

2. Click the Explore button. Create a full backup every Friday using only Tape 1. At some point in the simulation, an event will cause data loss on the simulated computer system. Use the simulation to restore as much data as you can. After you restore the data, print the Backup Audit Report.

3. In Explore, create a full backup every Friday on Tape 1, and a differential backup every Wednesday on Tape 2. At some point in the simulation, an event will cause data loss on the simulated computer system. Use the simulation to restore as much data as you can. Print the Backup Audit Report.

4. In Explore, create a full backup on Tape 1 every Monday. Make incremental backups on Tapes 2, 3, 4, and 5 each day for the rest of the week. Continue this cycle, reusing the same tapes each week. At some point in the simulation, an event will cause data loss on the simulated computer system. Use the simulation, to restore as much data as you can. Print the Backup Audit Report.

5. Photocopy a calendar for next month. On the calendar, indicate your best plan for backing up data. In Explore, implement your plan. Print out the Backup Audit Report. Write a paragraph or two discussing the effectiveness of your plan.

QUICK | CHECK ANSWERS

Session 11.1

1. They store more permanent data and are expensive to replace.

2. Virus

3. To prevent files from being stored inefficiently on the disk

4. One or more sectors of storage space—the minimum amount of space that an operating system reserves when saving the contents of a file to a disk

5. The FAT keeps track of the clusters on a disk and the status of each cluster.

6. False

7. A disk becomes fragmented when it contains files whose clusters are not next to each other.

Session 11.2

1. Copying a disk duplicates the disk contents, whereas backing up a disk compresses the files on the disk into a single, smaller file.

2. A backup job contains the list of files and folders you are backing up and the settings you are using; the backup itself is the compressed file that contains the data you backed up.

3. A partial backup is a backup of files that have changed since your last backup. An incremental backup backs up the files since the last backup, regardless of whether it was full or partial. A differential backup backs up the files since the last full backup.

4. It takes less time.

5. Yes.

CONNECTING COMPUTERS OVER A PHONE LINE

Windows 98 Dial-Up Accessories

Windows 98 makes communicating over computers easier than ever, because it provides accessories that allow you to connect your own computers to other computers and to the Internet. If you are using a computer on a university or institutional network, you are probably already connected to the Internet, and you can skip this appendix. This appendix is useful for people who are not connected to the Internet but who have their own computer, access to a phone line, and a modem.

Computers at universities or large companies are likely to be connected to the Internet via expensive, high-speed wiring that transmits data very quickly. Home computer owners, however, usually can't afford to run similar cables and wires to their homes, and instead rely on phone lines that are already in place, as shown in Figure A-1.

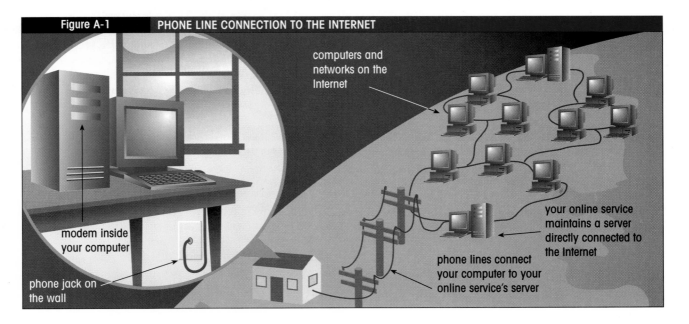

Figure A-1 PHONE LINE CONNECTION TO THE INTERNET

computers and networks on the Internet

modem inside your computer

phone jack on the wall

your online service maintains a server directly connected to the Internet

phone lines connect your computer to your online service's server

When a modem uses an ordinary voice phone line, which uses analog signals, it converts the modem's digital signals to analog, as shown in Figure A-2.

Figure A-2	DATA TRAVELING OVER A PHONE LINE

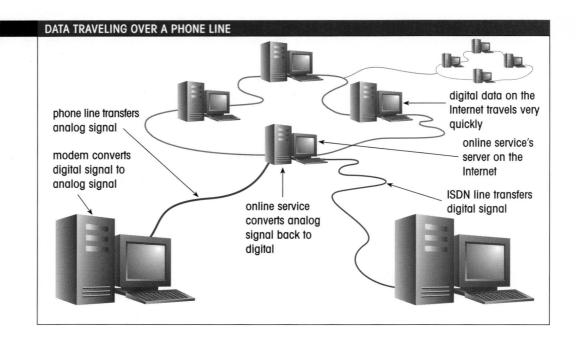

The receiving computer converts the analog signal back to digital. Data usually travels much more slowly over phone wires than over the networking infrastructure that makes up the Internet, and if there are any problems with the phone connection, data can be lost. But regular phone lines are often the only practical choice for homes and small businesses. In some areas, **ISDN lines**, wires that provide a completely digital path from one computer to another, are dropping in price to the point that some small businesses and homeowners can afford them. Whether you use a regular phone line or a faster ISDN line, Windows 98 can help you establish a connection between your home or office computer and the Internet. To do so you will need to select an Internet service provider (ISP), a company that sets up an Internet account for you that provides Internet access. ISPs maintain servers that are directly connected to the Internet 24 hours a day. You dial into your ISP's server over your phone line to use its Internet connection. You pay a fee for this service, sometimes by the hour, but more often with a flat monthly rate.

Figure A-3 shows the tools Windows 98 includes to help you connect to the Internet.

Figure A-3	WINDOWS 98 CONNECTION TOOLS
ACCESSORY	**DESCRIPTION**
Dial-Up Networking	Some computer users have one Internet account for home use and a different one for business use. The Dial-Up Networking accessory helps you manage the accounts that you use to connect to the Internet. You might have just one or several accounts listed in the Dial-Up Networking folder, which you can access through My Computer.
Connection Wizard	The Connection Wizard, available on the Internet Explorer menu, makes it easy for you to create an Internet account for the first time by prompting you for the needed information through a series of dialog boxes.
Online Services folder	The Online Services folder helps you install software for some of the major online services, such as America Online and CompuServe, all of which provide Internet service. If the online service you want to use is not listed in this folder, you will probably receive software from that service, or you can set up your account using the Connection Wizard.

Setting Up Dial-Up Networking

If you want to be able to connect to the Internet and other compatible networks using your home computer, you can set up a dial-up connection using the Internet Connection Wizard. If your ISP has provided you with an installation program that sets up the connection for you, install and run that program rather than using the Windows 98 Internet Connection Wizard.

To begin setting up a dial-up connection:

1. Click the **Start** button, point to **Programs**, point to **Internet Explorer**, and then click **Connection Wizard**.

2. Click the **I have an existing Internet account** option button, and then click **Next**. Choose this option when you have an account with an ISP. The first option would connect you to a referral service that helps you select an ISP, but you only use that option if you haven't already bought an account with an ISP. That option also requires that your telephone line be connected to your modem.

3. Click the **...Internet service provider** option button (the first one), and then click **Next**.

4. If necessary, click the **Connect using my phone line** option button, and then click **Next**. Choose this option when you are not on a local area network, which will be the case if you are connecting your home computer to an ISP.

5. If necessary, click the **Create a new dial-up connection** option button, and then click **Next**.

   TROUBLE? If you have no other dial-up connections established on your computer, the option discussed in Step 5 won't appear, so skip Step 5.

6. Type the area code and telephone number of your ISP in the appropriate boxes, and then click **Next**. Your ISP documentation will provide you with the numbers you should use. See Figure A-4; your numbers will be different.

   TROUBLE? If your service is in a different country, choose the country from the Country name and code list.

   TROUBLE? If the Connection Wizard looks different, you are probably using a different version of Internet Explorer.

| Figure A-4 | ENTERING ISP PHONE INFORMATION |

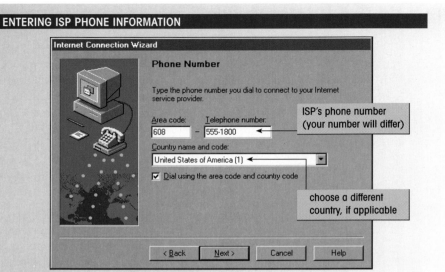

7. Type your username in the User name box, and then press **Tab**. Your ISP documentation will provide you with the username and password you should use.

TROUBLE? If you can't find your username in your documentation, it might be called User ID, Member ID, Login Name, or something similar.

8. Type your password in the Password box. As you type the password, asterisks appear instead of the letters you type, as shown in Figure A-5. This protects your password from the eyes of people who might be walking by your computer. You should keep your password secret so that unauthorized users cannot access your account.

| Figure A-5 | ENTERING A USERNAME AND PASSWORD |

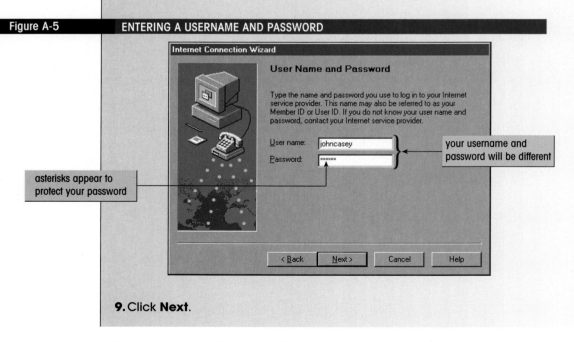

9. Click **Next**.

You now need to choose whether or not to work with advanced settings.

Using Connection Wizard Advanced Settings

When you are using the Internet Connection Wizard to set up an Internet connection, you can choose either to keep the default advanced settings or to change them. If you click No when asked about advanced settings, your connection will use the Windows 98 defaults. If you click Yes, you provide the settings from your ISP documentation. These steps use the Advanced Settings option, which allows you to ensure that your connection is using the settings provided by your ISP. If you choose not to change advanced settings, you might encounter problems with your connection if the Windows 98 default settings don't match those of your ISP. You can change the way your dial-up connection is **configured**, or set up, from the Dial-Up Networking window. Open the Dial-Up Networking window as directed in the next section, right-click the connection you want to modify, and then click Properties. Click the tabs to locate the settings you want to change.

To configure your dial-up connection:

1. Click the **Yes** option button when asked if you want to change advanced settings, and then click **Next**.

   TROUBLE? If you are sure you can proceed using the default settings, click the No button, and read through the rest of these steps without performing them.

2. Click the **PPP** or **SLIP** option button, depending on what your ISP's documentation specifies. A **connection type** is the kind of connection between your computer and your ISP's server. Windows 98 offers two connection types: PPP and SLIP. The preferred and more common connection type today is **Point-to-Point Protocol**, or **PPP**, which provides error checking and can cope with noisier phone lines than SLIP. **Serial Line Internet Protocol**, or **SLIP**, is a basic connection type that runs well on most systems but has no error-checking or security features. Most ISPs use a PPP connection, but some require SLIP; check your ISP documentation to see which one to use.

3. Click **Next**, and then click the appropriate **Logon Procedure** option button. Some ISPs require you to log on before you can use the service. In some cases, you must log on manually, providing the information required by your ISP when you attempt to connect. In other cases, you can use a **logon script**, a program that runs on your computer and logs you on to the service automatically.

4. If you need to use a logon script, click **Use this logon script option button**, click **Browse**, locate and select the logon script specified by your documentation, and then click **Open**. By default, Windows 98 stores logon scripts in the C:\Program Files\Accessories folder. Your ISP's documentation will tell you which logon script to use or will provide you with a different one. See Figure A-6.

Figure A-6 CHOOSING A LOGON PROCEDURE

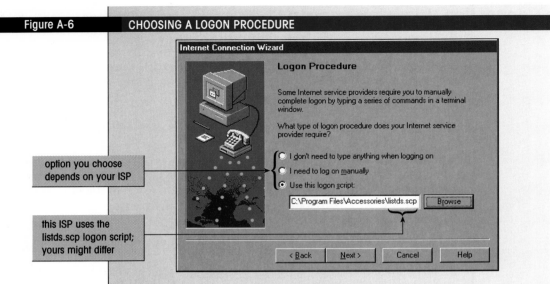

option you choose depends on your ISP

this ISP uses the listds.scp logon script; yours might differ

5. Click **Next**, choose the appropriate IP address option, and then, if you selected the second option, enter the IP address. An **Internet Protocol**, or **IP**, is a unique address that identifies a server on the Internet. Usually your ISP automatically assigns you one when you log on, because you are only a temporary user of the address (only over the period of time that you are logged on).

6. Click **Next**, choose the appropriate DNS Server address option, and then, if you selected the second option, enter the DNS numbers. The **Domain Name System**, or **DNS**, is a database service that helps computers look up the names of other computers and locate their corresponding IP addresses. If your ISP documentation provides you with a primary and secondary DNS server address, enter them here, as shown in Figure A-7.

Figure A-7 ENTERING DNS SERVER INFORMATION

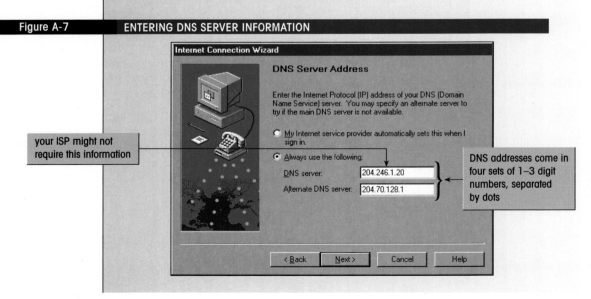

your ISP might not require this information

DNS addresses come in four sets of 1–3 digit numbers, separated by dots

7. Click **Next**, type **a name for your connection** (such as your ISP's name), and then click **Next**. Since you are only trying to set up your dial-up connection, not your mail and news options, proceed through the next three dialog boxes by clicking **No** and then clicking **Next**, and then click **Finish**. The Internet Connection Wizard closes, and you return to the desktop.

TROUBLE? If you want to set up your mail and news options now on your own computer, you can do so by clicking Yes and following the prompts.

Although the steps didn't direct you to set up your mail and news options, you can do that from within Outlook Express, Outlook (if you have Microsoft Office), or whatever mail and news software you are using.

Connecting to a Dial-Up Service

Once you have established a dial-up connection, you are ready to use it to connect to the Internet or another network or computer. You can have more than one dial-up service, in which case multiple icons appear in the Dial-Up Networking window. One connection might provide your business Internet service, another might be for home or family use, and another might access a university or institutional account.

To connect to your dial-up service:

1. Connect your phone line to your computer's modem.

2. Open **My Computer**, and then open **Dial-Up Networking**. The Dial-Up Networking window, shown in Figure A-8, displays icons for each dial-up networking connection you have.

Figure A-8	DIAL-UP NETWORKING WINDOW

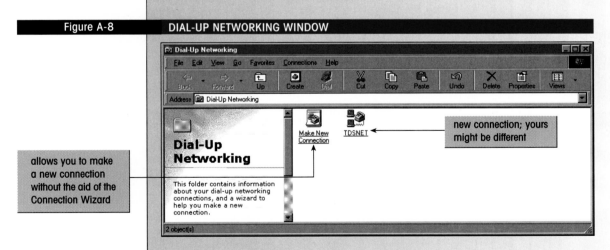

allows you to make a new connection without the aid of the Connection Wizard

new connection; yours might be different

3. Open the connection you just created. The Connect To dialog box opens. See Figure A-9; yours will reflect the information you entered in the wizard.

Figure A-9 | **CONNECTING TO THE INTERNET**

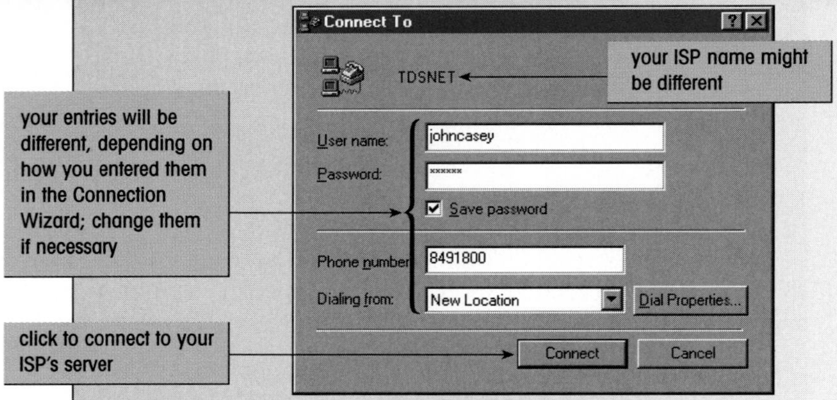

your ISP name might be different

your entries will be different, depending on how you entered them in the Connection Wizard; change them if necessary

click to connect to your ISP's server

Connect To

TDSNET

User name: johncasey
Password: ××××××
☑ Save password

Phone number: 8491800
Dialing from: New Location   Dial Properties...

Connect   Cancel

4. Click **Connect**, and then wait as your modem connects. The Connecting dialog box appears and identifies the steps of establishing a connection. First it uses your modem to dial the number, then it verifies your username and password, and finally it establishes a connection. A Connection Established dialog box (or something similar) may open, indicating that you are connected to your ISP.

   TROUBLE? If a Pre-Dial Terminal Screen dialog box opens after you click Connect, click Continue.

5. Close the Dial-Up Networking window. An icon 🖳 appears on your taskbar that indicates you are connected. You can now start your Internet browser to view Web pages, check your e-mail, or use any of the other Windows 98 communications features. Now you'll disconnect.

6. Right-click the Connection icon 🖳 on the taskbar. A pop-up menu appears, shown in Figure A-10.

   TROUBLE? If your shortcut menu doesn't have Disconnect as an option, you right-clicked the clock, the taskbar, or some other icon instead of the Connection icon. Click outside the pop-up menu to close it, and then repeat Step 7.

Figure A-10 | **DISCONNECTING FROM YOUR ISP**

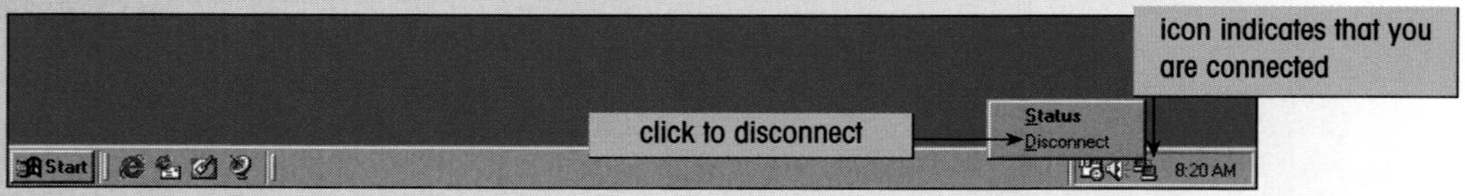

icon indicates that you are connected

click to disconnect

Status
Disconnect

Start | 🌐 📧 📁 📄 | 🔌 8:20 AM

7. Click **Disconnect**.

Installing the MSN Online Service

The steps so far have directed you to set up a dial-up service with an ISP. You can also choose to set up an account with one of the online services available in the Online Services folder, which appears when you first install Windows 98. Installation procedures for these services are included on the Windows 98 CD-ROM. You've probably heard of these services—America Online, AT&T, CompuServe, Prodigy, and MSN. These online services offer a variety of communications features—e-mail, newsgroups, Internet service, chat groups and forums, and other individualized features—and are available nationwide. When you select one of these services, the installation routine guides you through setting up an account with that service. In setting up an account, you will also have to set up payment options. These steps show you how to begin installing the MSN online service; if you choose to use the service, you can complete the installation by following the prompts on the screen.

To install the MSN online service:

1. Insert your Windows 98 installation CD into your CD-ROM drive, and then click the **Close** button in the Windows 98 CD-ROM title bar. You will need files from the CD as you load the MSN program.

2. Click the **Start** button, point to **Programs**, and then point to **Online Services**. The Online Services menu, shown in Figure A-11, shows the services available through Windows 98.

Figure A-11	ONLINE SERVICES

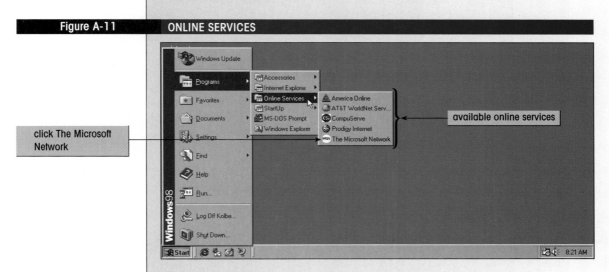

click The Microsoft Network

available online services

3. Click **The Microsoft Network**.

   TROUBLE? If you select a different service, your setup procedure will differ from the procedure in these steps.

4. Read the two opening screens and click **Next** on each screen. These screens inform you of the service to which you are subscribing and then warn you to close any programs that are running that might interfere with the MSN setup.

5. If necessary, select your country from the country list, and then click **Next**.

6. Read the MSN Member Agreement, and then click **I Agree**. By clicking "I Agree," you accept the terms Microsoft has outlined in the member agreement.

7. Click **Next** to start installing the Microsoft Network. The installation files are copied from the CD to the hard drive.

8. When the installation is finished, answer the questions shown in Figure A-12. If you have already set up an account using Dial-Up Networking, you need to request a new MSN account, but you can use your existing connection. Thus, you might use TDSNet to connect to the Internet, but you will also receive the benefits of the MSN online service.

Figure A-12   **COMPLETING THE MSN INSTALLATION**

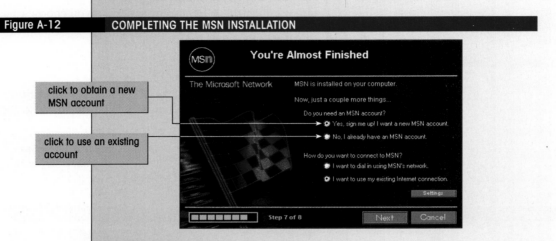

click to obtain a new MSN account

click to use an existing account

9. Click **Next**, then complete the procedure as directed on the screen. The service guides you through setting up an account. Each screen provides you with instructions; read them carefully before you proceed. When you are finished, your service is set up. Icons for the service are installed on your desktop that you can use to start the service.

Once you have installed an online service, you can connect to the service and use its features. The online services market is changing very rapidly, so make sure you compare prices and features before choosing the service you want.

Serial Line Internet Protocol (SLIP), WIN 98 A.5
serial ports, WIN 98 9.13
servers
  attaching to, WIN 98 10.14
service component
  in networks, WIN 98 10.9
Settings property sheet, WIN 98 4.23–26
shapes
  creating, WIN 98 7.25–27
  foreground and background colors for, WIN 98 7.31–32
shape tools, WIN 98 7.25–27
Shared As option button, WIN 98 10.21
share-level access control, WIN 98 10.19–20
Shift key
  holding down with StickyKeys, WIN 98 4.36–38
shortcut icons
  defined, WIN 98 4.6
  deleting, WIN 98 4.11, WIN 98 4.14
  document icons *vs.*, WIN 98 4.6, WIN 98 4.11
  identifying on desktop, WIN 98 4.13–14
  types of, WIN 98 4.14
  using, WIN 98 4.8–9
shortcut menus
  copying files to folders with, WIN 98 3.29
  cutting and pasting files with, WIN 98 3.29–31
  moving files between folders with, WIN 98 3.28
  opening, WIN 98 1.9–10
shortcuts, WIN 98 4.6–14
  adding to Quick Launch toolbar, WIN 98 5.40–41
  to documents, creating, WIN 98 4.10–11
  to drives, creating, WIN 98 4.7–8
  to printers, creating, WIN 98 4.11–13
  testing, WIN 98 4.8, WIN 98 4.10
  using, WIN 98 4.8–9
  vs. copies of documents, WIN 98 4.6
Show Desktop button, WIN 98 1.14
Shut Down command, WIN 98 10.16–17
Shut Down option, WIN 98 1.15–16
16 Color Bitmap file type, WIN 98 7.9
Size button
  arranging files by size with, WIN 98 3.20, WIN 98 3.21
sizing
  bitmapped graphics, WIN 98 7.10–11
  embedded objects, WIN 98 8.12
  graphic images, WIN 98 7.7
  shapes, WIN 98 7.27
  windows, WIN 98 1.21
sizing buttons, WIN 98 1.17

sizing coordinates
  for shapes, WIN 98 7.27
sizing handles, WIN 98 1.21
  for graphic images, WIN 98 7.7
SLIP (Serial Line Internet Protocol), WIN 98 A.5
Sound Recorder, WIN 98 8.27
sounds
  for StickyKeys, WIN 98 4.37
source disk, WIN 98 3.33–34
source files
  defined, WIN 98 8.9
  embedded object editing and, WIN 98 8.14
source programs
  defined, WIN 98 8.9
  editing linked objects in, WIN 98 8.23
special needs
  accessibility options, WIN 98 4.33
specialty search services, WIN 98 6.29
spin boxes
  in dialog boxes, WIN 98 1.26
Standard toolbar
  controlling display in Exploring window, WIN 98 3.6
  display options, WIN 98 2.17–18
  navigation buttons, WIN 98 2.23, WIN 98 3.17
standards
  network, WIN 98 10.8
Standard view
  in Calculator accessory, WIN 98 8.5
Standby mode, WIN 98 10.17
standby power scheme, WIN 98 4.28, WIN 98 4.29
Start menu
  defined, WIN 98 1.7
  opening, WIN 98 1.7
  starting Find utility from, WIN 98 6.5
startup disk
  creating, WIN 98 11.17–18
status bar, WIN 98 1.17, WIN 98 1.18
  activity shown by, WIN 98 5.10
  controlling display in Exploring window, WIN 98 3.6, WIN 98 3.7
StickyKeys
  testing effect of, WIN 98 4.37–38
  turning on, WIN 98 4.37
storage devices
  viewing list in Exploring window, WIN 98 3.7–8
straight lines
  drawing, WIN 98 7.23–24
stretching
  graphic images, WIN 98 7.24–25
Stretch/Skew option, WIN 98 7.24–25
Student Disk
  adding practice files to, WIN 98 2.15
  copying, WIN 98 2.25–26
  creating, WIN 98 2.15, WIN 98 3.5, WIN 98 4.7–8
  exploring contents of, WIN 98 2.16–17

formatting with Quick Format, WIN 98 3.4–5
  preparing for graphics tutorial, WIN 98 7.2
  preparing for search tutorial, WIN 98 6.4
subfolders, WIN 98 2.21
  defined, WIN 98 3.7
  viewing, WIN 98 3.9–10
subject guides, WIN 98 6.32–34
subject searches
  Internet, WIN 98 6.32–34
submenus
  selecting options on, WIN 98 1.8–9
subnets, WIN 98 10.3
subscribing to channels, WIN 98 5.25–27
  unsubscribing, WIN 98 5.29–30
subscribing to Web sites
  advantages of, WIN 98 5.18
  with Internet Explorer, WIN 98 5.17–19
Subscriptions folder
  restoring, WIN 98 5.29–30
  viewing update schedule in, WIN 98 5.28
System Information, WIN 98 9.30

T

tabs
  in dialog boxes, WIN 98 1.26
targets
  of links, WIN 98 5.10
taskbar
  accessing Web with, WIN 98 5.38–40
  adding toolbars to, WIN 98 5.38–39
  closing inactive programs from, WIN 98 1.14–15
  locating information about in Help, WIN 98 1.29
  rearranging toolbars on, WIN 98 5.39–40
  restoring size, WIN 98 4.39
Task Scheduler, WIN 98 11.2, WIN 98 11.16
TCP/IP, WIN 98 10.9
technical support staff, WIN 98 9.30
telephone lines
  communications over, WIN 98 A.1–10
text
  adding to graphic images, WIN 98 7.32–35
  customizing size in Accessibility Wizard, WIN 98 4.41
  highlighting, WIN 98 2.6
  selecting, WIN 98 2.5–6
  typing in, WIN 98 2.4
  working with, WIN 98 2.4–6
text boxes
  in dialog boxes, WIN 98 1.26
text document icons, WIN 98 4.14

TASK REFERENCE

TASK	PAGE #	RECOMMENDED METHOD
Accessibility options, activate	WIN 98 4.33	Open the Control Panel, click Accessibility Properties, select settings you want, click OK
Accessibility options, idle	WIN 98 4.40	In Accessibility Options, click General tab, click Turn off accessibility features after idle for, specify number of minutes, click OK
Accessibility Wizard, use	WIN 98 4.40	Click **Start**, point to Programs, point to Accessories, point to Accessibility, click Accessibility Wizard
Active Desktop, enable	WIN 98 5.20	Right-click a blank area of the desktop, point to Active Desktop, click View As Web Page
Active Desktop item, add	WIN 98 5.21	Right-click a blank area of the desktop, point to Active Desktop, click Customize my Desktop, click New, click Yes, click item you want to add, click Add to Active Desktop, click Yes, click OK
Active Desktop item, close	WIN 98 5.24	Point to item and wait for a title bar to appear, then click ☒
Active Desktop item, move	WIN 98 5.23	Point to item and wait for a title bar to appear, then drag title bar
Active Desktop item, remove	WIN 98 5.24	Right-click a blank area of the desktop, point to Active Desktop, click Customize my Desktop, click item, click Delete, click Yes, click OK
Active Desktop item, resize	WIN 98 5.23	Point to item and wait for a border to appear, then drag border or border corner
Backup, perform	WIN 98 11.23	Click **Start**, point to Programs, point to Accessories, point to System Tools, click Backup, if necessary click Create a new backup job and click OK, click Back up selected files, folders and drives, then follow directions on screen
Backup, restore files from	WIN 98 11.29	Click **Start**, point to Programs, point to Accessories, point to System Tools, click Backup, click Restore backed up files, click OK, then follow directions on screen
Calculator, start	WIN 98 8.5	Click **Start**, point to Programs, point to Accessories, click Calculator
Channel, subscribe to	WIN 98 5.26	Click button on Channel bar, click icon, click Add Active Channel, click one of the Yes buttons, click OK
Channel, unsubscribe from	WIN 98 5.29	In Internet Explorer, click Favorites, click Organize Favorites, right-click subscription, click Delete, click Yes if prompted
Channel, update manually	WIN 98 5.29	In Internet Explorer, click Favorites, click Manage Subscriptions, right-click subscription, click Update Now
Channel bar, view	WIN 98 5.25	Right-click a blank area of the desktop, point to Active Desktop, click Customize my Desktop, click Internet Explorer Channel Bar check box, click OK
Channel updates, schedule	WIN 98 5.28	In Internet Explorer, click Favorites, click Manage Subscriptions, right-click subscription, click Properties, change schedule settings on the Schedule tab, click OK

TASK	PAGE #	RECOMMENDED METHOD
Character, insert	WIN 98 2.6	Click where you want to insert the text, type the text
Clipboard, view contents	WIN 98 8.8	Click 🅰Start, point to Programs, point to Accessories, point to System Tools, click Clipboard Viewer
Computer, dial over a network		See "Dial-up service, connect to"
Computer, identify on a network	WIN 98 10.11	Open the network property sheet, click the Identification tab
Control Panel, use	WIN 98 4.27	See Reference Window: Using the Control Panel to Customize Settings
Data, transfer using Cut, Copy, and Paste	WIN 98 8.3	See Reference Window: Using Paste to Transfer Data from One Document to Another
Desktop, access	WIN 98 1.14	Click 🖉 on the Quick Launch toolbar
Desktop, change appearance	WIN 98 4.19	Right-click a blank area of the desktop, click Properties, click Appearance tab, choose a different scheme, or click Item list arrow, change size or color, click OK
Desktop background, change	WIN 98 4.16	Right-click a blank area of the desktop, click Properties, click Background tab, select pattern or wallpaper you want, click OK
Desktop color palette, change	WIN 98 4.25	Right-click a blank area of the desktop, click Properties, click Settings tab, click Colors list arrow, click palette you want, click OK
Desktop document, create	WIN 98 4.2	See Reference Window: Creating a New Document on the Desktop
Desktop document, open	WIN 98 4.4	In Web style, click the document icon; in Classic style, click the document icon, then press Enter
Desktop resolution, change	WIN 98 4.24	Right-click a blank area of the desktop, click Properties, click Settings tab, drag Screen area slider, click OK
Desktop, use Web page as background	WIN 98 5.32	Right-click a blank area of the desktop, click Properties, click Background tab, click Browse, locate and select Web page, click Open, click OK
Device, select	WIN 98 3.11	Click the icon that represents the device or folder to select it and highlight it
Devices, view or hide	WIN 98 3.8	See Reference Window: Displaying or Hiding Devices or Folders in the All Folders Explorer Bar
Dial-up networking, set up	WIN 98 A.3	Click 🅰Start, point to Programs, point to Internet Explorer, click Connection Wizard, then follow directions on screen
Dial-up service, connect to	WIN 98 A.7	Open My Computer, open Dial-Up Networking, right-click connection, click Connect
Disk, clean up	WIN 98 11.3	Click 🅰Start, point to Programs, point to Accessories, point to System Tools, click Disk Cleanup, click Drives list arrow, click drive, click OK

TASK	PAGE #	RECOMMENDED METHOD
Disk, copy	WIN 98 2.25	See Reference Window: Copying a Disk
Disk, defragment	WIN 98 11.15	See Reference Window: Defragmenting a Disk
Disk, format	WIN 98 2.2	Open My Computer, right-click 3½ Floppy (A:), click Format, click Start
Disk, Quick format	WIN 98 3.4	From My Computer, right-click disk icon, click Format, click Quick (erase), click Start
Disk, scan for errors	WIN 98 11.10	See Reference Window: Using ScanDisk
Explorer bar, view	WIN 98 3.6	Click View, point to Explorer Bar, click Explorer Bar you want
Explorer windows, navigate	WIN 98 2.23	Click ⇦, ⇨, or 🔼
File, copy	WIN 98 2.22 WIN 98 3.29	See Reference Window: Copying a File *or* Copying One or More Files
File, copy from one floppy disk to another	WIN 98 3.33	See Reference Window: Copying a File from One Floppy Disk to Another
File, delete	WIN 98 2.24	Right-click the file, click Delete
File, download from Web	WIN 98 5.16	In Internet Explorer, right-click file you want to download, click Save As (or Save Picture As, or something similar), enter a location, click OK
File, locate by contents	WIN 98 6.13	In Find, click the Containing text box on the Name & Location tab, type the text you want to search for, click Find Now
File, locate by date	WIN 98 6.19	See Reference Window: Locating Files by Date
File, locate by name	WIN 98 6.7	See Reference Window: Searching for a File by Name
File, locate in a specific folder	WIN 98 6.14	See Reference Window: Searching for Files in a Specific Folder
File, locate one you were working with recently using the Documents menu	WIN 98 6.23	Click 🏁 Start, point to Documents, click the file
File, locate using multiple criteria	WIN 98 6.22	In Find, enter the criteria you want to use on the three Find tabs, then click Find Now
File, move	WIN 98 2.21 WIN 98 3.27	See Reference Window: Moving a File *or* Moving One or More Files Between Folders
File, move or copy from floppy disk to hard disk	WIN 98 3.32	In Windows Explorer, select files on floppy disk you want to move, right-click selection, click Cut or Copy, right-click folder on hard drive, click Paste
File, move or copy with Cut and Paste	WIN 98 3.30	See Reference Window: Moving or Copying Files with Cut, Copy, and Paste
File, open from Find	WIN 98 6.11	Locate the file using Find, right-click the file in the Results list, then click Open
File, open from My Computer	WIN 98 2.9	Open My Computer, open the window containing the file; in Web style, click the file; in Classic style, click the file, then press Enter

TASK REFERENCE

TASK	PAGE #	RECOMMENDED METHOD
File, print	WIN 98 2.10	Click 🖨
File, print to a different printer	WIN 98 9.19	See Reference Window: Printing to a Different Printer
File, rename	WIN 98 2.24	See Reference Window: Renaming a File
File, restore deleted	WIN 98 11.5	See Reference Window: Restoring a File Deleted from a Local Drive
File, save	WIN 98 2.7	Click 💾
File, select	WIN 98 3.23	See Reference Window: Selecting Files
File, select all but a certain one	WIN 98 3.24	See Reference Window: Selecting All Files Except Certain Ones
File, view with Quick View	WIN 98 6.24	See Reference Window: Viewing Files Using Quick View
File extensions, hide	WIN 98 2.20	Open My Computer, click View, click Folder Options, click View tab, make sure the Hide file extensions for known file types check box is checked, click OK
File on the Web, locate by query	WIN 98 6.30	See Reference Window: Searching by Query
File on the Web, locate by subject	WIN 98 6.33	See Reference Window: Searching by Subject
File on the Web, locate using the Search Explorer bar	WIN 98 6.34	In Windows Explorer, click View, point to Explorer Bar, click Search, choose a search service, type a keyword, then click the corresponding search button
File or folder, delete	WIN 98 3.34	See Reference Window: Deleting a File or Folder
Files, arrange	WIN 98 3.20	See Reference Window: Arranging Files by Name, Size, Date, or Type
Files, back up		See "Backup, perform"
Files, locate by type or size	WIN 98 6.20	See Reference Window: Using Advanced Search Criteria
Files, restore from backup		See "Backup, restore files from"
Files, view list	WIN 98 3.15	See Reference Window: Viewing a List of Files
Find, start	WIN 98 6.6	Click ▣Start, point to Find, click the option you want
Folder, create	WIN 98 2.21 WIN 98 3.11	See Reference Window: Creating a New Folder *or* Creating a Folder in Windows Explorer
Folder, rename	WIN 98 3.12	See Reference Window: Renaming a Folder
Folder, select	WIN 98 3.11	Click the icon that represents the device or folder to select it and highlight it
Folder, view as Web page	WIN 98 5.35	In My Computer, open folder, click View, click as Web Page
Folder, view contents	WIN 98 3.15	See Reference Window: Viewing a List of Files

TASK	PAGE #	RECOMMENDED METHOD
Folder background, display image	WIN 98 5.36	Open folder window, click View, click Customize this Folder, click Choose a background picture, click Next, click Browse, locate and select image, click Open, click Next, click Finish
Folder or device, share on a network	WIN 98 10.21	In Windows Explorer, right-click folder or device you want to share, click Sharing, enter a share name, click the access type you want to grant, click OK
Folder settings, change	WIN 98 5.33	Click Start, point to Settings, click Folder Options, click Custom, click Settings, change settings, click OK twice
Folders, view or hide	WIN 98 3.8	See Reference Window: Displaying or Hiding Devices or Folders in the All Folders Explorer Bar
Font, delete	WIN 98 9.29	See Reference Window: Deleting a Font
Font, install	WIN 98 9.28	See Reference Window: Installing a New Font
Font, open	WIN 98 9.27	In Fonts window, right-click font, then click Open
Font size, change in Quick View	WIN 98 6.26	Click A or A
Fonts window, open	WIN 98 9.25	Click Start, point to Settings, click Control Panel, right-click Fonts, click Open
Graphic, add text	WIN 98 7.32	See Reference Window: Adding Text to a Graphic
Graphic, change foreground or background color	WIN 98 7.31	In Paint, click color in color box with left mouse button to change foreground color or with right mouse button to change background color
Graphic, color	WIN 98 7.28	See Reference Window: Filling an Area with Color
Graphic, copy, paste, and move portions	WIN 98 7.21	See Reference Window: Copying, Cutting, and Pasting Graphics
Graphic, crop	WIN 98 7.5	See Reference Window: Cropping a Graphic
Graphic, erase	WIN 98 7.7	In Paint, click ⬜, drag area you want to erase
Graphic, flip	WIN 98 7.22	In Paint, click Image, click Flip/Rotate, click option button you want, click OK
Graphic, magnify	WIN 98 7.14	See Reference Window: Magnifying a Graphic
Graphic, save in a different format	WIN 98 7.11	Click File, click Save As, click Save as type, click file type you want, type file name, click Save
Grid, show (this option available only in magnified view)	WIN 98 7.15	In Paint, click View, point to Zoom, click Show Grid
Graphic, stretch	WIN 98 7.24	In Paint, click Image, click Stretch/Skew, enter a stretch or skew percentage, click OK

TASK	PAGE #	RECOMMENDED METHOD
Hardware device, install	WIN 98 9.12	See page WIN 98 9.12
Help, display topic from Contents tab	WIN 98 1.28	From Help, click the Contents tab, click 📖 until you see the topic you want, click [?] to display topic
Help, display topic from Index tab	WIN 98 1.28	From Help, click the Index tab, scroll to locate topic, click topic, click Display
Help, return to previous Help topic	WIN 98 1.30	Click ⬅
Help, start	WIN 98 1.27	Click Start , click Help
High contrast, enable	WIN 98 4.38	In Accessibility Options, click Display tab, click Use High Contrast, click OK
Home page, view	WIN 98 5.15	In Internet Explorer, click 🏠
Icon, change	WIN 98 8.17	See Reference Window: Changing an Icon
Insertion point, move	WIN 98 2.5	Click the location in the document to which you want to move
Keyboard shortcuts, control with StickyKeys	WIN 98 4.37	In Accessibility Options, click Keyboard tab, click Use StickyKeys, click OK
Links, manage and update	WIN 98 8.23	See Reference Window: Managing Links
List box, change option	WIN 98 1.24	Click ▼, then click option you want in list that appears
LOG file, create	WIN 98 4.5	In Notepad, type .LOG
Maintenance tasks, schedule	WIN 98 11.16	Click Start , point to Programs, point to Accessories, point to System Tools, click Maintenance Wizard, then follow directions on screen
Menu option, select	WIN 98 1.8	Click the menu option, or, if it is a submenu, point to it
Mouse, customize for right- or left-handed use	WIN 98 4.30	Open the Control Panel, open the Mouse window, select settings you want, click OK
My Computer, open	WIN 98 2.14	In Web style, click My Computer on the desktop; in Classic style, click My Computer on the desktop, then press Enter
Navigation keys, use to navigate documents	WIN 98 6.26	Press key or key combination shown in Figure 6-19
Network, log off	WIN 98 10.17	Click Start , click Log Off
Network, troubleshoot	WIN 98 10.26	Click Start , click Help, click Contents tab, click Troubleshooting, click Windows 98 Troubleshooters, click Networking
Network, view	WIN 98 10.5	Right-click 🖳 on desktop or in Windows Explorer, click Open, click 🌐 to view entire network
Network folder or device, map to a drive letter	WIN 98 10.22	In Windows Explorer, right-click the icon representing the network folder you want to map, click Map Network Drive, click Drive list arrow, click drive letter you want to use, click OK

TASK	PAGE #	RECOMMENDED METHOD
Network properties, view	WIN 98 10.9	Right-click ▣, click Properties
Object, display embedded or linked object as icon	WIN 98 8.16	Right-click object, click Object Properties, click View tab, click Display as icon, click OK
Object, edit in-place	WIN 98 8.13	See Reference Window: In-place Editing
Object, embed using Insert Object	WIN 98 8.14	See Reference Window: Embedding an Object Using Insert Object
Object, embed using paste	WIN 98 8.10	Select object, cut or copy to the Clipboard, click destination document, click ▣
Object, embed with different methods	WIN 98 8.19	See Reference Window: Methods of Embedding
Object, link	WIN 98 8.21	See Reference Window: Linking an Object
Object, resize	WIN 98 8.12	See Reference Window: Resizing an Embedded Object
Online service, install	WIN 98 A.9	Click ▣Start, point to Programs, point to Online Services, click the service you want, then follow the directions on screen
Paint, start	WIN 98 7.3	Click ▣Start, point to Programs, point to Accessories, click Paint
Paint tools, use	WIN 98 7.4	See Figure 7-2
Panes, adjusting width	WIN 98 3.13	See Reference Window: Adjusting the Width of the Exploring Window Panes
Password, change	WIN 98 10.14	See Reference Window: Changing Your Windows 98 Password
Pattern, apply to desktop	WIN 98 4.16	Right-click a blank area of the desktop, click Properties, click Background tab, click Pattern, click pattern you want, click OK, click OK
People, locate on the Web	WIN 98 6.35	Click ▣Start, point to Find, click People, choose the service you want, type the name you want to search for, click Find Now
Pointer, control with MouseKeys	WIN 98 4.34	In Accessibility Options, click Mouse tab, click Use MouseKeys, click OK
Power management features, use	WIN 98 4.28	Open the Control Panel, open the Power Management window, select settings you want, click OK
Print job, pause	WIN 98 9.9	In the print queue, click Printer, click Pause Printing
Print job, remove from the print queue	WIN 98 9.9	See Reference Window: Removing Print Jobs from the Print Queue
Print job, troubleshoot	WIN 98 9.22	Click ▣Start, click Help, click Contents tab, click Troubleshooting, click Windows 98 Troubleshooters, click Print, follow steps
Print queue, open	WIN 98 9.5	Click ▣Start, point to Settings, click Printers, right-click printer, click Open
Print queue, use	WIN 98 9.4	See Reference Window: Using the Print Queue

TASK	PAGE #	RECOMMENDED METHOD
Printer, add	WIN 98 9.15	Open Printers window, select Add Printer icon to start Add Printer Wizard, follow steps
Printer, change default	WIN 98 9.20	In Printers window, right-click printer, click Set as Default
Printer, locate on a network	WIN 98 10.25	In Printers folder, right-click printer, click Properties, click Details tab
Printer property sheet, view	WIN 98 9.11	Click ![Start], point to Settings, click Printers, right-click printer, click Properties
Printers window, open	WIN 98 9.5	Click ![Start], point to Settings, click Printers
Program, close	WIN 98 1.12	Click ![X]
Program, close inactive	WIN 98 1.15	Right-click program button, then click Close
Program, start	WIN 98 1.11	See Reference Window: Starting a Program
Program, switch to another	WIN 98 1.14	Click the program button on the taskbar that contains the name of the program to which you want to switch
Properties, view	WIN 98 4.15	Right-click the object, click Properties
Quick Launch toolbar, add button to	WIN 98 5.40	Open My Computer, locate file or program you want to add, drag icon to Quick Launch toolbar
Quick View, start	WIN 98 6.24	See Reference Window: Viewing Files Using Quick View
Results list, sort	WIN 98 6.16	See Reference Window: Sorting the Results List
Screen, magnify portion	WIN 98 4.42	Click ![Start], point to Programs, point to Accessories, point to Accessibility, click Magnifier
Screen, print	WIN 98 3.25	Press Print Screen, start WordPad, click ![icon], click ![icon]
Screen saver, activate	WIN 98 4.22	Right-click a blank area of the desktop, click Properties, click Screen Saver tab, click Screen Saver list arrow, click screen saver you want, click OK
Search, clear	WIN 98 6.15	In Find, click the New Search button
Search criteria, specify	WIN 98 6.7	See Reference Window: Specifying Search Criteria
Search page, view on the Internet	WIN 98 6.29	Click ![Start], point to Find, click On the Internet
Shortcut, create	WIN 98 4.7	See Reference Window: Creating a Shortcut
Shortcut icon, delete	WIN 98 4.14	Select the shortcut icon, press Delete, click Yes
Start menu, open	WIN 98 1.7	Click ![Start], or press Ctrl-Esc
Startup disk, create	WIN 98 11.18	Click ![Start], point to Settings, click Control Panel, open Add/Remove Programs, click Startup Disk tab, click Create Disk, then follow directions on screen
Student Disk, create		Click ![Start], point to Programs, point to the NP on Microsoft Windows 98 option that corresponds to the level you are using, then click the disk you want to create. Follow the instructions that appear.

TASK	PAGE #	RECOMMENDED METHOD
Subfolders, view or hide	WIN 98 3.9	Click ⊞ or ⊟
System information, view	WIN 98 9.30	Click ▓Start , point to Programs, point to Accessories, point to System Tools, click System Information
Taskbar toolbars, rearrange	WIN 98 5.40	Drag toolbar to new location
Taskbar toolbars, view	WIN 98 5.38	Right-click a blank area of the taskbar, point to Toolbars, click toolbar
Text, select	WIN 98 2.6	Drag the pointer over the text
Thumbnail, show (this option available only in magnified view)	WIN 98 7.16	In Paint, click View, point to Zoom, click Show Thumbnail
Toolbar button, select	WIN 98 1.24	Click the toolbar button
Toolbars, control display	WIN 98 2.17	Click View, point to Toolbars, then select the toolbar options you want
ToolTip, view	WIN 98 1.7	Position the pointer over the tool
Video clip, change settings	WIN 98 8.28	Right-click video clip, click Linked Video Clip Object if an OLE object, click Edit, or just click Edit
Video clip, play	WIN 98 8.25	Right-click video clip object or file, click Linked Video Clip Object if an OLE object, click Play, or just click Play
View, change	WIN 98 2.18	Click View, then click the view option you want
Wallpaper, use graphic image	WIN 98 4.18	Right-click a blank area of the desktop, click Properties, click Background tab, click Browse, locate and select file, click Open, click OK
Web page, activate link	WIN 98 5.11	In Internet Explorer, click link on Web page
Web page, open with URL	WIN 98 5.8	See Reference Window: Opening a Page with a URL
Web page, print	WIN 98 5.15	In Internet Explorer, view page, click File, click Print, then click OK
Web page, return to previous	WIN 98 5.14	In Internet Explorer, click ⇐
Web page, view	WIN 98 5.6	See Reference Window: Viewing a Web Page with Windows Explorer
Web site, subscribe to	WIN 98 5.18	In Internet Explorer, view page, click Favorites, click Add to Favorites, click one of the two Yes options, click OK
Web style, switch to	WIN 98 2.12	Click ▓Start , point to Settings, click Folder Options, click Web style, click OK
Web view, switch to	WIN 98 2.18	Open My Computer, click View, then click as Web Page
Wildcards, use to find files by name	WIN 98 6.12	Start Find, type search string in Named box, using ? in place of single characters and * in place of multiple characters
Window, maximize	WIN 98 1.20	Click ▢
Window, minimize	WIN 98 1.18	Click ▬

TASK	PAGE #	RECOMMENDED METHOD
Window, move	WIN 98 1.21	Drag the title bar
Window, redisplay	WIN 98 1.20	Click the program button on the taskbar
Window, resize	WIN 98 1.21	Drag ⬜
Window, restore	WIN 98 1.20	Click ⬚
Windows Explorer, start	WIN 98 3.6	Click [Start], point to Programs, click Windows Explorer
Windows 98, shut down	WIN 98 1.15	Click [Start], click Shut Down, click the Shut Down option button, click OK
Windows 98, start	WIN 98 1.4	Turn on the computer